*Poetry and Experience*

# WILHELM DILTHEY

SELECTED WORKS · VOLUME V

---

# *Poetry and Experience*

EDITED BY

RUDOLF A. MAKKREEL

AND

FRITHJOF RODI

---

PRINCETON UNIVERSITY PRESS

PRINCETON, NEW JERSEY

Published by Princeton University Press, 41 William Street
Princeton, New Jersey 08540
In the United Kingdom
Princeton University Press, Guildford, Surrey



Library of Congress Cataloging in Publication Data will be
found on the last printed page of this book

ISBN 0-691-07297-3

This book has been composed in Linotron Sabon

Clothbound editions of Princeton University Press books
are printed on acid-free paper, and binding materials
are chosen for strength and durability

Printed in the United States of America
by Princeton University Press
Princeton, New Jersey

# CONTENTS

PREFACE TO ALL VOLUMES vii

EDITORIAL NOTE TO VOLUME V xi

ABBREVIATIONS xiii

INTRODUCTION TO VOLUME V 3

PART I

POETICS

1 The Imagination of the Poet: Elements for a Poetics (1887) 29

*Translated by Louis Agosta and Rudolf A. Makkreel*

SECTION ONE

Traditional Insights and New Tasks of Poetics 37

SECTION TWO

Chapter One: Description of the Poet's Constitution 56

Chapter Two: An Attempt to Explain Poetic Creativity Psychologically 68

Chapter Three: Corroboration Provided by the Testimony of Poets Themselves 107

SECTION THREE

The Typical in Poetry 115

SECTION FOUR

Prospects for a Theory of Poetic Technique to be Derived from These Psychological Foundations 119

Chapter One: Poetic Creativity and Aesthetic Impression 120

Chapter Two: The Poet's Technique 127

Chapter Three: The Historicity of Poetic Technique 160

2 The Three Epochs of Modern Aesthetics and Its Present Task (1892) 175

*Translated by Michael Neville*

I. The Three Preceding Methods of Aesthetics 180

II. Ideas Concerning the Solution of the Present Task of Aesthetics 205

3 Fragments for a Poetics (1907-1908) 223
*Translated by Rudolf A. Makkreel*

Lived Experience 223
Structural Psychology 228

PART II
POETRY AND LIVED EXPERIENCE

4 Goethe and the Poetic Imagination (1910) 235
*Translated by Christopher Rodie*

Life 237
The Poetic Imagination 238
Goethe's Poetic Imagination 244
Poetry and Lived Experience 250
Shakespeare 254
Rousseau 264
Goethe 269

5 Friedrich Hölderlin (1910) 303
*Translated by Joseph Ross*

Homeland and First Playful Poetic Efforts 305
Hölderlin As a Young Man 308
Maturity 321
The Novel *Hyperion* 334
The Tragedy of *Empedocles* 350
The Poems 368
The End 379

GLOSSARY 385
INDEX 389

# PREFACE TO ALL VOLUMES

This six-volume translation of the main writings of Wilhelm Dilthey (1833-1911) is intended to meet a longstanding need. It makes available to English readers translations of complete texts representing the full range of Dilthey's philosophy. The multi-volume edition will thereby provide a wider basis for research not only in the history and theory of the human sciences but also in Dilthey's philosophical understanding of history, life, and world-views. His principal writings on psychology, aesthetics, ethics, and pedagogy are also included, together with some historical essays and literary criticism.

Whereas the Spanish-speaking world, which assimilated Dilthey early and intensively under the influence of Ortega y Gasset, has had an eight-volume translation since 1944-45, the English-speaking world has approached Dilthey more hesitantly. The efforts made by H. A. Hodges to acquaint the British public with Dilthey met with only limited success. H. P. Rickman has translated parts of Dilthey's writings, and his introductions have sought to dispel the distrust of Continental philosophy which characterized the early phases of the Analytical Movement. While a few individual works have also been translated, a systematically collected edition will provide a more consistent rendering of important terms and concepts.

An increasing interest in Continental thought (Husserl, Heidegger, Sartre, Hermeneutics, Structuralism, and Critical Theory) has created a climate in which the still not adequately recognized philosophy of Dilthey can be appropriated. As phenomenological and hermeneutical theories are being applied to more complex and problematic questions, it is becoming more evident that the nineteenth-century roots of these philosophical theories must be re-examined. This is especially the case with problems surrounding the theory of the *Geisteswissenschaften*. As given its classical formulation by Dilthey, this theory has been entitled in English as that of the "human studies" in order to differentiate it from the positivistic ideal of a "unified science." Currently, the more forthright title, "human sciences," has been adopted—but at the risk of becoming submerged in a universal hermeneutics and post-Kuhnian philosophy of science. Given this new situation, the difference between the natural sciences and the human sciences will need to be reconsidered. If interpretation and the circularity associated with it are inherent to both the natural and human sciences, then the task will be to determine what kind of interpretation is involved in each and at what level.

The translations of Dilthey's main theoretical works on the human sciences will show that Dilthey's overall position was more flexible than has been realized. His distinction between understanding (*Verstehen*) and explaining, for example, was not intended to exclude explanations from the human sciences, but only to delimit their scope. Moreover, the importance of methodological reflection in the human sciences should become more evident and serve to eliminate the persistent misconceptions of understanding as empathy, or worse still, as a mode of irrationalism. The German term *Geisteswissenschaften* encompasses both the humanities and the social sciences, and Dilthey's theory and works assume no sterile dichotomies rooted in a presumed opposition between the arts and the sciences.

The limits of a six-volume edition did not permit inclusion of some significant works: full-scale historical monographs such as the *Leben Schleiermachers*, major essays from *Weltanschauung und Analyse des Menschen seit Renaissance und Reformation*, and *Die Jugendgeschichte Hegels*. We trust that our volumes will generate enough interest in Dilthey's thought to justify the future translation of these and other works as well.

This edition arose through a close cooperation between the editors, their respective universities (Emory University, Atlanta, and Ruhr-Universität Bochum) and a great number of colleagues from various disciplines who served as translators. This kind of large-scale cooperation required an organizational framework. A group of Dilthey scholars consisting of Professors O. F. Bollnow, K. Gründer, U. Herrmann, B. E. Jensen, H. Johach, O. Pöggeler, and H. P. Rickman met twice in Bochum to assist the editors in selecting the content of this edition. Several translation sessions were held at Emory University to bring the translators together to discuss terminological difficulties, and other scholars have advised us as well (see list of Advisory Board in the front matter).

Dilthey is difficult to translate. In an effort to render the translations as coherent as possible, the editors prepared a comprehensive lexicon for the use of the translators. To guarantee the quality of the translations, they have been carefully edited. First the assistant editor scrutinized the translations for problems with the lexicon and prepared bibliographical references. Then we went over each text, making revisions where necessary (1) to ensure that the allusions and idiomatic meanings of the original German have been preserved, and (2) to make Dilthey's complex and indirect prose accessible to the modern English reader.

An Alexander von Humboldt Fellowship in 1978-79 made it possible for the editors to begin their cooperative efforts. The Fritz Thyssen Stiftung in Cologne enabled them to execute this project through a five-year grant. The Translations Program of the National Endowment for the Humanities and Emory University have also made substantial means available for this project. The editors are grateful to all these institutions for their very generous support. Of course, this project would not have borne fruit were it not for the commitment of Princeton University Press and the encouragement of Sanford Thatcher. Our appreciation to all who have helped us in this time-consuming but worthwhile endeavor.

RUDOLF A. MAKKREEL
FRITHJOF RODI
*May 1984*

# EDITORIAL NOTE TO VOLUME V

In the preface we have already described our general procedures in revising translations for this edition. Coherence in the use of terminology has been our aim throughout, but when Dilthey uses terms nontechnically, as he often does in this volume, we have allowed the context to determine the best English equivalent. Thus, while we normally translate "Erlebnis" as "lived experience," when Dilthey uses it together with other adjectives such as "personal," we tend to drop the "lived" to avoid awkwardness. Brief notes about some of our most important terminological decisions have been provided where such terms first occur.

Words and phrases added by the editors of Dilthey's *Gesammelte Schriften* have been placed in ⟨ ⟩; those added by the editors of *Selected Works* in [ ].

The titles of works have been left in German (with English in parentheses) if they have not been translated into English. Otherwise, only the English title is used. When figures and works which are now no longer so well known are mentioned by Dilthey, we have provided brief annotations. But since they are not repeated from essay to essay, the index should be consulted for the first mention of names.

We have attempted to identify the many passages quoted by Dilthey without any citation. This has sometimes proved to be especially difficult; some passages could not be located even by the experts we consulted.

Since the number of our editorial notes greatly exceeds those in Dilthey's original texts, the former will remain unmarked and the latter will have a (D) at the end.

Our task has been facilitated by our assistant editor, Kenneth Heiges, but others have provided invaluable help as well. We are especially grateful to Dr. John Krois of Emory University, the staff of the Goethe Wörterbuch in Tübingen, and Professor W. Keller of the University of Cologne. Our thanks also to Ms. Vicki Shadix at Emory University for her skill in preparing the manuscript for this volume, and to Dennis Dugan for preparing the index.

Permission to quote from *Hölderlin: Poems and Fragments*, translated by Michael Hamburger (1980), has been granted by Cambridge University Press, New York.

# ABBREVIATIONS

| | |
|---|---|
| *CE* | *Conversations of Goethe with Eckermann*, trans. by John Oxenford. |
| (D) | Dilthey's own footnote. All others have been added by the editors. |
| *ED* | Dilthey, *Das Erlebnis und die Dichtung.* |
| *F* | Goethe, *Faust*, trans. by Walter Kaufman. |
| *GCE* | *Goethe: Conversations and Encounters*, ed. and trans. by David Luke and Robert Pick. |
| *GS* | Dilthey, *Gesammelte Schriften.* |
| *GSA* | Hölderlin, *Sämtliche Werke*, Grosse Stuttgarter Ausgabe. |
| *GSM* | Ludwig Lewisohn, *Goethe: The Story of a Man.* |
| *H* | Hölderlin, *Hyperion: Or the Hermit of Greece*, trans. by Willard R. Trask. |
| *HPF* | Hölderlin, *Poems and Fragments*, trans. by Michael Hamburger. |
| *SW* | Dilthey, *Selected Works.* |
| *TF* | *The Autobiography of Goethe, Truth and Fiction: Relating to My Life*, trans. by John Oxenford. |
| *WA* | *Goethes Werke*, Weimarer Ausgabe. |

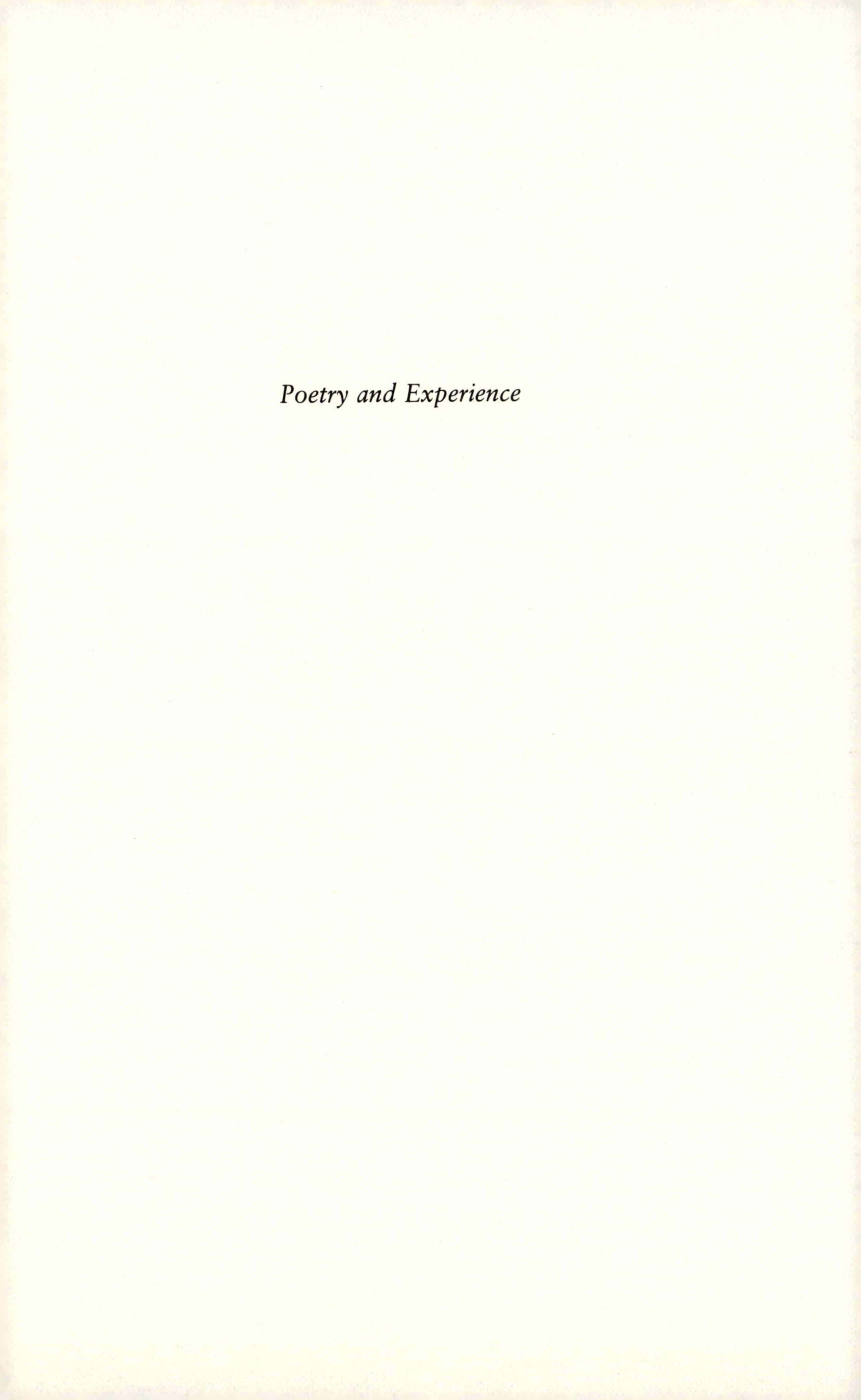

*Poetry and Experience*

# INTRODUCTION TO VOLUME V

In this volume we have selected those essays by Dilthey that contain his most important contributions to a philosophical understanding of poetry and to literary criticism. We have also included the essay on "The Three Epochs of Modern Aesthetics and Its Present Task," which deals with aesthetics in the more general sense.

Although a philosopher by profession, Dilthey felt a special affinity to poets and poet-philosophers such as Goethe, Schiller, and Hölderlin. Dilthey claims that since the Renaissance, when the visual arts were still capable of embodying the world-view of the times, our conception of reality has become so complex that only literature can still give expression to it. Whereas music is limited by the succession of tones in time, and the visual arts by what can be encompassed in one momentary frame, the medium of words can guide our imagination in several directions at once.

All the arts serve to intensify our experience, but poetry is so much more successful in this that one could simply call any heightening of our experience a "poetic effect" whether or not it is achieved through poetry. According to Dilthey, this poetic effect allows us to continue the natural process of reflecting on the meaning of our existence—a process that is part of life itself. Poetry completes life in a nonscientific way, allowing life to explicate itself, as it were. This poetically enhanced life is then articulated conceptually by philosophy in accordance with the methods of the human sciences.

Dilthey was able to delineate this close relation between poetry and philosophy especially well for German culture at the turn of the nineteenth century. As he has shown in many essays, the great literature of that age, beginning with Lessing, Goethe, and Schiller and continuing through the Romantic period, is inseparable from the great philosophical developments of Kantian idealism through Fichte, Schelling, Hegel, and Schopenhauer. Dilthey first sketched this reciprocal background in his Schleiermacher biography, which he began when still a theology student. Dilthey sought to understand Schleiermacher's relation to contemporary Romantic literary figures, and it is this historical task that inspired his *geistesgeschichtliche* approach to literature. This approach gradually found its most perfect form in the four literary essays of *Das Erlebnis und die Dichtung* of which two, those on Goethe and Hölderlin, have been translated for this volume. Dilthey's *geistesgeschichtliche* mode of literary study, which became extremely influential in the early twentieth century, combines an analysis of the great works of an author with an understanding of his intellectual development and other relevant cultural movements of his epoch.

One of the reasons for Dilthey's success as a historian was his ability to make the romanticism of Schleiermacher and his generation accessible to a later generation for whom radically different scientific and political concerns had become predominant. He was able to render the insights of these Romantic poets and idealist philosophers meaningful, without assenting to their speculative assumptions and systematic claims. Dilthey was also able to renew that sensitivity to historical contexts which had been developed by the Historical School of that earlier period. But he did not seek to merely revive the great ideas of a previous cultural epoch, for they also served as important reminders that the contemporary positivistic approach to the human sciences "truncates" the full reality of life. The answer to positivism lay not in a return to idealism or historicism, but in developing a more adequate conception of experience which would do justice to its fullness and integrate its intellectual content with its affective and volitional energy. The clue to such an improved theory of experience lies in the experience of the poets, but the formulation of the theory requires philosophical reflection. In the following, where the individual essays in this volume will be discussed in more detail, we will periodically return to the theme of the development of this concept of experience as "lived experience."

## POETICS

Dilthey's essay "The Imagination of the Poet," usually referred to as his *Poetics*, represents his single most important work in aesthetics. Not only does it examine the main historical contributions to the interpretation of literary works, but it also gives the fullest expression to Dilthey's own conception of the significance of poetry. His analysis of the role of technique and form in literature discloses an unusually acute awareness of the multiple conditions that intersect in the work of art and render its style not some ideal abstraction but a concrete extraction from reality. Published in 1887, when Dilthey still thought it possible to develop special explanative laws for the human sciences, the essay sets forth three psychological laws of metamorphosis in an effort to explain the peculiar creative power of the poet's imagination.[1]

The more general theoretical significance of the *Poetics* for Dilthey's work as a whole can be summed up in the following three points:

1. Poetics provides an analytic model whose findings have systematic import for the other human sciences. Literary works, like scientific works, have been preserved in terms of well-articulated and stratified traditions. Such traditions make it possible for a work that has influenced others to continue to coexist with them. But the literary tradition has a further advantage. Poets have left us detailed accounts of their creative processes, while scientists, who are primarily concerned with the confirmation of their results, seldom report on their processes of discovery and invention. All this leads Dilthey to think that he can use poetics to examine what influences are exerted in the human world, and how creative impulses manifest themselves in the historical world of human objectifications. Dilthey writes: "Our philosophical conception of history was developed from literary history. Perhaps poetics will have a similar significance for the systematic study of historical expressions of life" (see p. 36).

2. Dilthey's attempt to understand the creativity of the poet makes the *Poetics* the first full-scale account of his conception of psychology as a human science. But beyond that, the essay shows perhaps more clearly than any other how Dilthey conceived the relation between psychology and history. Poetics stands at the midpoint between the historical human sciences on the one hand and the more systematic human sciences on the other. Yet unlike many of the systematic human sciences such as sociology and political science, where economic and social institutions exert a direct influence on the events and objectifications of history, in literature and art these influences are always filtered through the psyche of an individual creative mind. Here more than in any other domain is it possible to study how individuals come to terms with their historical context and how some can even typify their epoch.

3. To the extent that it is possible to obtain a sense of the re-

[1] These laws of imaginative metamorphosis have been discussed at length in Frithjof Rodi, *Morphologie und Hermeneutik: Zur Methode von Diltheys Aesthetik* (Stuttgart: Kohlhammer, 1969) and in Rudolf Makkreel, *Dilthey, Philosopher of the Human Studies* (Princeton: Princeton University Press, 1975).

spective psychological and historical contributions to the work of art, Dilthey attempts to define what is universally valid for aesthetics and what is historically conditioned and relative. Dilthey is often seen as a historical relativist, but it is clear that he believed it possible to identify universally valid aesthetic traits which justify us in considering certain works of art as classics. A work is a classic if despite the unavoidable historicity of its technique it can still move us today. Our access to the content of great art that can speak to all human beings is through the kind of psychology which was first formulated in this essay and then further refined seven years later in his "Ideas Concerning a Descriptive and Analytic Psychology."[2]

One of the ways in which Dilthey's search for universally valid aesthetic traits manifested itself was in his analysis of six elementary spheres of feeling that are relevant to our response to a literary work (see pp. 77-86). These range from purely sensuous feelings, to formal feelings aroused by the rhythmic relations of sounds, to feelings aroused by various aspects of the meaning-content of a poem. Dilthey describes and analyzes these feelings prior to explaining how they are produced. Before proposing hypotheses about why repetition in rhythm is experienced as pleasurable, he insists on the importance of thorough descriptions of the normal psychological responses to the different levels of a work which can be codified in elementary aesthetic laws. One conclusion Dilthey draws from his descriptive analysis of the spheres of feelings is that pleasure cannot be considered their common denominator. The utilitarian conception that the poetic impression must be designed to maximize our pleasure is specifically criticized (see p. 123). We are not simply rational creatures constantly calculating means of accumulating pleasures and avoiding pains. The observation of everyday experience shows that we seek to satisfy drives that do not at all produce pleasure, but instead cause sorrow, frustration. Our overriding, even irrational drive is not to maximize pleasure, but to heighten our sense of life. What we seek from poetry is "powerful stimuli, even when mixed with strong pains" (see p. 124). The purpose of poetry is to expand the scope of our lived experience.

Although the intense pain experienced in observing a tragedy must be assuaged so that the observer is finally put in a state of equilibrium, what makes tragedy such an important literary form

[2] Dilthey, *Selected Works* (hereafter *SW*), 6 vols. (Princeton: Princeton University Press, 1985–), vol. 2.

is that its inherently powerful effects on us lead us to dispense with the trivial and to focus on what is essential in life.[3]

However, in a section that provides psychological explanations for certain general aesthetic principles established by Gustav Fechner (see pp. 86-93), Dilthey does formulate a so-called higher law of aesthetic reconciliation according to which compensation for unpleasurable stimuli can be provided by succeeding pleasurable stimuli (see p. 92). In so doing Dilthey falls back into a kind of calculative aesthetics which constructs total effects from elementary stimuli. The implicit assumption here is that particular stimuli have a constant effect regardless of their context. This stands in conflict with passages in the same essay where Dilthey describes psychic life as continuously formative and developmental. The same stimulus can thus never have the same effect on us. When Dilthey made plans in 1907-1908 to revise his *Poetics,* he acknowledged that this whole section on psychological explanations would have to be dropped (see *GS*, VI, 312).

If one takes this subsequent rejection of so-called higher level laws together with the recognition already formulated in the *Poetics* that aesthetic analysis into elementary feelings can never be exhaustive, then we see that it is impossible to account for the total effect of a work by means of universally valid rules. Analysis does locate elements whose effect is universally valid. Yet "the number of such elements is unlimited because of the infinite divisibility of the total aesthetic effect" (see p. 86). Thus the general psychological laws of aesthetics that Dilthey formulated in conjunction with his analysis of the six elementary spheres of feeling can illuminate only partial aspects of an art work. Our understanding of its overall meaning requires a different approach, one which examines the work of art as a psychohistorical product. We conclude from this that the thesis of point 3 above, namely, that psychology can provide access to what is universal, is limited by the thesis of point 2 concerning the intersection of the psychological and the historical. We can find what is universally valid in art only by artificially isolating its constituents. But to understand the fullness of the work of art as an expression of life, we must examine it within a concrete psychohistorical context. This is the approach Dilthey takes in the following section of the *Poetics* (see pp. 93-106).

[3] Dilthey, *Gesammelte Schriften* (hereafter *GS*), 19 vols., 1914-1982. Vols. I-XII (Stuttgart: B. G. Teubner, and Göttingen: Vandenhoeck & Ruprecht); Vols. XIII-XIX (Göttingen: Vandenhoeck & Ruprecht), XIX, 258; *SW*, vol. 1.

We have indicated the possible contribution of psychological description and explanation to a poetics. However, Dilthey's approach to the poetic imagination is not psychological in the commonly held subjective sense, for he never isolates the psychic life of the poet from his historical context. Thus he writes that "the activities and functions of the imagination do not arise in a vacuum. They should originate in a healthy, powerful psyche filled with reality. . . . All genuine poetry feeds on historical fact" (see p. 57). It feeds on such facts as they are appropriated in the lived experience of the poet. His experiences of reality are accumulated and ordered in terms of a gradually developing acquired psychic nexus. Past experiences are structured by this acquired or psychohistorical nexus which "consists not only of contents, but also of the connections which are established among these contents; these connections are just as real as the contents. The connections are lived and experienced as relations between representational contents, as relationships of values to one another, and as structures of ends and means" (see p. 72). The self relates to the world through this acquired psychic nexus, selects what is of interest, and establishes its purposes. The acquired psychic nexus embodies our overall response or attitude to reality, which can then be expressed in what Dilthey calls a world-view.

What is of concern here is the way the acquired psychic nexus informs the poetic imagination. It provides the framework for explaining how images are transformed by an artist. The most important process of the metamorphosis of images is the process of completion whereby the imagination draws on the fullness and richness of this overall nexus. "Only when the whole acquired psychic nexus becomes active can images be transformed on the basis of it: innumerable, immeasurable, almost imperceptible changes occur in their nucleus. . . . Thus we obtain from images and their connections what is essential about a state of affairs: what gives it its meaning in the nexus of reality. Even the style of the artist is influenced in this way" (see p. 104).

Whereas this acquired psychic nexus normally functions to focus our attention on those representations which are best adapted to the reality at hand and the particular purposes of the moment, in the artist it also serves to complete and enrich what is represented. A particular image becomes charged with the energy of the acquired psychic nexus and thus comes to typify it. The process of completion is especially central in the poetic imagination as it transforms lived experience so that "something outer is enlivened by something inner or something inner is made visible and intuitable by something outer . . ." (see p. 104). By means of this mutual reinforcement of the inner life of feeling and the outer reality of the world, the poetic process of completion taps the basic unity of man's psychophysical being—a unity that is then developed not only in poetic world-views but also in language, myth, and metaphysics.

As the theory of world-views to be published in volume 6 will make clear, Dilthey attached great importance to poetry for its ability to complete our lived experience of reality without attempting to make it absolute. This distinguishes the poetic expressions of world-views from their religious and philosophical expressions. Religious world-views attempt to define the meaning of human existence by appealing to an invisible transcendent framework. Philosophical world-views attempt to comprehend the mystery of the universe by means of a conceptual metaphysical system. In both cases an absolute total framework is created for life which distorts its dynamic essence. The fullness and openness of life are sacrificed either to some absolute transcendent being or to some absolute conceptual principle. In poetry, on the other hand, our life-experience is completed by being typified rather than totalized. By claiming less, the poetic world-view actually proves to have a more lasting value. Poetry being the imaginative condensation of the life-experience of the poet, which in turn is the integration of historical and psychological forces intersecting in the life of that individual, can at best have a typical significance.[4] The work of the poet cannot claim to have a universal validity as such, even though its specific constituents may exert an effect on the reader in terms of the kinds of universal laws we analyzed earlier.

Poetry is the meaningful articulation of lived experience and therefore never reducible to general ideas. Similarly, when Dilthey speaks of the poetic mood that pervades a literary work, he is not referring merely to a general psychological attitude expressed in the work, but to a meta-physical disposition which makes the work at the same time an expression of reality.[5]

Dilthey claims that the poet is in touch with reality, but it could be argued that the common man is even more in contact with reality. This is the point of dispute between Dilthey and the naturalists of his time, as we will see in "The Three Epochs of Modern Aes-

[4] For a discussion of the various senses of type in Dilthey, see Makkreel, *Dilthey*, pp. 112, 240-242.

[5] For a discussion of the difference between metaphysics and our meta-physical disposition, see *Introduction to the Human Sciences*, Book II, in *SW*, vol. 1.

thetics." The naturalists reacted against the Romantic glorification of the poet as a solitary genius who is removed from ordinary life, alienated from contemporary society, and nostalgic for the nobility of existence associated with the classical ideal of the Greeks. Instead, naturalists wished to describe the life of ordinary people in contemporary society in their effort to replace an idealistic aesthetics of beauty with an aesthetics of truth. Although Dilthey, too, is critical of idealistic aesthetics and the Romantic conception of genius as a divinely inspired madness, he believes that the naturalists have reacted more violently than is warranted. The poet should not be restricted to describing and exposing the world as it is. He must have a vision which will make his images transcend what is simply given in experience. But unlike the madman, whose images depart from reality arbitrarily because his acquired psychic nexus has become inactive, the images of the poet transform reality precisely to uncover what is typical in it. Instead of reproducing reality as experienced, the metamorphosis of a poetic image intensifies certain aspects, excludes other less relevant aspects, and finally completes it to conform to the overall structure of the acquired psychic nexus. Dilthey assumes that a poet like Goethe has an acquired nexus that is broad enough in scope to typify his historical situation. But however broad it may be, it also involves a perspective which can never be fully representative. The psyche of the poet is rarely as isolated as Hölderlin's, but even when it encompasses reality, idiosyncratic distortions cannot be ruled out. Dilthey's psychohistorical approach to poetry does not encourage the isolation of the poet, but it cannot assure that the poet's contact with reality is adequate. Every acquired psychic nexus is selective, which entails that it is a function of subjective feelings.

Dilthey's primary goal was to propose an account of creativity which would allow us to appreciate artistic genius without idealizing it. Yet he also gives an extended analysis of poetic technique which considers poetry from the side of reception-aesthetics. Dilthey admits that it would also have been possible for him to start with the impression of a work of literature on the public and from there to work back to the creative process of the poet. But that kind of approach from the outside to the inside tends to consider the creative process too much in terms of the calculation of effects on the reader or audience. Dilthey prefers to proceed from the inside out so that the calculation of effects characteristic of poetic technique can be seen to be a mere moment within the more encompassing spontaneous processes of poetic image-formation. The intention that refines an effect should not destroy the semblance of unintended formative processes. Nor should poetic technique remove what is incommensurable in a poetic formation. This means that technique must be defined historically. There can be no universally valid techniques for the various genres of literature.

Dilthey began his own *Poetics* with the claim that Aristotle's *Poetics* is dead. Yet, he follows this with an unusually perceptive analysis of Aristotle's work which shows that its value lay in articulating the technique of classical Greek drama. Aristotle's *Poetics* is no longer viable as the basis for a universally valid theory of drama. It can, however, remain a powerful model for us if we interpret it as a historically limited formulation of the ideals of Greek dramatic technique. Every age needs its own theory of technique and can learn from the way Aristotle performed this task. In the age of the French classical drama, aestheticians had mechanically derived rules from Aristotle, but Dilthey shows how Lessing, Goethe, and Schiller were able to appropriate aspects of his *Poetics* creatively as part of their own efforts to produce a living poetic theory.

In "The Three Epochs of Modern Aesthetics and Its Present Task" Dilthey relates the historicity of technique to the problem of style. It is precisely an awareness of style that Dilthey finds lacking in the proponents of naturalism in the arts. Their search for truth and rejection of otherworldly ideals are commendable, but their main thrust is too negative to appreciate the contributions of a stylistic unity. Instead of completing reality, naturalism dissects it. According to Dilthey, naturalism is a recurring phenomenon that appears whenever there is a crisis in the arts. Such a crisis occurs when the dominant styles of one age begin to break down and a sense of what is characteristic about a new age has not yet been developed.

To produce a proper understanding of style is the "present task" of aesthetics, and it can only be arrived at by a cooperative interchange among the creative artist, the aesthetician, the critic, and the public. A case could be made for the thesis that the deficiencies of the past epochs of aesthetics derive from the fact that what should have been a four-way debate was reduced to a series of dialogues initiated by philosophical aestheticians. Thus it may be said that the rationalist aesthetics of the seventeenth century paid adequate attention only to the perspective of the critic; the eighteenth-century analysis of aesthetic impressions only to the perspective of the spectator or public; the historically conscious aesthetics of nineteenth-century Germany only to the perspective of the creative artist. But Dilthey was too good a historian to be satisfied with such a simple formula, and he at the same time shows that the greatest representative of each of these epochs transcended its respective limits.

Cartesian rationalism produced what Dilthey called the natural system of aesthetic laws. France was the home of this system. It found its embodiment in such works as Boileau's *Art of Poetry*, which provides rules of criticism that regulate our judgment of poetry. French classicism allowed the critic to impose rules of order and perfection derived from the nature of things rather than from the imagination of the poet.

Dilthey provides further insight into this epoch by showing how Leibniz developed and advanced this system of aesthetics. What informed Leibniz's metaphysics of a rational, harmonious universe was an inspired intuition about the nature of psychic life which allowed him to argue that behind the discursive order of nature there exists a prediscursive, felt order. Even sensory perception displays a hidden intelligibility. Perceptions are not just givens of sense on which logical order must be imposed but are spontaneous activities with certain implicit dispositions to preserve and perfect themselves (see pp. 182-184). According to Leibniz our aesthetic consciousness of order and harmony goes much deeper than had been recognized. Leibniz's view is characterized in a way which lets us see him as a predecessor of Dilthey's own psychological aesthetics: "Delight in beauty is thus the result of a consciousness of the augmented activity of psychical power in accord with its inherent law which requires it to produce unity in plurality" (see p. 184). In this way Leibniz was able to extend the relation between aesthetics and a critical principle of unity to the artist and the public as well.

The next epoch of aesthetics blossomed in eighteenth-century Britain. It studied the aesthetic impression that a work of art makes on the public and analyzed it into a number of elementary feelings. This approach developed what Dilthey called a spectator psychology, which, although important for its "delineation of the feelings as the true locus of aesthetic apprehension" (see p. 193), was nevertheless incapable of understanding the creative processes of an artist. Dilthey regards Kames' *Elements of Criticism* as one of the best embodiments of this approach.[6] Its aim was to explain general

[6] In "The Imagination of the Poet," Fechner's *Vorschule der Ästhetik* was used as its most up-to-date representative.

agreement about taste by analyzing the work of art into its elementary components, each of which can be tested for its effect on the spectator. But the work of art is conceived as no more than a mass of impressions, so that such features as its style, which pertain to the overall effect, are not accounted for. Moreover, Dilthey finds it naive to assume that the several parts into which a work can be analyzed would have an isolated and constant effect. He claims that many of our apparently natural or immediate responses of feeling are, in fact, historically conditioned and thus not necessarily constant (see p. 199).

Despite the limitations of this empirical approach to aesthetics, Dilthey finds a greatness in Kames' *Elements of Criticism* that has relevance beyond his own epoch. Although Kames recognized the importance of feeling for aesthetic apprehensions, he did not, like Kant, posit a special aesthetic contemplative or disinterested feeling of pleasure. Instead he distinguished between the emotions caused by the ideal presence of objects in works of art and the passions caused by the real presence of objects. Emotions are internal motions; passions are emotions that arouse desire and thus lead to external motion as well. Dilthey regards Kames' notion of ideal presence as a more positive formulation of a similar idea to be found later in Schiller's theory of aesthetic semblance. Although Dilthey does not elaborate why he considers it superior (see p. 193), if we examine Kames' account of ideal presence, the reason becomes clear. The abstractly conceived relation between subject and object in Schiller's aesthetic semblance is represented by Kames as a more immediate relation in which the subject loses himself in the object. In ideal presence a mere representation of something past is transformed into a complete image where there is no past as distinct from the present. It is this capacity of art to preserve the past in the present that allows us to respond emotionally to what rushes by in real life. As Kames says, "our emotions are never instantaneous."[7] The ideal presence created in art allows us to fashion a more coherent emotional response to reality than would otherwise be possible. This anticipates Dilthey's own life-oriented theory of art and, in particular, his theory of the presence of the past in lived experience (see "Fragments for a Poetics," p. 226).

The third epoch of modern aesthetics was characterized by a historical method which had its roots in Winckelmann but only came to full growth in nineteenth-century Germany. The ordinary

[7] Kames, Lord Henry Home, *Elements of Criticism* (London: B. Blake, 1839), p. 35.

meaning of the term "historical" is too narrow to convey how Dilthey understands this epoch, for he sees in it the conjunction of four different factors. The *first* of these is transcendental philosophy and its conception of the role of the mind in actively shaping and producing our world-view. This also contributed greatly to the understanding of artistic creativity and genius. The *second* factor involves a more systematic concern with the relation between natural beauty and artistic beauty. Here Dilthey refers to Schelling and alludes to his speculative claim that what is created unconsciously in nature can be imitated and made conscious by the artist. This claim is reminiscent of Leibniz's conception of a harmony between an aesthetically ordered universe and an individual apprehending mind, but Schelling adds a historical dimension and suggests that the evolving world-order stands in need of completion by the human mind. The active formative powers disclosed by transcendental philosophy are now seen as complementing natural developmental processes. This leads away from the fixed a priori framework established in Kant's first *Critique* and toward a critical perspective on history.

Dilthey criticizes the first two components of the historical method for being too abstract and speculative—not grounded in a psychological understanding of individual artists and oblivious to the concrete differences among the various arts. The *third* factor implicit in the historical method concerns precisely this last point. It encompasses those special inquiries made by painters, poets, and architects into the way the specific medium and means of representation of their respective arts condition the forms that actually have been produced. The medium and means of representation of a particular art place certain material and formal limitations on what it is possible to create.

The *fourth* factor is the most obviously historical. It involves the attempts by Schiller, Friedrich Schlegel, and Hegel to distinguish "the main *epochs of art* in human history as a sequence of artistic attitudes towards reality" (see p. 203). These types of attitude are discerned on the basis of the meaning-content expressed in great art. According to Dilthey, this is also too speculative. The idea of a pattern of development common to all the arts ignores the different formal and material conditions of the various arts. We can delineate a series of epochs within the history of a specific art, but not for the history of art in general.[8]

[8] For an attempt to summarize Dilthey's contribution to the analysis of epochs, see Makkreel, *Dilthey*, pp. 394-399.

Although each art has its own form and mode of being, at times the conditions exist for the creation of a *Gesamtkunstwerk* (total work of art) in which several arts intersect. We usually associate the idea of a *Gesamtkunstwerk* with Wagner's "Music Drama" where music, poetry, and staging are more thoroughly fused than in traditional opera and made subservient to the cardinal interest of the dramatic action. Dilthey, however, sees it as a more pervasive phenomenon that is also exemplified in ancient Teutonic hymns. In *Von deutscher Dichtung und Musik* (Of German Poetry and Music), he writes: "The hymn is the *Gesamtkunstwerk* in the sphere of expression . . .—the same emotion is simultaneously expressed in poetry, music, and rhythmic movement."[9] Dilthey also points to Semper's idea of architecture as a spatial *Gesamtkunstwerk* integrating other visual arts as well (see pp. 213-214). Such works are bold attempts to articulate the spirit of an age which Dilthey sees as the main task of art. But even if a work is not totalistic in this sense, it can be significant if its style serves to reinforce what contemporaries experience as meaningful in their own lives.

In the "Fragments for a Poetics," which are notes from 1907-1908 for use in revising the *Poetics,* Dilthey reexamines the search for meaning in art. One of the fragments, entitled "Meaning as a Category of Life," warns that meaning should not be regarded as a special aesthetic category but as rooted in life itself. "The meaning of things is already inherent in them" (see p. 230). But as Dilthey says elsewhere, this meaning as given in lived experience (*Erlebnis*) is still somewhat indeterminate and it is the task of the poet to explicate it. In the "Fragments" Dilthey compares lived experiences to the motifs in an andante that must be unfolded (explicated) and then recapitulated in such a way as to be drawn back together again (implication).

In other related notes for revising the *Poetics,* Dilthey indicates that his previous analysis of spheres of feelings is to be recast as an analysis of spheres of lived experience. Although the term "lived experience" was already used in the *Poetics* of 1887, it is subjected to an extended reexamination in the "Fragments." Whereas a feeling is a relatively fleeting subjective state related to representational consciousness, a lived experience is now described as a more lasting mode in which reality is possessed. A lived experience is "not given

[9] *Von deutscher Dichtung und Musik*, (Stuttgart: B. G. Teubner, and Göttingen: Vandenhoeck & Ruprecht, 1957), p. 45.

to me" like a representation which is an index to some other reality beyond it. Instead, a lived experience is directly "there-for-me" as its own reality. In its most basic mode, a lived experience involves a reflexive or "self-given" awareness which is an immediate, prereflective consciousness where there is not yet the distinction between act and content, subject and object that characterizes representational consciousness. The *reflexive* awareness (*Innewerden*) inherent in lived experience is thus not to be confused with *reflection* (*Besinnung*). Yet because of the temporal structure of lived experience, it naturally goes over into reflection whereby we compare related experiences. The significance of Dilthey's extended analysis of time in the "Fragments" is to show that for lived experience the present is not a fleetingly felt now-state, but "the continuously advancing being ful-filled with reality in the course of time" (see p. 225). Lived experience is a structural nexus which preserves the past as a "presence" in the present. Every lived experience becomes part of a system of contextually related experiences explicated from it through a process of reflection on its meaning. Implicit in the structural analysis of lived experience is the part-whole relation that is central to Dilthey's hermeneutic approach.

As can be seen from volume 4, Dilthey's interest in hermeneutics goes back to the 1860s. In an earlier version of the Goethe essay already published in 1877, Dilthey had argued for the importance of incorporating the hermeneutical insights of Schleiermacher and Boeckh into poetics. There Dilthey spoke of understanding as reliving psychological states of mind, which suggests that he did not consider hermeneutics and psychology as inherently antithetical. What is clear, however, is that as the hermeneutical approach becomes increasingly prominent in Dilthey's later writings, the explanative pretensions of psychology must be placed in question. In the "Ideas Concerning a Descriptive and Analytic Psychology" of 1894 the role of explanation in psychology is already much more limited than in the *Poetics* of 1887. And in the "Fragments" we find Dilthey explicitly distancing himself from the claim in the *Poetics* that it is best to proceed from the inside out, from the psychohistorical explanation of the creative process of poetic metamorphosis to the analysis of historical technique exhibited by the poetic product.

Hermeneutics proceeds instead from the outside to the inside, and Dilthey now adds that this inside need not always be understood psychologically. Hermeneutics is the study of human expressions and objectifications to determine the meanings embodied in them.

Since what we produce always has unintended implications and consequences, the meanings embodied in human products gain independence from their creators. The author is no longer a privileged interpreter of his work. This is the significance of Dilthey's claim that disinterestedness is a property of the lived experience of the creative artist (see p. 227).

The lived experience of the poet assumes an impersonal quality that makes it more than the result of his own consciousness. Thus Dilthey strengthens his earlier claim that the nexus of lived experiences is not merely psychological. The language, myths, and songs with which we grow up already provide ways of gathering and organizing our lived experiences, which are more primordial than purely psychological descriptions and accounts. Moreover, Dilthey claims that because lived experiences conceived as psychic states tend to merge into each other, their delimitation must rely less on direct descriptions and more on the indirect method of studying their expressions and objectifications. It is only through expression that the fullness of lived experience can be captured. Expression is thus not secondary in the sense of merely communicating or displaying what is first in the poet's consciousness. "It brings out something new" (see p. 228) that neither introspection nor psychological description could discern.

This emphasis on expression and objectification as necessary for the articulation or the uncovering of lived experience adds further urgency to Dilthey's call for a more serious study by aestheticians of the distinctive medium and means of representation used in a particular art. As Dilthey wrote in an even later discussion of music, there is no clear way of demarcating the composer's lived experience from its expression because his experience is thoroughly musical: "There is no duality of lived experience and music, no double world, no carry-over from the one into the other. Genius involves simply living in the tonal sphere as though this sphere alone existed" (see "The Understanding of Other Persons," *GS*, VII, 222; *SW*, vol. 3). This link between the imagination of the artist and his medium also manifests itself in a 1908 outline for revising the *Poetics*. There it becomes clear that the general descriptions of the poetic imagination need to be specified in terms of a "linguistic imagination" which includes a "rhythmic and tonal imagination" (see *GS*, VI, 310). But this outline still preserves the order of the original *Poetics* by proceeding from an examination of the poet's lived experience, imagination, and creative processes to an examination of the work.

However, on the basis of Dilthey's final hermeneutic perspective the structure of the *Poetics* would need to be revised more radically. Although Dilthey never produced a revised *Poetics*, we can see some of the changes indicated in other works. In the *Formation of the Historical World in the Human Sciences* (1910), he writes: "The object which the history of literature or poetics deals with at first is completely distinct from the psychic processes in the poet or his readers" (*GS*, VII, 85; *SW*, vol. 3). Here we see Dilthey renounce his own earlier procedure of beginning with an aesthetics of genius. But he does not replace it with a reception-aesthetics, which orients everything to the impression the work makes on the psyche of the reader. Instead, poetics must start with an examination of the work as a part of objective spirit. It must first attempt to understand the relation of the words in the text to the meaning expressed by them. This meaning is not reducible to what was meant by the creator, but constitutes an independent inner nexus. Once this meaning has been determined objectively, the intentions of the creator may be considered. This then involves the transition from understanding (*Verstehen*) to re-experiencing (*Nacherleben*). In everything that we find meaningful, that which possesses the highest value is individuality, whether it be that of a great literary character like Hamlet or a great poet like Goethe. It is for this reason that Dilthey considers re-experiencing as the highest hermeneutic task.

Poetics should not ignore the poet's creative contribution, but it can be appreciated only after understanding the meaning embodied in a poem and determining how it stands in relation to a tradition. Precisely when we reach that point where the work organizes lived experiences differently from the way the conventions of a shared language and artistic technique would have us expect, we must appeal to psychological understanding. Thus Dilthey's earlier psychological approach is not to be discarded, but to be integrated into a larger hermeneutic approach. It is not the case as René Wellek would have us believe that near the end of his life, Dilthey came to the tragic realization that his psychological approach to literature had to be abandoned.[10] Instead, Dilthey was forced to make a further revision in his psychological program. But this represents only one more phase in a long series of reevaluations.[11] Since Dilthey's hermeneutical motto is to understand an author better than

[10] René Wellek, "Wilhelm Dilthey's Poetics and Literary Theory," *Wächter und Hüter, Festschrift für Hermann J. Weigand* (New Haven: Yale University Press, 1957), pp. 126-127.

[11] For a more detailed consideration of Dilthey's reevaluation of psychology, see Makkreel, *Dilthey*, pp. 294-304, 322-332.

he understood himself, re-experiencing can no longer be conceived in terms of reproducing either the actual process of creation or the actual state of mind of the author. Nevertheless, a psychological context for understanding remains relevant. To be sure, Dilthey's hopes for establishing poetics as a special human science had been set too high, but many of his earlier psychological contributions to poetics remain relevant and must be seen to play a delayed role in the overall process of understanding literature.

## POETRY AND LIVED EXPERIENCE

Dilthey wrote innumerable literary studies which have now been collected in such volumes as *Die große Phantasiedichtung* (The Great Poetry of the Imagination), *Von deutscher Dichtung und Musik* (Of German Poetry and Music), and volumes 15 and 16 of the *Gesammelte Schriften*. The only volume of literary essays that was published by Dilthey's students during his own lifetime was *Das Erlebnis und die Dichtung* (Poetry and Lived Experience). It appeared in 1906 and contains Dilthey's four best-known literary essays: "Gotthold Ephraim Lessing," "Goethe and the Poetic Imagination," "Novalis," and "Friedrich Hölderlin." The volume was instantly acclaimed and established a model for the *geistesgeschichtliche* approach to literary history that was subsequently developed by Hermann Nohl, Rudolf Unger, Emil Ermatinger, and Julius Petersen. Undoubtedly it also influenced such works as Ernst Cassirer's *Idee und Gestalt* (Idea and Gestalt) and Georg Lukács' *Soul and Form*.

We have selected the two essays in *Das Erlebnis und die Dichtung* which have the most direct bearing on poetic theory: those on Goethe and on Hölderlin. Goethe provides Dilthey with the ideal illustration of his *Poetics*, and Hölderlin forces Dilthey to move beyond his own initial standpoint.

The Goethe essay is a central work for several reasons. Not only does one of its sections provide the title for the whole volume in which it appeared, but also its history is intimately tied to Dilthey's *Poetics*. Just as the original 1877 form of the Goethe essay contains the seeds of Dilthey's *Poetics*, so the final 1910 form translated here stands as a last, somewhat more expression-oriented formulation of the same theory. The special affinity between the *Poetics* and the Goethe essay lies in the fact that both have as their core a theory of the poetic imagination. It was Goethe's extraordinarily powerful visual imagination and his reflections on the quasi-organic vitality of intuition that led Dilthey to the physiological studies on which he hoped to ground his own aesthetics. The concept of metamorphosis, developed in Goethe's studies in botany and zoology, had been refined by the German physiologist Johannes Müller, and two of the laws of the metamorphosis of poetic imagination clearly bear the mark of this influence.

Throughout his life Dilthey manifested a keen interest in Goethe and a particular sympathy with his vision. The diary of the nineteen-year-old student of theology in Heidelberg starts off with a kind of typology of world-views where the pantheism of Goethe and Spinoza plays an important role. Some years later he included in his book on Schleiermacher a central chapter on German literature as the formation of a new world-view. There Goethe is given the prominent role of initiating a new method of "Anschauung" (intuition). This idea was also expressed in Dilthey's public lecture of 1867 in Basel where he claims that "Goethe's searching eye still directs what we are doing today"[12]—an allusion to his own endeavor to sum up the achievements of what he called "the literary and philosophical movement in Germany between 1770 and 1800."

There is, however, another line of thought which connects Dilthey's ideas on poetics to Goethe. When Dilthey holds up the "totality of human nature" against any kind of "truncated" account put forward by one-sided intellectualism, it is Goethe above all whom he is championing. In fact, a good number of concepts through which Dilthey tried to express the fullness and vitality of concrete human experience are derived from Goethe, who coined most of Dilthey's terms, beginning with *Leben*: i.e., *Lebenserfahrung* (life-experience), *Lebensbezug* (life-relation), *Lebensgefühl* (feeling of life), and so forth. The life-root in all these terms points to the "togetherness" of man and his world in lived experience. Although the key term in this line of Dilthey's thought, namely *Erlebnis* (lived experience), is not of Goethean origin, it epitomizes Goethe's holistic approach. The word itself is a comparatively late derivation of the verb *erleben* (similar to *erfahren* = experience) and comes into use around the middle of the nineteenth century. Dilthey makes use of it occasionally after the early 1870s, but adopts it as a technical term only in the last decade of his life when he speaks of the triad *Erlebnis, Ausdruck, Verstehen* (lived experience, expression, understanding). In his early epistemological inquiries,

[12] *GS*, V, 24.

in his reflections on the method of the historiographer, and above all in the first sketches of an aesthetic theory, the words *Erlebnis* and *Nacherleben*, are not strictly defined, but they suggest various ideas: the idea that an experience can be a kind of unity with its own immanent teleology; the idea that such a unity can be communicated in such a way that we are able to re-experience and relive to a certain degree what has been experienced and expressed by other people even generations ago; and, finally, the idea that the conception of a work of art is rooted in a particularly intense kind of contact with reality where a unification of outer and inner experience takes place.

Despite his subsequent efforts to introduce stricter definitions for some of his basic concepts, Dilthey never overcame a certain vagueness and even an ambiguity in his use of the concept "lived experience." This is in part due to his efforts to use terms which are still rooted in everyday experience and language. Because the Goethe essay contains passages from various stages in Dilthey's development, it discloses several inconsistencies in terminology which have already been shown to exist in the *Poetics*.[13] They especially concern the question whether lived experience is an inner process involving feeling, emotion, and mood, or whether it is to be understood as that unity of inner and outer in which a mutual reinforcement of the inner life of feeling and the outer reality of the world takes place. In fact, both interpretations are correct, depending on the meaning of "inner" and "outer" that one applies. In the *Poetics*, Dilthey compares the process of experiencing to that of breathing: "Just as our body needs to breathe, our soul requires the fulfillment and expansion of its existence in the reverberations of emotional life. Our feeling of life desires to resound in tone, word, and image. Perception satisfies us fully only insofar as it is filled with such content of life and with reverberations of feeling. This to and fro of life at its fullest, of perception enlivened and saturated by feeling, and of the feeling of life shining forth in the clarity of an image: that is the essential characteristic of the content of all poetry" (see p. 59). This comparison with the breathing process is more than a vague analogy: the "totality of lived experience" (p. 106) is not a static relationship of inner and outer, but a dynamic process moving to and fro between acts of enlivening

[13] See Frithjof Rodi, "Grundzüge der Poetik Wilhelm Diltheys," in *Beiträge zur Theorie der Künste im 19. Jahrhundert*, ed. by H. Koopmann and J. A. Schmoll, gen. Eisenwerth (Frankfurt a.M.: V. Klostermann, 1972), p. 81f.; and Makkreel, *Dilthey*, pp. 147ff.

outer experience and visualizing inner feeling. It is here that Dilthey distinguishes between (1) poets who usually start with a vivid experience of situations, actions, and characters which they then enliven with their own feelings, and (2) poets whose major achievement lies in finding perceptual analogues that help to give shape to their inner life. Although Dilthey gives a vivid description of the typical differences between writers such as Shakespeare and Dickens on the one hand and Rousseau and Goethe on the other (a typification that is one of the earliest ideas of his poetics), he again and again emphasizes that every great work of art must be rooted in the totality of lived experience and must contain, as it were, both the inward and outward movements of the breathing process.

In this natural context the words "inner" and "outer" refer to two realms of reality and, accordingly, to two ways of experiencing which give rise to the creative process. But a second sense is added as soon as we speak of lived experience as expressed in a work of art. The expression as the objective structure of the poet's lived experience cannot be referred to as "outer" in the same way that we speak of the poet giving shape to his inner emotional life through visual images. We must distinguish more sharply than Dilthey between the two aspects which one might call the integration of lived experience (unity of inner and outer experience) and the meaning relationship between lived experience and expression. The claim that the meaning of the poet's lived experience (as something inner) can only be ascertained through its expression in the literary work (as something outer) is central to Dilthey's later hermeneutical theory. But this expression can be related back to the various ways in which the poet brings together his inner and outer experience. This integrative aspect is dealt with above all in those passages of the *Poetics* and the Goethe essay where the short sketches of Shakespeare and Rousseau serve to illustrate the contrast between objective and subjective poets.

By distinguishing between these two senses of inner and outer it is possible to avoid misunderstandings which might occur if the reader does not take into account the different phases of Dilthey's development in which the essays in this volume were written. In the *Poetics*, for example, Dilthey speaks of "the constant translation of lived experience into form and form into lived experience" (see p. 45). A contextual analysis can easily show that here Dilthey refers to the two acts of "breathing" within the totality of lived experience and not to the meaning relationship between lived experience, expression, and understanding. But when we read in the

Goethe essay about the structural nexus between lived experience and its expression, where it is said that the poet can express his personal experience fully and totally without any reflection intervening between lived experience and expression, Dilthey is considering poetry from a hermeneutical perspective. It should also be noted that Dilthey's final aesthetic reflections are not so much oriented toward the paradigm of the metamorphosis of images as to that of musical expression and its relation to the lyrical.

This important shift can be seen in the essay on Goethe, but even more so in the one on Hölderlin. Both essays focus on the nature of lyric poetry and explore how the poet makes visible—or rather, audible—the inner flux of his moods and feelings through the melody of his verses. Here the two senses of inner and outer overlap. Dilthey speaks of the inner or "personal" experience which is to be given shape through the poem, and he concentrates on the power of objectifications and their "inner form" to disclose the typical structures of lived experience. The essay on Hölderlin gives especially good examples of Dilthey's analysis of this structural relationship between lived experience and the form of the poem. His literary criticism is by no means limited to a "philosophical" approach in the narrow sense of the word: he is not interested merely in "ideas" but in the particular way the poet gives expression to his lived experience. In the case of Hölderlin, what is expressed is predominantly the poet's inner experience. Hölderlin belongs to the family of subjective poets, in contrast with objective poets such as Shakespeare and Dickens. He is described by Dilthey as a "musical genius," but Dilthey emphasizes that by "musicality" he does not mean simply the "treatment of language or of verse, but also the particular form of the inner processes and their structure" (see p. 374). In Hölderlin and his Romantic contemporaries (above all Novalis and Tieck) Dilthey sees the beginning of a new lyric poetry, "which expresses the exuberance of feeling, the nonobjective power of mood which arises from the inner recesses of the mind itself, the infinite melody of a psychic movement which seems to emanate from indiscernible distances only to disappear in them again" (see p. 376).

The passage just quoted is from a section of the Hölderlin essay entitled "The Poems," which contains the outlines of a theory of lyric poetry. It is an important supplement to the *Poetics* where Dilthey was obviously more interested in problems of drama and the novel than in those of lyric poetry. In one of the concluding passages of the *Poetics*, Dilthey claimed that the "theory of the novel is the most immediate, and by far the most pressing and important task of contemporary poetics" (see p. 172). The essay on Hölderlin, written some twenty years later, reveals a subtle understanding of the possibilities of modern lyrical language. Dilthey draws a line from Hölderlin to the "rhythmical style of Nietzsche" and to the poetry of Verlaine, Baudelaire, and Swinburne—poets of his own generation whom he had not yet recognized in his earlier aesthetic writings. His analysis of Hölderlin's poems therefore aims not so much at emphasizing Hölderlin's singularity, but rather at disclosing the possibilities of modern poetry in general.

His main points are the following: the lyric poem is rooted in a "psychic process that has been lived through" (see p. 372) and objectifies its "teleological" structures, the rising and falling of moods, the contrast of tension and resolution, the rhythm of unrest and tranquility. But the objectification is not normally an immediate verbal expression of inner movement (in this regard Goethe is an exception). The "musical" poet, like the composer, gradually articulates the rhythm of moods and feelings by artistic means which are not directly rooted in our inner life in the way that gestures and exclamations stem from our emotions. Just as the composer makes use of technical means such as repetition, variation, change of key—means which have been developed through centuries—the poet has at his disposal similarly refined linguistic devices such as the sophisticated economy in the use of particular words, the deliberate use of stressed and unstressed syllables in accordance with their semantic value, the application of historically developed meters, and so forth.

Apart from these direct contributions to poetics, the essays on Goethe and Hölderlin contain a number of biographical observations which can be considered as illustrations of Dilthey's theory of world-views. This again is not philosophy in the narrower sense of concentrating on the philosophical content of a literary work and classifying it as a particular type of thought. Literary criticism as it is displayed in Dilthey's essays examines the poet's attitude toward life, the ways in which a poet relates to the present moment, either submitting wholly to it and giving full expression to his immediate feelings (Goethe), or living in the shadow of "the great past of the Greeks" and longing for a better and purer life in the future (Hölderlin). These attitudes are of interest philosophically as far as they can be interpreted as different modes of articulating the meaning of life. Hölderlin, who is said to have lived always "in the totality of his inner life" (see p. 370), tends toward a poetry which expresses "the rhythm of life itself." This "rhythm" happens to be very similar to the law of historical growth and unfolding that Hegel used as the basic formula of his philosophy. But in Hölderlin, according to Dilthey, it is not expressed by an abstract idea or applied to history in order to give unity to the multiplicity of cultural phenomena: it is the very structure of his poetry. Hölderlin "saw how an initial state of feeling unfolds in its parts and ultimately returns to itself, and no longer with its initial indeterminateness. By recollecting the process of its unfolding, the feeling can be integrated into a harmony in which the individual parts resonate" (see p. 373). This process of unfolding and recollecting is like the musical progression from the explication of lived experience to its final implication that we mentioned in our discussion of the "Fragments for a Poetics." But the implication of experience should not be treated as a definite result. Neither in music, nor in poetry, nor in life itself do we reach a conclusion from which a definite meaning can be abstracted. Here Dilthey is in full agreement with Nietzsche who mocked those who considered the final chord in music as the telos of musical development. The meaning is implied and modified at every single stage, but there are moments where the implications produce an expression by which the fullness of lived experience can be communicated to others.

The implications of lived experience should not be seen as final solutions, but must be interpreted in light of what was said earlier about the presence of the past in the present. From this perspective the alternative between Goethe's submitting wholly to the present and Hölderlin's inability to cope with the present is not exhaustive. It is possible to be interested in the past without extinguishing our feeling for the present. Hölderlin's intense awareness of the past could have enriched, rather than detracted from, his present. However, his despair at the failure of the French Revolution led him to conclude that the ideals of humanity as first expressed by the Greeks had died with them. Thus Hölderlin's ideals are not alive in history, but are buried in nature.

Although the momentary present for Hölderlin is normally overshadowed by the past, there are also special moments as described in *Hyperion* which are enjoyed. They are enjoyed not as the fulfilling presence of the past, but as a kind of presence of the divine in nature. Thus Hölderlin speaks of a moment of love in which Diotima appears to Hyperion as a disclosure of the infinite in the midst of finitude, the divine in time. He then compares it to "the light of the southern noontime sun" poured out in "moments in which life itself seems to stand still" (see p. 341). This account of presence clearly prefigures similar passages in Nietzsche's *Thus Spoke Zarathustra.*

But Hyperion's joy in the present already contains within it the consciousness of mortality. "In the moment of greatest happiness when Hyperion first touches the lips of Diotima, he already knows this happiness will end" (see p. 344). Love can only be realized through a harmony with nature and, ultimately, the willingness to die.

Although Dilthey was often critical of Nietzsche's philosophy and its contemptuous attitude toward history, it seems fair to claim not only that Hölderlin influenced Nietzsche, as Dilthey points out, but that works such as the *Birth of Tragedy* and *Zarathustra* served in turn to heighten Dilthey's sensitivity to Hölderlin's poetic achievements. Dilthey refers to the theme of duality in Hölderlin that marks all individual existence, the tragic feeling of mortality that must permeate even a life-affirming pantheism. Is Nietzsche's Apollonian-Dionysian polarity being anticipated here? Certainly the other main figure of Hölderlin's literary imagination, Empedocles, fits the mold of a tragic Dionysian hero. He is, as Dilthey says, ready to sacrifice his life to revive his lost happiness. Empedocles' superhuman heart "feels nature's vitality so intensely that it no longer fears a return to her" (see p. 364).

Dilthey points to another affinity between Hölderlin and Nietzsche: they both felt "the great antithesis between a higher, future humanity . . . and the vulgarity surrounding them and the hundred ways in which it has deformed the human psyche" (see p. 350). On the one hand, this seems to be an admission that the Goethean ideal of full integration, which is so attractive to Dilthey, may no longer be possible for man in the twentieth century. On the other hand, Dilthey preserves the hope that a poetic style can be found that moves beyond the antitheses dwelt upon by Hölderlin and Nietzsche. "Their dithyrambs are poems in prose, and through their irony they play a sovereign artistic game with their enemies" (see p. 350). Irony may be an artistic device, but it is a destructive weapon, and therefore cannot be productive or poetic in the true sense. Although Dilthey's account of the Hölderlin-Nietzsche aesthetic is surprisingly sympathetic, Dilthey finally concludes that figures such as Hyperion and Zarathustra are ahistorical shadows. A genuine poet or novelist must be able to give his figures a lasting visibility grounded in historical facticity. In this respect, Dilthey remained true to one of the central claims of his *Poetics.*

# I

# POETICS

# I

## *The Imagination of the Poet: Elements for a Poetics (1887)*[1]

VI, 103

TRANSLATED BY LOUIS AGOSTA AND RUDOLF A. MAKKREEL

The *Poetics* of Aristotle was the organon for all poetic technique through the second half of the eighteenth century, and the feared standard of critics until Boileau, Gottsched,[2] and Lessing. It was the most effective instrument of philology for the interpretation, criticism, and evaluation of Greek literature. Together with grammar, rhetoric, and logic, the *Poetics* was a constituent of the curriculum of higher education. But then a new aesthetics, born of the spirit of the great period of German literature, came to guide Goethe and Schiller in their work; it was also able to raise the level of understanding in Humboldt,[3] Körner,[4] and the Schlegels, and to secure their aesthetic judgments. This aesthetics dominated the entire realm of German poetry: Goethe and Schiller were its princely rulers while Humboldt, Moritz,[5] Körner, Schelling, the Schlegels,

[1] This is a translation of "Die Einbildungskraft des Dichters: Bausteine für eine Poetik," originally published in a *Festschrift* for Eduard Zeller and reprinted in *GS*, VI, 103-241. Pagination in the margins refers to this volume.

[2] Johann Christoph Gottsched (1700-66). A follower of Christian Wolff, he upheld form and rules in literature over against the excesses of the later Baroque period.

[3] Wilhelm von Humboldt (1767-1835). Philologist and statesman; brother of Alexander von Humboldt; one of the founders of the University of Berlin and the modern *Gymnasium*; a friend of Schiller and Goethe.

[4] Christian Gottfried Körner (1756-1831). Official in the Prussian Ministry of Culture and a friend, admirer, and benefactor of Schiller. An exchange of letters between them discussing aesthetic matters exercised considerable influence.

[5] Karl Philipp Moritz (1756-93). Author and aesthetic theorist. He became closely acquainted with Goethe during the latter's stay in Italy (1786) and later in Weimar (1788). A defender of the autonomy of art, his best-known aesthetic writings are *Versuch einer deutschen Poesie* (1786) and *Über die bildende Nachahmung des Schönen* (1788).

and finally Hegel, served as their ministers of the fine arts, so to speak. This new aesthetics transformed philology, for it supplemented rational hermeneutics, which had been created in the controversy between Trentine Catholicism and Protestantism and developed by Ernesti,[6] with a hermeneutics along aesthetic lines. Schleiermacher, using Friedrich Schlegel's method, derived the rules of this aesthetic hermeneutics from the principle of the form of a literary work. It replaced a mode of evaluation and criticism which had prescribed rules to the understanding and had established corresponding grammatical, metrical, and rhetorical techniques, with a mode of aesthetic criticism proceeding from an analysis of form. The major achievements of this criticism are found in Wolf,[7] Lachmann,[8] and their successors. This German aesthetics hastened the decline of the old forms in France and England, and influenced the first creations, still tentative and unsure, of a new poetic age.

Today anarchy rules the wide field of literature in every country. 104 The poetics created by Aristotle is dead. Its forms and rules were models drawn from past artistic genres, which had already become powerless shadows of unreality when juxtaposed with the beautiful literary wonders of a Fielding or Sterne, a Rousseau or Diderot. Our German aesthetics does indeed still survive in some universities, but no longer in the consciousness of the leading artists and critics where it should live above all. In France, David[9] lost his influence in the visual arts; instead Delaroche[10] and Gallait[11] came to the

[6] Johann August Ernesti (1707-81). German theologian and philologist; he rejected both mystical interpretation and extreme rationalism, upholding instead the grammatical—and thus the logical and historical—interpretation of Scripture. His most influential work was the *Institutio Interpretis N. T.* (1761).

[7] Friedrich August Wolf (1759-1824). A classical philologist especially influential through his *Prolegomena ad Homerum* (1796), which concerns the origins of Homeric poetry. See also his *Vorlesungen über die Altertumswissenschaft* (5 vols., 1831-35), where he develops a broad, comprehensive view of the nature of classical studies.

[8] Karl Lachmann (1793-1851). A classical philologist who applied the methods of classical philology to early German texts. See especially his work on the *Nibelungenlied* (1826).

[9] Jacques Louis David (1748-1825). French classicist painter who often painted political themes ("Marat Assassinated," 1793) and classical subjects, such as the "Rape of the Sabines."

[10] Paul [Hippolyte] Delaroche (1797-1856). A French painter whose work falls midway between classicism and romanticism. Some of his paintings are "The Death of Queen Elizabeth" (1827) and the monumental mural of the "École des Beaux-Arts" (finished in 1841).

[11] Louis Gallait (1810-82). Belgian painter known for his classical tableaus and his historical paintings. Some of his paintings are "La mort du Maréchal de Biron" (1835) and "La conquête d'Antioche par Godefroy de Bouillon" (1840).

fore. In Germany, the fresco designs of Cornelius[12] vanished into the obscurity of the museum and made way for the realistic depictions of people found in works by Schadow[13] and Menzel.[14] Both changes meant that the code of ideal beauty adopted by Goethe, Meyer,[15] and their Weimar circle had been rescinded. Since the French Revolution a new poetry current in London and Paris has attracted the interest of poets and public alike. As soon as Dickens and Balzac began to write the epic of modern life as found in these cities, the basic poetic principles once debated by Schiller, Goethe, and Humboldt in idyllic Weimar became irrevelant. Today a colorful mixture of forms from all periods and peoples is breaking in upon us and seems to undo every delimitation of literary genres and every rule. Especially from the East,[16] we are inundated by elemental, formless literature, music, and painting—half barbaric but filled with vital emotional energy of peoples who still fight the battles of spirit in novels and twenty-foot-wide paintings. In this anarchy, the artist is forsaken by rules; the critic is thrown back upon his personal feeling as the only remaining standard of evaluation. The public rules. The masses throng into colossal exhibition halls, theaters of all shapes and sizes, and lending libraries. They make or break the artist's reputation.

This anarchy of taste always characterizes periods when a new way of feeling reality has shattered the existing forms and rules, and when new forms of art are striving to unfold. It can, however, not be permitted to last. And it is thus one of the vital tasks of contemporary philosophy, art history, and literary history to reestablish a healthy relationship between aesthetic thought and art.

The artist's need for honesty and gripping effects of all kinds today drives him onto a path whose goal is still unknown to him. It leads him to sacrifice the clear delimitation of forms and the pure elevation of ideal beauty above common reality. In this way he feels in tune with a transformed society. The struggle for existence and

105

[12] Peter von Cornelius (1783-1867). German painter commissioned by Ludwig I of Bavaria to paint the fresco decorations in the Glyptothek of Munich; also designed decorations for the mausoleum of Frederick William II of Prussia.

[13] Gottfried Schadow (1764-1850). Perhaps the most important sculptor of German classicism, also known for his graphic work and lithography. Some of his best-known works are his statue of Frederick the Great (Stettin, 1793) and the Blücher Monument (Rostock, 1819).

[14] Adolph von Menzel (1815-1905). Painter and graphic artist who was famous for his historical paintings of the court life of Frederick the Great.

[15] Johann Heinrich Meyer (1760-1832). An art historian and painter who met Goethe in Italy and then lived in Weimar as Goethe's friend.

[16] Dilthey means Eastern Europe, especially Russia.

influence in this society has become more ruthless and demands the exploitation of the strongest effects. The masses have obtained recognition and now have a voice. They assemble with great facility at central places where they demand the satisfaction of their desire for gripping, heart-rending effects. The spirit of scientific investigation is applied to all objects. It penetrates every kind of spiritual process and produces the need to see through every kind of disguise or mask to apprehend reality truthfully. In the eighteenth century our ideal was a literature in which a poet invested his true nature. The necessary expression of this was a representative art which perfected inner beauty. Today our ideal does not lie in form, but rather in the power which addresses us through forms and movements. Thus today art is becoming democratic, like everything else around us, and is filled with the thirst for reality and scientifically secure truth. Today's artists and poets feel that true and great art of the present ought to express the core or secret of our age, which must be as powerful as that which confronts the eye in the Madonnas or tapestries of Raphael, or speaks to us in *Iphigenia*. The artist feels a passionate resistance—all the more passionate, the more unclear his notion of the goal of his own art—against a reactionary aesthetics which derives a concept of ideal beauty from works of that past or from abstract ideas, and he measures the productive work of the struggling artist by it.

These influences have completely transformed poetry, but they have also debased it. Great geniuses of narrative literature such as Dickens and Balzac have accommodated themselves all too easily to a public voracious for reading matter. Tragedy is languishing for lack of an audience in which aesthetic reflection could preserve the consciousness of the highest task of poetry. Under the same circumstances, the comedy of manners has lost its subtlety in the structure of its plot and refinement of resolution. That tragic element with which Molière seasoned his great comedies (and which lent them their depth) has been replaced by superficial sentimentality to suit the taste of the masses. In the German visual arts a misology has arisen from the conflict with an aesthetics which has become unproductive—for an aesthetics which no longer works coopera- 106 tively toward the ideal of an age is unproductive. Artists have developed an aversion to thinking about art, sometimes even to every kind of higher culture. Today the results of this aversion are as evident to the artists themselves as to the public.

But there exist strong impulses in our art that lead to truthfulness, to the apprehension of power behind all form, and to efficacy; if these impulses are not to atrophy, then the natural relationship between art, aesthetic *raisonnement*, and an engaged public must be reestablished. Aesthetic discussion enhances the position of art in society, and it invigorates the working artist. The artists of Greece and of the Renaissance as well as Corneille, Racine, Molière, Schiller, and Goethe worked in just such a lively milieu. During the period of their greatest artistic exertions we find Goethe and Schiller completely surrounded and thus supported by such national aesthetic vigor in criticism, aesthetic judgment, and lively debate. The entire history of art and literature shows how the thoughtful apprehension of the functions and laws of art maintains the consciousness of its significance and ideal goals, whereas the lower instincts of human nature constantly strive to lead art astray. German aesthetics, especially, has given serious reasons to support the belief that art is an immortal human occupation. Only if what is lasting in this aesthetics, particularly its insight into the function of art for the life of society, is grounded more deeply, can the artist also maintain the high position in the esteem of society which the poet attained in the hundred years between the misery of poor Günther[17] and the state funeral of Goethe. In every golden age of the visual arts or literature, aesthetic reflection about the goals and techniques of the particular arts has provided essential support for the unfolding of a lasting style and a coherent artistic tradition. From the remains of the poetics and rhetoric of the Greeks we see how the unfolding of a lasting style for the poet and orator went hand in hand with the framing of rules. It is worth noting how the long golden age of the French theater was promoted by the aesthetic *raisonnement* made possible by Cartesian philosophy. Lessing, Schiller, and Goethe prepared for their literary work by intense aesthetic and technical reflection; this reflection played an active role in the development of *Wallenstein, Hermann and Dorothea, Wilhelm Meister*, and *Faust*; and it also assured a sympathetic reception of these works by the public. In short, art requires the thorough schooling and education of the artist and the public through aesthetic reflection if its higher aspirations are to be unfolded, appreciated, and defended in the face of the vulgar instincts of the masses. Is it not the case that the grand style of German literature was preserved only because of the majestic power of those two authors who lived in Weimar? By means of their comprehensive aesthetic influence, emanating from Weimar, supported by several

107

[17] Johann Christian Günther (1695-1723). Poet from Silesia.

journals, even resorting to terror-inspiring satire in the *Xenien*[18]—these two authors kept Kotzebue, Iffland, and Nicolai[19] in their place and encouraged a benign German public to place their faith in *Hermann and Dorothea* and *The Bride of Messina.* Such faith did not come naturally to the public.

The task of a poetics which derives from this living relationship to the artistic pursuit itself is to determine whether it can attain universally valid laws that are useful as rules of creativity and as norms for criticism. And how is the technique of a particular period and nation related to these universal rules? How do we overcome the difficulty, which all the human sciences[20] must face, of deriving universally valid principles from inner experiences, which are personally limited, composite, and yet incapable of analysis? The old task of poetics reappears here, and the question is now whether it can be carried out by means of those tools which the expansion of our scientific horizons puts at our disposal. For contemporary empirical and technical horizons do indeed allow us to ascend from poetics and the other particular aesthetic disciplines to a universal aesthetics.

From another perspective as well, a poetics has become an undeniable need of the present. The immense stock of literary works of all nations must be classified in light of its contribution to our education, spontaneous enjoyment, or knowledge of historical causes; accordingly it must be assessed in value, and applied to the study of man and history. This task can be carried out only if a

[18] Goethe and Schiller published a collection of *Xenien* (1797) in which they used satire about other authors while asserting their own literary position.

[19] August v. Kotzebue (1761-1819), August Wilhelm Iffland (1759-1814), and Friedrich Nicolai (1733-1811). Kotzebue was the author of over two hundred dramatic pieces of secondary import. Together with Iffland, he dominated the popular stage of his day. A foe of Goethe and Schiller, he was also anti-Romantic. Because of his later opposition to German unity and to the political student organizations, he was assassinated by a student radical.

Iffland was an actor, theater director, and playwright, with over sixty pieces to his credit. After 1811 he was the General Director of the Berlin *Nationaltheater*.

Nicolai was an author and a publisher who worked with Lessing and Moses Mendelssohn. He wrote several works critical of romanticism, *Sturm und Drang*, and classicism, and a number of satirical parodies aimed at Goethe, Schiller, Kant, Herder, and Fichte; the best known was the *Freuden des jungen Werthers* (1775).

[20] The human sciences (*Geisteswissenschaften*) encompass both the humanities and the social sciences. All previous translations of Dilthey and most of the writings on Dilthey in English have used the term "human studies." But current conceptions about the role of interpretation in all science have made it possible to refer to the *Geisteswissenschaften* as either human sciences or human studies.

general science of the elements and laws on the basis of which literature is formed accompanies the history of literature. "The material is the same in both cases. No mistake of method is more disastrous than the renunciation of the scope of historical and biographical facts in the formation of a general science of human nature. The achievements of human nature exist for us and can be studied only in the midst of society. This same relationship obtains between universal science and the analysis of historical phenomena for all other major expressions of social life."[21] The starting point of such a theory must lie in the analysis of the creative capacity, whose processes condition literature. "The poet's imagination and his attitude toward the world of experience provide the point of departure for every theory seriously directed to explaining the manifold world of poetry and literature in the succession of its manifestations. Poetics in this sense is the true introduction to the history of literature, just as the theory of science is the introduction to the history of spiritual or intellectual movements."[22] The artist and his public need such an evaluation of literature on the basis of a standard that is as secure as possible. We have entered an age of historical consciousness. We feel surrounded by our entire past—this is also true in the field of literature. The poet must come to terms with it, and only a historical perspective applied to poetics can emancipate him. Furthermore, philology, which first produced an understanding of the inner coherence among the literary products of a nation and their relation to the vitality of the national spirit, constantly finds historically limited poetic techniques. The problem of the relation of technique to the general laws of literature necessarily leads philology to the principles of poetics.

108

We thus arrive at the same basic question, but in its historical form: Can we come to know how processes grounded in human nature and, consequently, of universal scope yield these various kinds of poetry, which are separated according to nations and periods? Here we touch on the most fundamental fact of the human sciences: the historicity of psychic life as it is manifested in every system of culture produced by man. How is the sameness of our human nature, as expressed in uniformities, related to its variability, its historical character?

Poetics may have a great advantage over the theories of religion

[21] This is how, in an 1877 essay in the *Zeitschrift für Völkerpsychologie* on the poet's faculty of imagination, I justified the need to take up again the old task of a poetics. (D)

[22] *Ibid.*

or ethics with respect to the study of the basic fact of the human sciences, which is the historicity of free human nature. In no other area except that of science have the products of human activities been so perfectly preserved. The history of literature has preserved them as successive strata. Active powers still appear to pulsate vigorously in such products. Today poetic processes occur in just the same way as in the past. The poet is alive before our eyes; we 109 see evidence of his creative work. Thus the poetic formative process, its psychological structure, and its historical variability can be studied especially well. The hope arises that the role of psychological processes in historical products will be explained in detail through poetics. Our philosophical conception of history was developed from literary history. Perhaps poetics will have a similar significance for the systematic study of historical expressions of life.

The formation of such a science would also have a great practical significance for our system of higher education. Before the reform of philology through Humboldt's and Wolf's conception of the Greeks from the perspective of an ideal of humanity, the *Gymnasium*[23] aimed to derive from the classics a rational consciousness of rules of language and thought, of rhetorical and literary style, as well as a secure technique based on this. This legitimate idea was replaced by another during the heyday of our humanistic rediscovery of the Greeks, but its validity was more limited. The historical knowledge of the Greek spirit in its ideality was now supposed to educate one to attain full humanity. If the *Gymnasium* is to return to its former basic aim in a more mature form, which takes into account our historical consciousness, then it will also need a new poetics, a new rhetoric, and a more developed logic.

[23] Secondary school with a classical emphasis.

## SECTION ONE

# TRADITIONAL INSIGHTS AND NEW TASKS OF POETICS

### 1. Poetics As a Theory of Forms and Technique

The poetics founded by Aristotle, used and enriched in succeeding times until the eighteenth century, was a theory of forms and a technique based thereon.

Aristotle always applied the method of generalization which derives forms from particular facts and coordinates them, and the method of analysis which shows how forms are composed from units. His method provides description, not genuine causal explanation. His grammar, logic, rhetoric, and poetics are clearly based on observations, analyses, concepts of form, and rules, all of which arose from the practice of the respective art itself and which were refined by the systematizations of the Sophists. In identifying and ordering constant forms, and analyzing them in such a way as to [110] make manifest how units come together into basic connections and these, in turn, into higher systems, Aristotle was able to utilize the results of practice itself as well as the technical rules developed by the Sophists. A major part of Greek education consisted of instruction in analyzing language in terms of basic sounds as its units, analyzing metrical or musical wholes into basic tempi, analyzing proofs into terms; then in arranging and classifying the forms as they arose through composition; finally in recognizing and applying the rules according to which the means available in such forms must be combined for certain purposes. The *Poetics* of Aristotle was a theory of form and technique in this sense. Throughout the fragments of this work we discern a coming-to-terms with the results of the technique acquired in literary practice and academic analysis. And it is to this that the *Poetics* owes its systematic completeness and its didactic perfection.

Although the extant text of the *Poetics* lacks coherent organization and is remarkably silent about its relationship to its predecessors and to the rest of the Aristotelian corpus, the logical connections discernible in what is extant warrant the conclusion that Aristotle's theory of poetic forms and technique was not derived from general aesthetic principles, whether of beauty or of an artistic faculty. Instead, it seems to be abstracted from actual works of literature and their effects, and based on generalizations about technical relations between the means of imitation, the objects of imitation, and the possible modes of imitation.

The rules for this poetics were derived without exception from the properties of literature which consist in the imitation of men in action, as presented in speech (to which rhythm and pitch can be added), in the various manners in which this presentation can be carried out. This principle of imitation is objectivistic like Aristotle's logic and theory of knowledge. According to the latter, perception and thought correspond to being, so that being manifests itself in thought. This objectivistic principle was the expression of a naturalistic conception of knowledge as well as of art. On the one hand, this principle of imitation is the simplest expression of a kind of artistic practice and appreciation—which pertains, to be sure, only to the visual arts and poetry, not to music, decorative art, and architecture. On the other hand, this principle, in accord with this objectivistic mode of regarding the world, subordinates the pleasure of poetry to that of learning and contemplation. Although this principle is not without implications which reach back to more fundamental levels, the technical perspective predominates when 111 this poetics finds it sufficient to explain the origin of poetry by a delight in imitation and in perceiving imitations, combined with enjoyment of harmony and rhythm.

All further effects to be produced by poetry then follow from the nature of the object that is imitated, namely, man in action. In this context, poetics has recourse at important places to the psychological and ethical nature of the process to be imitated. Thus it grounds a theory which is merely an abstract formulation of a peculiarity of Greek tragedy, viz., that the plot is the principle or soul, as it were, of tragedy, and that character is secondary. This is grounded in the ethical axiom that the goal and happiness of man lies in action. Accordingly, in tragedy's concentrated reproduction of life, actions must not occur solely for the sake of character portrayal. Furthermore, this poetics views the peculiarity of tragedy as lying in the kind of effect produced by the objects to be imitated, i.e., fear and pity. It notes explicitly that the definition, to which this characterization of the tragic effect belongs, was based on an earlier discussion. This grounding, which has unfortunately been lost, must have derived this effect in an ethical-psychological manner from the nature of the process to be imitated.

So in the end, we may assume that the *Poetics* takes for granted a multiplicity of effects corresponding to the changes in the objects imitated, just as another familiar passage from Aristotle empirically enumerates a variety of completely different effects of musical art: pleasures of various kinds, and values, ethical education, and catharsis. In a spirit of empirical impartiality, the *Poetics* thus recognized a multiplicity of poetic effects. But it based these effects only on the relation between imitation, its object, and its means. From this relationship alone did it derive the forms and rules of literature. In this relation it found its unifying principle. The poet was conceived as producing his work according to rules for the purpose of a definite effect. It was a technique in which the intellect dominates. From its simple and basic idea, the *Poetics* defined the forms of literature with unsurpassed clarity, analyzed its parts, and established the rules according to which these parts must be formed and composed.

We have here a theory of the elements and technique of poetry which is constrained by the limits of the above-mentioned principle and by the available literature. But within these limits it is exemplary and highly effective. The schema by which it operates regards each of the arts as a kind of imitation. The arts which depict reality by means of color and form are distinguished from those which have their means of representation in speech, rhythm, and harmony. Literature finds its determinate place among the latter. The distinction between narrative and dramatic literature is based on the mode of reproduction employed by each. In particular, a technical view of tragedy was based on the theory of unity of action, the intricacies of plot development and its denouement, peripety, and recognition—even though the discussion of these possibilities frequently degenerated into casuistry.

112

Although this technique of the drama has been contested as an abstraction from the limited sphere of Greek theatrical art, it nevertheless did serve to develop in later dramatists an aesthetic awareness of the technique of the stage. The creator of the Spanish theater, Lope de Vega,[24] contrasted Aristotle's technique with rules such as that of the connection between the serious and the comic, which he took from the actual practice of the Spanish theater. He justified his own technique by claiming that the rules and models of the ancients could not be brought into agreement with the taste of his

[24] Félix Lope de Vega Carpio (1562-1635); see his *New Art of Writing Plays* (1609), trans. by W. T. Brewster (New York: Columbia University Press, 1914).

contemporaries. The poetics of Corneille and Boileau, which had been influenced by Descartes, developed the structure of French drama into a rigorous technique by coming to terms with the tradition of Aristotelian theory. The more closely we look at the form of Shakespearian tragedy, which is in essence quite regular, the more we are led to surmise that the process—itself historically unknown to us—by which the early English theater up to Shakespeare's immediate predecessors, Marlowe and Greene, developed its formal rigor required a coming-to-terms with extant technical theories. Gottsched and the conflict between Aristotelian-French poetics and the poetic theory of the Swiss mark the beginning of modern German literature. Lessing planned a commentary on the *Poetics* of Aristotle: he wanted to restore and vindicate it in its purity. He built further on the foundation of this poetics in his *Laocoön* and *Hamburg Dramaturgy,* in a genuine Aristotelian spirit but with his own characteristic independence. Later, when the storm against all rules had subsided, our two great poets, Goethe and Schiller, strove to produce a technique for German poetry; in the 113 1790s they carried on their remarkable debates about epic and drama which contain a wealth of observations about literary form that is still not fully exploited. They were astonished and delighted to find themselves in harmony with Aristotle in so many respects.

On April 28, 1797, Goethe wrote: "I read through Aristotle's *Poetics* again with the greatest pleasure. It is a beautiful thing to witness the human intellect in its highest manifestation. It is very noteworthy how Aristotle sticks exclusively to experience and this is, perhaps, a little too concrete; yet just for this reason, his work appears all the more solid." Likewise, in his reply of May 5, Schiller is very satisfied with Aristotle and is happy about his agreement with him. With true sensitivity he notes how this is not a philosophy of literature of the kind produced by modern aestheticians. Rather it is a conception "of the elements from which a poetic work is composed," how it would have to arise if one "had an individual tragedy to consider and inquired into every aspect that could be found in it." "But surely he can never be completely understood or appreciated. His entire view of tragedy rests on empirical grounds. He had access to a great number of staged tragedies which are no longer available to us. He reasons on the basis of this experience. For the most part, we lack the entire basis of his judgment." Schiller was right here, and this insight could have led him to discern the technical accomplishments of the Greek artists, commentators, and art critics prior to Aristotle. But when we read further, we notice that Schiller is an interested party, and that his judgment about Aristotle must therefore be more favorable than ours today: "And if his judgments . . . are genuine laws of art, this lucky accident is due to the fact that there were then artworks which represented their genre in an individual case." This is precisely the familiar, ahistorical conception of an idea that is realized in a single instance, of a species that is embodied in one exemplar.

The legacy of this poetics has been considerably extended, not only by Lessing, but also by Goethe and Schiller. On the basis of the way technique is conditioned by the means of representation, Lessing, like Aristotle, had derived the highest laws of the visual arts and, even more successfully, those of poetry. In contrast to the French, Lessing exhibited the true unity of the dramatic action in an exemplary analysis that agrees with the text of Aristotle, but is simultaneously supported by his own dramatic sense of life. Then Goethe derived, with great insight, the basic differences in the artistic practices of epic poets and dramatic poets from the divergence in their respective overall attitudes toward their material. He did this by gathering the technical reflections which had accompanied Schiller's and his own creative work into a common framework. "Both the epic writer and the dramatist are subject to general poetic laws, especially the law of unity and the law of development. Furthermore, both treat similar objects and both are able to use all kinds of motives. The essential difference consists in the fact that the epic writer recites an event as something completely past and the dramatist represents it as completely present. If one wanted to derive from the nature of man the details of the laws according to which each must proceed, it would be necessary to conjure up first a rhapsodist, surrounded by a quietly attentive circle of listeners, and then a mime, surrounded by a group impatiently watching and listening."[25] Schiller adds the following distinctions: because of the way the narrator represents his material as past, he is able to conceive the action statically, as it were. He already knows the beginning, middle, and end. He moves freely around the action, can put himself out of step with it, anticipate, and refer back. However, "When dramatic action transpires before me . . . I am strictly bound by the present, and my imagination loses all its freedom. An en-

114

[25] "Über epische und dramatische Dichtung von Goethe und Schiller," supplement to a Letter to Schiller, 23 December 1797. (D) See Johann Wolfgang von Goethe, *Goethes Werke* (Weimar: Hermann Böhlau, 1887-1919), 143 vols. (Weimarer Ausgabe, hereafter *WA*), I, 41(2):220-224.

during disquietude wells up in me."[26] Goethe and Schiller combine these fundamental propositions with extremely valuable detailed technical observations. It only remains for us to identify what it is in their ideal of form that can be derived with universal validity from the relation between the productive process, the object, and the means of representation, and separate it from that which was influenced by their historical situation.[27] The further influence by Herder and F. A. Wolf helped to generate a series of fruitful studies of epic poetry: one by Friedrich Schlegel in his *Die Griechen und Römer* (The Greeks and Romans) (1797), one by A. W. Schlegel in a review of Goethe's *Hermann and Dorothea*, which was influenced by his brother Friedrich, and another by Humboldt in a well-known essay of 1798, which also deals with *Hermann and Dorothea*. In Aristotle the epic was overshadowed by tragedy, which he preferred and which was still vigorous in his day. But these German writers carried the study of the fundamental difference between these two kinds of literature beyond Aristotle's poetics. Also at the same time, Friedrich Schlegel applied his aesthetic genius to produce the first study of form in prose literature.

115

## 2. Inquiries into the Creative Power from Which Works of Art, Including Literature, Arise

Aristotelian poetics as a theory of forms and technique proved to be inadequate. The technique it derived by abstraction from the Greek poets clashed with the technique of the Spanish and English theaters as well as that of the modern novel. Thus the universality of Greek poetics had to be called into question, and solutions to the disputes arising therefrom had to be sought on the basis of principles. The models of Greek art had furnished a firm foundation for aesthetic debate for a long time. When they became doubtful, a foundation had to be sought in principles. It was finally found in human nature. The Aristotelian principle of imitation was objectivistic—an analogue of the Aristotelian theory of knowledge. Ever

[26] Schiller to Goethe, 26 December 1797, *Der Briefwechsel zwischen Schiller und Goethe*, 3 vols. (Frankfurt a.M.: Insel Verlag, 1912). (D)

[27] I should particularly like to draw attention to the following letters in the *Briefwechsel Schiller-Goethe*: 28 June 1796; 28 November 1796; 4 April 1797; 7 April 1797; 8 April 1797; 19 April 1797; 21 April 1797; 24 April 1797; 25 April 1797; 7 July 1797; 20 October 1797; 25 November 1797; 9 December 1797; 30 June 1798; 22 August 1798; 24 August 1798; 1 March 1799; 29 May 1799; 23 October 1799; 6 March 1800; 27 March 1801. (D)

since philosophers began to probe the subjective power of human nature and grasp the independent force whereby it transforms what is given in the senses, the principle of imitation became untenable in aesthetics. The new standpoint of consciousness, expressed in epistemology since Descartes and Locke, also asserted itself in modern aesthetics. Here too, as in the fields of religion, law, and science, investigation into causes or virtual relations sought to determine the faculty or power from which art and literature originate. Bacon and Hobbes—genuine contemporaries of Shakespeare and his school—had already glimpsed this power in the imagination. Addison recognized the faculty of imagination as the power which contains the particular basis of literary creations: a kind of extended sense of vision which makes the absent present. David Young, Shaftesbury, and Dubos (who has not been adequately recognized) derived the basic features of a modern aesthetics from this creative power. In Germany, this aesthetics then became a systematic whole. It proceeded from the perspective of a creative power found in man and in nature as a whole—a power which produces beauty. We will now briefly describe what German aesthetics, the highest expression of this perspective, has contributed to the progress of poetics, and to what extent it still needs to be supplemented.

The accomplishments of German aesthetics can be correctly evaluated only when it is not investigated solely in terms of abstract systems. Rather, we should also examine the lively observations and discussions found in Herder's early writings, in the entire life's work of Goethe and Schiller, in the literary and critical achievements of the Schlegels, etc. The historical and critical works of Zimmermann[28] and Lotze[29] found the contributions to aesthetic knowledge made in this golden age of German literature in precisely those theories which are most abstract and controversial. However, the actual significance of this aesthetics for literature consisted in the fact that, when our poetry reached its peak, both poets and philosophers were reflecting on the productive power, the goal and the means of literature. German poetics of that time must be recognized as a nexus or system[30] that included the most general aesthetic principles, the debate between Goethe and Schiller about technique, as well as the analyses of form and composition by the Schlegels

116

[28] Robert Zimmermann, *Geschichte der Ästhetik als philosophischer Wissenschaft* (Vienna, 1858).

[29] Hermann Lotze, *Geschichte der Ästhetik in Deutschland* (Munich, 1868).

[30] *Zusammenhang* can be translated as both nexus (especially in a psychological context) and system (especially in a historical context).

and Schleiermacher. It was a vigorous, fertile mode of thought that influenced poetry and literature, criticism, understanding, and literary-historical or philological research. Only insofar as philosophical thought exerts an influence does it have a right to exist.

The *first* achievement of German aesthetics was an important *tenet* that was abstracted from the development of poetry in modern times and that could be clearly seen in the epoch of Goethe and Schiller. In the process of differentiation by which the particular cultural systems of modern nations have become increasingly separated from each other since the beginning of the Middle Ages, art too developed as an independent expression of life with its own characteristic content. In the eighteenth century, poetry became a dominant power in Germany; it became conscious of a capacity—rooted in genius—to generate a world of its own. This capacity was embodied in Goethe. Thus poetry was led to recognize the following fundamental truth: poetry is not the imitation of a reality which already exists prior to it; nor is it the adornment of truths or spiritual meanings which could have been expressed independently. The aesthetic capacity is a creative power for the production of a meaning that transcends reality and that could never be found in abstract thought. Indeed, it is a way or mode of viewing the world. Thus poetry was acknowledged as an independent power for intuiting the world and life. It was raised to an organon for understanding the world, alongside science and religion. Both truths and exaggerations were mixed in this tenet and it is clear that any future poetics will have great difficulty in separating the two.

Schiller was the first to attempt to express the nature of aesthetic 117 genius in a formula. We will explicate it by ignoring its imperfect basis in a theory of drives or impulses. For Schiller, beauty is living form. This is produced whenever we intuit life in an image, or whenever form is endowed with life. Form must become life, and life form.

> . . . a human being, though he may live and have form, is far from being on that account a living form. In order to be so, his form would have to be life, and his life form. As long as we merely think about his form, it is lifeless, a mere abstraction; as long as we merely feel his life, it is formless, a mere impression. Only when his form lives in our feeling and his life takes on form in our understanding, does he become living form; and this will always be the case whenever we adjudge him beautiful.[31]

[31] Friedrich Schiller, *On the Aesthetic Education of Man; In a Series of Letters,*

I shall designate as Schiller's law the thesis that the aesthetic process can either discern a liveliness of feeling in outer form and thus enliven what is visible, or make life visible in outer form and thus give life form. This law thus involves the constant translation of lived experience into form and form into lived experience. We shall later seek to formulate this principle in more exact psychological terms and to provide a proper foundation for it. What Herder says in his *Kalligone* [32] is akin to Schiller's thesis. According to Herder, beauty is perceived when the perfection of things that is sensed in feeling as satisfaction resonates in our own satisfaction.

This thesis concerning the unity of inner and outer, of life and form, became, as is well known, the vehicle for a world-view or a way of philosophizing. This aesthetic world-view, stimulated by reflection on the poetic process—especially on what operated so powerfully in Goethe—was reinforced by Schiller's power of reflection and brought into connection with the requirements of speculation by Schelling. Our aesthetic capacity consists in vivifying the relationship we experience between inner and outer and in also extending it to nature, which is regarded as dead by the intellect. This experienced relationship then becomes a formula for the ground and nexus of the world in the system of identity. Naturally it could then be employed in the reverse direction as an objective principle for deriving beauty in nature and the creativity of the artist, which serves to highlight this beauty and to intensify it.

Schelling's aesthetic world-view was first developed in his *Darstellung meines Systems der Philosophie* (Exposition of My System of Philosophy)[33] which conceives the world as the product of genius, i.e., absolute reason—a world in which nature and spirit are one. The creative capacity to which Schiller referred has here become the ground of the world. In November 1801, A. W. Schlegel began his lectures on literature and art, which constitute a fully worked-out aesthetics in our sense; here beauty is defined as the symbolic presentation of the infinite. Partly based on Schlegel's lectures, Schelling began his 1802 lectures on art, which derive the creativity of the artist from "art in itself," the root of art in the absolute—without, however, adding anything of importance to the richness of A. W. Schlegel's lectures. The most complete exposition of this metaphysical principle of art is contained in Schelling's later discourse on *The Philosophy of Art: An Oration on the Relation*

118

trans. by E. M. Wilkensen and L. A. Willoughby (Oxford: The Clarendon Press, 1967), p. 101.

[32] Published in 1800 as a metacritique of Kant's *Critique of Judgment.*

[33] *Zeitschrift für spekulative Physik*, II, 2 (1801). S. W., IV, pp. 105ff. (D)

*Between the Plastic Arts and Nature.*[34] The artist must "emulate the creative spirit of nature active in the inner nature of things." The aesthetics of Hegel and his school has applied this metaphysical principle to the entire realm of art. Negatively, this aesthetic philosophy has the virtue of doing away with the principle of imitation. And yet its positive formulation, which went beyond that of Schiller, has blurred the boundaries that separate the aesthetic vivacity of intuition from scientific thought and philosophic knowledge.

The *second tenet* of German aesthetics provides the basic foundation for Schiller's law. It was convincingly enunciated by Kant in his analyses of taste and pleasure. It can be extended to the creative process by means of the claim that the same complex process is involved in aesthetic receptivity as in aesthetic creativity, though the former is less strong. The judgment of taste is aesthetic, i.e., it has its determining ground in the relation of the object to the feelings of pleasure and displeasure,[35] but without any relation to the faculty of desire "this mere representation of the object is accompanied in me with satisfaction, however indifferent I may be as regards the existence of the object of this representation." "The satisfaction which determines the judgment of taste is disinterested."[36] "Taste is the faculty of judging of an object or a method of representing it by an *entirely disinterested* satisfaction or dissatisfaction. The object of such satisfaction is called *beautiful.*"[37] Since there is no conceptual transition to pleasure or displeasure, the further condition is added that aesthetic satisfaction does not arise through the mediation of concepts. Thus, the Kantian analysis completely negates the views that beauty is a mode of truth or a representation of the perfection of things in a sensuous form. It focuses on the significance of feelings for the aesthetic processes.

119

This second tenet of German aesthetics has been presented especially brilliantly by Schopenhauer. The task is to supply a completion and deeper grounding by investigating the significance of feelings for the processes of creativity, the metamorphosis of images, and composition. Only then can this most certain part of the foundation of aesthetics to date, receive the requisite universality and psychological grounding.

[34] Trans. of *Über das Verhältnis der bildenden Künste zu der Natur* (Munich, 1807).

[35] Kant, *Critique of Judgment*, section 1. (D)

[36] *Ibid.*, section 2, trans. by J. H. Bernard (New York: Hafner Press, 1956), pp. 43, 58.

[37] *Ibid.*, section 5, p. 45.

A *third tenet* of German aesthetics is derived by proceeding regressively from Schiller's law to the conditions which external reality must satisfy in order for it to be aesthetically intuitable as something living. This tenet also points back to the philosophy of identity as well as to aesthetical metaphysics. It immediately follows from this that it will be very difficult to give adequate formulation to it. Very diverse accounts of the relationship of artistic creativity to external reality have been given. They go back to Herder's discussion of sculpture and Moritz's *Über die bildende Nachahmung des Schönen* (On the Artistic Imitation of the Beautiful), which is known to have influenced Goethe while he was in Italy. They can also be found in Kant, Schiller, Goethe, Schelling, and Hegel, among others. They are either very thin and lacking in content or are open to doubt. Art constantly works out problems for whose solution the conditions must lie in external reality. There must be a relationship between external reality and the eye that perceives beauty which makes it possible to behold beauty in the world. The creativity of the artist intensifies qualities that already exist in reality. The task is to recognize these qualities as well as the relationship which obtains here; and only the modern theory of evolution, combined with psychology, seems to make that possible.

A *fourth tenet* can be empirically abstracted from aesthetic impressions in an indeterminate form. But its more exact determination on the basis of principles already expounded offers considerable difficulties.

The Aristotelian theory of technique claimed universal validity, and subsequent poetics preserved this claim. Kant formulated this presupposition of a natural system of art in the following way: ". . . in a judgment of taste (about the beautiful) the satisfaction in the object is imputed to *everyone*, without being based on a concept (for then it would be the good). Further, this claim to universal validity so essentially belongs to a judgment by which we describe anything as *beautiful* that, if this were not thought in it, it would never come into our thoughts to use the expression at all, but everything which pleases without a concept would be counted as pleasant."[38] This proposition transfers the concept of universal validity from the field of knowledge to that of taste. In both cases Kant envisions a timelessly valid system of determinations. Further, not only here, but also in the fields of law, religion, and morality, Kant accepted a natural or rational system timelessly valid in its

120

[38] *Ibid.*, p. 48.

determinations. This is why neither Kant's hypotheses about the origin and development of the planetary system nor his views on the historical development of a perfect cosmopolitan constitution lead us to conceive of his standpoint as developmental. In agreement with Kant, Goethe and Schiller undertook to derive a universally valid technique for all poetry from a foundation of aesthetic concepts. In the same vein, we find Schiller's ideal human being realizing the highest freedom by means of the beautiful in himself. Further, this ideal person then emerged in Goethe, though not without Schiller's influence, as the goal of development in his two great literary works, *Faust* and *Wilhelm Meister*, with which he was occupied throughout his whole life. The wonderful spell of these two works originates in part from the way in which Goethe's realistic nature accepts human strivings as conditioned by the confines of the real, and yet raises them to this pure ideality. Historically considered, this universal ideal of humanity is the most profound meaning-content of German poetry.

In contrast to this standpoint we find Herder, the founder of the Historical School, who emphasized no less one-sidedly the historical multiplicity of national tastes. He took as his starting point literary works completely beyond the scope of technical poetics, which as we saw had proceeded by abstracting forms and rules from the literature of the ancients. Herder found the germ of poetry in the natural tones and lyrical cadences of the folk song, in Hebrew poetry, and in the poetic art of primitive peoples. He saw the nucleus of poetry in the musical and the lyrical. Thus he captured the other nonintuitive aspect of poetry which had not previously been attended to. Further, he was able to recapture, with a unique subtlety of feeling, how indigenous national poetry originated from the language of a people. Hamann had already said: "The field of language 121 extends from the art of spelling all the way to the masterpieces of literary art, and the most subtle philosophy of taste and criticism."[39] Herder wrote: "The genius of language is also the genius of the literature of a nation."[40] How poetry is produced by language as the first expression of psychic life had also been observed earlier. The ancients had seen how the formation of poetry preceded the development of prose. In his life of Homer, Blackwell[41] had ex-

[39] Johann Georg Hamann, *Schriften*, vol. 2 (Berlin: Reimer, 1821), p. 128. (D)

[40] Johann Gottfried Herder, *Sämmtliche Werke*, vol. 1, ed. by Bernhard Suphan (Berlin: Weidmann, 1877), p. 148. (D)

[41] Thomas Blackwell, *An Enquiry into the Life and Writings of Homer*, 2nd ed. (London, 1735).

pressed the view that in the earliest times humans were able to hear tones much more keenly than we in our present-day speech. Their speech was a kind of singing. Original language was full of metaphors, and the rule of poetry that instructs us to use metaphors expresses the original nature of language. Hamann collected these observations in his *Aesthetica in nuce*: "Poetry is the mother tongue of the human race. As barter preceded commerce, song preceded speech. The senses and passions speak and understand nothing but images." Ever since his essay on the life stages of language, Herder developed the historical causal nexus in which poetry grows indigenously from the foundation of language in every nation. Herder immersed himself fully in the ancient poetry of the most diverse peoples by translating, recreating, and analyzing it with congenial vivacity. He became the founder of the historical study of literature in its relationship to language and national life, because he sensed the pulse of national life in language and literature. The perspective of historical poetics thus begins to open up with Herder. The infinite variations of man's sensuous-spiritual constitution in its relation to the external world is for him the condition of beauty as of taste, and these change as man's disposition changes.

Herder is historically justified—not only over against Aristotle, but also against Kant and Schiller. But he was overwhelmed by these opponents because he lacked clarity of concepts and a firm foundation. The embryonic thought of this genius did not solve the problem inherent in the relation of the universal elements of poetry to those which change historically—indeed, it even failed to recognize the problem fully. Instead, he wasted his energy on one-sided polemics against the idea of a rational system and universal validity. The important works of Schiller and the Schlegels, wherein the historical forms of literature were recognized and distinguished in terms of naive and sentimental, classical and romantic poetry, were also not employed, either by the authors themselves or by subsequent aestheticians, to deal with this problem.

122

On the basis of these still imperfectly formulated and grounded tenets that were partially distorted by one-sided explication in terms of discrete claims and counterclaims, German aesthetics developed a great treasury of profound and sensitive insights into the poetic realm, ranging from the concept of beauty to the forms of individual literary genres. The tenets that we exposited indicate that this aesthetics always sought to establish a causal relation between the psychic state which produces a literary work and the form of that work. This was undoubtedly the main advance which distinguished the study of literary works in this epoch; we can therefore call the philology and criticism of this period "aesthetical." The analysis of form according to this explanative method which proceeds from inner psychic life has since been extended to all European literatures. After Humboldt analyzed the epic, he applied this aesthetic mode of analysis to language itself in terms of his concept of the inner form of language. Goethe and Schiller alternate between creative work and aesthetic reflection. The Schlegels were the first to recognize the form of the Spanish and Renaissance English drama and to investigate the form in the prose of Lessing, Boccaccio, and Goethe. Schleiermacher understood Plato as a philosophical artist by this method and transformed hermeneutics by means of it.[42] The great period of German philology, criticism, and aesthetics began when Kant, for whose critical method the distinction between form and content and the relation of form to the active process of the mind were always central, encountered these tendencies in aesthetic and philological analysis.

Yet at the same time, German literature and poetics tended to overestimate the importance of form. Schiller, who revered a realm of pure and ideal forms separate from reality as a region of freedom and beauty, was finally led to consider it an advantage of Greek tragedy that its characters were "ideal masks." He regarded the prose form of *Wilhelm Meister* as a limitation, and even told Goethe that in the future he should present beautiful content only in metrical form. The Romantic world of beautiful illusion emerged. Otto Ludwig wrote: "Through my understanding of Shakespeare, I have overcome the unnatural separation introduced by Goethe, Schiller, and the Romantics who followed their lead in separating the aesthetic and the beautiful from the good and the true, making poetry into a fata morgana, an imaginary island of dreams, which estranges man from the world and from himself, robbing him both of his 123 feeling at home in the world and of his ability to act. I have overcome this unnatural separation, which stamps our culture with an effeminate character, and my endeavor is to impart my cure to other

[42] What Dilthey's brief references to Humboldt, Goethe, Schiller, and the Schlegels point to is the expansion of the notion of form from the strictly objective sense of classical drama. Since, according to German aesthetics, form is rooted in the mind, it can also be embodied in epic, ordinary language, prose writing, philosophy, and nonclassical modes of literature. This leads to the notion of inner form which is not only more subjective than the traditional concept of form, but also more encompassing. It allows us to discern form where previously literary criticism saw only formlessness or disorder.

patients."[43] German aesthetic theory was also negatively influenced by its use of the metaphysical method.[44] If today we were to attempt to ascertain the mental states which produce and manifest themselves in literary forms, then only a psychology which leads us to recognize the historical nature of man could do so. Since such a psychology was not available then, these mental states were merely surveyed intuitively or by arbitrary methods. This holds for the way Schiller juxtaposed naive and sentimental poetry as well as for the way in which the aesthetics of the Hegelian school brought poetic states of mind in relation to one another by means of an external dialectic.

## 3. Problems and Resources of a Contemporary Poetics

A threefold task arises: first, to transport the problems on which this period of aesthetic speculation worked into the context of modern empirical science; second, to exploit the great wealth of inspired observations and generalizations which were accumulated then for purposes of empirical research; and third, to put the findings of technical poetics into a scientific relation to those of aesthetic speculation. What resources and methods do we have at our disposal for these tasks?

Poetics, which has remained far behind in generating empirical causal knowledge, will at first seek to learn from the methods and resources of *related disciplines*.

The most closely related discipline, rhetoric, has unfortunately remained at the point which it reached in antiquity. It is a theory of elementary forms and technique. It has taken no steps in the direction of causal knowledge. However, rhetoric could be useful for philology and everyday life, both in the limited sense in which it was understood in antiquity as well as in the wider sense of a theory of practical discourse (i.e., prose designed to demonstrate and persuade). The resources provided by grammar and metrics, by our sense of logical coherence, and by the aesthetic sensitivity of philology have nearly been exhausted. Only through comparison and psychological grounding can it be established to what extent and in what proportions the elements of style vary within an in- 124

[43] Otto Ludwig, *Skizzen und Fragmente* (Leipzig: C. Chobloch, 1874), p. 84.

[44] Dilthey never defines what a metaphysical method is, but he seems to mean by this the construction of polarities and dialectical opposites.

dividual. This would create a systematic foundation for investigating certain questions of lower and higher criticism.

Hermeneutics is also closely related to poetics. Although hermeneutics advanced to the standpoint of the aesthetic contemplation of form under Schleiermacher, neither it nor poetics has since then progressed beyond this standpoint.

Grammar and metrics, however, can provide the groundwork for poetics and the models for a comparative approach to poetics which will first establish individual causal relations in their uniformity and thus gradually allow us to attain a thorough knowledge of the causal nexus.

The distinction which must now be developed between the methods of grammar and those of poetics should not be underrated. The grammarian is presented with very elementary phonetic transformations and he is able to establish series of these transformations within diverse languages and compare them with one another. He can obtain help from the genealogical relations among languages. He is able to ascertain the physiological conditions for the uniformities in these elementary phonetic transformations. Poetics, however, cannot employ a genealogical analysis of literary schools. Nor is it able to order the transformations of a type or a motif into fixed sequences. The physiological aspect of the poetic process cannot be used for the elementary grounding of a poetics in the same way that the physiological aspect of the linguistic process grounds grammar. Changes in phoneme, accent, and tempo do indeed pervade all poetry as well as literary prose. But this side of poetry is manifestly less well suited for the elementary foundation of poetry than is phonology for that of grammar. Attempts to detect the physiological phenomena that accompany the higher poetic processes (such as those made by the French in their theories of hallucination) are at present still without results. So poetics can hardly expect results as favorable as those in grammar if it uses the latter as a model and remains content with external empirical observation, with the reciprocal elucidation of one causal nexus through another, with generalization by means of comparison, and with a mere physiological grounding. We must attempt to proceed as far as possible with such means; but the following reasons warrant our going beyond the sphere of these resources and methods.

The grammarian encounters language as a basically fixed system, 125 in which changes take place so slowly that they escape direct apprehension through observation. The productive powers involved in the process of language formation are indeed the same as those which can be apprehended in psychic life in general. Their relationship to speech processes is never experienced, but is obtained through inference. This is the basis for the kinship between the methods of linguistic research and those of the natural sciences. By contrast, the living process in which poetry originates can be observed from its inception to its completed form in our contemporary poets. Every person with a developed poetic sense is capable of fully recapturing the feeling of this process. In addition, we have the poet's own testimony about his process of creation. This provides literary documentation, which permits us to establish the life histories, as it were, of the development of outstanding poetic works. The results of these creative processes are preserved in an immense mass of literature which is nearly unlimited. Poetic works possess properties which make them—compared to prose works—most suited for causal investigation. The creative life that produced literary works still visibly pulsates in them. Frequently, the law of their formation can still be apprehended in the final form *(Gestalt)*. These observations about poetic creativity and aesthetic receptivity, and the testimony about these processes, must be made available to us; the psychological insights thus attained must be transferred to the external history of the development of literature; and finally the finished, transparent form of literary works must be analyzed to complete and confirm our insight into their genesis—when all this has been done, an exciting prospect will open up in this field. Perhaps we can here succeed for the first time in deriving a causal explanation from productive processes. Poetics seems to be at a stage that may perhaps make it possible to give an inner explanation of a spiritual and historical product according to a causal method.

Only through such an inner causal explanation can we hope to answer the central questions of poetics—with which we saw speculative aesthetics struggling in vain—and thus reconstitute poetics so that it will become usable. The relation of this inner or psychological method to the central questions of poetics and its actual utilization can here be indicated only with reference to the following three problems.

The independent value of poetry and the *function* which it has in society can never be brought to light by an external, empirical method. If spirit were to confront its own creations only as objective, empirical phenomena and analyze them according to the external method of the natural sciences, then a self-alienation of spirit from its own creations would arise. Socratic self-knowledge would give way to an external descriptive method. Poetics would be unable

126

to recognize the living function of poetry in society and thereby to secure its place and dignity in society.

The central question of all poetics—that concerning the *universal validity* or historical variability of the judgment of taste, of the concept of beauty, of technique and its rules—must be answered if poetics is to be of use to the creative poet, to guide the public's judgment, or to furnish a firm foundation for aesthetic criticism and philology. But every empirical, comparative method can only derive a rule from the historical past, whose validity is thus historically restricted. It cannot make any binding claims or judgments about what is new and belongs to the future. Such a rule applies only retrospectively, and contains no law for the future. Since we have ceased to presuppose the paradigmatic value of ancient literature, the law of beauty and the rules of poetry can be derived only from human nature. At first, poetics had a firm basis in a classical model from which it abstracted, then later in some kind of a metaphysical concept of the beautiful. Now poetics must seek this firm basis in the life of the psyche.

There exists a general relation between the psychological and the historical which pervades all fields. The uniform conditions under which all poetic creation occurs and the universally valid rules to which it is bound originate from the poetic process, from the means of representation which the poet employs, and from the objects he portrays. Special conditions are then added to attain the individual forms of poetry. Thus the universally valid norms of lyrical, epic, and dramatic literature arise. In these forms and according to these rules, a poetic technique develops—the techniques of the Greek, Spanish, or the Renaissance English theater. Technique can also be developed into a theory of forms and rules, which, however, is historically conditioned, not universal for mankind as such. It works with the givens of historical life, the overall state of mind of the poet, and traditions of representation. Thus a mode of portraying persons and connecting their actions arises that is specific to a nation and a time. The technique developed in great poetry by creative geniuses remains bound by these determinations and is able to achieve unity, necessity, and heightened artistic effect only through the factual and historical character of poetry. The poet's imagination is historically conditioned, not only in its material, but also in its technique. Poetic technique is regarded as universally valid only due to a lack of historical consciousness. Without doubt the Renaissance English poets—especially Shakespeare, as well as the Spanish and French poets—invested much reflection into the mas-

127

terful techniques they created. Otto Ludwig performed a great service by analyzing this technique with the congenial sensitivity of a genuine dramatic poet, but he failed to recognize its historical origins and limits.

The particular forms of literature cannot be explained, as regards their inner impulses, by the method of external observation and comparison; nor can they be brought under universally valid rules in this way. But what can be discerned in all poetry, beginning with the most elementary creations, is a fundamental psychological distinction between expression of one's own inner life and submission to what is objective.

Thus poetics must make use of the advantage it has, and relate all the tools of external observation, cross-illumination, generalization through comparison—also the construction of a series of related moments into a developmental sequence and its completion—to the psychological study of poetic creativity. Because of our concern with a foundation for poetics, psychological considerations will predominate in what follows. But the complete working out of a poetics would make clear what can be gained from that other side of the modern method—especially when the oldest accessible documents and the literary accomplishments of primitive peoples become the basis for a comparative approach.

SECTION TWO

## Chapter One. Description of the Poet's Constitution

### *1. The Processes of His Psychic Life (Disregarding His Private Disposition)*

Our first and simplest task is to observe, collect, and unite, according to literary or biographical methods, all the traits that poets manifest in common. They are brought into focus against the background of what appears not only in the poet, but also in the philosopher, natural scientist, or politician. This comparison would be 128 superfluous if both the classical and Romantic orientations had not failed to recognize these facts and falsely placed the poet in an ethereal realm of ideal forms or in an illusory world cut off from reality.

According to Aristotle, the objects of literature are human actions. Although this formula is too narrow, we may nevertheless say that only to the extent that a psychic element, or a combination of them, stands in relation to a lived experience and its presentation can it be a constituent of literature. Consequently, the substratum of all true poetry is a lived or living experience[45] and whatever psychic constituents are related to it. Every image of the external world can indirectly become the material for the creativity of the poet through just such a relationship. Every operation of the understanding which generalizes experience, orders it, and increases its applicability assists the work of the poet. This sphere of experience in which the poet operates is no different than that from which the philosopher or politician draws. The youthful letters of Frederick the Great or of any contemporary statesman are full of elements also to be found in the psyche of a great poet; many of Schiller's thoughts could have been those of a political orator. A powerful psychic life, intense experiences of the heart and of the world, a capacity for generalization and demonstration—all these

[45] *Erlebnis, lebendige Erfahrung. Erlebnis* will be translated as "lived experience" to distinguish it from *Erfahrung* except when other adjectives render "lived" awkward.

form the fertile ground for human accomplishments of the most diverse kinds, including those of the poet. One of the few things we can infer from Shakespeare's works about what he read is that he must have liked Montaigne. This primordial relation of a powerful intellect to life-experience[46] and generalizations derived from it must exist in every great poet. According to Goethe, "all depends upon this: one must *be* something in order to *do* something."[47] "Generally, the personal character of the writer influences the public rather than his talents as an artist."[48]

Thus representations of life are always the soil from which literature draws its essential constituents. The elements of poetry—motif, plot, character, and action—are transformations of representations of life. We immediately sense the difference between heroes constructed from stage props—paste, paper, and glitter—no matter how their armor may shimmer, and those composed from reality. Particular or general representations of characters whose elements already exist either in ourselves or in reality as constituted by others need only undergo a transformation for the *personae* of a drama or a novel to be created. Similarly, the nexus of events provided by our experiences of life need only undergo a transformation in order to become an aesthetic plot. There is no special morality of the theater, there are no resolutions which satisfy us in a novel but not in life itself. That is precisely what is powerfully gripping about a work of literature—that it originates in a psyche similar to ours, only greater and more vigorous. It expands our heart beyond its actual confines without displacing us into the thin, rarefied atmosphere of a world unfamiliar to us. The activities and functions of the imagination do not arise in a vacuum. They should originate in a healthy, powerful psyche filled with reality; accordingly they should foster and strengthen whatever is best in the reader or listener, teach him to better understand his own emotions, to look for hidden life in the monotonous stretches of his own path, to tend his modest garden, as it were, and then also to be equal to whatever extraordinary things occur there.

129

All genuine poetry feeds on historical fact. A specific way of viewing people, enduring character types, complexities of human

[46] *Lebenserfahrung* is more encompassing than *Erlebnis* and includes the understanding of life obtained through others.

[47] Johann Peter Eckermann, *Gespräche mit Goethe*, 20 October 1828 (Leipzig: Brockhaus, 1836), trans. by John Oxenford as *Conversations of Goethe with Eckermann* (hereafter *CE*) (London: George Bell and Sons, 1909), p. 341.

[48] Eckermann, *Gespräche*, 30 March 1824; *CE*, p. 77.

action, and their resolution in accordance with the moral feeling of a period and a nation, and finally the contrasts and relations among the images and symbols that are especially prominent at a given time: these are the already naturally powerful elements that all poetic technique must accept and transform into a product which is necessary, unified, and whose effect is focused. Poetic technique is historically conditioned.

### 2. *The Primary Function of the Poet*

How does poetic creativity develop within this historical matrix? If we are to answer this question on the basis of the facts of literature, then we must first provide a description of the characteristic achievement of the poet—his function, as it were—on the basis of biographical and literary facts. Only then can we observe and describe the particular features of the specific processes that go into his achievement.

We cannot follow idealistic aesthetics when it defines the essence and function of art in terms of the highest ideal of art that we are capable of conceiving today. Most of the theories of culture stemming from the period of German speculation suffer from this defect. What has been developed under the most favorable conditions may not be projected as the impulse that explains the entire series of phenomena constitutive of art as a sphere of life. Art is to be found wherever something is exhibited—be it in tones or in a more lasting medium—and is not expected either to serve our knowledge of 130 reality or to be converted into reality, but satisfies our intuitive interest for its own sake. Art encompasses a domain which extends from the outlines of reindeers and whales with which eskimos adorn their weapons and the images of idols made by Africans on the one extreme, to the creations of Goethe and Raphael on the other. It is a domain in which what is presented is at the same time developed and transformed, and which has at least one common feature, namely, that mere presentation as such, and its contemplation, provide satisfaction. This feature—satisfaction in perceiving what is presented—belongs to every work of art. However, we must guard against the temptation to see the essence of art in this simple feature—a danger which Aristotle did not escape. We must also beware of trying to define what else belongs to the work of art by means of blanket statements.

The poet depicts through a sequence of words. One could think that in the course of time those objects better represented by another art form would have been ceded to that art, and that those objects which were most suited for the medium of speech would have been allotted to literature to comprise its subject matter. One could thus argue that the description of nature as such, and the beauty of the human body, are not appropriate objects of literature, although they can very well affect the emotions very deeply in paintings and can delight the eye in marble. Competition among the arts has certainly worked in such a direction. However, what has separated poetry from the other arts and determined its function in society is not the medium of speech, but rather a peculiar core content which is poetry's own.

The comparative method can ultimately arrive at archetypal units, as it were, at simple life-forms of poetry. Although I am here postponing this investigation, I shall nevertheless try to describe the core content of poetry which is common to all literature beginning with its simplest forms. The poet's creative work always depends on the intensity of lived experience. Through his constitution, which maintains a strong resonance with the moods of life, even an impersonal notice in a newspaper about a crime, a dry report of a chronicler, or a strange, grotesque tale can be transformed into lived experience. Just as our body needs to breathe, our soul requires the fulfillment and expansion of its existence in the reverberations of emotional life. Our feeling of life desires to resound in tone, word, and image. Perception satisfies us fully only insofar as it is filled with such content of life and with reverberations of feeling. This to and fro of life at its fullest, of perception enlivened and saturated by feeling, and of the feeling of life shining forth in the clarity of an image: that is the essential characteristic of the content of all poetry. Such lived experience is fully possessed only when it is brought into an inner relation with other lived experiences and its meaning is grasped thereby. Lived experience can never be reduced to thoughts or ideas. However, it can be related to the totality of human existence through reflection, especially through generalization and the establishment of relationships, and thus it can be understood in its essence, that is, its meaning. All poetry—its elements and their forms of connection—is composed of lived experience understood in this sense. A vital mood permeates and shapes every outer intuition of the poet. A poet possesses and enjoys his own existence through a strong sense of life which oscillates between pleasure and suffering, and over against the clear, pure background of his circumstances and of the symbols of human existence *(des Daseins)*. We therefore say that someone has a poetic nature who,

131

even without being creative, allows us to enjoy this beautiful sense of life or vitality. Accordingly, we call a work from another art form poetic if its soul is lived experience or life, even though it addresses us through the medium of color or line, in sculptural forms, or in music.

The function of poetry is thus, at its root, one of preserving, strengthening, and awakening this sense of life in us. Poetry continually leads us back to this intensity of the feeling of life, which fills us in our finest moments, to this inwardness of vision through which we enjoy the world. Our real existence is one of restless movement between desire and enjoyment; a more restful happiness is only possible on these rare occasions when we take a holiday from ordinary existence. But the poet can bring us a more healthful appreciation of life. He can furnish us with long-lasting satisfaction through his creations, without any bitter aftertaste, and can teach us to feel and enjoy the whole world as lived experience—always as full, whole, healthy human beings.

### *3. This Function is Conditioned by the Greater Intensity of the Poet's Psychic Processes*

This function, like every other function of an individual or a class of people in society, does not involve a special process or combination of processes peculiar to that individual or class. Rather, we find here the same processes which occur in every psyche—they only differ in their intensity. The creative imagination of the poet confronts us as a phenomenon totally transcending the everyday life of mankind. Nevertheless, this imagination is merely a function of the more powerful constitution of certain human beings, originating from the unusual intensity and duration of certain of their elementary processes. The life of the mind is constituted from the same processes and according to identical laws, and yet it manifests forms and functions widely divergent from each other by means of these mere differences in the intensity, duration, and integration of these processes. A great poet arises in this way too. He is a being who differs from every other class of human beings to a much greater extent than is usually assumed. Even the average writer displays none of the demonic might or incalculable, passionate power with which Rousseau, Alfieri, Byron, or Dickens have gone through life. At first, psychology was so preoccupied with the investigation of uniformities that the explication of different types of human beings was necessarily neglected. Literary history has had

132

to wait for the assistance of the psychological aesthetician. Only with the aid of his exploration of the poetic imagination will literary history be able to provide a thorough and exact account of the special kind of creative life that characterizes those poets about whom we have sufficient information.

The poet is distinguished first of all by the intensity and precision of his *perceptual images*, their multiplicity, and the interest which accompanies them. That is the first constituent of lived experience, and it emerges with unusual forcefulness in the poet. The first reason for this lies in the sensory constitution of the poet—the eye with which he views the world and the sensitive ear with which he hears it. If we want to take stock of the wealth of precise images accumulated by the poet, we must consider how they are stored in memory. According to Max Müller's calculation, Shakespeare had some 15,000 words at his disposal. Goethe too had just as impressive a command of his mother tongue. Shakespeare's acquaintance with jurisprudence has been traced back to the special training of a law clerk, and psychiatrists believe they can learn from his descriptions of insanity as from nature itself. We see Goethe dealing as an expert with an anatomist one day, with a botanist the next, and then with a historian of art or philosopher. In addition to this sort of talent, a special sort of interest is also necessary. For a person whose images stand in relation to intended actions or knowledge to be attained, images are signs for something which occupies a determinate place in the calculation of his intentions or in the relations to what is knowable. But a poetic genius yields himself to lived experience or to an image, with an independent interest in [133] them, with a quiet satisfaction in intuition, however frequently he may be distracted by external life or by science. A poetic genius is like a traveler in a foreign land, who, with great enjoyment and complete freedom, abandons himself, without any utilitarian motives, to the surrounding impressions. This lends him the character of childlike naiveté evident in Mozart, Goethe, and many other great artists, which is very much compatible with an accompanying system of goal-directed actions.

The poet is then further set apart by the clarity of delineation, strength of sensation, and energy of projection peculiar to his memory images and their formations. When a stimulus ceases, the excitation in the sensory organ can nevertheless continue. The perception then becomes an after-image. When this excitation of the sensory nerves no longer exists, the content of perception can continue to exist as a representation or be reproduced as one. The representation which immediately follows a perception, without the intervention of another representation, is most closely related to it as regards its character. Fechner calls it a "memory after-image." If other representations intervene between the impression and its reproduction, the vivacity, clarity, and distinctness of the representation is reduced. However, this difference between sensory perception and representation varies considerably in different persons, as Fechner has established through a survey. From nearly colorless and indistinctly formed images of recollection—which are indeed mere shadows of reality—we find transitions to sharply delineated, intensively colored forms projected into sensory space, of which artists and most poets are capable. Balzac spoke about the persons in his *Comédie humaine* as if they were alive. He scolded, praised, and analyzed their actions as if they belonged to the same respectable society that he was part of. The basis of this attitude was Balzac's sensory constitution. Even as a child he had memory images which were realistically delineated and colored. Accordingly, his descriptions were able to attain photographic accuracy. At the same time, he was astonished to discover in himself the ability "like the dervish in the *Thousand and One Nights* to assume the body and soul of the persons he wanted to present." Indeed, he compared this ability, which was frightening even to himself, "of relinquishing his own moral habits and transforming himself into something else, to being able to dream while awake or to a second sight."[49] This reminds us of Goethe's statement that "If I have spoken to someone for a quarter of an hour, I want to let him talk for two hours."[50] Turgenev told friends he so lived the roles of his heroes that for a time he thought, spoke, and walked as they did. When he was writing *Fathers and Sons* he spoke like Bazarov for a considerable time. Goethe said the following about such innate capacities in general: "That is what is inherent to great talent. Napoleon controlled the world as Hummel[51] played his grand piano."[52] That is the facility which always exists wherever there is real talent. Flaubert writes—and why should we doubt his word?—"The figures of my

134

[49] See Théophile Gautier, *Honoré de Balzac, sa vie et ses oeuvres* (Brussels: Melline, Cans & Co., 1858); Balzac's literary presentation of it in his *Louis Lambert*; as well as Alexandre J.F.B. de Boismont, *Des hallucinations, ou histoire des apparitions . . .* (Paris, 1845), pp. 461ff. (D)

[50] Eckermann, *Gespräche*, 26 February 1824.

[51] Johann N. Hummel (1778-1837). Famous pianist and composer.

[52] Eckermann, *Gespräche*, 7 April 1829.

imagination affect and pursue me; or, rather, I am the one who lives in them. As I described how Emma Bovary poisoned herself, I had such a distinct taste of arsenic that I suffered two attacks of indigestion."[53] And, the biography of Dickens, too, is filled with evidence about how his characters confronted his imagination with incomparable sensory vividness and, at the same time, how close they were to his heart.

Even more than by the intensity of his memory images, the poet distinguishes himself by the power with which he ⟨expresses or⟩ *re-creates psychic states*, both states experienced in himself and those observed in others, and, consequently, the situation and characters constituted by the interconnection of such states. In the field of inner experience, the distinction between a lived experience and its re-creation corresponds to that between external perception and its representation. One's own psychic state becomes an object in this re-creation. First, those external perceptions which are conjoined with affective or volitional states become representations. Images of persons, of the environment, and of the situation are reproduced as representations connected with one's state of mind. On the basis of this complex of representations, the re-creation of feelings and volitional processes is then initiated. If the effect that a state of affairs has on feeling and will persists, then the affective and volitional acts deriving from that state of affairs will naturally appear anew when it is vividly reproduced. But beyond that there is a re-creation of the affective or volitional process which is as distinct from the original lived experience as representation is from perception. New formations (*Neubildungen*) of feelings or of volitional forces are as a rule mixed in with these re-creations (*Nachbildungen*), thus lending them a certain vivacity. But these new formations disturb the purity of the re-creation, especially in literary works. Such are the associations which falsify pity and fear in middle-class drama because they evoke a recollection of one's own painful predicament or one's apprehension about it. This is not the least of the reasons why tragedy needed aristocratic heroes who are separated from the viewer by great distance. Here we enter the poet's ownmost domain: lived experience and its expression or re-creation in the imagination. First, the vivacity of these re-creations depends on the original force of feelings, emotions, and volitional

135

[53] Communication by Flaubert to Taine, quoted in Hippolyte Adolphe Taine, *De l'Intelligence*, vol. 2, 4th ed. (Paris: Hachette & Co., 1883), p. 1. (D)

processes. Second, these re-creations differ in various degrees from the original processes with respect to their distinctness, energy, and the resonance of one's own inner state. Since these re-creations are never separated from the memory of external perceptions, we have already given an indication about the possible vivacity of these re-creations with our earlier examples of the intensity of memory images. Let me add to that a remark by Dickens. As he was approaching the end of his story "The Chimes," he wrote: "Since I conceived, at the beginning of the second part, what must happen in the third, I have undergone as much sorrow and agitation as if the thing were real; and have wakened up with it at night. I was obliged to lock myself in when I finished it yesterday, for my face was swollen for the time to twice its proper size, and was hugely ridiculous."[54]

On October [19], 1786, Goethe relates how he discovered the plot of *Iphigenia in Delphi* when he was midway between sleeping and waking. About the recognition scene he writes: "I myself cried like a child over it."[55] Goethe told Schiller that he did not know if he was capable of writing an authentic tragedy, that the very endeavor terrified him, and that he was nearly convinced the mere attempt might destroy him. In the childhood years of a poet, the lively power to re-create causes the poetic figures from fairy tales, novels, and plays to be interwoven with reality itself, as we know from the cases of Goethe and Dickens. Obviously drawing on his own experience, Goethe described the limits of the imagination in re-creating as follows: "The imagination can never conceive of a virtue as perfectly as it actually appears in an individual. The imagination conceives of it more vaguely, hazily, indeterminately, and less sharply delineated—but never with the completeness characteristic of reality."[56]

136 The poet is also set apart by a capacity to truly *enliven images,* and the attendant satisfaction gained from perception is *saturated with feeling*. The intensity of his feeling of life permits images of the circumstances of the many phases of his life to arise and remain present to him. Goethe says, "Claude Lorrain knew by heart the smallest details of the real world, and he used them as the means

[54] John Forster, *The Life of Charles Dickens*, vol. 2 (London: Chapman & Hall, 1873), p. 132. (D)

[55] Goethe, *Tagebuch*, Bologna, 19 October 1786, in *WA*, III, 1:304.

[56] *Goethes Unterhaltungen mit dem Kanzler Friedrich von Müller*, ed. by Carl August Hugo Burkhardt (Stuttgart, 1870), p. 81.

with which to express the world of his beautiful soul. That is true ideality."[57] The same thing holds for the poet. Chamisso,[58] asked about the significance of *Peter Schlemihl*, declined to make any pronouncement about it and noted instead: "He seldom wanted to express anything through poetry. But if an anecdote, a word, or an image (in this case a joking conversation with Fouqué)[59] made his left paw itch, he reckoned it might strike home for others as well. Then he would struggle laboriously with language until he had it."

What we have said above makes it clear that great poets are driven by an irresistible impulse to undergo every kind of powerful experience suitable to their nature, to repeat it and gather it in themselves. Shakespeare rushed through his life filled by experiences with the feverish tempo of his heroes. The son of a well-to-do landowner, then apprentice to a lawyer, he was married at eighteen and burdened with a family the next year. Almost still a boy, he already had the experiences of love and marriage behind him. He was cast upon the sea of London life and existed from then on in that highly complex situation of actor, poet, and theater proprietor with difficult relations to the court and nobles of England. He attained the height of fame and prosperity in his thirties, and at forty he was a well-to-do landed gentleman in Stratford, recovering in his stately house from the storm of his life. All this occurred in the age of Elizabeth, in that heroic epoch of England's history filled with powerful figures and bloody political events, while England became the predominant sea power. In fact, these political events were taking place on the streets of London. It was possible for Shakespeare to be an unbiased and clear observer, thanks to the influence of Renaissance authors. Similarly, we find the career of Cervantes also filled with change and adventure. He was the secretary to a papal envoy and a soldier in the most diverse campaigns and then fell in captivity. Aeschylus and Sophocles, no less than the great English poets, acquired their understanding of the world through an active life. Corneille and Racine learned at the most powerful and splendid court of the world how to depict the heroic 137 dispositions and tragic destinies of kings and princes in such a way that this age of royalty saw its mirror image in their work. In

[57] Eckermann, *Gespräche*, 10 April 1829.

[58] Adalbert von Chamisso (1781-1838). Romantic author of ballads and other folk narratives, including *Peter Schlemihls wundersame Geschichte* (1814).

[59] Friedrich de la Motte Fouqué (1777-1843). German Romantic poet of French origin. See also footnote 131.

Weimar, Goethe exemplified and expounded the joy of a true poet about the broadening of experience through an active life. Finally, Dickens, the creator of our contemporary novel, accumulated an incredible stock of images and lived experiences as an apprentice, law clerk, reporter in Parliament, and on the highways and byways of England, and finally on long journeys to two continents, constantly studying society and people, from those in schools and prisons up to those in the palaces of Italy. He controlled these images and lived experiences with an authority equal to that of Rubens over the colors of his palette.

Other poets have focused their existence on the fullness of inner experience. They directed their attention inwards to their own subjective states, and they turned away from external reality and the colorful changes of characters and adventures in it. The best embodiment of this kind of poet is Jean Jacques Rousseau. We know from his own words how, when he was forty-four and living in the Hermitage of La Chevrette Park, he formed the figure of Héloïse from the dreams of his lonely heart and from his love for the Countess d'Houdetot—which, to be sure, was also little more than a dream. He infused Héloïse with a powerful stream of passions which he found in himself, with his lived experience of a dynamic nature, and with the inner dreamlike lived experiences of his own lonely heart. However, with *Emile* he wrote an even more deeply felt inner history of a psyche which sought truth in the age of the Encyclopedists. If we turn to antiquity, we also find such an inwardly related poet in Euripides: he lived with the writings of the philosophers. In the Middle Ages, we find Dante. His lived experiences were completely intertwined with the great theological, philosophical, and political battles of his age, and his psyche was their stage. Whereas we find a balance between inner and outer in Goethe, inner experience seems to predominate in the early Schiller. The second half of Schiller's short life is characterized by an undertone of resignation and an overriding concern to raise the soul to a free ideal state through philosophical and historical thought, while he increasingly lost touch with external reality.

Finally, the poet stands apart in that his images and their connections unfold freely *beyond the bounds of reality.* He creates situations, figures, and fates, which transcend this real world. The main problem of this investigation is to determine how these processes, in which the genuinely creative work of the poet is completed, are constituted. The designation "poetic imagination" provides us with a mere word which hides these processes from us.

138

### *4. The Relation of the Poet's Imagination to Dreams, Insanity, and Other States that Deviate from the Norm of Waking Life*

First of all we must observe and describe these processes in which a metamorphosis of reality is accomplished, and apprehend how they both resemble and differ from those processes that are most closely related to them. These closely related processes emerge in dreams, madness, and, in general, in states that deviate from the norm of waking life.

It seems to have been one of the accepted principles of ancient poetics that poetic creativity was a kind of madness. Democritus, Plato, Horace, and Aristotle are in accord on this point. Subsequently, the Romantics have repeatedly emphasized the affinity between genius and madness, dreams and all kinds of ecstatic states. Here as elsewhere Schopenhauer has sought to furnish scientific evidence for a Romantic idea. He gave a complete description of the personality of a genius. Of course, it was very subjective indeed, because he used himself as a model. A high and broad forehead, an energetic heartbeat, small stature, a short neck—he found these characteristics to be especially favorable. According to him, a genius should even have a strong stomach. When the very great intelligence of the genius, conditioned by tremendous cerebral vitality, frees itself from the service of the will, the abnormal disposition of genius emerges. In particular, genius elevates itself above time and temporal relations. It produces phenomena akin to madness because, according to Schopenhauer, madness involves a disorder of the memory where the temporal continuum is suspended. Genius also involves an intensified sensitivity of the functions of the brain, and a complete alienation from the ways of the world and of the man on the street. This accounts for the melancholy loneliness of the genius. Such a bleak way of praising genius does, as we can see, capture some of the traits of Byron and Alfieri. Richard Wagner, following Schopenhauer, also exalted "madness" and thereby placed all noble achievements and sacrifices on the same level with pathological phenomena. Then French psychiatry made this affinity of genius and madness the theme of a whole series of psychiatric fantasies. I am not going to discuss all that can be said about the similarities between genius and madness; I intend only to indicate 139 the points of contact between the creative work of the poet and the delusions, dreams, and fantasies that occur in other abnormal conditions. In all these conditions, images arise which transcend experience. It is the mark of the great writer that his constructive imagination produces—out of elements of experience and based on analogies with experience—a type of person or plot which surpasses experience and yet through which we nevertheless come to understand it better. Moreover, the writer is like a dreamer or madman in that he views situations and events with a clarity and vividness approaching that of hallucinations. He lives with figures who reside solely in his imagination just as if they were real persons—he loves them and fears for them. A further analogy between genius and insanity lies in the capacity to transform one's own ego into that of the hero and to speak from his perspective much as an actor does. One of the most interesting problems of psychology is implicit in these relations.

## Chapter Two. An Attempt to Explain Poetic Creativity Psychologically

Today, established psychological theory starts with representations as fixed quantities. Changes in representations are allowed to occur externally through association, fusion, and apperception. I maintain that this psychology is incapable of explaining the images of the dreamer, the madman, or the artist. If one conceives, through abstraction, mere relations of representations in a purely representational being, no one can say which laws these representations would follow. But as perceptions or representations appear in the real nexus of psychic life they are permeated, colored, and enlivened by feelings. The distribution of feelings, interests, and the way they influence our attentiveness, bring about, in conjunction with other causes, the appearance, the gradual unfolding, and the disappearance of representations. Efforts of attention—which derive from feelings, but are forms of volitional activity—impart an impulsive energy to individual images or permit them to fade away again. In the real psyche, therefore, every representation is a *process*. Even the sensations which are connected in an image, and the relations existing among them, are subject to *inner transformations*. Perception and the image itself are also processes subject to lively transformations. Perception manifests properties which stem from these processes and cannot be understood on the basis of representations as such.

140

### 1. *Elementary Processes Relating Individual Representations*

Despite these circumstances, the real, living psyche first manifests certain elementary processes that relate individual representations and can be explicated without considering the inner transformations in these representations.

The first class of these processes relate perceptions and representations which are already in consciousness, as a consequence of their existing together in the unity of this consciousness, and insofar as conditions of interest and attention operate in a determinate direction. Representations held together by attention in this way are *distinguished* from one another. Their divergence is sensed in terms of *degrees*; their kinship in terms of *similarity* or likeness. These relations can be sensed or possessed in an immediate reflexive awareness[60] just as much as the sensory contents that are thus held together. Such reflexive awareness implicit in sense also apprehends elementary relations between perceptions and representations as they coexist in space or succeed each other in time.

The second class of these processes comes into play wherever perceptions and representations, or their constituents, are evoked by one another in consciousness. Here the laws of *fusion* and of *association* apply. The pervasive significance of these two laws for psychic life can be compared to that of the laws of motion for our explanation of external nature. They designate elementary properties of psychic life which decisively distinguish it from the course of nature. Therefore, every attempt to determine these laws more precisely by analogies with mechanics will fail. To be sure, it is necessary to borrow illustrations from the external world to characterize psychic processes. This is because the latter only recently came under observation and were first apprehended in light of the already developed natural sciences. But this should not deceive us about how basically unsuitable these illustrations, taken from the spatial realm and its motions, are for grasping laws whose characteristic features are conditioned by the totally different nature of psychic processes.

First law: perceptions, representations, or their constituents, which are similar or alike, interpenetrate one another, independently of the position which they occupy in the psychic nexus. They 141

[60] Reflexive awareness (*Innewerden*) is an immediate prereflective mode of self-givenness in which the dichotomies of form and content, subject and object characteristic of reflective consciousness do not yet exist. See the Introduction.

produce a content, which, as a rule, is connected with a consciousness of the different acts that constitute it, and which incorporates the differences among the constituent contents unless they are purposely disregarded. In contradistinction to the causal nexus of the external world, all representations involved in this psychic process are equally near and equally far from one another. Even those representations which are farthest from each other in the psychic nexus interpenetrate one another simply because they are akin. Because consciousness is led from the similar to the dissimilar according to the conditions of interest and attention, it can reproduce contents that are either similar, alike, unlike, or even opposed from a given perception or representation.

Second law: perceptions, representations, or their constituents, which were unified in the unity of one process of consciousness, can reproduce each other reciprocally under certain conditions of interest and attention. We characterize this basic relationship as "association," but we use this expression in a narrow sense, since Hume and his English successors also included that conjunction which makes possible a reproduction through likeness or contrast. This law too should not be interpreted mechanistically or atomistically. For we see how, on the basis of association, contents are linked with one another in perception and thought in the most varied ways to form a nexus of psychic life which continually orients, as it were, whatever occurs in consciousness. Thus reproduction is not instigated by a contiguous representation or perception. Rather, it is conditioned by this overall psychic nexus, in which, to be sure, the parts are not clearly and sharply distinguished. Although the relations of these parts are not brought to complete consciousness, they are active nevertheless. This has certain consequences for the reproduction of composite images which are also important for artistic creativity. Furthermore, the factors that cooperate to make reproduction possible are very complicated. The following processes condition reproduction: first, the constituting process of experience which produced a complex of contents; then, subsequent acts in which this complex occurred again, either in full or in part, taking into account the intervening intervals; finally, the present state of consciousness which instigates the reproduction, again taking into account the interval separating it from the previous instance of 142 reproduction. Concerning these processes, we also distinguish the following as properties influencing reproduction: the character of the contents and their modes of connection; the interest that individual psychic acts bestow on these contents and the stimulation of consciousness conditioned thereby; the frequency of their recurrence; and finally, the amount of time separating these individual acts from one another. Feelings and acts of will express themselves in interest and attention to raise representations into consciousness.

## 2. *The Nexus of Psychic Life and the Formative Processes Produced By It*

We shall no longer ignore the more comprehensive and subtle nexus in which individual representations function. Only by abstracting from this nexus could we isolate the elementary processes just presented from the life of the psyche. We shall also no longer ignore the inner transformations which take place in perceptions, representations, or their constituents. Only by means of such an abstraction could we regard these perceptions, etc., as fixed, self-subsisting elements which can merely be distinguished, fused, related, brought to consciousness, or suppressed from it.[61] In reality a psychic process is usually—I do not say always—at the same time a formative process. It is conditioned by the entire nexus of psychic life; and it also contains inner transformations of perceptions, representations, or their constituents which are brought about by this nexus.

All the more complex psychic processes, insofar as they are produced by the nexus of psychic life, are thus *formative processes*. They do not just distinguish, fuse, or relate fixed representations, raise them to consciousness or suppress them, but also effect changes in these perceptions or representations. In fact, such changes never consist in the creation of new contents that have not been previously experienced, but rather in excluding particular contents or connections, intensifying or diminishing them, or in their completion, i.e., the addition of contents or connections drawn from experience to a perception or representation. In addition to this, we find a constant variation in the arousal of consciousness and in the strength of interest focused on individual constituents at a given moment, as well as in the related distribution of the involvement of feeling and will.

[61] The fusion of discrete representations, the raising of some into consciousness and the suppression of others, defines apperception for Johann F. Herbart (1776-1841). Herbart's theory of apperception is based on the mechanistic hypothesis that representations are discrete elements, each having a tendency to preserve itself. In the next chapter we will see Dilthey redefining apperception as a dynamic formative process rooted in the overall continuum of psychic life. Apperception will be used not to explain constancy, but to describe change.

143 The entire *acquired nexus* of psychic life acts on these formative processes. It transforms and shapes those perceptions, representations, and states on which the attention is directly focused, and which thus engage our consciousness most strongly. This acquired nexus of our psychic life encompasses not only our representations, but also evaluations derived from our feelings and ideas of purpose which have arisen from our acts of will—indeed, the habits of our feeling and will. This nexus consists not only of contents, but also of the connections which are established among these contents; these connections are just as real as the contents. The connections are lived and experienced as relations between representational contents, as relations of values to one another, and as relations of ends and means.

This complex nexus is characterized by an *articulation* which is rooted in the structure of psychic life. The play of stimuli stemming from the external world is projected in psychic life as sensation, perception, and representation. The changes so produced are experienced and judged in a multiplicity of feelings, according to their value for our own life. Then our feelings activate certain drives, desires, and processes of the will. Either reality is adjusted to our own life (the self in turn influencing external reality) or our own life adapts itself to a hard and intransigent reality. Thus there is a constant interaction between the self and the milieu of external reality in which the self is placed, and our life consists of this interaction. In this life, the reality of perceptions and the truth of representations are interwoven with a hierarchy of values projected onto the whole of reality by the feelings. These are then linked with the energy and consistency of the expressions of the will—and the normative concerns that constitute the system of ends and means.

Despite the highly composite nature of this nexus of psychic life, *it works as a whole* on the representations or states on which our attention is focused. The individual constituents of the nexus are not clearly conceived or distinctly differentiated, nor are the relations between them raised to the light of consciousness. Yet we possess this acquired nexus and it is effective. Whatever is to be found in consciousness is oriented toward it, bounded and determined by it, and grounded in it. Through it principles derive their certainty, concepts receive their sharp delineation, and our position in space and time obtains its orientation. Likewise, it is from this 144 nexus that feelings receive their significance for the totality of our life. Finally, it is because of this same nexus that our will, which is usually occupied with means, remains constantly certain about the system of ends in which the means are grounded. These are the ways in which the acquired psychic nexus works in us, although we possess it obscurely. It even regulates and controls those fervent, momentary wishes which seem to absorb consciousness completely as well as new concepts or facts which are still alien or hostile to it.

### *3. Three Main Types of Formative Processes: The Place of Artistic Creativity in the Nexus of Psychic Life*

We accept the distinctions between representation, feeling, and willing as a fact of inner experience. Our descriptive attitude in laying the foundations of poetics excludes explanatory hypotheses, and allows us to preserve these empirically given distinctions. To be sure, these three classes of processes as we find them in the structure of psychic life are connected with one another. They constitute three major domains of formative processes.

The formative processes of *thinking* and knowing proceed first of all in the ways we have already indicated. But if we move beyond distinguishing, unifying, relating, reproducing, and suppressing representations, then we immediately encounter apperception among these kinds of formative processes. It constitutes the simplest case in which the nexus of psychic life acts on an individual process and receives a reciprocal influence from it. By "apperception" we mean the process whereby—through the direction of attention—experiential contents, sensations, or inner states are incorporated into the nexus of consciousness. Apperception is first conditioned by the total or partial interpenetration of experiential contents into an already given representation. It mediates the incorporation of the resulting perceptual representation into the nexus of the original representation. This can produce a change either in the content of experience or in the nexus of psychic life. Other formative processes are initiated by inner impulses, which are inherent in the play of representations. These processes take control of our perceptions and reshape them. The development of our psychic life consists of 145 the continual modification of external stimuli through perceptual contents and inner impulses.[62] Furthermore, there exist formative

[62] Heymann Steinthal, *Abriß der Sprachwissenschaft* (Outline of Linguistics), vol. 1 (Berlin: Dümmler, 1871), p. 166f., and Moritz Lazarus, *Das Leben der Seele* (The Life of the Soul), vol. 1 (Berlin: Dümmler, 1876), pp. 253ff., employ the expression "apperception" to characterize the more complex formative processes as such. Wil-

processes which relate only reproduced representations. Thus a poet characterizes an invented figure through further features which he borrows from his memory. Or a scientist derives from data, which he already possessed, an explanation of a fact with which he has long been acquainted.

When the will controls these elementary and formative processes with intense energy and with a consciousness of its goal, a fundamental distinction arises which differentiates the play of our representations from logical thought. If psychology begins with the totality of life, if it grasps the intermeshing of volitional and representational processes, then it does not need to separate the play of representations from relational thought and to posit a higher form of spiritual life above the involuntary processes. For it would be most peculiar to acknowledge a process of fusion and then posit over and above it, and completely separate from it, a logical process of identification; it would be equally peculiar to acknowledge a process of the association of ideas and then place over this a completely independent, logical connection of representations.[63] In real-

---

helm Wundt, in his *Grundzüge der physiologischen Psychologie* (Principles of Physiological Psychology), vol. II (Leipzig: W. Engelmann, 1874), pp. 210ff., characterizes every process in representation which is guided by an inner volitional act of attention as "apperception." However, since this expression received a fixed sense through Leibniz and his school and since other expressions are available for the group of processes identified by the researchers just cited, I have preserved the older usage. (D)

Moritz Lazarus (1824-1903) and Heymann Steinthal (1823-1899) were followers of Herbart. They applied Herbart's concept of apperception to the development of language (see Dilthey, *GS*, XVII, 155). In 1859, Lazarus and Steinthal founded the *Zeitschrift für Völkerpsychologie und Sprachwissenschaft* (Journal for Ethno-psychology and Linguistics). Dilthey was critical of Herbart's mechanistic hypothesis that apperception is a function of representations striving to preserve themselves. He was even more skeptical about the spiritual hypothesis of a soul of a people as proposed by Lazarus and Steinthal.

According to Dilthey, Wilhelm Wundt (1832-1920) places too much emphasis on the role of the will in apperception. Wundt's conception of apperception is less mechanistic than Herbart's, yet it appeals to special acts of will to produce what are called "creative syntheses." Through such a synthesis, a perception can have an effect which is greater than the sum of its components. If one starts with fixed elements of psychic life, then the hypothesis of creative synthesis becomes necessary. However, if one starts with the overall continuum of psychic life, the hypothesis becomes dispensable and the nature of apperception changes from being a synthetic act to an articulative process.

[63] Dilthey is here arguing for a continuity between psychological and logical processes. All processes of consciousness are inherently formative and do not need to have a logical form imposed from above as claimed by the Kantians.

ity, the latter are only more advanced stages, as it were, of the processes we have described. The processes of thought involve a higher degree of complexity, but especially a greater participation of the will. Thus we obtain first of all a sphere of elementary logical operations. The more complex logical processes, forms, and rules of thought are conditioned by it. Their development is borne by language, which preserves the acquisitions of the life of the psyche, fixes them in forms, and transmits them from one generation to another. The sciences emerge as powerful organs of the formative processes that render representations adaptable to the description and explanation of reality. In this context hypotheses also arise, i.e., concepts and combinations of concepts that transcend the sphere of experience in the interest of explanation. If we were to apply the concept of imagination, then hypotheses would have to be subsumed under the concept of the scientific imagination.

146 When impressions from the external world produce changes in our representational life which induce formative processes of perception or thought and, of course, also change the state of our feelings, then impulses originate which react back upon the external world. For, under certain conditions of the psychic nexus, feelings evoke volitional processes. Another class of formative processes arises on the basis of these *volitional processes*. A volitional process does not derive from representations and feelings by means of the mere addition of a physiological process from our motor system, as is shown by inner volitional acts. Rather, volitional processes are just as important as emotional processes for inner experience. This suffices for the requirements of our descriptive procedure. There are outer volitional acts aimed at adjusting the external world to our own inner life and its need to control the processes of nature and direct those of society; from these we now distinguish inner volitional acts which direct the course of our representations, feelings, and passions. Outer volitional acts are the source of our economic life, our legal and political institutions, and our domination of nature. Among other things, inner volitional acts are the source of our inner moral development and the religious practices supported by it. To be sure, our religious practices were at first intertwined with outer volitional acts. Man wanted to ensure the success of his undertakings through his religious acts. Religion is also bound up with the problem of knowledge in its primitive form. Man wished to penetrate the darkness that surrounds, conditions, and burdens him. But inner volitional acts become the authentic nucleus of the religious attitude in more developed cultures.

Acts of will are connected with a multitude of representational formative processes. Their common feature is that the contents of will and their relation in the will find their expression in representations. First of all, in every volitional act there is a relation, conditioned by the feelings, between the will and an anticipatory image of an effect. This image of an effect is formed naturally by the will in a manner that transcends reality. Consequently, these purposes stand to one another in a relationship whose basis is the structure of the will extending back to elementary impulses. The sum total of these practical representational contents and their connections is comprised in the relations of these purposes to the manifold of possible means and in the relations of domination and subordi- 147 nation that exist between wills. Then practical categories such as "good," "purpose," "means," or "independence" arise through abstraction, and are then applied throughout the sphere of human volition. Ideals originate from inner acts of the will. We see thus that formative processes of this class also produce representations which transcend reality. If we were to classify them under the concept of the imagination, we would have to speak of a "practical imagination."

Between these two domains of thought and action there is a third region comprising those formative processes in which representational contents and their connections are determined and formed *by the feelings*, without producing an impulse either to adapt external reality to the will or the will to reality. This can occur only in two cases. The first involves a temporary equilibrium of feelings, in which life takes a holiday, as it were. Such an affective state is amplified, intensified, and formed by festive enjoyment, social life, games, and art. To the extent that this state of mind includes a relation to reality, our mood seeks to subordinate all representations to itself. The second case comes about when our affective state encompasses a tension which cannot be overcome either by an outer or an inner act of will. Unnerving and ineradicable facts impart their somber quality to all things, and images corresponding to them are produced in melancholy brooding.

The formative processes which occur in our representations under the influence of the feelings under such circumstances also constitute a very extensive sphere. It extends from the gloomy projections of the hypochondriac about his eye infection or the image that an insulted person develops about someone who has offended him, on the one hand, to the Venus of Milo, Raphael's Madonnas, and *Faust,* on the other. This entire sphere is governed by the basic law that representations which have been formed by a certain state of feeling are regularly able to evoke it again. In particular, intense states of feeling are discharged, so to speak, in gestures, vocalizations, and representational complexes, which then, as symbols of these affective contents again arouse these states of feeling in the viewer or listener. Thus a lowering or raising of the voice, a specific tempo, a change in volume, pitch, or speed evokes a feeling that corresponds to the state of feeling from which it arose. The schemata used in music are of this nature.

These formative processes make possible the establishment of continuity in the development of the higher feelings, both for the existence of the individual and for the evolution of humanity. Here too, as in the spheres of representing and thinking, the will contributes to the formation of coherent images. Fixed forms of social life, festivity, and art thus arise. And here, too, images transcend the bounds of reality. We can characterize the capacity to produce such processes very simply: it is the artistic or the poetic imagination. We now move to the consideration of that topic. 148

### 4. *Spheres of Feelings and the Elementary Laws of Aesthetics Originating from Them*

Since the formative processes of the artistic imagination are produced by the play of feelings, the basis of their explanation must be sought in an analysis of feelings. The significance of our affective life for artistic creativity has never been completely overlooked. The experience of the relations of forms to our feelings is the source of the significance possessed by relations of line, by the distribution of force, weight, and symmetry in architectural and pictorial compositions. From the perception of the relations between our feelings and vocal changes in pitch, rhythm, and volume, we develop accentuated speech and melody. Acquired insights about the effects of characters, fates, and actions on our feelings have produced ideal formations of character and plot. What is ideal in the plastic arts emerges from mysterious relations between felt distinctions in psychic life and the manifold of corporeal forms. An analysis of feeling thus contains the key to the explanation of artistic creativity.

In real life, feelings always confront us with intricate complexities. Just as a perceptual image is composed of a manifold of sensory contents, so too does an affective state arise from elementary feelings which must be studied through analysis. Suppose I am standing in front of Raphael's painting *The School of Athens*. Each individual color has its own affective tone. Then I notice that the harmony of the colors and their contrasts, the beauty of the lines and the expression of the persons in the picture all have their special feelings. All of these aspects come together in the feeling with which the painting completely fills and satisfies me. These feelings appear in forms which are shaped by a specific kind of combination of elementary feelings. Joy, sorrow, or hatred are examples of such forms. But 149 these forms do not relate to one another in any obvious, purposive nexus, nor can they be arranged into a system.

Differences among feelings manifest themselves first of all as differences in degree. Feelings can be arranged in a series according to their intensity, proceeding from a zero-point of indifference to increasingly intense degrees of pleasure, satisfaction, and approval in one direction, and to degrees of displeasure, dissatisfaction, and disapproval in the other. But feelings also display qualitative distinctions. For the time being, we cannot determine whether these qualitative distinctions originate exclusively from the representational content and from the will, or whether the life of the feelings can on its own generate distinctions over and above those of the degree of pleasure or displeasure. This is so because life consists precisely in the reciprocity of the different aspects of the psyche. We are not able to say which representational processes remain when we exclude the participation of feeling and will in interest and attention. Nor are we able to say whether, taken by itself, the function manifested in affective processes would provide us with a mere monotonous scale of pleasures and pains. We will investigate the elementary affective processes within the given qualitative manifold content of the feelings.

The simpler constituents from which our feelings are composed recur in the way that sensations or the constituents of perception do. Indeed, we find that a determinate class of affective processes regularly arises in the causal nexus of psychic life from a determinate class of antecedents. Just as a class of stimuli corresponds to a sphere of sensory qualities, so too a determinate class of affective antecedents corresponds to a determinate sphere of feeling. I can thus arrange the elementary feelings into spheres, and, in this sense, they form an easily surveyed manifold.

Stimuli unmediated by representations are only antecedents of feelings of sensory pain and pleasure. Their connection is a problem for psychophysics, which seeks out the mediating processes within the body, leading from a stimulus to a feeling. But, naturally, the transition from the last phase of a physiological process to feeling as such cannot be grasped any more readily than the transition from the former to sensation. However, in all other cases psychic processes are the antecedents of feelings. The transition from a psychic process as antecedent to a feeling as consequence contains the self-evidence which always accompanies one's inner awareness of producing an effect. This connection can be assigned the inner compulsion that we characterize as "necessity." Finally, there is a con- 150 stancy according to which a given sensory or representational content always produces a specific feeling under otherwise identical circumstances. However, we know nothing about how that happens and why a specific class of processes is connected with just this particular class of elementary feelings. Also, this relationship does not illuminate the rule according to which the value of a state or a transformation is experienced in a feeling. For value is indeed only the representational expression of what is experienced in feeling. And precisely because certain processes produce feelings with a constancy similar to that with which certain stimuli produce sensations, do the elementary feelings disclose a sphere of experience whose objects we can characterize as evaluations. In pleasure we partly enjoy the properties of objects—their beauty and their meaning—and partly the intensification of our own existence—properties of our own person that give value to our existence. This twofold relation is based on the interaction between ourselves and the external world. Just as we experience the external world through sensations, we experience value, meaning, and an increase or decrease of existence in ourselves or in something outside of ourselves through feelings.

Let us survey the spheres of feeling by proceeding from the outside to the inside, as it were.

The *first sphere* of elementary feelings comprises those that make up general and sensuous feelings. What is characteristic about them is that a physiological process evokes pain or pleasure without the mediation of representations. Meynert has made plausible conjectures about the constituents of this causal nexus.[64]

The *second sphere of feelings* is constituted by those elementary feelings which emerge from the *contents of sensation* when accompanied by a concentrated interest. The degree of intensity of a sensation already stands in a regular relation to pleasure and displeasure. Degrees of intensity which are too great or too small have

[64] Meynert, *Psychiatrie; Klinik der Erkrankungen des Vorderhirns begründet auf dessen Bau, Leistungen und Ernährung* (Vienna: Braumüller, 1884), pp. 176ff. (D)

a disagreeable effect, while those in the middle range are inherently enjoyable. However, the qualities of a sensation are also related in a regular way to an affective tone which accompanies the sensation when concentrated attention is given to it. Goethe carried out experiments about these sorts of effects of simple colors. Such an effect also exists in the sensation of simple tones. Here the effort to establish which sensations are elementary and which are the result 151 of a fusion of several sensations but are nevertheless separable through attentiveness and practice presents the familiar difficulties that surround the elementary theory of music. In poetry, these feelings condition the aesthetic effect in that the mere predominance of soft sounds in the phonetic material of many lyric poems—Goethe's in particular—already provides an unexpected charm. We can designate the aesthetic *principle* according to which the simple sensory elements employed in art are suited to produce an effect as the *principle of sensuous charm.*

The *third sphere of feeling* encompasses those feelings which originate in perceptions, and are evoked by the *relations* of *sensuous contents* to one another. This is how harmony and contrast affect us in tone and color. The enjoyment of symmetry is the most common of the spatial feelings, and that of rhythm the most common among temporal feelings. But an immeasurable expanse of a uniformly blue sky or of the sea also evokes a strong aesthetic feeling. Through the relations of tones to one another in its linguistic material, quite apart from the meaning of individual words, poetry produces a sensuous enjoyment of great diversity and strength. One of the most important foundations of poetics lies in the investigation of these elementary feelings. In particular, poetics must search how the rhythmic feeling is rooted in the feeling of life itself. For, just as our body displays symmetry on its surface, rhythm pervades its internal functions. Our heartbeat and breathing are rhythmical. Walking is a regular, pendulumlike motion. Waking and sleep, hunger and eating follow one another in more protracted, but still regular, alternation. Our work is facilitated by rhythmic movements. Water dripping in regular drops, the rhythm of recurring waves, or the monotonous rhythms with which the nurse sings to the child all have a soothing effect on the feelings and so induce sleep. The explanation of the general psychic significance of rhythm is still an unsolved problem. For, the fact that we more easily and uniformly apprehend the totality of sensory change by means of rhythm does not seem to explain the primal power of rhythm. If we consider the relationship of a simple sensation to what is rhythmical in the movements which affect vision and hearing, then we can regard the enjoyment of rhythm as the repetition of a similar relationship at a higher level (since the parts of this rhythmical process are sensations). But this is only a hypothesis which—at least for the time being—is undemonstrable. There poetics must provide a comparative treatment—at first empirically—of the extensive field [152] stretching from the songs, melodies, and dances of primitive peoples to the structure of the Greek chorus. Only then will the study of rhythm and meter, as abstracted from highly developed literature, enter a wider context which will furnish the means for deciding between the conflicting psychological hypotheses.

We designate the principle according to which the elements of sensation of an artwork must stand in relations that stimulate feeling positively as the principle of the *pleasurable proportion among sensations*. In poetry, one's pleasure in what is rhythmical as well as in phonetic combinations is, to be sure, conditioned not only by these elementary relationships, but also by associations that provide meaning to rhythmical patterns and phonetic combinations based on content.

The *fourth sphere of feelings* comprises the great variety of feelings that spring from the cognitive *connection* of our *representations* and which are aroused by the mere forms of our representational and thought processes, without regard to the relationship of their content to our being. In this wide sphere of feelings we find, among others, gradations in the feeling of success which accompanies our representing and thinking, the agreeable feeling of confirming evidence and the disturbing one of contradiction, pleasure in the unity underlying the manifold, enjoyment in comprehending change, the feeling of boredom, the enjoyment of jokes and of the comical, the surprise evoked by a penetrating judgment, and so forth.

It is worth noting how an analysis into elementary feelings becomes significant for poetics in that it illuminates the extent to which feelings are integrated in a poetic impression. Since one sphere of feelings is joined to another, it becomes clear how elementary feelings as yet uninfluenced by the meaning-content of a poem can combine to produce an effect whereby even a sorrowful content can be conveyed in a medium characterized by melody, harmony, rhythm, and forms of representation and thought which are lively and uplifting. We now recognize how *form in poetry is something composite*, and how, precisely by combining feelings, form becomes most effective.

This is why the fourth sphere of feelings is very important, and poetics encounters problems of considerable scope here. From the relations of representations to one another in thought there originate forms and their constituents which are important for poetry: 153 the joke, the comical, the simile, the antithesis, and the relation between how thought comprehends the unity of a manifold and the richness actually presented by this manifold. This relationship makes it possible for us to find satisfaction in a receptive attitude, equally far removed from chaotic confusion and boring monotony.[65] Similarly, the following feelings emanate from the relations among representations in thought: "When there exist two diverging occasions for representing one and the same matter, it is pleasing to become aware that they really lead to a harmonious representation, and displeasing to become aware that they lead to a contradictory representation."[66] Naturally, the relations among representations in thought, such as identity and difference, agreement and contradiction, must be elevated into clear consciousness if these relations are to have an effect on one's aesthetic feeling.[67] In summary, we find an artwork pleasing because the forms of the representational and thinking processes which occasion its apprehension by the recipient are accompanied by pleasure, still quite apart from the relation of the content to our concrete impulses. I characterize this as the *principle of pleasure in the cognitive connection of representations*. Special principles of historical significance are contained in it: the unity of interest; Leibniz's idea that plurality must emerge *from unity* and reemerge *in unity;* unity in multiplicity; intelligibility. At the end of the seventeenth century and the beginning of the eighteenth, this principle was made the basis for art and poetry especially. The rules implicit in the principle were explicated to make its importance for the work of art fully obvious—although one-sidedly. It is in the spirit of this period that one must understand the secret of its poetry as formulated by Montesquieu: to say much with one word. According to him, a great thought is one that encompasses much; with one stroke it makes us conscious of an abundance of representations. Here greatness is conceived as a form

[65] The best treatment of this since ancient times can be found in Fechner's *Vorschule der Aesthetik*, vol. 1 (Leipzig: Breitkopf und Härtel, 1876), pp. 53ff. See his principle of the unified connection of what is manifold. (D)

[66] This is Fechner's formulation of the principle of *noncontradiction*, agreement, or truth. See *ibid.*, pp. 80ff. (D)

[67] This principle is characterized by Fechner as that of *clarity* (*ibid.*). The three principles mentioned above are grouped together by Fechner as the "three highest formal principles." (D)

of cognitive apprehension. That was the spirit of the poetry of Voltaire and Frederick the Great.

The *form* of literature is naturally related to its meaning-content, and when the many elementary feelings pertaining to the form of literature work together so that even the most cruel and bitter destiny is elevated into a sphere of harmony—as is manifested in so many of the verses of Homer or Shakespeare, or also in Goethe's *Elective Affinities*—then we enter the sphere of feelings in which the aesthetic effects stem from the meaning-content of literature. The *fifth sphere of feelings* results from the particular *material impulses* which pervade the whole of life and whose entire content is possessed in a reflexive awareness obtained through feelings. These feelings emerge when elementary drives are either obstructed or aided by the surrounding milieu or by inner states. They pervade the entire moral world and are interwoven with our instincts, welling up from the depths of our sensory feelings. The list of drives that emerge from the depths of sensory feeling includes the drives for nourishment, for self-preservation or the will-to-live, for procreation, and love of offspring. These are the strongest springs in the clockwork of life, the muscles which propel that immense leviathan, society. The sensuous force of these impulses is almost matched by the power of motives belonging to a higher region. What presents itself as self-consciousness becomes, from the practical side, a striving for the preservation and perfection of the person and for self-esteem. These are only different sides of the same state of affairs, and feelings of the most powerful sort are attached to it. When these feelings are either obstructed or furthered and their relations are apprehended, then particular, and often composite, feelings of vanity, honor, pride, shame, and envy arise. But society is just as thoroughly dominated by a second group of feelings in which we experience the pain and pleasure of others as our own. We appropriate another's life in our own ego, as it were, through sympathy, pity, or love. The more subtle activities and attitudes of society rest primarily upon these two major traits of human feeling.

154

The elementary material of poetry is to be found in this sphere of feelings. The more firmly motif and plot are rooted in life, the more powerfully do they move our senses. The great elemental drives of human existence, the passions that derive from them and the fate of these passions in the world, these constitute the authentic basis of all poetic ability when they are lived and experienced in their essential psychological power. What makes a poet great is the fact that these drives operate much more powerfully, extensively,

and concretely in him than in his reader or listener; this produces
155 an expansion and intensification of the sense of life which is the most elementary effect of all poetry on the reader or listener. If, like Fechner, we are to formulate principles (laws) that regulate creativity and are embodied in what is beautiful, then we must here establish a *principle of truthfulness* in the sense of the powerful reality of a person and of the elementary drives in him.[68] This principle will hold for all the arts. For, where no external truth, in the sense of a depiction of reality, is aimed at, as in architecture and music, there the forms are rooted in the inner power of a substantial human being, rather than in the mere imitation of the life of others or even the forms created by them. It is this power which provides a musical work or a cathedral its truthfulness.

The will, through which the drives work themselves out and evoke passions, has, however, general properties that express themselves in these drives and passions. We can also obtain a reflexive awareness of these properties through impressions which are to be distinguished from the groups of feelings just described, no matter how closely related they may be. Thus the *last sphere of feelings* arises when *we possess a reflexive awareness of the general properties of acts of will* and experience their value. The very great diversity in this sphere of feelings originates from the multiplicity of these properties, from the relations into which they break up, as it were, or from the differences in our experience of them, depending on whether we merely feel these properties powerfully or experience their value through judgments made about us or about others. Let us briefly enumerate some examples: the enjoyment of power; the reflexive awareness of consistently adhering to what the will holds to be essential despite changes in circumstances—an awareness that persists through time, even negates it for the purposes of the will, and defines what we mean by character and steadfastness. To these examples we may add the following: loyalty, courage, disregard of danger or suffering in upholding what is essential to one's character; the rich content of life appropriated and unified by the will, and enjoyed in a joyous expansion of the feeling of life; responsibility which honors an obligation to another will, and which recognizes
156 this obligation regardless of whether it is derived from an act of receiving, or of enjoyment or of positing—namely, responsibility

[68] Fechner's principle of truth (*ibid.*, pp. 80ff.) is connected with that of noncontradiction and says that we are only satisfied by artworks which meet the demand for external reality to the extent that we can presuppose an agreement of the artwork with external objects according to an idea or purpose of the latter. (D)

rooted in integrity or faithfulness to duty; related to these are gratitude and devotion. And just as I esteem myself as a person and defend the domain of my rights, I also am constrained to acknowledge that the other's personality is valuable in itself and, thus, to respect his domain. Thus we develop a sense of justice and lawfulness. Many feelings are involved in this process, ranging from the impulse to punish wrongdoing, on the one hand, to a sense of fairness on the other. Finally, the power of the will contains, as the highest expression of all this, the capacity of a person to dedicate himself to and sacrifice himself for a cause or for people to whom he is bound by strong attachments. This highest attribute of the will, its peculiar capacity for transcendence, elevates it above the law of self-preservation and the entire course of nature.

The moral ideas posited by Herbart are only shadowy abstractions derived from apprehending the properties of the will and their value. But the overall life or vigor of the will can never be completely penetrated by the intellect.[69] Because we can apprehend and grasp the value of this life of the will only through such specific properties, and because the inner structure in which these properties coexist is very difficult to penetrate—indeed, may be impossible to penetrate fully—Herbart settled for an account of elementary moral ideas gained from an analysis of moral judgments.

The feelings pertaining to the life of the will can be refracted in various ways: they appear sometimes as the consciousness of one's own worth, sometimes as a judgment about other persons, and sometimes as the enjoyment of the intuition of perfection in its pure types. It is important to realize that these feelings and their refractions have a special significance for the poet's way of seeing things. When the images of these grand attributes of the will and the feelings stemming from them are at work in the poet, an ideal of life becomes the soul of his poetry.[70] This process of idealization shapes his characters and story. At the same time, it is the source of ideality in the structure of the plot which is grounded in the will; in particular, it accounts for the scope and nobility of the plots of Schiller's dramas. Since, through processes we will soon be discussing, this

[69] "Verstand" is translated as "intellect" to distinguish it from Dilthey's "Verstehen" (understanding).

[70] I first analyzed the meaning of the poet's ideal of life and how it contributes to the forming of his world-view in "Lessing," *Preußische Jahrbücher* [Berlin: G. Reimer, 1867], pp. 117-161 ⟨republished in *Das Erlebnis und die Dichtung*⟩. See also "Scherer zum persönlichen Gedächtnis," *Deutsche Rundschau* (October 1886). (D)

ideality is also imparted to the formal elements which are freely combined in other arts, a general principle of the efficacy of all the arts stems from this feeling-sphere. We may designate this as the *principle of ideality*.

157 All of these feeling-spheres produce elementary aesthetic effects; and every artistic effect is first of all based on a combination of them. Some of the principles (laws) that Fechner abstracted from empirical considerations of aesthetic effects have been given a psychological derivation in the preceding discussion. But our derivation has, at the same time, shown that other principles could have been established along with them with equal justification. It is here that we first obtain a firm footing in the domain of aesthetic laws which, independently of changes in taste and technique, receive enduring validity from a constant human nature. We now recognize that the problem facing modern poetics, which first emerged in the opposition between Herder and Kant, is soluble. The analysis of human nature yields laws which, independently of temporal change, determine both aesthetic receptivity and poetic creativity. The state of consciousness of a nation at a given time conditions a poetic technique which can be presented in rules whose validity is historically circumscribed; but from our human nature there arise principles that regulate taste and creativity just as universally and necessarily as logical principles regulate thought and science. The number of these principles, norms, or laws is indeterminate. They are, after all, merely rules specifying the conditions of the individual elements that can produce aesthetic effects. The number of such elements is unlimited because of the infinite divisibility of the total aesthetic effect. Some of these elementary laws were presented in our discussion of the spheres of feeling. However, when the elementary feelings enter into higher connections, then higher laws of poetics also result.

### *5. Uniformities in the Causal Nexus of the Life of the Feelings and Some Higher Laws of Poetics*

We have seen how particular classes of antecedents produce particular spheres of feeling. However, these elementary feelings are related to one another. Just as sensations are reproduced as representations, so too are feelings recalled. Further, since these feelings can be converted into impulses, they themselves constitute a cause of transformation. These three causal relationships are the source of laws of aesthetic effects and aesthetic creativity, which must now be established for poetics.

158 The way in which *elementary feelings combine* is different from the way in which sensations or representations are connected. Our feelings fuse into an undifferentiated general life-feeling when they are not kept separate by means of representations. When pleasurable feelings of disparate character, deriving from utterly different antecedents, are aroused by an object, the intensity of the pleasure grows; thus when the aesthetic pleasures within the various spheres of feeling we have described—pleasures associated with a particular tone, a melodic line, rhythm, the connection of images into a unity, and the power of this unity—combine, the result is an intensity of total effect which we feel as a unity. It is highly noteworthy that a considerable poetic effect is elicited when what are in themselves small effects of a particular sound, rhyme, and rhythm are combined with the aesthetic effects of the content. If one reduces the most beautiful poem to prose, its aesthetic effect is almost entirely lost. Fechner believed that this warranted the derivation of the following aesthetic principle—which, to be sure, would then have a very striking psychological law as its background.

> When conditions of pleasure, which do not amount to much in themselves, come together without conflict, this releases a greater—very often much greater—pleasurable result than that corresponding to the value of the individual elements of pleasure—greater than what could be explained as the sum of the individual effects. Indeed, a positive pleasurable result can be attained by a combination of this sort, which exceeds the threshold of pleasure where the individual elements were too weak to do so; it is only necessary that these elements show a comparative advantage over against others in regard to satisfaction-inducing properties.[71]

But Fechner's example, taken from the lyrical poem, can be explained without the assumption of this striking law. When rhythm and rhyme are regularly used to reinforce the expression of feeling in poetry so that we expect it, its absence elicits a feeling of deprivation—thus of displeasure—which diminishes or cancels one's pleasure in the affective content. This can be observed in the well-known polymetric verses of Jean Paul. The same applies to the other example mentioned by Fechner, in which meter, rhythm, and

[71] Fechner, *Vorschule*, vol. 1, p. 50. (D)

rhyme elicit only a small effect without an affective content which we can grasp. Further, the relation of the affective content to the form appropriate to it is the source of a new feeling that intensifies the strength of the pleasure. So Fechner's principle might be replaced by the more cautious *principle of total effect*, according to which a manifold of elementary feelings combines to form a total strength which is further enhanced through the relations of these elementary 159 feelings to one another, since these relations produce a feeling which augments the sum total of pleasure.

On the basis of the affective state that arose in this way, the *change* in our *state of consciousness* is manifested in a *new feeling*. When a vital stimulus appears, then the transition from the existing affective state is experienced as a new feeling. From this there results first of all a general condition for the emergence of the aesthetic impression. Fechner designates the relationship expressed by this condition as the *principle of the aesthetic threshold*.

> For every determinate degree of receptivity and attention there is a determinate degree of external influence that must be exceeded, i.e., a corresponding determinate external threshold. But as the internal conditions change, a greater or lesser external influence becomes necessary, and the external threshold is thereby raised or lowered.[72]

And when this relation is such that the stimulus is able to evoke a feeling, then the strength and type of this feeling is a function of the relations to the existing affective state and the other stimuli appearing at the same time. This principle can be designated as that of the *relativity of feeling*. Fechner then derives the following particular aesthetic principles: the *principle of aesthetic contrast*, according to which "what furnishes pleasure does so all the more when it is contrasted with what gives displeasure or less pleasure, and vice versa,"[73] and the *principle of aesthetic sequence*, according to which, in a (positive) series from a smaller to a larger pleasure or from larger to smaller displeasure, the total pleasurable result is greater or the unpleasurable result is smaller than in the opposite case of a (negative) series.[74] For example, the feeling of getting better that accompanies convalescence can offset or outweigh the discomfort still existing in the convalescent's situation, however great it

[72] *Ibid.*, p. 49f. (D)
[73] *Ibid.*, vol. 2, pp. 231ff. (D)
[74] *Ibid.*, pp. 234ff. (D)

may be. Further, since art can often bring pleasurable stimuli into play only in connection with unpleasurable stimuli, this same relationship holds for the *principle of aesthetic reconciliation*, according to which unpleasant stimuli can be offset by subsequent pleasant stimuli through proper arrangement. So a disharmonious chord is resolved into a harmonious one, and in literature a situation full of danger and distress is brought to a happy conclusion—the displeasure vanishes in the subsequent pleasure.[75] Finally, there are properties of feelings in relation to their duration, their growth and decay, which likewise regulate the aesthetic effect and which are treated by Fechner in the *principles of summation*, *satiation*, *habituation*, *dulling*, and *change*. 160

We now turn from the connection and succession of elementary feelings and the relationships arising from them to the problem of their *reproduction* or renewal. Here we enter a very obscure domain. To the reproduction based on associations that relate representations, there correspond processes which at the same time indicate another kind of relation of feelings to each other and to representations. Let us here stay with what is simple and certain. Feelings are revived by the conditions which produced them previously, as long as these conditions retain the same relationship to the life-needs of the individual. This renewal can be regarded as a reproduction or as a repeated product from the same antecedents. A loss evokes a painful feeling when the representation is recalled as long as the loss remains linked to a diminution of the self. If this is no longer the case, the loss is represented with indifference. However, when one representation is related by the laws of association and fusion to another which provides a stimulus for feeling, then the first representation becomes the bearer of an affective content through a principle of association. Each thing integrally connected to our life embodies, as it were, all that we have experienced about it or about things similar to it. How much a fragrance we inhale or a leaf blowing in the autumn wind can mean to us! This dry leaf, floating slowly to the ground, contains little—when considered merely as a sensible image—that could evoke an aesthetic impression; but all the thoughts that are evoked by it revive feelings in us which unite to form a strong aesthetic impression. In addition, by means of a kind of transference, the affective content from one part

[75] *Ibid.*, p. 238. In subsequent sections of Fechner's *Vorschule der Aesthetik* one can obtain an overview of the relationship of the summation of aesthetic impressions, satiation, habituation, dulling, change, proportion, etc. Their psychological place is indicated by the next sentence in our text. (D)

of the representational structure of an image can also spread to other parts that are not related to it. A great portion of all aesthetic effects is a function of this process. Insofar as both aesthetic receptivity and aesthetic creation depend on this process of the stimulation of aesthetic pleasure through association (and fusion), a *principle of association* can be established. Fechner formulates it as follows:

161

> In proportion to whether we are pleased or displeased in recalling something, the recollection also contributes an element of pleasure or displeasure to the aesthetic impression of the thing, which can either conflict or agree with the other moments of recollection and the direct impression of the thing.[76]

This principle is extraordinarily important for all aesthetic impressions. The immediate impressions of feeling which are connected with sensations receive continual support through association. It is on this basis that in music sensory satisfaction in tone is augmented by the principle of meaning of tone and rhythm, since changes in the volume and pitch of the notes or in the rapidity of their succession stand in regular psychological relations to changes in feeling. This can already be perceived in both children and animals. A very fertile field for experimental psychology and aesthetics opens up here. This principle is of great significance for poetics as well. For, lived experience, which forms the essential content of all literature, always involves a state of mind as something inner and an image or a nexus of images, a place, situation, or person as something outer. The living power of poetry resides in the indissoluble unity of these two aspects. Thus an image itself or something akin to it represents a mental content, and this mental content takes on sensory concreteness in this image or one akin to it. All literary metaphors and symbols work in this way. When Shakespeare wants to represent Hamlet's deep attachment and sense of duty to his father, these inner states evoke powerful visual images which correspond to these states.

Let us again proceed further. Another cause of the change of our feelings is quite peculiar to them; it is grounded in their *relations* to the *impulses* which extend over our reflexive awareness of the life of the drives and the will, of what obstructs them and aids them. This reflexive awareness of the states of the will through affective states produces the elementary feelings of the last two spheres. On

[76] *Ibid.*, vol. 1, p. 94. (D)

the other hand, the volitional process is always activated by the feelings, which are constantly being converted into impulses, desires, and acts of will. In the same way that in many states of feeling or reflexive awareness an unnoticeable transition of feelings takes place, we also find, within the sphere of desires and emotions of various kinds, transitions from feelings to volitional processes. Without becoming entangled in hypotheses, we are here only concerned to justify a distinction for empirical observation, based on 162 the inner experience of the difference between feeling and willing, and on the fact that the intensity of feelings is by no means a measure of the power of the will. Indeed, strong feelings may be linked with very weak volitional processes. The conversion of our feelings into volitional processes is regulated by the law that we strive to preserve pleasant feelings and to diminish unpleasant feelings, at least to the extent of attaining a state of equilibrium. The first way in which the will seeks to diminish a feeling of displeasure into a state of equilibrium consists in the adaptation of the external conditions of life to inner needs: this is how external actions of the will arise. Another way, however, consists in the will seeking to adapt itself to a reality it cannot change. Our inner nature strives to be in harmony with unalterable external conditions. This happens by means of inner acts of will. In the beginning, the religious process is predominantly a way of coming to terms with mysterious powers that surround us, a way of distancing ourselves from what is oppressive and threatening, or of attaining what we wish—i.e., an external mode of volitional action. The development of religion into something higher occurs when a reconciliation with what is insuperable is sought in the mind itself, in the moral capacities, and in the inner volitional act of changing one's life. Superstition must therefore give way if a true inner religiosity is to unfold powerfully. Obtrusive sensations of displeasure are constantly guided toward equilibrium or pleasure through the deepest struggles of the will.

The process of diminishing unpleasant feelings proceeds very differently in aesthetic creativity and aesthetic receptivity. Here, where everything takes place in the imagination, there is nothing to prevent displeasure from moving freely into a state of equilibrium, just as all dissonances in a musical composition are resolved into harmony. It follows from the principle of truthfulness that literature, as the depiction of the world, cannot dispense with pain, that the highest expression of human nature, its transfiguration, can be made visible only in suffering. The privileged position of tragedy is based ultimately on the fact that only here can the highest power and transfiguration of the will be expressed. From the tendency, as already discussed, to convert displeasure into a state of equilibrium or of pleasure, there results *the aesthetic principle of reconciliation.* According to this principle, every poetic work that expresses more than transient sentiments but aims instead to produce a lasting satisfaction must end with a state of equilibrium or pleasure, in any case with a final state of reconciliation, even if this end-state consists of a mere idea which transcends life. Even the schema of a metaphysical myth, as invented by Plotinus, Spinoza, or Schopenhauer, displays this return to peace and reconciled unity. Lyric poetry—to the extent that it not only resounds musically but also permits an inner process to be lived out—strives for such a state of equilibrium. The most beautiful examples of this are provided by Goethe. The tragedies of Shakespeare have been frequently and exhaustively shown to correspond to this principle. Although the structure of *Faust* is lacking in technique, it does at least correspond fully to this schema of the process of feeling. Even great epic literature, which somehow permits the entire world and its order to be viewed, must be compared to a symphony in which one dissonance after another is resolved until finally the whole resounds in powerfully harmonious chords.[77]

163

This relationship also grounds the important aesthetic *principle of tension or suspense* (*Spannung*). Of course, tension involves many diverse phenomena. In it the inner re-creation of strong impulses such as fear or anticipation are at work. A thought process in which one seeks to answer a stated question can also result in tension or suspense—most especially in novels whose complication consists of an event that transpired before its beginning; and where our becoming aware of this event then occasions the resolution of the suspense. The way in which this sort of motif can lead to invention is shown by Goethe's remark that Manzoni[78] uses fear to produce an emotional suspense; and that if he himself were younger, he would write something in which fear is aroused, to which he would then add admiration through the hero's exemplary conduct, whereby the fear would be resolved into this admiration.[79] Thereby

[77] This aesthetic principle has also been referred to by Fechner as the principle of aesthetic reconciliation; see *Vorschule*, vol. 2, p. 238. (D)

[78] Alessandro Manzoni (1785-1873). The leader of the Italian Romantic school.

[79] Eckermann, *Gespräche mit Goethe*, vol. 1, p. 377 (D); 21 July 1827; *CE*, p. 271.

Goethe would also have revived the motif of many Arthurian romances.

### *6. Laws Governing the Free Transformation of Representations Beyond the Bounds of Reality under the Influence of the Life of the Feelings. The Poet's Creative Work. The Resources of Poetic Technique.*

We have seen how elementary feelings arise, are combined, intensified, and renewed; how displeasure evokes the impulse to go over into a state of equilibrium or pleasure; and finally how pleasure strives to maintain itself. This entire web of feelings, conditioned as it is by representations and impulses, in turn conditions the formation of representations and the force of our impulses. We have already been able to derive elementary and secondary aesthetic principles. We will now look more carefully into the origin of a poetic work and its impression by considering how representational elements are changed under the influence of the feelings and transformed beyond the bounds of reality. Initially an aesthetic impression develops from the constituents of consciousness as they exist in life. We have derived the principles according to which these impressions are combined, connected, and strengthened. But the powerful effect of art and literature does not depend solely on our enjoyment of those constituents of consciousness that already possess an aesthetic effect in the course of our life; it also depends on *images that are formed to evoke a still purer kind of aesthetic pleasure*. These images are unconcerned about their relationship to reality, and are produced merely to satisfy the need for the *feeling of life*. We now encounter and shall attempt to solve the most difficult problem of the psychological foundation of a poetics. 164

For this we transpose ourselves into the reality of a psyche filled with life-experiences and reflection on them—for such is the poet's psyche.

> *All products of psychic life, including literature, are composed of perceptions as their elements.*

This tenet is established through the following consideration: Even when acts of will, scientific inventions, or artistic images transcend what is real, we will not be able to find any constituents in them that could not be drawn from perception. I hold the same view about combinations of such constituents. However, according to this view, it is essential that inner experience inform outer perception if we are to be able to posit substances standing in causal relations. The proof of this is too involved to allow me to furnish it here.[80]

When the physicist constructs his concept of the atom, he can only combine elements of experience on the basis of relations drawn from experience, while disregarding others which are usually connected with them. When Homer, Dante, or Milton transcend our earth to show Olympus and Hades, heaven and hell, they must take the colors and impressions for their sensory images from the radiance of the sky which delights us in this world and from the darkness and the fire which terrify us here and now. In order to portray the beatitude of the gods and of pure angels, the helplessness of the departed souls, or the torments of the damned, they must connect and intensify the inner states of pleasure and pain which they have lived and experienced themselves. When Walter Scott or Conrad Ferdinand Meyer[81] transpose us into historical circumstances that are completely foreign to our own, they can employ no elementary feelings or representations that are not created from our own present life and the states experienced in it. Locke and Hume had already attempted to formulate the psychological basis for this. We are not able to invent any element of the life of the psyche, but rather must draw every element from our experience. To be sure, this proposition holds only within certain limits, which we will discuss later.

165

From this proposition, we obtain a rule for artistic creation, namely, that an appropriate relationship must exist between the poet's task and the energy, scope, and interest of the experiences that contain the material for its execution. Thus in this respect, one must already be born an artist or poet. The poet is governed by the law that only the power and richness of his lived experiences furnish the material for genuine poetry. This is the source of a principle according to which the basis for the poet's specific effects must be sought within the sphere of the richness and energy of his experience. This is the point at which the objective poet is distinguished from the subjective—indeed, even the pathological poet.

[80] See this essay on p. 104f. For Dilthey's attempt to demonstrate how categories like substance and cause are rooted in inner experience, see "Life and Knowledge" in *SW*, vol. 2.

[81] Swiss poet (1825-98). Many of his novellas are about the Italian Renaissance.

*The images of reality consisting of these elements, and the connections among such images which obtain in reality, are freely transformed by the creativity of the poet, unrestricted by the conditions of reality. This creativity is therefore akin to dreams and other related states, including insanity.*

I designate that which the poet or artist has in common with one who is dreaming, hypnotized, or mad as a *free formation of images,* unrestricted by conditions of reality. The kinship which exists here between the poetic process and those states which diverge from the norm of waking life touch precisely on what is essential about the poetic process of imagination. A scientific invention, or the project of a man of practical genius, takes its standard from reality, to which thinking and acting conform in order to comprehend and be effective. By contrast, the developments of representations we are discussing are not restricted by reality.

Goethe gave a moving account of this kinship between the poetic and the abnormal in *Torquato Tasso.* It also emerges in the two greatest subjective poets of the eighteenth and nineteenth centuries: Rousseau and Byron. If we read about Rousseau's life beginning April 9, 1756, when he went to the Hermitage in La Chevrette Park and "began to live," till his death, which put an end to his dreams, disappointments, and delusions of persecution, it is impossible to separate his delusions from the real facts of his life. Byron's demonic hypersensitivity enormously amplified all the processes of his life; and the reproach of insanity was hurled back and forth between him and his wife in their quarrels. But even in the most normal achievements of a poet, the following traits show a kinship with states that diverge from the norm of waking life. Mere representational images can receive the mark of reality and appear in the visual field or as part of the world of sounds. In this respect, the poet's image approaches a hallucination. Then, through a process of metamorphosis, images receive a shape which diverges from reality, and even when transformed in this way, they are accompanied by an illusion. Images are transformed under the influence of feelings. They are shaped by our emotions, just as the uncertain outlines of rocks and trees are transformed by the influence of the emotions of a traveler in the woods at night. Goethe describes the experience:

166

> And the cliffs that bow with ease,
> Craggy noses, long and short,
> How they snore and how they snort!

And the roots, as serpents, coil
From the rocks through sandy soil
With their eerie bonds would scare us,
Block our path and then ensnare us;
Hungry as a starving leech,
Their strong polyp's tendrils reach
For the wanderer.[82]

Indeed, it is a characteristic mark of the poetic genius that he is capable not only of convincingly reproducing experience, but also that by means of a kind of constructive spiritual power he can produce a figure which could not be given to him in any experience, and through which the experiences of daily life become more comprehensible and meaningful to the heart. Pleasant effects can be created by apt descriptions of social life, but only those figures, situations, and actions that completely transcend the horizon of everyday experience live for mankind at large. Finally, a kind of splitting of the self, a transformation into another person, can take place in the poet.

A curious *problem* is contained in the kinship between the poetic process and those states which diverge from the norm of waking life. Nature herself offers us certain experiments by means of states which display—under circumstances otherwise extremely diverse—
167 the same strength, vivacity and free development of representations of the imagination beyond the bounds of reality. For all these quite diverse cases, we find ourselves forced to seek the causes for the absence of those conditions which normally regulate representations and keep them clearly and correctly oriented to reality.

*This kinship arises from the absence of conditions which otherwise regulate representations. However, in one who is dreaming, insane, or hypnotized they are produced by causes of a completely different kind than in the artist or poet. In the former case, the strength of the acquired nexus of psychic life is diminished, while in the latter, its entire energy is directed toward free creativity.*

There is a *structure* of psychic life which is as clearly recognizable as that of the physical body. Life always consists in the interaction of a living body and an external world which constitutes its milieu. Sensations, perceptions, and thoughts constantly originate from the

[82] *Faust, Part I*, lines 3878-80, 3894-3900; in *Faust*, trans. by W. Kaufmann (Garden City, N.Y.: Doubleday, 1961) (hereafter *F*), pp. 361, 363.

play of external stimuli. Changes in our affective state on the basis of a general feeling are also aroused. The feelings then evoke volitions and the strivings of desire and will. Volitions result in external actions of the will, and among them the most powerful are those that are permanently embedded in bodily states—such as the impulse for self-preservation, the need for nourishment, the impulse to propagate, and the love of offspring. Almost as powerful are the need for esteem and the social instincts, which are embedded in the will. Other volitions produce inner changes in consciousness. The hierarchy of the animal kingdom is based on this structure. We see the most simple, bare form of life where a stimulus, in which feeling and sensation are undifferentiated, produces a movement in an animal. In the child, we see the transition from stimuli to desires by means of sensations. Accompanying this, there is a separate transition through feelings to desires. In the child, both transitions produce movements, but without the interpolation of representations stored in the memory. However, sensations do eventually leave behind traces. Habits of feeling and desire are formed. Gradually, as the psyche develops, an *acquired nexus* of psychic life emerges between sensation and movement.

Experience furnishes us only with processes and the way they affect each other. The latter also falls within the scope of immediate experience. Indeed, our concepts of freedom and necessity are grounded in the manner in which one process is produced by another. *A nexus of processes* is the most comprehensive state of affairs that falls within our psychic experience or that can be derived from it through indubitable combinations. Whether one affirms or denies that this nexus of processes is held together by hidden forces that lie behind them or by a psychic unity that operates beneath them, in either case one transcends the sphere of empirical psychology and resorts to transcendent hypotheses. In accordance with this methodological insight we propose the concept of the *acquired nexus of psychic life*—encountered in experience itself—and of its effects on the individual processes occurring in consciousness. We have already shown above how this nexus operates as a whole upon the transformations which take place in consciousness. Although its constituents are not represented clearly and distinctly and its connections are not explicit, nevertheless its acquired picture of reality regulates our understanding of whatever impression our consciousness is occupied with. Its acquired standard of evaluation determines the feeling of the moment; and its acquired system of

168

the purposes of our will, of their interrelations and of the means required by them, controls our passions of the moment.

Naturally, the effect of this entire nexus, composite as it is, on the changes in consciousness is the *most difficult* and, accordingly, the *highest function* of psychic life. It requires the greatest energy and health of the cerebral functions. The conditions for the reproduction of representations and their connections are assembled in the cerebral cortex. Only the highest energy of cerebral life makes it possible for this entire apparatus to have a wide-ranging efficacy allowing even the most remote representations to come into contact and to be used. A logical inference requires much less energy from consciousness than the operation of the acquired psychic nexus. For inference involves relating only a few concepts with the assistance of the attention that is concentrated upon them. The great achievements of genius and the control of a powerful mind are grounded in the efficacy of the acquired psychic nexus. Precisely when there is a period of relaxation after a stretch of long, deep stimulation of the overall acquired nexus through intense work, then creative combinations suddenly emerge from the depths of this nexus.

This *apparatus functions* unintentionally, as it were, to keep our 169 representations and desires *adapted* to the acquired nexus of psychic life, in which *reality* is represented. When this operation of the regulatory apparatus breaks down in those states which diverge from the norm of waking life, this involves completely different causes than when the regulatory operation is suspended as the poet creates figures and situations that transcend reality. The first case involves a diminution in the efficacy of this acquired nexus, the second, a utilization of the nexus, which at the same time intentionally transcends the reality represented within it.

A *diminution* of the operation of the acquired psychic nexus is exemplified first of all by *insanity*. In contrast to the particular stimuli which the subcortical centers project into the brain hemispheres, the cerebral cortex operates as an apparatus of classification, inhibition, and regulation. In the case of insanity, the normal functioning of this apparatus breaks down as a result of pathological irritability and weakness. Stimuli such as those involved in hallucinations, which can as such be accompanied by awareness of their subjective origin, now receive the mark of reality due to the breakdown of the regulatory apparatus and become the basis for delusions. Pathological changes in our general state of feeling or any morbid changes in its intensity are modifications, which would otherwise be regulated by the acquired nexus of evaluations and which are acknowledged as having a subjective origin, now escape from its control and similarly become themselves the substratum for further delusions. Next, especially when the memory becomes fragmentary, we encounter interpretations and inferences that are prompted by pathological changes in our general state of feeling and are supported by hallucinations. They are no longer regulated by the acquired nexus of psychic life as it represents and harmonizes with reality. Surely we are all familiar with the overly subtle reasoning of the insane, who on the basis of such a foundation demonstrate their delusions with logically impeccable form. We are accustomed to regard thought, in the sense of logical inference, as the highest achievement of intelligence. Metaphysical philosophy, with its cult of reason as abstract thinking, has also exercised its influence in this direction. It is therefore often considered surprising to see a deranged person who is proficient in making inferences. An inference is a process through which one compares or relates, by means of a middle term, that which cannot be directly compared or related. If one includes within the scope of the inference the discovery of the middle term, then a materially correct inference, which captures a relationship actually existing in reality, requires the highest achievement of psychic life, namely, the contribution of the entire acquired nexus. What is peculiar about the madman is that his inferences lack objective reference, which is to say that neither the process of connecting the subject and predicate in the conclusion nor that of discovering the middle term is controlled by the acquired psychic nexus. His conclusions are therefore often materially false and indeed frequently ridiculous. They are so due to his failure to utilize facts provided by his experience. When confronted with this oversight or error, he is forced to raise objections which, for their part, contain the same error. For this reason it is generally futile to attempt to correct someone who is insane. But his inferences are unobjectionable with respect to the external relationships among the terms he has chosen. His thinking is formally correct. 170

No one can deny that there are *transitions* which gradually lead *from mental health* to states no longer regulated by the acquired nexus and its representation of reality. Already in ordinary life, when hypersensitivity about something specific in psychic life is combined with a low capacity to see things in perspective, a distortion of the true value of things occurs, from which there stems in turn a one-sided hypersensitivity and something like a despotism of a particular attitude that ignores reality. If someone criticizes the tulips of a passionate gardener who is like this, the gardener may come to hate him. We are inclined to regard this as a mild form of craziness. The limit of insanity lies in the pathological state of the brain, and the only outer symptom of this limit that forensic medicine may apply to living subjects is a decrease in the functioning of the brain which is so great that the acquired psychic nexus, and the way it represents our current view of reality and the harmony of feelings and actions with it, can no longer serve as a basis for responsible action. This occurs when, as a consequence of such a diminution of the energy of the nexus, the actions of the person in question no longer allow us to presuppose an adequate number of reasons or motives necessary to ascribe moral responsibility.

*Dreams* also present images which transcend the bounds of reality, but which are nevertheless accompanied by a belief in their reality. They, too, are a function of a diminution of the energy of the psychic nexus and the accompanying change in the functioning of the brain. A change in the circulation of blood in the brain takes place during the onset and duration of sleep.[83] The functioning of the cerebral cortex is modified. At the same time, only isolated and indefinite impressions pass through the sense organs. These impressions and the changes induced in the organism itself produce associations and inferences which are not determined and regulated by the acquired psychic nexus. So, for example, feelings connected with a specific organ, which have a fixed reference when a person is awake, now appear indefinite in their spatial location, and without the causal relations which would normally be recognized to hold; thus shortness of breath could evoke images of a heavy object weighing one down. Similarly, combinations established by thought between particular dream images are unregulated and, therefore, frequently odd. *Sleepwalking,* where the course of a dream is acted out as a complete drama, is perhaps the most noteworthy example of the imagination active in states which diverge from the norm of waking life and yet are akin to its poetic use. It provides the transition between dreams and hypnotic states. In hypnotism, too, the acquired nexus of psychic life is set aside. But the dreamlike action which dominates here is characterized by its dependence on a hypnotizing will. One who is hypnotized is, so to speak, an imitative mechanism.

The transcendence of reality in creative work of the poet has

171

[83] See the studies of Donders, von Rählmann, Wittkowski, and Mosso. (D)

causes of a completely different kind. The total energy of a healthy and powerful psyche is active here. A rich and extensive fund of experience is employed, which has been ordered and generalized by thought. The transformation of images is effected in a psyche in which the entire acquired nexus that represents reality is present and efficacious. A will conscious of its purpose modifies the images beyond the bounds of reality. Consequently, there are considerable differences between the metamorphosis of images in the creative work of the poet and in those states which diverge from the norm of everyday life. The poet is aware of the nexus of reality and he distinguishes his images from it. He differentiates reality from the realm of beauty and illusion. However much these images approximate the character of reality, they nevertheless remain separated from it by a fine line. During his creative work, the poet lives in a dream world where these images receive the mark of reality. But they do not receive this through the obscure natural power of hallucinations, but rather through the freedom of a creative capacity 172 in possession of itself. Further, because the nexus of psychic life actively affects the formation of these images, they acquire a relationship to reality appropriate to the purpose of the artwork. When images lose this relation they cease to move us. The typical and the ideal in poetry transcend experience so that it can be felt and understood more profoundly than in the most faithful copies of reality.

This kind of belief in images of things that are unreal, and the illusion that results, can best be compared with what takes place in *children at play*. Literature is akin to play, as Schiller has demonstrated. In play, the energy of the child's psychic life becomes active and free, inasmuch as it does not as yet possess any other channel. The will, which has not yet been given serious purposes by reality, sets ends for itself which lie outside the nexus of reality. In later stages of life the distinguishing trait of play is that its activities stand in no causal relation to the purposive nexus of this life. Thus play becomes separated from the seriousness of real life; and, in that respect, it is like art and literature. The illusion which thus arises is grounded in voluntary or deliberate psychic processes and, accordingly, has its bounds in the consciousness of this origin.

The laws according to which images and their connections freely unfold beyond the bounds of reality under such diverse conditions will also be more easily grasped if we begin by comparing these conditions. Nature permits us to perceive everywhere the free unfolding of images under otherwise completely varying circumstances.

These processes are not as different from those of memory as is usually assumed. Every memory image is constituted from acquired constituents, but the momentary state of consciousness determines which of these constituents are employed in the formation of the image. For the same image can no more return than the same leaf can grow back on a tree the following spring. If I make present in imagination a person who is absent, the current state of my consciousness determines the position of the figure and the expression on his face.

*Images are transformed when constituents either disappear or are excluded.*

173 In dreams and in mental disturbances certain properties of images disappear which in reality are inseparable from them because they are given and fixed, so to speak, by the acquired nexus of psychic life that represents reality. Thus dreams are not constrained by time, space, and the law of gravity. A madman connects constituents of images with a seemingly extraordinary power to combine, without being aware of the contradictions in the properties of these constituents. In contrast, the creative work of the artist and poet involves the deliberate exclusion of refractory traits. It strives for clarity and harmony in the constituents of images—which, to be sure, would in itself only be the superficial harmony of an empty ideal if other laws did not also operate in transforming images.

*Images are transformed when they expand or contract, when the intensity of the sensations of which they are composed is increased or decreased.*

*Dreams* permit images to be expanded or intensified in accordance with the influence of our feelings. Aside from the direct intervention of physiological functions in sensation, dream representations are free from the competition of external images, and the intervention of the acquired nexus of reality is cancelled to a certain degree. Also, under the influence of feelings, the colors in our dreams glow more intensively; sounds resound more powerfully and charmingly. Barely audible stimuli are amplified enormously. Figures seem to grow in size before our very eyes. Alternatively, the number of analogous images is multiplied while we dream. Hope and fear similarly lend images a quality which transcends reality. *Melancholy,* on the other hand, makes the colors of reality fade. Hypochondria intensifies beyond actuality those images which are viewed as the cause of the mental stress. And yet for the hypochondriac the acquired nexus of psychic life still acts as a corrective, particularly through its evaluations. As long as the hypochondriac retains his social contacts his feelings remain regulated. His condition deteriorates when he seeks solitude in order to escape such intrusions on his imagination. With insanity such controls no longer exist. In paranoia the image of a person whose action thwarts the will of the patient is intensified and expanded into a caricature of a hostile power.

The same process of modifying the intensity and extension of elements through the influence of feelings can be observed in the case of the *poet*. In particular, one perceives how feeling colored the vision of the English poets, even of historians such as Macaulay and Carlyle. Even a simple letter by Dickens, Carlyle, or Kingsley[84] contains examples of this nervous intensification of reality where things become larger than life. Cliffs become more steep and meadows more lush. This emotional power contained in images is then discharged in that peculiar English mode of humor which works through exaggeration, one moment reducing something delicate to a mere shadow, the next capriciously expanding something powerful into bizarre extremes of force or frenzy. In Shakespeare and Dickens this is intensified into a kind of artificial illumination. It is as if images were exposed to electrical light and magnifying glasses. The transfiguration of memory images and the intensification involved in representations of the future are conditioned by the fact that representational contents are expanded and transformed as if they existed in open space. There thus exists an inner affinity through which memory images and dreams of the future prepare the poet for creating his representations.

174

*Exclusion* and *intensification* result in the idealization of images in all the arts. Indeed, for a sensitive person this occurs even in the unintentional processes of recollection. The image of a landscape or a person is not called back by a mechanical memory process, but rather is formed anew on the basis of an affective state. Not every constituent of the earlier perception contributes to the new image, but only what is of interest in the present state of consciousness. Nor do the elements appear in exactly the same strength or scope that characterized the image of perception. Rather, in this respect, too, they are determined to a certain extent by their relationship to one's present state. Since the poet has no intention of

[84] Probably Charles Kingsley (1819-75), English clergyman, novelist, and poet, whose novels *Alton Locke* and *Yeast* dealt with Christian socialism.

producing a faithful reproduction, the will supervenes and shapes these images in a way that is satisfying to one's feelings, and exclusion, intensification, and diminution generate a progressive idealization of images. Even in the greatest achievements of the imagination, exclusion leads to harmonious characters and actions, and intensification strengthens the affective content. However, both of these processes would not be sufficient to fill a poem with satisfying life. The most important process of all now comes into play:

> *Images and their connections are transformed when new components and connections penetrate into their innermost core and thus complete them.*

175 An imagination which only excludes, intensifies or diminishes, increases or decreases, is feeble and attains only a superficial idealization or caricature of reality. Wherever a true work of art emerges, we find an unfolding of the nucleus of an image through positive completion. It is difficult to make this process intelligible. A perception or representation is first of all transformed according to the laws of association or fusion so that another image penetrates it or is associated with it. But association contains no principle that goes beyond the efficacy of actual contiguity, and fusion produces mere integration. *Only when the whole acquired psychic nexus becomes active* can images be transformed on the basis of it: *innumerable, immeasurable, almost imperceptible changes* occur in their nucleus. And in this way, the completion of the particular originates from the fullness of psychic life. Thus we obtain from images and their connections what is essential about a state of affairs: what gives it its meaning in the nexus of reality. Even the style of the artist is influenced in this way.

That process of completion, by which *something outer is enlivened by something inner* or *something inner is made visible and intuitable by something outer*, is especially important for poetry which proceeds from lived experience. Contents and relations acquired in inner experience are transferred to outer experience. And this is what makes possible the metaphysical constructions of natural thought through which the relations of thing and property, cause and effect, essence and accident are constituted. The application of such forms of relation to our experience always depends on the completion of something outer by something inner which is often connected with it, and this rests on the primary fact that we ourselves are simultaneously inner and outer. Abstract conceptual categories gradually emerge from this animation of aggregates of sensations in evolutionary stages, which proceed through language and scientific thought.

This relationship to something outer is in general the most essential and central connection by which we join our experiences into a whole. The way in which state and image are interwoven as inner and outer is not acquired, but rather is rooted in the psychophysical nature of man. We might say that an extension or projection of what we find in our own life takes place here; this is then developed throughout our life. Here we find the deepest basis for language, myth, metaphysics—the concepts through which we conceive the world, even our basic legal conceptions. For example, the idea of property is the necessary external expression for a lived experience of the will. Here we also find the reason that the poet can form images as the expression of an inner state in such a way that they can evoke the same inner life in others.

176

We can now make a more general observation. The metamorphosis, effected through these three kinds of transformation on the basis of feelings and impulses proceeding from the overall acquired nexus of psychic life is a living process, for the image which is thus produced is not formed in a single act. Rather, it follows from the law that attentiveness involves a limited quantum of energy, that psychic life is only able to produce these image formations in a temporal sequence. Familiar elements are connected in these formations, but the constructive dimension that differentiates the artist from the mathematician lies in the way these elements are joined, certain desired ones being preserved and new ones added. Now, since the artist's constructive process stems from his mood, his affective state, it has something instinctive or impulsive about it. The mode and manner in which the transformations occur is that of *unfolding*. Impulse and unfolding correspond to one another. At this point we recognize that the whole of spiritual life is *not* dominated by mechanical relationships of association and reproduction. The emergence of an image is a living process. Images do not simply recur without change. Furthermore, certain relations among processes become habitual. As images become more easily reproduced, we get used to certain relations and to certain ways of advancing from one element to another. The style of an artist is such a habit based in his nature—for instance, his tendency to imagine and model garments in wood or other materials may lead him to elongate the lines of the body.

Accordingly we call the regular relationship which links a satisfying arousal of feeling (or a constituent of such an arousal) to a state of affairs, and through which, correspondingly, artistic creativity seeks satisfaction in the production of such a state, an aesthetic *principle*. At first such a principle operates spontaneously in the inner formative processes of an artistic, poetic soul, without the intention of making an impression on someone else. Insofar as such a principle (as we will soon see in more detail) simultaneously appears as the basis for making a pleasing impression on someone else, an impression which no reader or listener is able to evade, the formulation of this principle assumes the form of a *rule* to which 177 the impression is universally connected. The principle can thus be characterized as a universally valid *norm*. When these principles produce transformations of images on the basis of the acquired psychic nexus of a poet, aesthetic laws of a higher level arise.

The satisfaction that a creative artist finds in his work depends on the extent to which the entire nexus of his acquired psychic life has influenced his creative processes and their end product. Corresponding to this, regarded from the side of the impression, is the principle that a poetic work only satisfies to the extent that it also does justice to what it arouses and activates in the acquired psychic nexus of the listener or reader. Since this nexus becomes more and more complex with the progress of the human race, it follows that both poetic creativity and receptivity demand and produce an *ascending development of poetry*. These tenets indicate a principle which can be formulated more exactly only after more thorough analysis of the nature of the aesthetic impression. In particular, the full reality of the employed constituents and their relations, exclusion, intensification, diminution, and completion constitute principles to which both the process of creativity and the aesthetic impression are bound. A poet's style depends on the predominance of one or another of these principles. We recognize here the psychological factors which condition important differences in style. In literature, the relations between a psychic state and a nexus of images, between inner and outer, are to be developed through completion; this important law of completion has as a consequence the further principle that all poetry gives visual shape to life as it is enjoyed in feeling, and (conversely) transfers the vivacity enjoyed in feeling into what is visible in perception. In short, poetry constantly restores the totality of lived experience. We find in these principles and their grounding the more complete psychological formulation of what was designated as "Schiller's law" in the historical introduction.

## Chapter Three. Corroboration Provided by the Testimony of Poets Themselves

178

Let us now elucidate the way the processes of exclusion, intensification, and completion work together as we examine the field in which images become free and unfold unhampered, as in empty space. We will proceed here from the simple to the complex, and thus arrive at the poets' own accounts of their aesthetic creativity. I shall offer only some accounts. Others might want to add more to produce a complete collection.

The simplest case of such an unfolding is provided by hypnagogic or slumber images. We can regard these, following Goethe's lead, as the basic phenomena of poetic creativity. They can apparently *not* be reduced to the processes of differentiation, comparison, fusion, association, apperception, etc. Goethe describes them as follows:

> I had the gift of imagining a flower in the center of my visual field when I closed my eyes and lowered my head. It did not remain in its first shape for even one moment. But it immediately disintegrated, and from its inner core new flowers would unfold, composed of both colored and green petals. They were not natural flowers, but rather fantastical ones, which nevertheless were regular like a sculptor's rosettes. It was impossible to stop this spontaneous creation; rather, it would last as long as I pleased, neither weakening nor strengthening. I could produce the same effect if I imagined the patterns on a stained-glass window, which would then similarly display continual changes proceeding from the center toward the periphery.[85]

If I am to compare both this and other descriptions of hypnagogic images—especially the classical one of Johannes Müller[86]—with my own experiences, then I must begin, for expository reasons, with our ability to attend calmly to our overall visual field and its colorful hazes. Given this mode of attention, the distribution of the sensory elements in this field makes it possible to project a common or customary configuration of these elements into it. But this configuration may also be varied in accordance with the laws discussed above. Indeed, according to our psychological account this involves

[85] *WA*, II, 11:282.

[86] *Über die phantastischen Gesichtserscheinungen* (Koblenz: J. Hölscher, 1826), p. 20. (D)

a process which is spontaneous and manifests itself as the unfolding of images. This unfolding of hypnagogic images beyond reality counts as a verification of our psychological account. In his *Elective Affinities*, which in the spirit of our century explicates the physiological conditions of the highest revelations of the life of the mind, this power of Goethe's imagination is transferred to Ottilie. Between waking and sleeping, she sees an illuminated space containing her absent lover in various locations and situations.

179

Let us broaden the context of discussion by considering contiguous data. The process exemplified by hypnagogic images is akin to that in which arabesques and patterns arise. In the latter, however, the will participates actively, thus generating intentional modes of formation and creation of an artistic sort. Habits of representation serve to produce symmetry and unity in multiplicity. Experiences of mechanical relations between bodies, between force and resistance, also exert their influence. But the process of creation ultimately transcends everything given in these experiences, however much it may have been conditioned by them.

To these phenomena of visual representation there corresponds another series in aural representation: the way children play with variations in sounds. As a function of the child's surplus energy, it is strongest in early morning. High and low pitch, strength and rapidity in the succession of tones, and even variations in vowels, stand in regular relations to the child's moods. They provide the basis for musical expression, certain natural elements of every language (namely, the way the symbolical aspect of phonetic material stands in fixed relations to spiritual processes), as well as accentuation and rhythm in speech.

The constant formation and transformation that take place in the poet become more readily discernible when we observe these simpler data of the imagination. Whenever we are able to get a glimpse into a poet's life we see how only a small part of this incessant inner shaping and experimenting is ever embodied in his works. This, too, has been expressed in a moving way in *Tasso*, and has its analogue in the incessant variation of shapes produced in a dream (that hidden poet in us).

Hypnagogic images are related to *dreams* on the one hand and to the creations of poets on the other. Johannes Müller himself emphasizes how these images make an imperceptible "transition into the dream images of sleep." The general pattern of what happens in dreams is that which was observed in hypnagogic images. The elements given in the sensory field are reproduced by images or the habitual configurations among image elements. Transformations take place according to the laws discussed above, but the attentiveness within the temporal flow that is required for the production of images induces a spontaneous unfolding and transformation of one image into another. In a passage related to the description already cited, Goethe relates hypnagogic images to the poet's creativity. "One can see more clearly what it means to say that the poet and every authentic artist must be born. Namely, the inner productive capacity must bring into prominence those after-images or images lingering in the sensory organ, memory, and imagination; it must do so spontaneously, without plan and intention, and vigorously. These after-images must unfold, grow, expand and contract in order to transform superficial schemata into true objective beings."[87] 180

This is related to the dreamlike quality that is sometimes discernible in the poet's creative work. Goethe says the following about some of his ballads: "I carried them all in my head for many years. They occupied my mind as charming images, as beautiful dreams that came and went." Then he adds: "At other times things went completely differently in writing my poems. I had absolutely no previous impression or intimation about them. Instead, they suddenly overwhelmed me and insisted that they be created immediately, with the result that I felt forced to write them down on the spot instinctively and in a dreamlike way."[88]

Carlyle attributes to Shakespeare this spontaneous aspect of dream formation in poetic creativity, although admitting it to be on the basis of honest, preparatory work: "Shakespeare is an example of what I might call an unconscious intellect. The works of such a man grow unconsciously from unfamiliar depths in him, however much he may also achieve by the greatest effort and deliberate activity."[89]

In a passage in his *Vorschule der Ästhetik* (Introductory Course in Aesthetics) which contains an account of his own poetic work in the form of an aesthetic principle, Jean Paul writes: "The character must be alive and control you in the hour of inspired production. You must hear, not merely see, him. He must inspire you as in a dream, and in such a way that, in a previous sober moment

[87] *WA*, II, 11:283.

[88] Eckermann, *Gespräche*, 14 March 1830.

[89] Carlyle, *Heroes and Hero-Worship*, 3rd lecture, "Dante and Shakespeare," in *Thomas Carlyle's Collected Works*, vol. 12 (London: Chapman & Hill, 1869), p. 126.

you could have approximately predicated the 'what,' but not the 'how.' If a poet has to reflect whether he is to make his character say 'Yes' or 'No' in a given situation, he should throw him away, for he is just a cold cadaver!"[90] The following remark can be added 181 from the notes to his letters: "While writing, the genuine poet (like the dreamer) does not prompt his characters but only watches them. He sees them as if they were in a dream, and then he listens to them. Viktor's remark that a dreamt opponent often made more difficult objections than a real one is also frequently made by the playwright who prior to becoming inspired could not at all have provided words for a group of actors, while he finds no difficulty in creating dramatic roles when he is inspired."[91]

It has been reported to me by Heinrich von Stein that when Wagner was in Paris engaged with work on the Teutonic legends, he simultaneously saw before him all of his material. *Siegfried, Tannhäuser, Lohengrin, Tristan, Parsifal*, and even the *Meistersinger* were given in quite determinate specific intuitions—such as, for instance, a scene from the *Meistersinger*, a determinate legendary confrontation.

In total agreement with Goethe's remarks and the related testimony we have cited is the testimony of the well-known Russian novelist Goncharov,[92] who writes:

> A specific figure always hovers before me, and at the same time a main motif. Guided by it, I proceed, and, along the way, I avail myself of whatever I happen to come across, although only what fits in. Then I work actively, assiduously, and so quickly that my pen can barely follow my thoughts, until I again run into a brick wall. Meanwhile, my head keeps working. My characters do not permit me any peace, and they appear to me in various scenes; I seem to hear fragments of their conversations. It often seems as if these things were not my thoughts, but rather outside me and that I only needed to watch in order to project myself into them.

Other reports allow still deeper insights into the process. They illustrate what we have said about the influence of the feelings on

[90] Jean Paul, *Vorschule der Ästhetik*, in *Jean Pauls Werke*, section 49-51 (Berlin: G. Hempel), p. 222. (D)

[91] *Ibid.*, section 38, p. 54. (D)

[92] Ivan Alexandrovich Goncharov (1812-91). His best-known novel is *Oblomov* (1855).

poetic creativity. These reports stress *moods* and *states of feeling* as the *starting point* of the process. Let us begin with Schiller:

> I do not believe that it is always the vivid representation of one's subject matter that generates works of inspiration, but frequently it is only a need for subject matter, an indefinite impulse to discharge aspiring feelings. The musical structure of a poem is much more often on my mind when I sit down to write it than a clear concept of the content, about which I have frequently not made up my mind.[93]

Regarding the origin of *Wallenstein* Schiller writes: "For me, feeling is at first without a clear or determinate object, which only takes shape later. A certain basic musical mood comes first, and the poetic idea follows upon the latter."[94] 182

In his autobiography, Alfieri relates that most of his tragedies originated either during or after listening to music. Kleist, too, remarks:

> I regard music as the root, or rather, (expressing myself more precisely) as the algebraic formula of all other arts. Just as we already have a poet (Goethe) who drew all his thoughts about art from a theory of colors, so with me since early youth all my general thoughts about the art of literature have regarded it in its relation to sound. I believe that the most important keys to the art of literature are contained in harmonics. . . . If a work comes freely from the human mind, it must necessarily belong to the whole of humanity.[95]

If one adds that which is contained in this testimony about the relationship of feelings and moods to poetic images, to that about the unfolding of images and their relations, then the frequently cited testimony of Otto Ludwig no longer seems so paradoxical, although the overstimulation of his nervous system is by no means without influence upon the processes of his poetic creativity as he describes them. Of the three accounts he has given us, the most complete and the clearest is the following:[96]

[93] Schiller to Körner, 25 May 1792. (D)

[94] Schiller to Goethe, 18 March 1796. (D)

[95] Heinrich von Kleist, *Sämtliche Werke und Briefe*, ed. by H. Sembder (Munich: Hanser, 1961), pp. 874-75.

[96] Otto Ludwig, *Skizzen und Fragmenten, ein Bericht aus dem Tagebuch des Dichters*, March 1840, in *Nachlass*, 1:45, ed. by Moritz Heydrich (Leipzig: C. Cnobloch, 1874); *Shakespearestudien*, 2:303; and "Zum Verständnis der eigentümlichen Methode von O. Ludwigs Schaffen," 1:134.

This is my procedure: A mood leads the way, a musical mood which turns into a color. Then I see one or more figures in a certain posture, with certain gestures, either by themselves or in relation to one another, as in a copperplate engraving done on paper of that color, or, more precisely expressed, as in a marble statue or group upon which the sun falls through a curtain of the color in question. I also experience such a color when I read a work of literature that has moved me. When I get into a mood such as those furnished by Goethe's poems, I have a saturated golden-yellow merging into golden-brown. Schiller's furnish a radiant crimson. In Shakespeare every scene manifests a nuance of the particular color of the entire work. Surprisingly enough, that image or group is usually not the image of a catastrophe, but sometimes merely a characteristic figure in some kind of emotionally charged situation. Immediately related to the latter is a whole series of figures and groups. I do not first discover the plot or narrative content, but rather some visible situation from which ever new sculptural shapes and groups move either backwards toward the 183 beginning or forwards toward the climax till, finally, I conceive the whole work in all its scenes. All of this happens with great speed, and my consciousness is quite passive as a kind of physical anxiety overcomes me. I can then also reproduce the content of all the successive individual scenes at will. But it is impossible for me to summarize and articulate the narrative content. Next, language is added to gesture and behavior. I write down what I can, but when the mood leaves me, what I have written is only a dead set of letters. Now I apply myself to filling in the gaps in the dialogue. I inspect the text with a critical eye. I seek the common denominator of all these individual aspects, or, if I may put it this way, I seek the idea that unconsciously furnished the creative force and the coherence of the phenomena. Then I similarly search out the pivotal points of the action in order to elucidate the causal nexus for myself, and I seek the psychological laws underlying the individual aspects and the complete content of the situations. I arrange whatever is confused, and construct a plan in which mere instinct is no longer a factor; everything is intentional and calculated, both as a whole and as regards the individual words. The piece then looks approximately like a work by Hebbel. Everything is abstractly expressed. Every change of situation, every piece of character evolution, is, as it were, a

> psychological model. The dialogue is no longer a real dialogue, but rather a series of psychological and characteristic traits, a series of pragmatic and higher motives. I could leave it just this way, and in this form it might appeal to the intellect more than subsequently. Nor does it lack popular passages that would please the public. But I cannot bring myself to consider such a piece a poetic artwork. Even Hebbel's pieces seem to me to be raw material for an artwork, not the work itself. It is not yet a living human being, but rather a skeleton with some flesh on it, yet with the manner of composition still discernible.

Finally, we can round off the testimony of genuine poets by considering that of an entertaining storyteller; this is comparable to the satyr-play that follows the seriousness of the tragic trilogy. It shows how the formation of images from the drives and desires, which flit before us in youth as wishes and hopes, could become the point of departure for a modest kind of literature. Anthony Trollope's *Autobiography* recalls:

184

> I will mention here another habit which had grown upon me from still earlier years,—which I myself often regarded with dismay when I thought of the hours devoted to it, but which, I suppose, must have tended to make me what I have been. As a boy, even as a child, I was thrown much upon myself. I have explained, when speaking of my school-days, how it came to pass that other boys would not play with me. I was therefore alone, and had to form my plays within myself. Play of some kind was necessary to me then, as it has always been. Study was not my bent, and I could not please myself by being all idle. Thus it came to pass that I was always going about with some castle in the air firmly built within my mind. Nor were these efforts in architecture spasmodic, or subject to constant change from day to day. For weeks, for months, if I remember rightly, from year to year, I would carry on the same tale, binding myself down to certain laws, to certain proportions, and proprieties, and unities. Nothing impossible was ever introduced,—nor even anything which, from outward circumstances, would seem to be violently improbable. I myself was of course my own hero. Such is a necessity of castle-building. But I never became a king, or a duke,—much less when my height and personal appearance were fixed could I be an Antinous, or six feet high. I never was a learned man, nor even

a philosopher. But I was a very clever person, and beautiful young women used to be fond of me. And I strove to be kind of heart, and open of hand, and noble in thought, despising mean things; and altogether I was a very much better fellow than I have ever succeeded in being since. This had been the occupation of my life for six or seven years before I went to the Post Office, and was by no means abandoned when I commenced my work. There can, I imagine, hardly be a more dangerous mental practice; but I have often doubted whether, had it not been my practice, I should ever have written a novel. I learned in this way to maintain an interest in a fictitious story, to dwell on a work created by my own imagination, and to lie in a world altogether outside the world of my own material life. In after years I have done the same,—with this difference, that I have discarded the hero of my early dreams, and have been able to lay my own identity aside.[97]

[97] From *An Autobiography by Anthony Trollope*, vol. 1 (London: Wm. Blackwood, 1883), pp. 56-58.

## THE TYPICAL IN POETRY

One last important trait must be added to this elementary psychological theory of poetry. Images and their connections are transformed by feeling. This does not happen in a vacuum, but amidst the activity of all the psychic processes that continually operate in our sphere of experience—indeed, amidst the entire acquired nexus of psychic life which influences spontaneous creativity. Images and their connections do indeed transcend the common experiences of life. But what thus arises still represents these experiences, teaches us to understand them more deeply, and enables us to draw them closer to our hearts.

This follows directly from our earlier discussions in which the *substratum of poetic creativity* was sought in the processes that develop our sphere of experience. The poet shares this substratum of his creativity with the philosopher or the statesman. For all of them the experience of what is human is the foundation; generalizations and inferences are applied to develop this experience further. A natural relationship between a powerful intellect and life-experiences must also have existed in every great poet. He must have formed his characters, plot, form, and technique from representations of life. This cannot be emphasized strongly enough in opposition to all modes of aestheticism which strive to separate beauty from the experience of life. Even Schiller—although he found himself on this precipitous path—expressed the wish that aesthetics might substitute the concept of truth for that of beauty.

With the participation of the will, the metamorphosis of representations attains its artistic application and a literary work arises from inwardly nurtured images. Only when the will incorporates its elaboration of the experience of life into these images can it give the literary work a meaning-content that furnishes lasting satisfaction. Only to the degree that the work succeeds in forming lived experience so that it contains many experiences in the most intensified form can it attract the attention of a reflective person experienced in the world and satisfy him. What is presented is at the same time supposed to move the mind of the reader or listener.

This cannot be accomplished through mere particulars. Otto Ludwig fully felt the desire for particular matters of fact and reality; 186 nevertheless, he was forced to realize that singularity as such is not what moves us. For, as such, it is still mixed with traits that the reader or listener cannot re-create without offense and which are, therefore, repulsive. If realism is to stir our hearts, it must work through generalization, exclusion of what is accidental, and through emphasis on what is essential and meaningful for the feeling of life. Then the mind and heart of the reader will accept the images produced by realism because he will feel his own heartbeat more fully, because the very stuff of his own being is encompassed by these images, and everything is excluded that, as particular, could be strange to him.

Thus, the works of the poet also possess *universal validity* and *necessity*. But here these features do not signify what they do in the propositions of science. "Universal validity" signifies that every heart with feelings can re-create and appreciate the work in question. That which is selected from our life and taken together as being necessary for the nexus of life as such, we call "essential." "Necessity" signifies that the nexus existing in a work of literature is as compelling for the spectator as for the creative artist. When these requirements are satisfied, then the real manifests the essential.

We designate those essential aspects of reality highlighted in this way as the "typical." Thinking produces concepts, artistic creativity produces types. These types embody first of all an intensification of what is experienced, but not in the direction of empty ideality. Rather, they represent multiplicity in an image whose powerful and clear structure makes intelligible the *meaning* of our ordinary, unfocused experiences of life. In a poetic work everything is typical. The characters are typical; what is essential in their structure—the law of their development, as it were—is highlighted. They are displayed forcefully (even where weaknesses are shown) and with a brilliance which extends to every expression, as if no one had really understood these people before. The passions are also typical; the inner nexus of the phases in which a passion runs its course in a human being and consumes him is rid of particularity in poetry and manifests itself as stemming from the innermost law of the feelings. Consequently, what is essential and majestic is felt in passion as an expansion of the psyche and can be completely re-created and experienced by the viewer or listener. The nexus of the action, both in itself and in its relation to fate, is also typical. Everything that 187 disturbs the transparency of the causal chain is removed from the plot. The necessary links in the chain are reduced to their smallest number and simplest form. Just as the worldly wisdom of a fable or a proverb expresses a rule by which events unfold and are interconnected, literature expresses with the greatest power and simplicity the proper relationship of the parts, connected in the plot according to their inherent law. Nowhere in reality do we find such intensity and the absence of what is accidental. Here, by contrast, what is irrelevant to poetic types is excluded, and every part of the plot is laid out in its highest reality and power. Even the mode of representation is typical, for the breath that keeps the hero, his passions, and his fate alive must also animate the entire work, including its rhythms and images. The work thus becomes an individual. In the story of Lear, the brutal dimensions of the age leave their mark upon every figure and every sentence; and even Cordelia belongs to that stock: she will not submit.

Furthermore, all literature is *symbolic* since the material and goal of poetic representation is always formed by lived experience, i.e., either something inner that manifests itself through something outer or an external image that is enlivened by something inner. Its basic form is the poetic image which displays an inner process in a situation, the symbol. In this sense, the symbolic is the basic property of poetry, which is proper to it by virtue of its subject matter. Goethe once told Eckermann, "A lively feeling for one's circumstances and the capacity to express them, that is what makes a poet."

It is evident that the problem of all poetic technique is to produce something typical. In scientific induction, running through cases is only a means for presenting the *necessity* of the causal nexus, which was already implicit in the first case but could not be extracted in its purity. The unconscious process of typification that has already run its course in the poet's life-experience before he comes across his particular subject matter, allows him to re-create its dead facticity in a necessary sequence of moments with the highest degree of liveliness and simplicity. Here, too, the necessity consists in a compelling connection that convincingly draws the listener or reader along with it, and universal validity consists in the way in which this necessity exists for everyone.

The characters act with necessity when the reader or viewer feels that he, too, would act in that way. Necessity thus does not contradict the impression of *freedom*. Shakespeare enhances this impression in a genuinely Protestant manner in that even his villains recognize the demands of the moral law as they voluntarily and knowingly violate it. This necessity is thus in accord with freedom. Every true and great work of literature allows us to feel both simultaneously. We recapture and re-create in ourselves a complex 188 of mental and emotional states which are produced one by the other in sequence and in which the thrust of a consistent passion extends through the whole. But this mode of efficacy is totally different from the way in which premises compel us to draw a conclusion. The reflexive awareness of this other way of connecting terms is the fact which we call freedom. Externally this is presented in the monologue in which a decision is being prepared. No one has more persistently struggled to express this coexistence of necessity and freedom in a tragedy than the noble Schiller in his *Wallenstein*—here, too, he was Kant's best disciple.

The category of the *essential,* like those of substance and cause, is transferred from inner to outer experience, and designates first of all the complex of traits in which our inner life apprehends the meaning of an object. On the basis of his feelings, the poet thus brings forth what is essential in the singular or typical. How the poet can exclude the frequently irregular traits of reality is precisely the major problem that can only be dealt with by starting with the nature of human life and its psychological analysis. We can then begin to answer questions about the types of human beings, the number of poetic motifs, the basic forms that link the components of a plot, etc., which technique could previously deal with only externally.

## SECTION FOUR

# PROSPECTS FOR A THEORY OF POETIC TECHNIQUE TO BE DERIVED FROM THESE PSYCHOLOGICAL FOUNDATIONS

### Universal Validity and Historical Limitations of Poetic Technique

We have analyzed the poetic process and derived the principles that follow from the nature of this process with universal validity. Their number is indeterminate. The expression "principle" (which we chose, following Fechner) can also be replaced by the designation "norm," "rule," or "law," because the occurrence of the aesthetic impression is bound by the lawful relation expressed in a principle. Since contemporary psychology—to the extent that it can be legitimated—involves empirical gathering of data, description, comparison, and partial causal connection, one cannot yet hope for the derivation of a limited number of well-defined aesthetic tenets. The situation is the same in the related fields of logical, ethical, legal, and pedagogical norms, although logical norms are more accessible to the intellect. Still less is it possible to obtain these norms or principles completely through Fechner's method of abstracting from artworks and their impressions. Even if we admit that some of the difficulty in discovering these principles is a function of the present imperfect state of psychology, the further question arises whether a complete technical theory of poetry, which would identify the constituents of poetry, the rules of combining them, and decide the answers to questions of interest to both poets and the public, could be established on the basis of these principles. To answer this question affirmatively, the principles for solving the problem we posed at the beginning would either need to be already available in their totality or ready to be compiled by some future psychology.



Here we confront the most fundamental question facing all historical life in general. Pedagogy and ethics, aesthetics and logic, are all searching for principles or norms capable of regulating life in an adequate way. These disciplines strive to derive them from the facts pervading the history of humanity. But the unfathomable multiplicity and singularity of historical phenomena make a mockery of every attempt to derive such rules, except in the one field of logic. For in the latter, thought is transparent to itself and is clear through and through. On the other hand, we have already concluded that there are generally valid norms which lie at the basis of all creativity and all aesthetic impressions. Happily we can thus dismiss the approach of the Historical School, which attempted only to be descriptive and repudiated intellectual guidance by scientific principles. For life categorically demands that thought guide it. If such guidance cannot be produced by way of metaphysics, life will seek another fixed point. If we cannot seek it, as the outmoded poetic technique did, in the paradigms of a classical period, then the only alternative is to investigate the depths of human nature itself and the nexus of historical life. Here, in fact, such universally valid norms have been discovered. Since the nature of the poetic process is transparent, we are able to describe the process of creativity and derive its norms here with a greater clarity than has been possible in any other field (excluding logic).

190

The extraordinary significance of poetics, and of aesthetics in general, for the study of all historical phenomena is thus confirmed. This significance derives from the fact that the conditions for a causal explanation are more favorable here, and that therefore the major questions of principle can first be decided here. But the above analysis permits us to take a further step. The relation of the historical multiplicity of poetic works to universal principles—the problem of how historicity and universal validity coexist in poetic technique—can be clarified up to a certain point.

## Chapter One.
## Poetic Creativity and Aesthetic Impression

Aesthetics, and within it poetics, can be constructed from a dual perspective. The beautiful can be taken either as aesthetic *pleasure* or as artistic *production*. The capacity for this pleasure is called "taste" and for this productivity "imagination." If aesthetics begins with the study of aesthetic impressions (as in the schools of Fechner and Herbart), it seems necessarily to become something different than when it begins with the analysis of creativity, as in our study. Until now the first approach, more fruitful for technical considerations, has consistently predominated. When we pose the question of a theory of technique, it is first of all necessary to determine the relationship of these two approaches within such a theory.

This *dual perspective* exists in all systems of culture.[98] For it originates from the relationship between creation and appropriation which occurs in historical life. Thus, the discovery and the evidential corroboration of logical relationships supplement each other, as do the moral incentive of the agent and the judgment of the observer, the inner striving of the person to improve himself and the demands that society makes on personal development, productivity, and consumption. One kind of aesthetician proceeds from the outside to the inside. He examines the aesthetic impression to infer the artist's intention to evoke it, and from this, in turn, the origin of a technique that determines the impression. In this he resembles the ethical theorist who derives the origin of the moral law from the judgment 191 of an impartial observer. The other sort of aesthetician proceeds from the inside to the outside. He locates the source of rules in man's creative capacity. To be consistent, he must regard the aesthetic impression as a faint copy of the creative process. How do we resolve this controversy?

The relation between feeling and image, between meaning and appearance, does not originate either in the taste of the listener or in the imagination of the artist. Rather, it emerges in the life of the human mind, which expresses its content in gestures and sound, transposes the power of its impulses to a beloved form or to nature, and enjoys the intensification of its existence in images of the conditions that produced it. In such moments beauty is present in life itself, existence becomes a celebration, and reality becomes poetry. Both taste and imagination receive elementary contents and relations from this reality of beauty in life itself. *The relations established* here between feeling and image, meaning and appearance, inner and outer, can be *freely* employed to produce *music* in the domain of aural representations, and arabesques, ornamentation, decoration, and *architecture* in the domain of visual representations. But when employed according to the law of *imitation, poetry* arises in the first domain and *sculpture and painting* in the second. One and the same human nature generates both artistic creation and taste that re-experiences feelings—both arise from the same laws and correspond to one another. To be sure, this process works much more powerfully in the creator than in the spectator; moreover, in the creator it is also guided by the will; but its constituents are predominantly the same.

[98] For Dilthey's account of cultural systems, see *Introduction to the Human Sciences*, Book I in *SW*, vol. 1.

It will suffice here to develop and ground this thesis more fully within the domain of poetry.

The *process* in which I *appropriate* a tragedy or an epic is extended and extraordinarily composite. It is an *aggregate* of all the aesthetic constituents that we surveyed. The feelings that are combined in it derive from all the spheres of feeling. This aggregate of states involves feelings of *displeasure* as well as of satisfaction and pleasure. This is a necessary feature of every aesthetic composition of greater scope, for a sequence of purely pleasurable impressions soon becomes boring. Since poetry depicts life, an impoverished 192 and diluted version of it results if one excludes pain, the major driving force of life and the will. Nevertheless, *pleasure* must *predominate* within the aggregate, and the listener or reader must finally be led from a painful stimulus to a state of equilibrium or pleasure. All the energies of a full human being must be satisfied. Our senses should be filled with the affective content of sensations and with the moods which arise from their relations. Our higher feelings must find themselves powerfully expanded through the significance of their object and be resolved harmoniously. Further, our reflective contemplation ought to be totally occupied and engaged by the universal validity and necessity of the object, its relations to the overall acquired nexus of psychic life, and the consequent infinity of the horizon which surrounds the significant object. Only then will we find the work adequate and will all our needs be silenced. The great, classical artists are those who produce a lasting and total satisfaction in people from the most diverse epochs and nations. In other cases, we find something missing—be it sensuous charm, the power of feeling, or depth of thought.

However, the impression of a poetic work, although it is highly composite, does have a *determinate structure*, which is conditioned by the essence and means of literature. Literature arises as a lived experience and is expressed in words, i.e., in a temporal sequence. This process is accompanied by much agitation and it also evokes such a response in the listener. The listener's imagination re-creates the other's lived experience from his words and is similarly stirred, although less intensely. The words project an intuitable whole in an airy and transparent medium, as it were. In this whole, whose constituents work together to produce an impression, the pleasurable predominates. Even what is painful is in the course of time transformed into a state of equilibrium or satisfaction, just as we would wish it in life itself. The proportion of pleasurable and displeasurable constituents is a function of the fundamental structure of the creative process. Consequently, a poetic impression is *not* a skillfully arranged *aggregate* of pleasurable constituents, but rather has its *necessary form.*

Similarly, we cannot *derive* the process in either the poet or the listener from the *task* of uniting as *many* pleasurable or satisfying *constituents* as possible. Our direct experience does indeed encounter only processes and how one process produces another; but we cannot deny facts of psychic life that are not as yet explicable on the basis of direct experience. We have a need for strong stimuli which increase our energy. People appear to be insatiable in their desire to explore the inner life of other people or nations, to apprehend characters by re-experiencing, to share suffering and joy, and to listen to stories—whether they merely could have happened or whether they are actual histories of the past or present. This inner impulse is characteristic of primitive peoples as well as contemporary Europeans. It provides the elementary basis for the work of the poets, the historian and biographer as well as for the enjoyment of their listeners and readers. And since any greatness in our nature also has its attendant weakness, the same impulse also accounts for the pernicious popularity of pulp novels. Just as in Hauff's parody,[99] the admirer of Clauren[100] reads a description of a champagne breakfast while himself breakfasting on plain bread, so, too, many people add spice to the thin repast of their lives with the powerful emotions cheaply obtainable from the lending library. Even what is horrible becomes a source of pleasure to crude people, through a loathsome trait of human nature by which the security of one's own warm hearth is increased and doubled when compared with the danger and pain of others. There is something irrational in all this, which cannot be reasoned away from our nature. We are, after all, not machines that seek uniformly to produce pleasure and exclude pain, to weigh the respective values of our pleasures, and in this way to program our volitional impulses to attain the greatest possible quantity of pleasure. For such a person life would, of course, become rational, a mere problem in calculation. But that is not what life is like. Indeed, the irrationality of the human character can be seen in every heroic human being, in every genuine tragedy, and in criminals of all kinds. Our everyday experience shows us the same thing. We do not try to avoid pain, but rather broodingly and misanthropically immerse ourselves in it. When we

193

[99] Wilhelm Hauff, 1802-27. The piece in question is *Der Mann im Mond* (1826).

[100] Heinrich Clauren, *nom de plume* of author Carl Heun (1771-1854).

risk our happiness, health, and life to gratify feelings of antipathy, irrespective of considerations of pleasure, we are driven by dark impulses. And this need of human nature for powerful stimuli, even when mixed with strong pains, which cannot be reduced to some mechanism for maximizing pleasure, also operates in the composition of a powerful poetic impression. In the latter, the expansion of the psyche evoked by the greatness of those who suffer must compensate for the painful stimulus and bring about a satisfying final state. In a tragedy, therefore, pain and death serve only to disclose the greatness of the human psyche.

All of this can only come about when from the most nimble, 194 ethereal, and transparent aural materials, and the representations connected with them, a nexus of images is formed in the imagination of the spectator. The great rule of poetry is, thus, to activate the imagination in a certain intended direction. The nexus of images that results must, however, also be plausible in its sensory presence. For only where we believe in the reality of this nexus of images do we have a lived experience.

This composite poetic *impression* must now be compared with the *creative work* as we have analyzed it. The following relationship results. The primary process is that of *creation*. Poetry arose from the urge to express lived experience, not from the need to make possible a poetic impression. Whatever is formed from feeling excites feeling again, and does so in the same manner, though with diminished force. Thus, the process in the poet is akin to that in his listener or reader. The conjunction of individual psychic processes in which a work of poetry is born is similar in its constituents and structure to that which is then evoked in the listener or reader. According to Voltaire, whoever wants to judge a poem must have strong feelings and be born with some of the sparks of the fire that inspired the poet whose critic he wants to be. In both, the same nexus of image elements evokes the same nexus of feelings. The relation between visual imagery, conceptual universals, and stimulus content determines the structure through which the constituents are connected in both cases. Yet the differences between creativity and receptivity are equally unmistakable. The poetic creative process is much more composite, its constituents more powerful, the participation of the will stronger, and it takes a much longer time than reading or listening to the completed work.

One consequence of the above is that *poetic technique has two sides* to it. It includes the operation of both an involuntary, incessant formative process and, simultaneously, a calculation of the aesthetic impression and of the means to produce it. Both can be united in the poet. This is because any rational technique aimed at evoking a certain poetic impression must strive for the same metamorphosis of images, which begins with involuntary and not completely conscious formative processes. It can thereby calculate and focus the effects more clearly and precisely. Accordingly, in those poets who were at home on the stage, such as the Greek tragedians, Shakespeare, or Molière, a calculating intellect is inseparably bound up with involuntary creativity. The following *technical law* results: the intention that calculates the means to attain an impression must disappear behind the illusion of completely involuntary formation and free reality. The artistic intellect is always at work in such great dramatists as Shakespeare and Molière, but they hide it as much as possible. Their wonderful theatrical effects rest upon this total interpenetration of the theatrical and the poetic. In contrast, Goethe sought an appropriate form for every new problem. While he was in Italy, he censured himself for this tendency toward dilettantism. Furthermore, he was unable to develop the new forms which he had created to fully correspond to his astounding poetic intention: this is true for both *Faust* and *Wilhelm Meister.* Yet his poetic formative imagination emerged all the more purely and powerfully. Schiller correctly described Goethe's method:

195

> Your own way of alternating between reflection and production is really enviable and admirable. These operations are completely separate in you, and that is the reason that they can both be executed so purely as operations. As long as you produce or work you are really in the dark; the light is in you alone; when you begin to reflect, the inner light begins to emerge from you and illuminates the objects, yourself and others.[101]

Accordingly, the *theory of technique* must *proceed from these two psychic processes* and their *interaction* in the poet. A poetics which begins with the impression makes literature more or less into the work of the intellect which calculates effects. That is what happened with the poetics dependent on Aristotle. On the other hand, if unconscious creation appears as the source of poetic form, then rules, acquired insights, and rational analysis are spurned. That is what happened during the second phase of our Romantic period,

[101] Schiller to Goethe, 2 January 1798, in *Briefwechsel Schiller-Goethe.*

that of Arnim and Brentano.[102] Let us hope that poetics will open both portals of its experience as widely as possible so that no kind of fact or approach is excluded. When poetics investigates aesthetic impressions, it enjoys the advantage of being able to produce intentional changes in these impressions by changing the object and being able to analyze the complex of processes into its constituents. This renders possible experimental aesthetics as it is now being developed by Fechner. On the other hand, when poetics proceeds from creation, the right material of literary history can finally be utilized. Countless philologists and literary historians work unceasingly to make the works of poets usable and intelligible. What we now need is a new poetics which does not want to legislate to literature as Boileau did, but which instead strives to explain and 196 encompass—through comparative studies—all literary phenomena beginning with the primary seeds of poetry in the expressions of primitive people. Then empirical literary history and comparative study will be used in a healthy reciprocal manner to clarify the nature of creation, to project its unchanging norms, to show the historicity of technique, and thus to comprehend the past and show the future the way. A poetics arising from such cooperation will create the means for literary history to provide a much more subtle characterization of poets. Perhaps then the overabundance of personal gossip in which literary history is currently wallowing will disappear.

The result of these psychological discussions can again be presented in *principles* or *rules*. If we consider the laws of metamorphosis in isolation, then there is, corresponding to the process of intensification or diminution, a *principle* of the differing *emphasis on constituents* relative to their importance for the whole and to the highest energy of the dominant constituents among them. The law of exclusion has corresponding to it a *principle* of the greatest possible approximation to *pure satisfaction* through the exclusion of whatever contradicts such an effect. The law of completion has corresponding to it the *principle of the articulation of what is essential and meaningful* according to the relation between a state of feeling and an image. Further, if we focus on the achievements of these principles relative to their tasks, then two supplementary principles emerge. *Plausibility* and *illusion* constitute the necessary conditions under which the poet can carry out his task. They thus

[102] Achim von Arnim (1781-1831) and Clemens Brentano (1778-1842) cooperated to edit the folksong collection, *Des Knaben Wunderhorn*.

designate the limits by which his creative work is bound. *Aesthetic freedom*, which produces a gratifying realm of forms and actions separated from the purposive actions of life, operates within these limits and according to these laws. The poet is indeed determined by the acquired nexus of psychic life and by the laws, value relations, and purposes of reality contained in this nexus. He is bound by them if he is to satisfy his reader or listener. But he is not required to make his images correspond to reality. Schleiermacher based his aesthetics upon this principle of aesthetic freedom. "It belongs to the nature of spirit that we take those activities which are determined from without and which accordingly represent something externally given, and liberate these activities from this attachment and elevate them to an independent presentation. This is what art does."[103] When overemphasized, this principle grounds the glorification of the imagination in the Romantic aesthetics of Ludwig Tieck[104] and his contemporaries. When we finally consider the order of the constituents that are involved in the common structure of poetic creativity and poetic receptivity, we can formulate the rules for poetic works of a larger scope—especially those developed for drama. The effect of an individual constituent part must be proportionate to the scope of the whole work. Thus the plot of a tragedy must convey the impression of *importance* and *magnitude*, and a comical theme must be treated differently in a comedy than in a humor magazine or in a joke among friends. Further, the constituents must produce a self-contained and *strict unity*. One application of this is the famous rule of the unity of dramatic action. Finally, the constituent parts must be so ordered that their effect will continue to *intensify* up to the conclusion of the work.[105]

197

## Chapter Two.
## The Poet's Technique

Psychology has dominated our previous discussions. Now that we have obtained a foundation for poetics, our method changes and a literary-historical empirical approach will guide us. In accord with

[103] Schleiermacher, *Vorlesungen über die Ästhetik,* edited by Carl Lommatzsch, in *Sämtliche Werke*, ser. 3, vol. 7 (Berlin: Reimer, 1842), p. 116. (D)

[104] 1773-1853. Tieck's novel, *Franz Sternbalds Wanderungen*, is the definitive German *Künstlerroman.*

[105] These three principles have been developed by Gustav Freytag in his *Technik des Drama* (Leipzig: S. Hirzel, 1863), pp. 24ff., as rules of drama in connection with the principle of probability. (D)

the spirit of modern scholarship, it must encompass the entire field of literature and seek elementary structures, especially in the artistic works of primitive peoples. This empirical literary history must establish causal relationships among these productions and forms, and will find it necessary to utilize a developmental-historical approach everywhere. It can thus not respect the limits of previous literary history, but rather must draw explanations from the wide field of human culture wherever they can be found. Literary history must supplement this empirical method with the method of "reciprocal illumination," as Scherer[106] called it, and thus elucidate the temporally distant and obscure through the proximate and the accessible. This empirical literary history must employ comparison to arrive at generalizations and to derive uniformities. In this it is always supported by what has been learned through the study of the psychological foundations and can, at no point, dispense with psychological explanation. For a poetics without a psychological grounding employs popular and untenable concepts and theses, instead of scientific and demonstrable ones. However, from now on psychology will only have the role of an accompanying voice. Since this treatise is already far too long, we shall limit ourselves 198 to some especially important applications of our psychological foundation. To be sure, the fruitfulness of the psychological approach can only become completely apparent after every single problem which empirical literary history poses for poetics has been considered from the psychological perspective and is solved. If we later have the opportunity to attempt this, then we will not have to bear the burden alone. The poetics of Scherer, who will long be remembered for his fertile and energetic mind, is now to be published from his lectures. The way he connected grammar with poetics, and the unique manner in which he was able to encompass the history of Germanic literature—which is such an instructive source for the primary structures and forms of poetry—will certainly provide us with invaluable assistance. How much better it would have been had we been able to work together with him while he was alive!

1. Our opposition to previous poetics has become increasingly clear. We rejected every universally valid concept of beauty, but we

[106] Wilhelm Scherer (1841-86). His *Geschichte der deutschen Literatur* (1880-83) was indebted to the spirit of positivism, and made famous the phrase "Ererbtes, Erlebtes und Erlerntes."

found a productive formative process in human nature. As this process proceeds from the nucleus of lived experiences to the medium of language, all peoples develop the rhythmical expressions of feelings, which the psyche needs just as much as the body needs to breathe. It also brings about the free presentation and transformation of the content of lived experience, and vital personal action in a plot that moves or stirs the soul. This poetic creativity, already differentiated into various kinds at its very root, initially has its standard and distinguishing characteristic in the fact that the nexus of images produced satisfies the creator himself. At the same time, however, the satisfaction of the reader or listener becomes the goal of the poet and the standard of his achievement. His work first becomes purposive through the latter and generates its technique as does every other purposive activity. By "poetic technique" we understand that creativity of the poet that is conscious and sure of its goal as well as of its means.

*The poet's technique is a transformation of the content of lived experience into an illusory whole existing merely in the reader's or listener's representations. The sensuous energy of this structure of images has a powerful feeling-content, is significant for thought, and produces a lasting satisfaction with the aid of other lesser means.*

It is constitutive of the *artist's character* that his work does not intrude into the purposive system of real life and is not limited by it. The common man goes through life engaged in the one major occupation of gratifying his needs or pursuing happiness. For him, every object or person relates to this task of his life. The genius yields himself to objects without reference to utility, and, accord- 199 ingly, does this in a truly disinterested manner. Apprehension as such is his concern. Theoretical intelligence subordinates its representations to reality, and practical intelligence sets them into an appropriate purposive relation to reality. Disinterestedness, together with the deep reflection stemming from it, for which everything becomes lived experience, and which hovers over its objects with a calm and contemplative eye, forms a more ideal reality that evokes belief and simultaneously satisfies both the heart and the head: these are the characteristics of the poet.

The process which takes place in the listener or reader corresponds to the one indicated above. The nexus of images, which emerges in the imagination, includes persons and actions which are not related to those of real life by either cause or effect. The listener is thus lifted out of the sphere of his direct interests. Art is play. The entire effect which it would like to produce consists of a present and lasting satisfaction. The fact that this play may have other effects must not be allowed to obtrude itself on the consciousness of the listener. Such a satisfaction, however, is bound to the illusion which makes imitation a lived experience of reality. The basis of all genuine art is the agreement of the product of the imagination with the laws and value determinations of reality contained in the acquired nexus of psychic life, the probability and plausibility stemming from them, and the sensory impact of the work. Modern technique, which consistently and capably strives to establish this foundation, is completely justified in its opposition to so-called poetry of ideas or illustrations of thoughts. Without this foundation, how would we be moved to experience the destinies of others as our own and what is invented as real? Today's poets forget all too often that their object must really move the heart and that its theoretical relations must be meaningful.

Noteworthy consequences follow from this basic property of poetic appreciation. The processes displayed in literature never evoke external volitional actions on our part. One hears of persons who have interrupted the performance of a play in order to castigate the villain or to rescue the innocent victim. This presupposes an error about the actual relationship of the persons who are acting to those depicted by them. No matter how deeply a process may affect us as reality, we never cease to be conscious of the illusion. Further, in reliving what is presented in this way we are able to make the transition from one state to another much more quickly than in real life. In a few hours we follow the astonishing contrasts in the fate of a novel's heroine. A bloodthirsty playwright can compress a half dozen deaths into a single evening at the theater. This can be explained by the fact that these events neither bind our thoughts and emotions as firmly, nor excite the real relations of our existence as powerfully as do the occurrences of natural life. Sympathy with another's toothache is very different from a toothache of one's own; if consciousness of the illusion is added, then the spectator's pain and pleasure about the other's fate does indeed become more pure, but also weaker.

In addition to the poet and the public there is a third person, the *critic*. His reaction is the same as that of an ideal listener or reader. At least that is the way it should be! How then does it happen that a critic notices an imperfection in a character? The critic finds that a certain setting of a poem produces the hero's affective state, and this in turn a volitional process. As he tries to reproduce it, however, a quiet, inexorable resistance sets in. This resistance stems from the depths of his acquired psychic nexus which in this respect surpasses that of the poet. Or how does he recognize what is defective in a resolution? Because the peaceful reconciliation of his excited feelings fails to occur. Once again, his acquired psychic nexus produces insights into the relations among values as well as among purposes without his being explicitly conscious of them, and they surpass the poet's insights. It is not subsequent reflection, but rather intense lived experience that makes a good critic as well as a good poet. The capacity to make a profound judgment about a poet, therefore, is akin to creative ability. Lessing's greatness as a poet cannot be explained by the fact that he was our greatest critic. Rather, the energy of his creative ability and the acumen of his analytical understanding combined to make him the greatest critic, and as a poet Lessing then utilized the artistic devices that had become apparent to him as a critic. He thus intensified his creative ability through conscious technique.

The fact that such a *transformation* of lived experience is possible is based on the fact that reality offers the material (namely, changing situations and characters) in which a creative mind finds the means to produce such effects, even if unusable material is mixed in with it. According to Goethe and Schelling, even the most perfect human body is only beautiful for a transitory moment, but it is just this that the visual arts immortalize. Similarly, what is poetically meaningful appears only seldom and fleetingly, but the poet notices and preserves it. What is universally valid for feeling is never free from the interference of chance. The fullness of life is constrained by the limits of time, space, and causality. The poet must complete, idealize, and purify on the basis of his powerful sense of life. 201

Two passages from Schiller and Goethe corroborate this conception of poetry. Schiller defines the poet as follows: "I call 'poet' anyone who is capable of projecting his state of feeling in an object with the consequence that this object compels me to go over into that state of feeling, i.e., affects me vitally." If this definition is thought to be too narrow because it does not include the poet who begins from his own subjectivity, we can cite Goethe's comprehensive claim: "Lively feelings of situations, and power to express them, make the poet."[107]

[107] Eckermann, *Gespräche,* 11 June 1825; *CE,* p. 159.

2. Also, the way in which *technique is established as a mode of knowledge* must be changed in modern poetics. As much as contemporary poetics owes to the two older methods and as forcefully as we emphasized this in the previous chapter, poetics must still take a decisive step in order to become a modern science. Poetics must recognize the productive factors, study their effects under varying conditions, and solve its practical problems by means of this *causal knowledge.*

> *Knowledge of technique is based on a causal approach, which not only describes the composition of poetic products and forms, but really explains them. From this it derives an indeterminate number of universally valid principles of the poetic effect and represents them as rules or norms. It shows how in the causal nexus of processes according to the laws of psychic life and in accordance with poetic norms, a poetic technique emerges under the conditions of a particular age and people; and, accordingly, it shows how it has only a relative and historical validity. Poetics thus grounds literary history and finds its completion in it.*

By giving our own sense to a term coined by Humboldt, we form a concept which connects the causal approach of contemporary poetics with the form analysis of earlier poetics. Thus we call the *distribution of changes* which occur in lived experiences according to the laws we have described, i.e., the restructuring of constituents, emerging relations of emphasis, power and expansion, as well as transformed relationships, "inner poetic form." This inner form is something unique in every case. If one relates individual works that are alike into groups, then an inner poetic form emerges, which is 202 common to a number of them, and the problem arises of explaining it from common conditions. On the other hand, comparison yields several elementary uniformities which remain constant within a sphere of feeling, and this leads to the task of inquiring into the regular antecedents of such a uniformity on the basis of the simplest attainable facts and the task of observing regularly coexisting phenomena and investigating their connections.

The poet's creative processes transform images in the direction of lasting satisfaction, and the elements of the images thus produced are the bearers of poetic effects upon others. These constant causes from which poetic effects originate have been formulated by us as *principles.* They can also be transformed into rules or norms. Their number is indeterminate because every constant cause of poetic effects can be formulated in terms of such a principle. In our formulations we took care to indicate the place of those principles already developed in traditional aesthetics, especially the historically significant ones.

If the ends and means of the genres of literature could be derived from the *combination* of these *rules*, then a *universally valid poetic technique* would arise. However, even the distinctions among the three kinds of literature can only be exhibited empirically in the original distinctions that we have been able to find in primitive peoples. The expressions of life in which lyric, epic, and dramatic poetry first appear here are, psychologically considered, so complex and their psychological significance is still so uncertain that there is, at the present, no hope of attaining a psychological interpretation for these distinctions. It would be inappropriate to derive these literary genres constructively from the essence, end, and means of literature in general. Although many aestheticians have defined drama as a higher unity of lyric and epic poetry, a mere glance at the available accounts of primitive peoples shows how much they err. Neither can the technique of particular genres of literature be derived from their end and means. Anyone can test this for himself by trying to determine the relation of the principles of poetic impression to one another, or by using them to conceive the most effective possible selection of ordered impressions, or by seeking the most favorable possible selection among the possibilities contained in the individual moments of inner form, mood, plot, action, character, etc. The result will be to confirm the indeterminateness of the principles and the impossibility of delimiting their number, of measuring their relative value, and of obtaining a final ordering of their inner relations. A universally valid poetic technique is thus impossible. 203 This is corroborated by considering the few works on the technique of particular genres of literature that exist. Otto Ludwig used his poetic insight and his perhaps too delicate aesthetic sensitivity to attempt to abstract a universally valid dramatic technique from his intimate study of Shakespeare. He was able to penetrate Shakespeare's technical secrets more deeply than any previous Shakespeare scholar. He showed how finely, securely, and consistently the technique of this greatest of all dramatists was developed. One can regard his book as an indirect, but very ingenious, proof that Shakespeare created the extraordinarily perfect form of classical English drama with the aid of his sense of technique. But Ludwig did not find the universally valid technique which he sought for the dramatists of his day, especially for his own use. What he has set forth as such a technique is only a vague ideal image of the historical technique of Shakespeare. Thus, his love of Shakespeare was also fated to be unproductive.

In his book on the technique of drama, Gustav Freytag reaffirmed the validity of the form of a closed plot which had been lost through dramatic abuses. Due to the penetrating consistency of its basic idea, Freytag's book is a true handbook of dramatic literature and critique. He develops the rules of drama from the requirements for the most effective form of action. Into the body of the action or plot he then retroactively inserts the tragic soul. He thus was able to derive only a particular, limited form of drama, in which a unified and closed action is led systematically through its stages. Within these limits, Freytag was able to make felicitous observations about the five parts of the drama and the three dramatic moments located between them. But the more intricate forms of Shakespeare's tragedies cannot be derived from Freytag's scheme of a closed plot. For, if one traces the line that leads from the simple, austere structure of *Macbeth* to the complicated and seemingly disintegrative structure of *King Lear,* a remarkable distinction appears in the tragic form. *King Lear* and *Hamlet* display a wealth of episodes and sharply delineated contrasts which stand in opposition to the basic tragic mood, and which can by no means be adequately explained by the intent to illuminate the main action by means of contrast. Indeed, they contain completely elaborated subplots, which interrupt the continuity of the play and cannot be there merely for the sake of a contrasting effect. One soon realizes that these works are 204 psychic portraits which neither require nor permit strict causal connections. One notices an inner relatedness of a special kind between these causally unrelated processes for which Hegel's "Idea" provides a mere point of comparison, and an inadequate one at that. It provides no real understanding of this inner relatedness. Herder has already called attention to the fact that every character and every scene in Shakespeare appears with such a specific coloration that we could not conceive of its being transferred into another work. The mysterious soul of the drama which is manifested in such facts does not issue from the individuality of the poet and enter into the closed form of the action; instead it autonomously determines the structure of a form in which it is able to come to expression. Only through the historically appropriated content of a drama is it possible to understand its proper form. Form is not universally valid, but relative and historical.

*3. Lived experience is the basis of poetry; the most primitive civilizations always show poetry to be connected with elemental and powerful forms of lived experience. Examples of such forms include rituals, festivities, dance going over into pantomime, and the commemoration of tribal ancestors. Here song, epic, and drama already exhibit separate roots.*

When strong psychic agitation does not lead to acts of will, it finds expression in sounds and gestures, in a combination of song and poetry; thus we find poetry connected with rituals and festivals, with dance and games in primitive peoples. Poetry's link to myth and religious cult, to the splendor of festivals and the joy of games, and to pleasant fellowship is therefore psychologically grounded. This link is visible from the first beginnings of civilization, and pervades the entire history of literature.

In primitive civilizations, *lyric poetry* is inseparable from song. Joy and sadness resound in the expansive, open, and bright nature of the Africans who accompany their routine activities with song. Literary historians will hopefully someday be able to establish the various stages of development of rhythm, rhyme, and form in song by the comparative method. American Indians east of the Rocky Mountains have a form of song wherein that which excites feeling is expressed in a single line; this is then sung in endless repetitions by individuals and choruses. "When I face the enemy, the earth trembles beneath my feet." Or, "My enemy's head has been cut off and falls at my feet." A favorite poetic figure in their songs is antiphrasis, which children enjoy regularly. The Dakota Indians praise a brave man with the words: "My friend, you have been defeated by the Ojibway." The natives of Danakil and Somali unite a definite rhythm with an incomplete cadence and rhyme in their many songs.[108]

205

Epic songs of primitive peoples extend from animal fables to the epic song as an element of the heroic epic. In Senegal there is a special hereditary class of bards called Griots. That their epic songs have a content akin to that of the Greek rhapsodists is shown by a report of the refusal of the princes of Kaarta to flee, because if they did the bards would bring public shame on them. At the courts of the kings of Dahomey and Suliman, these bards have at the same

[108] Details about the sources of our knowledge are to be found primarily in Theodor Waitz, *Anthropologie der Naturvölker,* 2nd ed. (Leipzig, 1877), vol. 2, pp. 236ff., 524; vol. 3, pp. 231ff.; vol. 4, p. 476; examples in vol. 2, pp. 240ff.; vol. 3, p. 232. (D)

time the function of preserving the history of the past. American Indians east of the Rocky Mountains preserve the memory of their tribal history in their epic legends, although they also create freely invented epic narratives comparable to our romances or ballads. In one such narrative, the soul of a departed warrior abandons the field of battle to see how deeply he is mourned; in another a beloved wife returns to earth from beyond the grave to determine whether her premature death has caused sorrow.[109]

The incipient forms of *drama* produced in less advanced civilizations completely confirm our information and inferences about the origin and development of dramatic art in more advanced nations. Joy and sorrow, love and anger, extreme passions, even religion and its grave solemnity are expressed by primitive peoples not only in sound and song, but also in gesture, rhythmic movement, and dance. Thus they represent encounters of love and clashes of war. Dance goes over into pantomime. Here, especially, Indian tribes intensify the effect by using masks. The religious and political transactions of the Indians are accompanied by such pantomimes. "If . . . any intercourse be necessary between two American tribes, the ambassadors of the one approach in solemn dance, and present the calumet or emblem of peace; the sachems of the other receive it with the same ceremony. . . ."[110] If they are celebrating the birth 206 of a child or mourning the death of a friend, this is done in pantomime dances that reflect the feeling of the moment. Indeed, such pantomimes constitute a major part of the Indians' rituals. They are often performed with masks and costumes, and are repeated annually. The Iroquois still have twenty-one such ceremonial pantomime dances today. In one of them a bear emerges from his cave, and he must retreat back into it three times after being hunted. Animal masks with their terrifying, but also comical, effects are especially popular. They are the primitive expression of that combination of what is frightening or ridiculous with what is ugly, which we will later recognize as one of the most effective of poetic formulas. At this less advanced stage of civilization there is no boundary between dance and mimetic representation. I would suggest that the dance gradually became the art form for dramatic pantomime in the same way as meter and rhyme did for poetic

[109] Details concerning sources in *ibid.*, vol. 2, pp. 237ff.; vol. 3, p. 234. (D)

[110] J. Lubbock (Lord Avebury), *On the Original Civilization and the Primitive Condition of Man*, 6th ed. (London: Longman, Green and Co., 1902), p. 549. Citing a report from Robertson's *America*, vol. 4, p. 133.

speech. The negroes of Akra already use jesters whose pranks are presented in mime.[111]

4. In what follows we will only discuss the technique of major poetic works, whether epic or dramatic.

*Every living work of major scope takes its subject matter from something factual that has been experienced. In the last analysis, it expresses only lived experience, transformed and generalized by the feelings. For this reason, no idea may be sought in literature.*

Goethe remarks that his *Elective Affinities* contains no line that has not been experienced—but also none that is just as it was experienced. There are similar comments by him about other works. Contemporary literary history has been of service in always looking for the material basis of literatures. Sometimes it finds personal experience, sometimes stories from the past or the present, sometimes—especially in the novella—previous literary works. In some cases, we find a simple underlying subject matter, in other cases, a combination of them. *Facticity* has always proved to be the ultimate fresh and firm nucleus of every poetic work.

Therefore, a poetic work always contains more than can be expressed in a general proposition, and its gripping force comes precisely from this surplus. Every attempt to locate the idea of a poetic work by Goethe contradicts Goethe's own express declarations: "The Germans . . . by their deep thoughts and ideas, which they seek in everything and fix upon everything . . . make life much more burdensome than is necessary. Only have the courage to give yourself up to your impressions, allow yourself to be delighted, moved, elevated, nay, instructed and inspired for something great; but do not imagine all is vanity, if it is not abstract thought and idea."[112] "If imagination did not originate things which must ever be problems to the understanding, there would be but little for the imagination to do."[113] "[T]he more incommensurable, and the more incomprehensible to the understanding, a poetic production is, so much the better it is."[114] He rejoiced over the incomprehensibility

207

[111] Details concerning sources in Edward Tylor, *Anfänge der Kultur*, vol. 2, pp. 133, 241; *idem, Anthropologie*, pp. 354ff.; and in Waitz, *Anthropologie der Naturvölker*, vol. 2, p. 243; vol. 3, pp. 137, 210; vol. 4, pp. 123, 476. (D)

[112] Eckermann, *Gespräche*, 6 May 1827; *CE*, pp. 258.

[113] Eckermann, *Gespräche*, 5 July 1827; *CE*, p. 266.

[114] Eckermann, *Gespräche*, 6 May 1827; *CE*, p. 259.

of his greatest works and correctly noted how various states of his life and changing ideas about them intersect in his most significant works and how this intensified their incomprehensibility. Already for this reason, he regarded *Wilhelm Meister* as "one of the most incalculable productions; I myself can scarcely be said to have the key to it."[115] He explicitly called *Faust* totally "incommensurable"[116] and found every attempt to bring it nearer to understanding futile. He expressed his view about the sense in which lived experience obtains a universally valid meaning in literature with reference to *Wilhelm Meister*: "Its inception sprang from an intimation of the great truth that man frequently wants to attempt something for which he is denied the capacity by nature. . . . However, it is still possible that all the false steps nevertheless lead to an inestimable good—an intuition that is gradually unfolded, clarified, and corroborated in *Wilhelm Meister* and is ultimately clearly expressed in the words: You remind me of Saul, the son of Kish,[117] who went out to seek his father's she-asses and found a kingdom."[118]

Thus the interpretation of literary works as presently dominated by *Hegelian aesthetics* must be opposed. Consider an example. The attempt to formulate the idea of *Hamlet* has been made again and again. But all we can do is to give a paltry description of the incommensurable facts which Shakespeare has given a universally valid meaning in his drama. Since he had developed in himself a keen and strong moral sense in the context of the Protestant religious feeling of his day, it often came into conflict with the dubious moral climate in which he advanced his career. This was the source of a very deep feeling of infirmity and moral degeneracy which was set over against the capacity of this great man to find pleasure in heroic passions and in the fortune and splendor of this world. Prior 208 to Shakespeare, English drama had produced its effects through the strongest contrasts and the boldest effects, through bloody adventure and comic situations, through sensuous vitality and tragic death. The force of Shakespeare's moral sense added to that an inner nexus of character, passion, tragic guilt, and decline, as well as the coordination of related actions, thereby creating the technique of the classical English tragedy. This very strength of his moral feelings already produced those early experiences and judgments about the nature of the world that are found in his sonnets. When

[115] Eckermann, *Gespräche*, 18 January 1825; *CE*, p. 110.

[116] Eckermann, *Gespräche*, 3 January 1830; *CE*, p. 422.

[117] I Samuel 9.

[118] *WA*, I, 35: 8.

he became acquainted with the legend of Hamlet, he saw in it the most terrible symbol for the moral infirmity of the world. A sensitive moral soul must find his own mother guilty, indeed, despise her, and avenge his father on her husband, the king. With this legend he conjoined images of courtly corruption which he knew all too well. The problem of insanity which had always interested him, he wove into the plot as a further symbol of human frailty. In Ophelia, he shows us a terrible kinship between the sensuous faculties of a pure maiden and the images which madness imposes upon her. The plot, developed on the basis of play and counterplay, permits various interpretations. But at least one thing is clear, namely, that the lived experience of the poet and its unnerving symbols constitute a dramatic core that cannot be expressed in any proposition. When the psyche of the spectator is stirred, everything comes together into a graphic, felt unity of the deepest life-experiences, and that is precisely the significance of poetry.

*The limits of the poetic imagination* manifest themselves in the way the poet's formative power is rooted in his material. The dependence of epic poetry on myth and legend during the heroic age has been established in detail by philology. Concerning tragedy, the following principle can now be asserted:

> *A powerful tragedy is produced when poetic creativity confronts external states of affairs, reports, stories, etc., as inexorable reality. Then the imagination strives to give unity, inwardness, and meaning to this reality. To the extent that the recalcitrance of the factical* (Faktischen) *proves invincible, the plot and the characters manifest a special kind of illusion and efficacy.*

5. The transformation of subject matter into a poetic work always must take into account the *medium in which* the nexus of images *appears*. The transformation is always conditioned by this medium. 209 But here it is crucial not to regard the medium as simply a linguistic expression, as a sequence of words.

> *The medium in which the nexus of images appears is, in its first moment or aspect, a sequence of words in time. In relation to our feeling, the poetic formation of this medium exists in the arrangement of tone qualities, in rhythm, and in phrasing. Since intensity of feeling conditions metrical relationships, comparative metrics must begin not with relations of temporal duration, but rather with the relations between the intensity*

*of the vocal processes excited by feeling, the resistances which it has to overcome, rising and falling movement, etc. The other moment of the medium in which a nexus of images is formed and exists as a whole is the nexus of processes in the imagination of the hearer or reader made possible by memory.*

We discovered principles of poetic effect in single tones, in relations between tones, in changing rhythm, and in the relations of these sensuous properties of word sequences to the play of psychic states. We perceive here the *first moment of the medium in which poetic images* that are initially an inner possession of the poet also *become visible* to a reader or listener. The psychological interpretation of this moment is dependent on the empirical, comparative study of such poetic means of representation. Aristotle was not yet able to see the link between the object of poetry and its metrical form. For him the two *aitiai physikai*[119] [physical causes] of the art of poetry, the impulse to imitate and our equally innate sense of measure and harmony, which includes the sense of metrical form, stand juxtaposed without mediation. The reason for this was his one-sided principle of imitation. Our psychological foundational studies have shown this connection. The affective content of action and character also emerges in the linguistic means of representation as intensified by the imagination. There exists an original relationship between the stirrings of our feelings, volitional tensions, the faster or slower sequence of representations, on the one hand, and tone, its volume, pitch, rapid or stately sequence, rise or fall, on the other. The strength and character of our feelings, the energy of
210 volitional tension, the easy and precipitate flow of representations when we are in high spirits, the interruption of this flow when we are in pain—all of these stand in fixed, physiologically conditioned relations to the pitch, volume, and velocity of tones. These are experienced in the intonations of speech. We may assume that in primitive times, speech which bore affective content of greater strength was also more closely related to the recitative. Music borrowed its schemata for melodies from this, as is clearly shown by national differences. Here also lies the source of meter, which was at first still linked with recitative, song, and dance. Thus we conclude that the relations of temporal duration as such are *not* to be regarded as the primary metrical facts, but rather the relations of intensity, resistance, rising and falling movement, etc. But the at-

[119] Vahlen, *Beiträge zu Aristoteles' Poetik* (Vienna: K.u.K Hof- und Staatsdruckerei, 1865) vol. 1, p. 11. (D)

tempt to discover principles of metrical form is futile as long as we lack a more detailed knowledge of the languages of primitive peoples and of their metrical forms. It is only with difficulty that we distinguish the metrical effect of the repetition of words, the refrain, and the simple counting of syllables, etc.[120]

The *other moment of the medium* in which an image is apprehended as a whole is the nexus produced by memory. The action and the fullness of the character possess their reality outside the poet, not in ethereal words, fading away and supplanting one another, but rather in what is formed in the listener by means of the words. In this medium the course of psychic life is represented in the most adequate way. Actions and psychic processes are the proper objects of poetry. However, the simultaneity of imagery can only be produced by a succession in which the individual constituents of the image are preserved, remembered, related to one another, and conjoined. Now since it is in the nature of an aesthetic impression that every moment ought to furnish satisfaction in and of itself, and since extended descriptions with incomplete constituents are tiresome, artistic skill must be employed to produce an imaginative nexus by means of actions whose parts already satisfy and appeal to our capacity to visualize. Thus *Lessing's law*[121] must be refined in its formulation and justification. From the fact that words succeed each other in time, it does not follow that the imaginative nexus arising in the mind is to be limited to a mere successive order.

*The action of a drama best corresponds to the sequence of words, since each individual part by itself already provides satisfaction, while at the same time each contributes something to the formation of the whole in the imagination. Therefore, the portrayal of what is simultaneous is the object of poetry only to the extent that it is either a natural effect of the action (disclosure of character) or artificially incorporated into the form of the action (descriptions of external objects and bodily beauty).* 211

[120] Tylor, *Anthropologie*, pp. 343ff.; Waitz, *Anthropologie der Naturvölker*, vol. 4, p. 476. (D)

[121] Dilthey here alludes to the following passage in Lessing's *Laocoön*: ". . . then signs arranged side by side can represent only objects existing side by side, or whose parts so exist, while consecutive signs can express only objects which succeed each other, or whose parts succeed each other in time." *Laocoön*, trans. by Ellen Frothingham (Boston: Little, Brown & Co., 1898), p. 91.

6. Let us now discuss the *way in which poetic creativity produces works* in accordance with the conditions of its medium. Here we encounter a twofold direction, which is embedded in the nature of lived experience.

*Just as in science the inductive and deductive methods are separated out and nevertheless cooperate in many ways, there are also two kinds of imaginative processes rooted in lived experience: either a subjective state is made visible in the symbol of an external process or an external facticity is enlivened. Subjective and objective poets are distinguished on this basis.*

I first discussed this distinction within the imagination in an essay, "Über die Einbildungskraft der Dichter" (On the Imagination of the Poets),[122] where I undertook to justify it by an analysis of literary history. Schiller already juxtaposed two basic moods of the imagination: the naive and the sentimental. This distinction was not used to designate epochs of literature, but rather basic dispositions of poets. Since the distinction established by Schiller is a very complex and historically conditioned one, I examined literary-historical materials in order to find the most *elementary division within the functions of the imagination.* The present investigation offers a psychological confirmation of this division discovered through the literary method.

Every composite investigation conjoins inductive and deductive methods. Similarly, every major poetic work must unite these two tendencies of the imaginative process. However, for poets such as Shakespeare and Dickens, the poetic enlivening of *images offered* 212 *to them by the external world* predominates. Shakespeare seems to be able to view the world with the eyes of every kind of human being. He uses his Montaigne[123] in analyzing human characters and passions. His major dramas offer models, as it were, of every important emotion. He seems to have become completely absorbed

[122] *Zeitschrift für Völkerpsychologie*, 10 (1877): 42ff. ⟨This treatise was revised as the essay, "Goethe and the Poetic Imagination."⟩ [See this volume, pp. 235-302.] Let me add that in a lecture of 1886 on poetic imagination and insanity [*GS*, VI, 90ff.], I gave a more popular account of some of the main points of the psychological foundation established in this essay. In my literary and historical essays on Lessing, Novalis ⟨now included in *ED*⟩, Dickens, Alfieri ⟨*Westermanns Monatshefte*, 41 (1876-77); 38 (1875)⟩, and elsewhere, I have tried to apply the multiplicity of psychological perspectives made possible by the foundation furnished here. These studies also supplement what is expounded here. (D)

[123] Montaigne's *Essays* appeared in English translation in 1603. Shakespeare was influenced by them and makes direct and significant quotations in *The Tempest.*

by the reality confronting him. While with Shakespeare we can merely infer this from his works, we can directly see it in the case of Dickens. He lived in the same society as Carlyle and John Stuart Mill. He loved Carlyle, but shared none of his inclination for melancholy brooding about the ultimate questions of life. Dickens found the fulfillment of his life in apprehending the society around him, with love and hate, in untiring observation of human nature with that penetrating glance born of his faith in humanity, and in developing every conceivable device of the modern novel through which he became the true creator of this art form.

In contrast, Goethe's *Faust* is composed of *moments of the poet's own life*. This is generally his procedure. An event or story of general interest is found for an inner lived experience. Their fusion occurs suddenly through inspiration, and then a slow process of metamorphosis and completion of the discovered symbol begins. For years he would press his sufferings and joys, the conflicts of his heart, and his mind's deepest agitations into the vessel of such an invented or real story. In many cases this process would last for half his lifetime. The characterization process in *Faust* is no exception. It is rather "the apotheosis of this art form. Goethe's wonderful ability to give the most sensitive expression to states of mind and their actual backgrounds, and to visualize them in tropes, is apparent in his most hastily written notes as well as in his lyric poems. He displays what moves him through the great trope of an action which dresses even the most intimate lived experience in beautiful garments. He describes all this with the transparency and purity of nature herself; never has anyone been more truthful. As he shows himself through this, Goethe becomes the embodied ideal of an age, and *Faust* is the comprehensive symbol in which he reveals his whole life."[124] In the same way as I approached Goethe's poetic technique in these remarks from the above-cited essay, so the two great "pathological" poets, Rousseau and Byron, could also be intuitively explained by means of this mode of operation of the imagination. In his early period, Schiller, too, created the inner life of his heroes predominantly from his own personal states.

7. The transformation of the subject matter takes place on the basis of feelings; these, however, are very composite. We shall des-

[124] Dilthey is quoting from his essay, "Über die Einbildungskraft der Dichter." See the almost verbatim passage in "Goethe and the Poetic Imagination" in this volume, p. 301.

213 ignate as a "mood" an aggregate of feelings whose components do not stand out prominently and strongly, but possess an extended duration and a great capacity to expand. Such complexes of feelings have properties which are conducive to poetic creativity and poetic impressions. We then call them *poetic moods.* The mood operative in the production of a work is also evoked by the apprehension of the work.

> *Poetic moods, aggregates of feelings, which do not effect us violently, but endure and are imparted to every process, produce transformations in images in accordance with the laws of imaginative metamorphosis. The number of such aggregates of feelings is unlimited. But the historical continuity of poetic technique has the consequence that poetic moods are developed and transmitted through the literature of a tradition, and thus stabilized around certain favorable points in this multiplicity which are especially conducive to poetic creativity and enjoyment. These moods are manifested in the aesthetic categories of the ideally beautiful, the sublime, and the tragic with which the ugly can then be combined and, on the other hand, the categories of the sentimental, the comical, the charming or the graceful.*

Psychology and the history of literature will both have to investigate the composition of these poetic moods, their relations to one another, and especially their effect upon the material of poetry on the basis of the laws of the imagination. In undertaking this serious task, they will have to contend with the dialectics of Hegel, Solger,[125] Weisse,[126] and others, who naturally found abundant material in these flexible phenomena. If the category of the beautiful characterizes the state in which the object is completely adequate to the psychic life of the spectator and in which the object fulfills and wholly gratifies the mind without disturbance and feelings of displeasure, then we find on the one side aggregates of feeling that reflect the overwhelming magnitude of their object, while on the other side there is a psychic state in which the subject feels itself superior to the object. On both ends of the spectrum, whose middle is formed by the *ideally beautiful*, there arises an admixture of

[125] Karl Wilhelm Ferdinand Solger (1780-1819). Like Tieck, Solger considered irony the highest principle of aesthetics. Hegel criticized this conception of irony as a mode of dialectic which is too negative.

[126] Christian Hermann Weisse (1801-66). A philosopher who attacked Hegel; his *Antrittsrede* of 1847 called for a reorientation to Kant.

displeasure, and from the dissolution of the latter, a peculiar agreeableness. In the one case, the feeling of something *immeasurably great* in the meaning of the object must be overcome; in the other case, the feeling of something *trifling*.

The mood in which an object appears as *sublime (erhaben)* contains, as Burke has shown beyond any doubt, something of fear, terror, and astonishment. Therefore, it is always combined with unpleasant stimuli. But because it expands the psyche in proportion to the magnitude of the object—whether this magnitude consists in what is spatially immeasurable, physically overwhelming, or spiritually and volitionally powerful—a persistent and strong stimulus develops, namely, a strangely agreeable feeling of exaltation (*Erhebung*). 214

*Tragedy* involves an even greater combination of feelings, for the misfortune of the hero not only evokes fear through his heroic character, but also pity through his role as the adversary of fate: "The grand and monstrous fate that exalts man by crushing him." Thus the stimuli involved in the sublime are intensified. Tragedy receives a privileged status, for it combines a gripping action with a decisive outcome. The tragic expresses the character of reality—many have sought to find in the tragic a law for the real world—and thus satisfies the intellect. Furthermore, a feeling of displeasure can enter into the tragic. It is characterized by the aesthetic category of ugliness. The question whether *ugliness* can be the subject of art arises only from an unfortunate and abstract manner of expression. For the property of ugliness is always a subordinate constituent of the aesthetic object presented by poetry. It can only have aesthetic effects indirectly. The displeasure contained in it must be outweighed by the overall aggregate of feelings, and in the sequence of feelings it must be displaced by satisfaction. Accordingly, there are determinate aesthetic loci where ugliness is permitted to emerge. One such locus is characterized by the combination of the sublime, as something fearful, and the ugly. Similarly, the body painting and masks of primitives used ugliness to intensify the impression of the fearful. The same intensification of terror is produced by Dante's description of Cerberus and of Minos, the Judge of Hell,[127] and of the deformity of Richard III. Victor Hugo and the French Romantics have made excessive use of the same strong medicine; and Dickens made his most villainous characters ugly. The sublimity of evil is the demonical. In the final analysis, even frightful evil is sublime.

[127] See Dante's *Inferno*: Cerberus, VI, lines 13-36; Minos, V, lines 1-16.

It is sublime when Adah, Cain's wife, says of Lucifer: "There is a power in his gaze which fastens my unsteady eye to his." The man whose will knows no bounds resembles the violence of nature herself. He generates terror all around him. He is alone in the midst of society like a beast of prey. To this mixture of the sublime, the tragic, and evil, ugliness can be added. Here we reach the limits of the aesthetic impression.

215 We represented the beautiful as the midpoint of a spectrum of poetic moods. The second of the two sides is formed by the moods in which a feeling of something trifling in the object must be overcome. The *sentimental* already lacks some of the glory of beauty, and so a slight feeling of displeasure of the indicated kind enters into it. The *comical* arises from, and is enjoyed in, a poetic mood that lies on the same side of the spectrum. To be sure, laughter is evoked by extraordinarily different representations or relations of representations. Laughter which is stimulated by what is incomprehensible, persistently vexing, or contemptible, and laughter evoked by a witty combination of ideas, share a very mysterious common structure as psychic processes. What leads from this psychic process to a subsequent sudden explosion is unknown. In each of these cases, a contrast evokes a psychic convulsion, which is discharged in the respiratory region where other psychic states such as sighing, sobbing, and angry fuming are also expressed. But the poetic mood in which the comical arises and is enjoyed as situation, process, or character is based on a special kind of laughter-producing contrast. Here what is trifling, humble, or foolish somehow asserts itself over against what is ideal, proper, or even merely superficially dignified. The privileged position of this poetic mood derives from the fact that only by its means can a serious realism show the discrepancy between outer appearance and inner reality, between pretense and true value, between an ideal and its manifestation, and indirectly resolve it into an aesthetic psychic state. This is where an admixture of ugliness can also be aesthetically effective, and where, indeed, a pinch of indecency can be added to the recipe. Jean Paul's *Katzenberger*[128] and many of Dickens' characters exemplify the former, while situations in Sterne and Swift illustrate the latter. We move further down the line of the trifling when we consider the moods in which the *gracefully charming*, the *naive*, and the *petite* are poetically presented or enjoyed.

Poetic moods are related to the laws of the metamorphosis of

[128] *Dr. Katzenbergers Badereise* (1809).

subject matter in ways that are fruitful for causal considerations. An idealizing mood results in things being excluded; the sublime produces intensifications; and we enjoy the graceful even as we disparage it. An extensive field for research in psychological aesthetics opens up here.

8. We distinguish the density, weight, and temperature of a physical object and then investigate these general properties of all objects in isolation; similarly, in the physiology of animals we distinguish the different functions of metabolism, sensation, and voluntary movement; so, too, in a poetic work we distinguish *subject matter, poetic mood, motif, plot, characterization, action*, and *means of representation*. The causal relations within each of these moments of a work of literature will have to be studied. Only in this way will a causal explanation of these creations of the imagination become possible. Let us now discuss *motif*. 216

*The significance of a life-relationship is apprehended in the material of reality through the poetic process. This produces a motivating force which then transforms what was found to be poetically moving. The life-relationship thus apprehended, felt, generalized, and thereby made into a force which is effective in this way is called a "motif." In a major work of literature a number of motifs operate together. Among them a dominating one must have the motivating force to produce the unity of the entire work of literature. The number of possible motifs is limited, and it is one of the tasks of comparative literary history to trace the evolution of particular motifs.*

The transformation of the subject matter by means of the poetic moods that the subject matter can arouse in manifold and contrasting ways is also further dependent on the fact that the life-relationships contained in the subject matter are comprehended in accordance with their significance or their universal value for human feelings. Insofar as a life-relationship is apprehended in its significance, and its representation accordingly receives the motivating force needed to produce a poetic transformation, we call it a "motif." Both Goethe and Schiller make use of this concept. In his maxims, Goethe defines it at least for the narrower domain of tragic literature. This definition is in agreement with the one we have just outlined. "The task and work of the tragic poet is nothing but a psycho-ethical phenomenon, identifiable in the past and presented in a comprehensible experiment."[129] "What we call 'motifs' are thus actually phenomena of the human spirit which have been repeated and will be repeated again and again, but to the poet they display themselves as merely historical."[130] One such motif is the fascination exerted by water, especially a dark body of water at night: it is embodied in the Undine legend.[131]

Reality provides only a *limited number* of motifs. Gozzi[132] has 217 pointed this out; he claimed that there can only be thirty-six (dominant) motifs in a tragedy. This was one of Goethe's favorite topics in his conversations: he discussed it with Eckermann, Schiller, and Kanzler Müller. The organization of motifs delimited in this way can be determined further only by connecting the comparative method of literary history with psychological analysis. Such an approach would also need to study the history of the development of such motifs.

Any major poetic work connects a multiplicity of such motifs, but *one* of them must *predominate*. Through highlighting and the conscious use of motifs, the dark ground of lived experience is illuminated, or its *significance* is at least made partly transparent. I shall illustrate this important relationship by considering *Faust*. Goethe and his contemporaries shared Rousseau's faith in the autonomy of the person and his overall capacities. He thus discovered in himself the lived experience of an individual striving for unlimited development through knowledge, enjoyment, and activity. This striving was supported by the courageous faith that Man "in his dark impulses is nevertheless conscious of the right way."[133] Since this lived experience had its origin in the spiritual condition of the time, it had an extraordinarily strong capacity to arouse interest. It possessed something approximating universal validity. Then Goethe found the symbol for it in the *Faust* legend: a receptacle that could absorb all of the storm and stress, all of the suffering and joy of that day. This content—darkly brilliant, particular, and universal—unfolded only with the course of Goethe's life itself, since life was its object. The poet experienced in succession the turbulent stress of youth and its frightful dangers; then, in Weimar, he ex-

[129] *Sprüche in Prosa*, ed. by Gustav von Löper (Berlin: Hempel, 1870), p. 772. (D)

[130] *Ibid.*, p. 773. (D)

[131] Water nymph legend. Famous fairy tale and opera libretto by the German Romantic poet, F. de la Motte Fouqué (1811).

[132] See Carlo Gozzi, *Mémoires*, 3 vols. (1797).

[133] Goethe, *Faust I*, lines 328-29.

perienced the purification of his heart through intuition and by possessing the world in intuition alone—that *cognitio intuitiva* and that *amor dei intellectualis* of Spinoza grounded in resignation, which in the poet becomes, at the same time, artistic contemplation. On the basis of his aesthetic education, he then developed the power to live and work within an ever more encompassing totality. It is his and Schiller's ideal of human development, drawn from their own deepest experiences and feelings, that determined the course of the Faust poem. To be sure, many motifs were already contained in the Faust legend and others were added by Goethe. This is the way the significance of lived experience is *articulated*. At this point, we again see that a great poem is as irrational and incommensurable at its nucleus as the life that it portrays. Indeed, Goethe has explicitly said this of his *Faust*.

9. When all the genetic moments cooperate, a poetic structure arises amidst the constant metamorphosis. This structure stands before the poet's eyes, as it were, before he can begin the detailed execution. Aristotle's *Poetics* designates this structure as *mythos*,[134] and in our poetics we call it plot (*Fabel* as derived from the Latin *fabula*). Characters and actions are interwoven with one another in the plot. For the person and what he does or undergoes, the hero and his actions are merely two sides of one and the same state of affairs. Without the concrete character of the murderer, the act of murder remains an abstraction. The imagination lives in concrete images alone. 218

*The plot, the developed basic structure of any major work of literature, already exists for the epic or dramatic poet before he begins the execution of the work. It is usually sketched in the form of notes. Literary history possesses sufficient materials to confirm this stage of creativity in such plots and to determine their basic properties and main forms by the comparative method.*

Just as in nature, so, too, within the realm of poetic creativity we find that only a few of the available seeds mature. Literary history has preserved a considerable number of *dramatic* outlines that were never executed. Still more instructive is the comparison

[134] Vahlen's *Beiträge zu Aristoteles' Poetik*, vol. 1, pp. 31ff., treats the dual use of the expression *mythos* in the *Poetics* both for the material which is available to the epic or dramatic poet (the *pragmata* to be worked on) as well as for this developed basic structure (*synthesis tōn pragmatōn*). (D)

of completed dramas with outlines or drafts. We can thereby look into the workshop of Schiller, Lessing, Goethe, Kleist, Otto Ludwig, and overhear some of their studio secrets. Schiller prefaced many outlines with an account of the historical and social situation. In outlining their plots, other poets immediately rush to the main scenes which contain the nucleus of the dramatic effect.

The epic poet does not need a plot which is as tightly structured as that of the dramatic poet. Therefore, the plot of the action which he has in mind does not necessarily require an outline. That Walter Scott generally wrote down his plots seems to be indicated by the following passage in the Introductory Epistle to *The Fortunes of Nigel:*[135]

> CAPTAIN: You should take time at least to arrange your story.
> AUTHOR: That is a sore point with me, my son. Believe me, I have not been fool enough to neglect ordinary precautions. I have repeatedly laid down my future work to scale, divided it into volumes and chapters, and endeavoured to construct a story which I meant should evolve itself gradually and strikingly, maintain suspense, and stimulate curiosity; and which, finally, should terminate in a striking catastrophe. But I think there is a demon who seats himself on the feather of my pen when I write, and leads it astray from the purpose. Characters expand under my hand; incidents are multiplied; the story lingers, while the materials increase; my regular mansion turns out a Gothic anomaly, and the work is closed long before I have attained the point I proposed.

219

Balzac not only wrote down a scenario, but he had it printed in narrow columns on wide sheets. His novel was formed by expanding these scenarios through at least a half dozen different printings.[136]

Spielhagen tells the following in his *Beiträge zur Theorie und Technik des Romans* (Contributions to a Theory and Technique of the Novel),[137] which is rich in technical insights as only the disclosures of a poet could be. Prior to writing he prepares a list of the characters, so far as he already knows them, including their personal characteristics. He also sketches an outline of the plan. A detailed outline is then soon interrupted by the irresistible impulse to proceed with the actual writing itself. During this writing, the plot of an

[135] *Works*, vol. 25 (Boston and New York: Houghton Mifflin Co., 1913), p. xxxi.
[136] See Gautier, p. 3. (D)
[137] Friedrich Spielhagen (Leipzig: L. Saackmann, 1883), p. 26. (D)

epic narrative undergoes changes more frequently than the plot of a drama, because its elements are not as tightly interconnected.

Since the plot is fashioned from characters and actions or events, *two basic forms of its structure* arise. We now advance the thesis that

> *the structure of the plot either has the focal point of its aesthetic effect, and accordingly of its form, in the development of the protagonist or in the play and counterplay of the action. The Latin nations have especially developed the second form both in the drama and the novel. The first form is predominantly represented in the Germanic peoples.*

The Greeks already placed special emphasis on structuring the action into play and counterplay. This was then developed into a peculiar equilibrium between strophe and antistrophe in the semi-musical form of their drama. The Spaniards expended their astonishing acumen in linking gripping and powerful situations into a suspenseful and unexpected action by means of ever new theatrical effects of play and counterplay. One of the most splendid examples of this is the *Weaver of Segovia* by Juan Ruiz de Alarcón [1581-1639]. Classical French tragedy merely simplifed the Spanish technique, and French comedy since Molière has given this form its highest perfection. It is the most poetic expression of the French spirit as such. Even the French novel is usually constructed around a crisis. Similarly, Goethe's *Elective Affinities* certainly is not a novella, but a novel with this structural form. 220

The drama and novel in Germany and England developed a form which did indeed often employ the device of play and counterplay, but in which the development of the hero constitutes the focal point of the poetic effect. What gives Shakespeare's hero his powerful superiority over the characters surrounding him is his ability to keep counsel with himself alone, to wrestle with his conscience, to understand his responsibility and his own nature, and to express it in a soliloquy. The same basic form of the plot is developed in the modern novel. The inexperienced soul who enters the world, the optimist still unfamiliar with the abyss of human nature, and the spirit who joyously rushes into the future only to find the world opposed to him—who needs more details? The epic of our individualistic epoch is built upon this contrast. It is our *Iliad* and *Odyssey*. This is what always happens anew whenever a fresh, young spirit enters the world, and what we all rediscover as our lost youth in *Wilhelm Meister* or *David Copperfield*. Smollett's *Roderick Ran-*

*dom* already shows such a development of a youth who must make his own way through life. Dickens then gave the novel the most perfect form which it has yet attained. His technically best works introduced play and counterplay, suspense and crisis into the development of the hero. Thus they integrate the resources of both approaches.

10. *All further processes in the poet* are permutations of experience from the base we have developed and in accordance with the laws of the imagination. They evoke images which are saturated with the power of feeling and have universal significance. As they strive to impress these images on the imagination of the hearer or reader, they must arouse the imagination into vigorous activity. For that reason too, it is important that the nexus of the literary work—consisting of characters, action, and presentation—provides adequate content for the imagination activated by feeling. Time, space, and the causal nexus must be treated in such a way that the figures can develop and move in the imagination with ease and without resistance. The words and sentences of a work of literature resemble the dabs of color in a late Rembrandt. Only through the cooperation of the imagination of the reader or listener do figures take shape from it. The meaning-content of literature develops as the emotionally barren constituents of life and their mechanically inflexible relations of space, time, and causality are transformed into a poetic world. Such a world is then ideally composed from purely feeling-producing constituents. The *time* that separates and unites these constituents is not measured by the clock, but rather by what happens. Here we find poetry making its own free use of the natural determination of time in accordance with the sequence of inner states. Therefore, the French "unity of time" belongs to a mechanical world, regulated by the clock, but not to the world of the emotions: it produces mathematical prose. An imaginary sense of time can be artificially upheld by avoiding the explicit and external measurement of time as much as possible. Similarly, *spatial locations* are brought closer to one another by invisible but strong relations between persons and actions. Here a good poet will avoid geographic exactness and would rather return, as Shakespeare did, to the geography of the world of fairy tales. The nexus of *cause and effect* is limited to a few necessary components. This nexus could not function this way in reality, and it is only intended to evoke the illusion of reality. Therefore, clever critics have readily pointed to gaps in the causal nexus of *Wilhelm Meister*, *Faust*, even

in the dramas of Shakespeare; but in doing so they have not touched either Goethe or Shakespeare; they only showed that they did not understand the difference between poetry and prose. We need only believe that there is a consistency in the nexus. It is merely the illusion of reality that is to be produced. And this happens not by carefully accounting for everything, but rather by a lean structuring of the action which reduces it to a few components and then expands these into broad scenes that are true to life. Such a fully developed scene leads from a state of tranquility to the highest emotion.

However, since this entire poetic world, including its characters and their destinies, is constituted only in the imagination of the hearer or reader and has its existence there, this world is at the same time subordinated to the laws of the psyche which it enters: the acquired psychic nexus must cooperate in its apprehension. This world must accord with the laws which our intellect has found in reality. It must accurately express the felt values of things as determined by a mature human being. It must display a coherence of will and a connectedness of purpose as acquired through a masculine sense of work. When these demands are met, then the poetic world will produce what is *plausible, probable*, and essential in the illusion of reality—that which characters and their destinies need if they are to arouse pity and fear. 222

*The principle of the production of a work of literature is to raise representations of life to poetically significant images and relations. The nexus of action or events must thus contain, as far as possible, only feeling-producing constituents. Time and space are measured only by the actions that fill them and the relations among these actions. The number of components of the action is reduced as much as possible, but the indispensable components are then unfolded expansively.*

11. From this principle a primary technical rule for action results: the action should not aim to copy reality, but should rather establish an economical nexus by separating out those components of the action that do not arouse feeling from those that do, and thus create the illusion of the movement of life. In a drama, processes are structured by a unifying action; in an epic poem, by an event. But this distinction is of no consequence here, for both the action and the event are unreal and produce an illusion. While in real life everything appears to be causally connected, the *most general law* of the structure of poetic action or events is that they must have a

beginning and an end, between which a uniform continuum must exist, just as we would wish it in real life. Without pain and obstacles the poetic image of life would be insipid and false. However, all discord should be resolved in a final, powerful, but tranquil harmonious chord. Thus the structure of the action is determined by the requirement of a universally valid feeling encompassing the overall scope of the work. When this action is complete, it proceeds from a state of tranquil striving through inner and outer counterforces, amidst increasing tension leading up to a crisis, which then winds down to a final reconciliation. This is also how the metaphysical and conceptual poetry of the declining ancient world, which was dominated by religious consciousness, conceived action in the cosmos: first blissful tranquility, then emerging forces that act against one another, then guilt and pain, and finally the restoration of all things to the original state of bliss. We find, however, that the way in which the *reconciliation* is brought about is *historically conditioned*. Accordingly, the form of the action or the event is not universally valid, but is dependent on the historical content.

The technique of action in the *drama* has been studied in great detail since the time of Aristotle; and recently it has been delineated with a fine sense of form by Freytag. He uncovered two basic configurations of dramatic form, and thereby made a genuine aesthetic discovery—a rare accomplishment. Every action transpires in play and counterplay, for the hero of the action needs an opposing force. This counterforce ought not to reduce our interest in the hero, but merely activate him. The action that results from this leads to a climax which is the decisive middle point of the drama. The action ascends to this point and descends from it. Play and counterplay can be distributed around this decisive point of the construction in two ways. If the protagonistic force predominates in the first part, then the tension of the hero's passions is intensified on the basis of the inner impulses of his character, to the point of action; then a reversal sets in; what he did reacts back upon him; and, as he is gradually overcome by the reaction of the outside world pressing in upon him, the action is dominated by the antagonistic forces. Alternatively, if the antagonistic forces are dominant in the first part, then the hero is driven forward to the climax by the intensifying activity of the forces opposing him; and only after the reversal, which sets in at this point, does the passion of the hero begin to dominate.[138]

223

[138] For a more detailed discussion of dramatic action (especially the demonstration

In the *epic*, processes are linked by an *event*. This event must represent the entire nexus of the world. The most general properties of the epic, which follow from this, have been presented with penetrating force by Humboldt, although he did so with a certain idealistic one-sidedness. The application of his principles to the modern novel, which is the legitimate heir of the epic and capable of being a rigorous artistic form, was first attempted by Spielhagen in his *Beiträge*. This is one of the main tasks for poetics in the future.

12. *The characters first receive an independent life in the poet, based on an as yet obscure property of psychic life, which we can also observe in dreams. Then they receive a second existence in the imagination of the spectator. The imagination forms a character from a nexus of processes, which as such would not be capable of life, by allowing essential traits to crystallize around certain highlighted points that arouse the strongest interest of the feelings, and allowing the others to fade into the twilight. Thus the poetic illusion of a complete reality arises. The comparative history of literature ought to determine the limited number of ways in which typical characters can be articulated, the development of individual types, and the different operations of the imagination in forming and portraying characters.* 224

In *dreams* we confront our own ego with other persons, become startled by them, even feel shame before their superior intellect. For example, an insane woman found herself in constant conflict with a judge whom she blamed for the loss of a lawsuit. This judge was stronger than she, she claimed. He used arguments and legal expressions that she was unable to refute, indeed unable even to understand. Such dissociation of our psychic life and the partial projection of our own spiritual substance into an imagined person presents unresolved difficulties, yet it does provide the basis for pantomime, drama, as well as the independent life of the characters in epic narratives. It can be observed in the theatrical actor, who projects himself into other persons in such a way that while he is acting, his own sense of self partially disappears. It is surely not accidental that two actors, Shakespeare and Molière, lent their characters the most independent life.

---

of the diversity of its structure, which is conditioned by the historical change of its content) I refer the reader to my review of the work by Freytag, *Allgemeine Zeitung*, 26 March, 29 March, 3 April, and 9 April 1863. (D) Reprinted in *Die große Phantasiedichtung*, pp. 132-159.

A character is raised from the given subject matter to the level of producing a universally valid affective response when constituents of human nature that resonate strongly in everyone are connected in essential relations through which they form a causal nexus. Every truly poetic character has, therefore, something *unreal* and *typical* about it. Thus the most effective of Shakespeare's characters provide models for the normal course of a passion in a person susceptible to it. Goethe's main characters, especially Faust, manifest the full reality of personal, lived experience in the diverse moments of their individual lives, but these images of their states are merely juxtaposed. The epic or dramatic portrayal of a character merely consists in the concrete presentation of individual scenes; the fullness of a character exists nowhere in the work, but first in the poet's head and then in the imagination of the hearer or listener. Although the character is unreal, he receives the illusion of reality through an artistic device which renders our perception of him similar to that of real persons. The most intense and bright light of our interest focuses on individual moments of life that arouse our feelings. These moments are related to one another in perceivable ways, and they permit the unity of the character to be surmised. Just as in real life, these moments are anticipated by less pronounced 225 moments. Thus there arises, so to speak, a rounding-off of life. [A counterexample is] a drama like *Emilia Galotti*,[139] which, being composed of purely emotional moments, lacks the serene and healthy qualities of human existence. What is essential and typical in the character must be clearly illuminated with everything else appearing to gradually fade into the background. Thus the poet works like the painter. He, too, exhibits only what falls within the scope of interest and attention, and the focused perception that results therefrom. Because of this he challenges our observation of reality itself. A painter who strives to show everything produces no illusion. The impression of reality is even further strengthened if, as in life itself, something impenetrable remains in the nucleus of the character. This is always the case when the poet's imagination is simultaneously both so powerful and so realistic that it does not smooth out the jagged edges or remove the irregularities from its material. The irrationality that results has an extremely lifelike effect. As in a Rembrandt painting the features emerge only partially, enigmatically, and not in perfect balance—they seem to emerge from a mysterious twilight.

[139] Lessing (1772).

The portrayal of what is typical and essential in a character is only made possible by the extreme liveliness of the poet's inner processes. Given that the conditions of the character portrayed are simplified, the imagination alone can activate these processes. One process then leads to another with such consistency that the illusion produced comes to resemble nature. Thus we can explain the repeated and somewhat curious remarks of Goethe that he "could anticipate a multiplicity of human states." "In general, I took pleasure in portraying my inner world before becoming acquainted with the outer one. When I subsequently found in reality that the world was the way I had conceived it to myself, I found it irksome, and I had no more desire to portray it, indeed I would say that had I waited until I was acquainted with the world before portraying it, my representation would have turned into persiflage."[140] "My idea of women is not abstracted from the phenomena of actual life, but has been born with me, or arisen in me, God knows how. The female characters . . . are all better than they could be found in reality."[141] He knew very well how the apprehension of the structure or typical essence of a character is grounded in this inner necessity with which this character's traits condition one another, but he failed to understand the basis of our acquaintance with it. "There is in characters a certain necessity, a certain coherence, by means of which certain secondary traits accompany this or that basic trait of a character. Empirical observation teaches us this sufficiently; however, the knowledge of this can also be innate in some individuals."[142] 226

*13. The means of poetic representation are generated when the goals of literature—sensuous intensity which creates illusion, the arousal of feeling which produces lasting satisfaction, the generalization and orientation of particulars relative to a reflective framework which gives significance to lived experience—enliven the entire body of the literary work, even the individual words, the finger tips of this body, as it were. Thus sensory illustrations or images, graphic expressions, figures, tropes, meter, and rhyme arise. Poetics has to show how the nature of poetic creativity, active in the nucleus of the plot, finally manifests itself in these means of representation. Thus, the strong movement of feeling which produced the action is*

[140] Eckermann, *Gespräche*, 26 February 1824.

[141] Eckermann, *Gespräche*, 22 October 1828; *CE*, p. 342.

[142] Eckermann, *Gespräche*, 26 February 1824.

*also finally expressed in figures of speech. Accordingly, the relation of inner states to images contained in the nucleus of lived experience and through which the plot becomes a symbol is at the same time so much the spiritual form of the creativity of great poets that many means of representation derive from this relation.*

In the rhetoric and poetics of the ancients, the theory of the means of representation underwent an exemplary development from the standpoint of the *analysis of form*. Scaliger's *Poetics*,[143] with its extraordinarily subtle treatment of these forms, was still related to the theory of the ancients, just as the classical French theory of tragic action was to Aristotle.

Still to be developed is a *dynamic mode of analyzing* means of representation based on the causal knowledge of linguistics. The principles for carrying out this task were sketched in our psychological foundation. Their application is governed by the following principle: the nature of poetic creativity which fashions the motifs, plot, characters, and actions from the subject matter is still operative in the individual means of representation—even in every single syllable—and the forms enumerated by classical rhetoric and poetics must be interpreted on the basis of this creativity.

Let us first illustrate the above with *tropes*. The real nucleus of poetry, lived experience, contains a relation of the inner and the outer. "Spirit and garment," animation and embodiment, the significance of a sequence of shapes or sounds, and the visual image for an ephemeral psychic state—an artist sees these relations everywhere. He even discerns and appreciates a tacit creative life and tranquil energy in stones and flowers. 227

The supreme principle of understanding the world does indeed lie in the psychophysical nature of man, which he then transfers to the entire world. There exist *stable lawful relations* between *inner states* and *outer images* which manifest themselves in dreams and insanity as well as in language, myth, and metaphysical and conceptual poetry. If we conceive a natural symbol as an image that stands in a stable, lawful relation to an inner state, then comparative considerations show that our psychological nature provides the basis for a sphere of natural symbols found in dreams and insanity, as well as for those found in language, myth, and poetry. For example, if one side of our body has become numb by lying on it,

[143] Julius Caesar Scaliger (1484-1558). Author of *Poetices Libri Septum* (1561), the most influential poetics of the Renaissance.

then we imagine in our dream that someone is lying next to us; or if pressure has put our hand to sleep, it will appear to belong to another body in our dream. Griesinger[144] has pointed out that certain inner states or feelings of an insane person manifest themselves in the belief that his ideas are either "produced by" or "derived from" someone else; and Lazarus has called attention to the fact that primitive peoples have similar beliefs.[145] Thus the inner states of the insane are expressed in a sphere of impoverished, truncated symbols. These relations are unfolded in a richer and freer manner in language, myth, and poetry, but still in accordance with laws. Even the basic myths that illuminate external, distant and transcendent phenomena by means of the lived experience of our own inner nature are limited in number.

These processes of embodiment and enlivening operate with the greatest energy and freedom in the psyche of the poet. That is shown in each of Goethe's notes to Frau von Stein: in every case there is a situation, a feeling about his state, and a trope in which he expresses himself. We learn from this that the image, the comparison, the trope, are not added in the presentation like a garment thrown over a body; rather they are its natural skin, so to speak. The formation of symbols, which is the heart of the poetic process, extends throughout the body of the literary work—it encompasses personification and metaphor, synecdoche and metonymy. What often offends our sense of taste in the abundance of images in Shakespeare or Calderón,[146] is precisely the uninhibited flow and stream of this constantly sparkling movement of the poetic imagination. The analyses of the forms of trope, which the ancients have bequeathed to us, can become the starting point for a deeper knowledge on the basis of our causal approach.

228

We can illustrate this with rhetorical-poetic *figures of speech*. All poetic creativity reveals the influence of feelings on the movement of representations. The feverish tempo of the characters and the action in Shakespeare, and the grandeur of Schiller's dramatic action, are the natural expressions of the affective and volitional styles of these great men. Even the ordering of the words in sentences and the choices of figures of speech derive from this natural movement

[144] Dilthey reviewed the 4th ed. of W. Griesinger's *Pathologie und Therapie der psychischen Krankheiten* (Braunschweig: F. Wreden, 1876). See *GS*, XVII, 71.

[145] Moritz Lazarus, *Das Leben der Seele, in Monographien über seine Erscheinungen und Gesetze*, vol. 1 (Berlin: Dümmler, 1876).

[146] Pedro Calderón de la Barca (1600-81). Spanish poet whose works (121 secular and 73 religious dramas) represent the high point of the Spanish theater.

of the soul. Hyperbole and understatement are thus merely the final and most palpable expressions of the laws according to which images are intensified or reduced, expanded or condensed, under the influence of feeling. Efforts to intensify the strength of a feeling by means of contrast produce those tensions in the actions or the characters which belong to the inner structure of a work, but they finally resonate in a rhetorical antithesis. We designate the inner form of a work, from the initial process of extricating the motifs from the subject matter to the working out of the tropes, figures, meter, and language, as the style of the work. Various attempts have been made to discover the basic distinctions of style. Vischer's distinction between *direct and indirect idealization* must be called a genuine aesthetic discovery.[147]

## Chapter Three. The Historicity of Poetic Technique

1. We have noted again and again that the goals and methods of the various literary genres cannot be derived through combining the principles of poetic receptivity. Thus, they do not contain a universally valid technique. If we take the principles of poetic receptivity, seek to arrange impressions according to them in an optimally perfect way, select from among the possibilities which contain the individual moments of inner form, mood, motif, plot, etc., those that are most favorable and correspond most to one another, even then a real decision as to their most perfect combination in a novel or drama will never result from these formal relations. They result in mere shadows and transient possibilities which are not clearly determined either in themselves or in their relations. If we dissect the impression which an artwork produces, we find that the principles of receptivity are highly composite and that the moments of inner form according to which it is composed are very numerous. The purity and magnitude of the impression are conditioned by all of these. But the impression is ultimately dependent on the inner *connection* which exists *between* the *meaning-content*, which has

[147] Friedrich Theodor Vischer (1807-87), author of the three-volume *Aesthetik, oder Wissenschaft des Schönen* (Reutlingen und Leipzig: Carl Mäcken's Verlag, 1846-57). The contrast between these two modes of idealization is formulated by Vischer in Section 657: According to the law of direct idealization, each particular form must be beautiful. This is superseded by the law of indirect idealization which produces beauty from the cooperation of a plurality of forms which need not themselves be beautiful. See vol. 3, pp. 533f., 1190f.

developed *historically*, and the *form belonging to it.* The principles of receptivity and their rule-governed connection in the inner form 229 operate throughout the whole work; but what gives it the character of great art is the link whereby this form proves to belong inseparably to a historically developed and powerful content.

Thus we obtain the first principle which expounds the historicity of technique. It expresses our opposition to every formalistic aesthetics, but also to every aesthetics which, like Fechner's, is based on the summation of effective elements.

*The principles of the poetic receptivity and the possibilities of effectively connecting powerful components into an inner form establish a technical framework for the poetic work only when a historically developed content attains its proper form by using these means.*

2. We would like to penetrate the nature of this historicity of poetic technique and comprehend more exactly the relation between the historically developed content and its form.

This meaning-content is presented as a unity. Accordingly, it might seem that the historical continuum could be developed in terms of logical relations between univocal positions. In this way, the Hegelians have ruined our understanding of modern philosophy with their fiction of the logical unfolding of one standpoint from another. In reality, *a historical situation* contains, first of all, *a multiplicity of particular facts.* They stand next to one another indifferently and cannot be traced back to one another. They reflect such givens as the original distribution of water and land, mountains and plains, climate, and perhaps even original variations among human beings. In the play and counterplay of historical forces that takes place against this backdrop, the effects become consolidated into impenetrable facts. Their coordination within a given period first constitutes the historical situation.

The causal nexus produces a relationship of mutual dependence and thus of inner relatedness between groups of these facts. Thus the constitution and education of a people of a given period stand in such a relationship of reciprocal dependence and affinity. Then an intensively and widely operative factor inevitably produces effects in a large number of these coordinated facts which impart a common imprint, a mark of kinship, to all of these. Thus, the rational and mechanistic spirit of the seventeenth century put its stamp on the poetry, the politics, and the warfare of that period. 230

Furthermore, human work always relates facts into the unity of a purposive whole, and where such a purposive whole is successful, it always becomes the model for many others. In the coordination of facts that constitute a historical age, these causes and a large number of others generate *reciprocities* and *affinities*, with the consequence that this *coordination can be compared to a system.* All of this is contained in Comte's concept of social consensus, which, of course, has still broader implications.

But the *unity* of a period and a people that we characterize as the *historical spirit* of an age can only arise from these elements through the *creative power* and self-assurance of a genius. Knowledge or artistic creativity can produce a unity in, among, and between these indifferent facts—a unity which is made possible by this coordination of facts in a given age. That happens through that most comprehensive and creative method of combination of which human genius is capable in the area of sensing, contemplating, and thinking. The genius of the ruler or the statesman forges isolated facts into a purposive unity which their coordination makes possible. The aim of this kind of genius is very different from that of the artist and the philosopher, but they are akin with respect to scope and greatness.

*In religion and philosophy, in art and especially in poetry, the coordination of constituents which exists in a particular time, and already contains in itself causal relations and affinities, is connected through a historically creative process into a unity which transcends what is given. Thus, it is the achievement of genius to first produce that unity which we characterize as the spirit of an age from an original manifold, its constituents, and their individual relations.*

3. This is the point at which we can bring together *historical* and *psychological* considerations. We have already expounded a psychological concept of the acquired nexus of our psychic life and related it to the creative work of the poet. In a great man this acquired nexus represents the available structure of coordinated facts, i.e., principles, value determinations, and purposes in a sensitive and accurate manner. It then influences the processes which occur in consciousness. The poetic work thus becomes the mirror of the period. In *Hamlet*, Shakespeare has formulated this achievement of poetry with artistic awareness, at least for drama: "[T]he purpose of playing, whose end, both at the first and now, was and is, to hold, as 'twere, the mirror up to nature, to show virtue her

231

own feature, scorn her own image, and the very age and body of the time his form and pressure."[148] Here we can solve the riddle of how an age can become thematic both to itself and to us in the plots, actions, and characters of its poets. The acquired nexus of the psychic life of a great man is causally conditioned and thus represents the coordination of the constituents of the life, thought, feeling, and striving of a period. Since the acquired nexus is formed in the processes we have been considering, those aspects of reality which are related to one another, or their causal structure, are already apprehended in this nexus, and thus it already accentuates what is essential in the phenomena of life. This overall nexus, although not clearly and distinctly differentiated according to constituents and relations, works as a whole to condition the processes in the poet through which representations of life are elevated to poetic images. We have described in detail how this occurs. The plot, action, and characters represent this nexus. Literary figures, filled with meaning, are surrounded by an aura of significance which derives from the framework of an understanding of the world, for this framework conditions the way the essential structure of the characters and their interrelations are brought into relief. Goethe sensed this about the figures of his great poem *Faust*, referring to "the magic breath that hovers round their course."[149] It is always the spirit of an age.

*Psychologically, the contribution of the poetic genius is made possible by the fact that the acquired nexus of his psychic life is conditioned by the coordination of the constituents of an age. The nexus thus represents this coordination. In turn, the poetic processes taking place in consciousness and their results—plot, action, character, means of representation—are conditioned by this acquired nexus and thus themselves represent this nexus.*

4. The historicity of poetic technique was already implicit in our psychological foundation. For its most significant result was that *the principles of poetic creativity as well as of poetic effect are pervasive properties of very complex processes* through which the lasting satisfaction of the creator and the spectator are attained. 232 These principles constitute a *numerically indeterminate manifold within which thought cannot produce the relations of a logical*

[148] *Hamlet*, act 3, scene 2, lines 19-23.

[149] From Dedication of *Faust*, line 8. *F*, p. 65.

*system*. This thesis provided us with the principle of an empirical and therefore psychological aesthetics, as opposed to idealistic aesthetics, which is fundamentally metaphysical. On the other hand, since we took the poet's creative process as our point of departure, rather than Herbart's simple enumeration of unrelated aesthetic ideas or Fechner's unrelated principles of pleasurable effect, we arrived at an even more fundamental unity for aesthetics through the psychological analysis of creation and understanding. But the necessary correlate of our thesis is the following: On the basis of the norms of poetic creativity as well as the principles of the poetic impression, it is the *achievement of the poetic genius* to produce a *form* and thus the *technique* of a *literary genre* from the factual *multiplicity of the given life of a period*; this form is thus *historically conditioned and relative*.

An insight into ultimate questions is opened up. If it were within the power of our knowledge and our attitude to the world to obtain a universally valid understanding of the world, then the works of poets would do so thousandfold as in more or less perfect mirrors. There are indeed universally valid features in our experience which point beyond us to an inner nexus of the world. A glance at the immeasurable expanse of the heavens show us the intelligibility of the cosmos. And turning back into ourselves, we find that whenever a person's will breaks through the nexus of perception, desire, impulse, and enjoyment, and is no longer concerned merely with himself, an experience results which I have characterized as metaphysical consciousness in contrast to the changing metaphysical systems.[150] It is also a consequence of this that all great and true poetry exhibits common traits. It requires the consciousnesss of the freedom and responsibility of our actions as well as the consciousness of the nexus of our actions in accordance with cause and effect. The theory that our actions are externally and mechanically determined will never evoke a lasting conviction in a great poet. But neither philosophical thought nor poetic creation can derive a universally valid understanding of the world from these obscure, disconnected traits. The understanding of the world which they are capable of producing is conditioned by, and relative to, the historical situation of consciousness. This, then, is what poetic form is dependent on.

233 Poetic form arises only through a transformation of representations of life into aesthetic constituents and relations. It is thus al-

[150] See *Introduction to the Human Sciences*, Book II, in *SW*, vol. 1.

ready conditioned by the coordination of the realities of life and their representations, which constitute the character of an age. The selection and exclusion of constituents, their transformation, accentuation, and overall connection are historically conditioned. The way in which a period understands the world determines both which representations of life are elicited by feeling and the direction in which it develops them into poetic constituents and relations. This understanding of the world brings out something essential in the characters. It gives significance to the action. It opens up broad perspectives through affinity and contrast between the characters. It creates a specific kind of unity in the dramatic action. And it does all this precisely on the basis of the actual affinities, contrasts, structural unities, and reciprocal effects which the life of the age places at its disposal.

The important concept of the *historical types of technique* in a literary genre arises from such considerations. Friedrich Schlegel characterized these types as schools—a characterization which, following Winckelmann,[151] he borrowed from the visual arts. I shall illustrate this concept using drama as an example.

Gustav Freytag derived the following schema of dramatic form from the simple relations of the disturbing forces within a unitary action, which are then relentlessly driven toward a tragic conclusion through passion. The drama has the structure of a pyramid: it ascends from the exposition through the increasing intensity of a disturbing moment, to the climax, and declines from this point to the catastrophe. Thus, two further parts—intensification and decline—are added to the three original parts—ascending exposition, climax, and catastrophe. These five parts are in turn articulated into scenes and groups of scenes, although the climax usually comprises one main scene. Three important points separate and connect these five parts: these are the disturbing moment between the exposition and intensification; the tragic moment between the climax and the reversal; and, finally, as a structural device, the moment of ultimate suspense between the reversal and the catastrophe. Thus eight phases of a drama are to be distinguished. Furthermore, every one of these eight phases has its own specific delineation according to its position in the whole of the dramatic structure. With the ease of a technically experienced playwright and of a fine critical mind, Gustav Freytag developed in this law of dramatic form the dynamic

[151] Johann Joachim Winckelmann (1717-68). German art historian and archeologist.

relations in an action driven forward by a passion, which then 234 encounters a reaction and thus hastens toward a catastrophe. However, those are not the characteristics of great drama in general, but rather of a specific type of drama.

The *technique of the Greek drama* is as much determined by a historical content of life as that of the Spanish or English. Stemming from the dithyrambs of the festival of Dionysus, the gripping content of Attic tragedy consists in the fact that the innermost, holy nucleus of faith suddenly confronted the contemporary Athenian with sensory reality and emotional power. And since the myths of the clans and the gods involved the fate of several generations, the encompassing form of the tragic trilogy—based on the organization of the stage, the participation of music and conventions of rhetoric—was developed in the creative mind of Aeschylus. When the understanding of these presuppositions gradually faded after the decline of the old clan structure and the old faith, the form of the tragic trilogy also dissolved.

Whereas the Attic trilogy was unfolded from a simple seed into well-tempered, rhythmical proportions, the Spanish and English theater progressed from the colorful, crude, and disorderly adventures of the popular stage to the creation of an integrated dramatic type. This development took place in those two nations through many original experiments, in constant confrontation with the form and theory inherited from the Greeks. In both cases it was a creative individual who succeeded in finding the type of a new form. However, the kinds of theater for which Lope de Vega and Shakespeare established their form were as different from each other as the life of the people in Spain and England at that time. Lope de Vega wrote in the *New Art of Writing Plays*: "In the happy age, when the glorious monarchs Ferdinand and Isabella conquered Granada, when Columbus discovered America, the Inquisition was launched and, at the same time, our comedy, so that everyone would be encouraged to perform good and heroic actions by being shown the deeds of great men." It is in this sense that Lope de Vega designated questions of honor and virtuous actions as the subject matter most suited to drama. Drama of this type is thus not characterized by a tragic ending, but rather begins with a conflict and generally proceeds through play and counterplay to a crisis in which honor is established or virtuous action is rewarded. It is not unusual for the monarch or his representative to make a *deus ex machina* appearance as an absolute Catholic presence in order to establish 235 justice or to repair whatever damage to honor that might remain.

The entire scope of a poet's talent is concentrated on complicating the action by means of ever new theatrical devices, on conjoining the most colorful contrasts of life, and on maintaining the suspense to the end. Lope de Vega notes expressly that since the Spanish want to see much in a few hours, the unities of time and place cannot be preserved; only the unity of action must be observed. "It is not possible to remove any part of the plot without thereby damaging the whole." Many attempts were made to tame the unruliness of the English popular stage with the methods of Seneca's theater and with the rules of the ancients. Then came Shakespeare, who, in a genuinely Protestant way, finds the nucleus of his dramatic form in the character, passion, and conscience of his hero.

*The form of a work of literature and the technique of a literary genre are historically conditioned on the basis of its meaning-content. The history of literature must elucidate the historical types of technique employed in the specific genres of literature.*

5. Amidst this historical variability of poetic form and technique as well as the variability of impression and taste, *stable lawful relationships* emerge, which the history of literature will gradually confirm through the comparative method. A particular type of literary genre develops at a determinate historical place, usually by means of a rapid formative process, and it receives its character, coloring, scope, and form from this soil. Since there exists a general process of consolidating what can be preserved in representations—which is limited only by inconsistencies in the tradition—specific moments of form develop and unfold in history. Poetic moods are expressed in major works and are passed on through these works, not only to the public, but also to the poets who follow. Motifs are extracted from the fullness of lived experience, and their motive force and applicability manifests itself. Character types are developed, their structure becomes transparent, and the art of intuiting characters poetically is handed down to poets by their predecessors. From the structuring of the action to the most intricate subtleties of meter, we find ever more ways in which technique is transmitted. If we now compare the historical types within a genre of literature, *two kinds of series* can be formed which display *constant relations.* Within the same nation there exists a lawlike progression from a religious, sublime style to a state of equilibrium and from there to the moving and passionate, technically effective and complex style, 236 as Scaliger, Winckelmann, and Friedrich Schlegel discovered. If we

construct a series of the types of form of a literary genre, proceeding through the entire continuum of our culture, but omitting those parts characterized by the imperfect assimilation of earlier culture, then another very important lawlike relation emerges. As life becomes more complex, as its constituents and their relations to one another grow more manifold, and especially as more and more emotionally impoverished technological factors intrude between those moments that we experience with feeling, it requires greater power to raise the content of life to poetic form. Correspondingly, the form which is to solve the problem must become, internally at least, more complicated. Popular modes of fiction, which play with this multiplicity informally, become more prevalent. Genuine works of literature, which attain an integral form through artistic simplification, require an ever greater degree of genius.

*Lawlike relations between these types of poetic form can be discovered by linking poetics to the comparative history of literature. Within a nation there exists a lawful sequence of style forms. To the extent that the constituents of life become more manifold in human history and the number of technical, emotionally impoverished moments increases, a greater power is required to elevate the content of life to poetic form.*

6. *The future of poetry* cannot be predicted on the basis of its past. But poetics teaches us to apprehend and appreciate with historical sensibility the living forces of the present and the coming-into-existence of art forms based on them. For the term "classical" does not designate what corresponds to certain rules; rather, a work is classical to the extent that it still provides us a complete satisfaction in the present and has a broad and continuing impact.

A poetics based upon psychology makes possible, above all, the recognition of the *social function of literature*; the feeling of the dignity of the poetic vocation rests upon this recognition. In antiquity, poetry was not yet distinguished from speech, religion, myth, and metaphysical thought. None of man's historical attitudes can ever be completely expressed in concepts. The urge to communicate the inexpressible is the source of symbols. Myths grasp the most important relationships of reality from a religious point of view. Since these relationships are all related to one another and since 237 the human heart is always the same, basic myths pervade humanity. They involve symbols such as the relationship of a father to his children, the relation of the sexes, battle, plunder and victory, images of the land of the blessed and of paradise. In such symbols the external, distant, and transcendent is always made visible on the basis of the lived experience of one's own inner life. Relationships which extend from reality to the beyond are interpreted on the basis of relations which are familiar to our emotional life. Just as the number of basic myths is limited, so too is the number of elementary symbols which recur in the religious rituals of all peoples. Examples of such ritual symbols include icons, sacrifices, funeral rites, banquets, and bonfires.

As if by an elemental power, lived experiences were elevated to poetic significance through speech, religion, and mythical thought; similarly, nature was animated, the spiritual was given embodiment, and reality was idealized. Only gradually did poetry free itself from this mythical context. Ever since then poetry has become increasingly independent. The unity of the spiritual realm created in the Middle Ages by connecting theology and metaphysics has been gradually dissolved since the fifteenth century. The extensive attention that was then given to metaphysical constructions is now given to religion and art. Shakespeare, Cervantes, or Ariosto[152] found unpretentious and naive ways of expressing the meaning of life without venturing to challenge theology or philosophy. Richardson, Sterne, and Swift, Rousseau and Diderot, Goethe and Schiller asserted the right of genius to expound the meaning of life in images derived from their feelings; but they still sought a relationship to metaphysical thought. In our day the path has been totally cleared for poetic genius. Since religion has lost the support of metaphysical arguments for the existence of God and the soul, for a great number of people today only art and literature can still provide an ideal conception of the meaning of life. Poetry is pervaded by the feeling that it itself must furnish the authentic interpretation of life. Indeed, even the extravagances of the French novel, which seems to be competing with the social sciences, are grounded in this consciousness. For the time being the French novel occupies a terrain surrounded by a morass: let us hope that someday genuine literature will come to bloom there.

The place assigned to poetry by modern man will be determined by the following considerations. Contemporary man wants to make of life whatever can be made of it by the art of living. For the faith of reflective experience in its unlimited capacity seems to be corroborated anew daily. But modern man can only fulfill his capacity 238

[152] Ludovico Ariosto (1474-1533). Italian poet of the Renaissance, and the father of Renaissance Italian comedy.

to the extent that he knows the nexus of causality and the meaning of life. The sciences of nature and of society have the causal nexus of all appearances as their object. Yet, the meaning of life and of external reality can never be grasped by them. This meaning can only be grasped individually and subjectively through life-experience. Literature gives an intensified expression to the experiences of life and of the heart. It presents the beauty of life amid its bitterness, the dignity of the person amid his limitations. Here we reach the highest of the successive levels of the functions of poetry. The connecting links that lead from the previously discussed most general and elementary function of all literature to this, its highest accomplishment, have been indicated everywhere; the reader can supplement what we have said.

Modern poetics renders a further service to the poetry of the present by recognizing the historical nature of technique and thus acquainting our contemporary poets with the rules flowing from the nature of man and the *artistic devices* acquired through historical experience. On the other hand, it *frees* poetry *from the shackles of inherited forms and rules*. The poetics of our great poets still strove to subject epic poetry to the basic laws of Homeric form, and the poetics of Freytag and Otto Ludwig still subjected our drama to the form of Shakespeare. The poetics which we have outlined offers the poet the principles which govern the poetic impression and the norms by which poetic creativity is bound. But it has at the same time demonstrated the historical relativity of even the most perfect form. Its aims are to encourage the contemporary poet to seek a new form and technique for the substance of his age and to see his highest law in a lasting, universally satisfying effect.

Furthermore, we can already see in vague outlines the new forms in which the poetic content of our age and our people can find its expression.

The Germanic peoples will always place a hero, rather than a destiny or a crisis, at the center of the work of literature. *Nathan the Wise*, *Iphigenia*, and *Faust* already completely transcend the nexus of passion, guilt, and catastrophe. Here we see the broad and free presentation of a heroic soul, conditioned in many ways, both guilty and guiltless, struggling with reality and finally overcoming it. This is also what is dramatically gripping in the tone-poems of Richard Wagner: they are capable of setting forth heroic images and expressing the fascination of heroism. Only the powerful, realistically portrayed whole person, the heroic man who struggles with himself and with reality and remains triumphant however badly he

239

has been bruised, can have the kind of elevating and redemptive effect on modern man that the tragic trilogy once had on the contemporaries of Aeschylus.

And what is this hero's world? Modern man, since the time that most of his literary works began to be preserved, has produced two great social systems and has portrayed their emotional content in two golden ages of literature. We are living at the dawn of a third age. Feudal society was based on the institution of permanent warfare, whether on a small or a large scale, the strength of its soldiers, and the resulting distribution of property. Courage in warfare, feudal fidelity, chivalrous love and honor, and the Catholic faith were the motives that activated men at that time. Epic poetry was the creation and the mirror of this age. Then monarchies created nation-states with administrative structures that subordinated the feudal lords. More latitude and freedom of movement was created for commerce, industry, and scientific thought in these centralized states. The modern theater was the creation and mirror of this age. One still hears the war cries of the last battles between the monarchy and the feudal lords on the stage of Shakespeare and Lope de Vega. The French theater represented the epoch of the absolute monarchy in its strongest and most refined feelings. During the crises of his life, as on the battlefields of the Seven Years War, Frederick the Great, the greatest king of modern Europe, found the expression for his heroic feeling of life in the verses of Racine. For Racine's characters both spoke and acted regally. Frederick also delighted in the sovereign way in which understanding plays with life and love in Voltaire's verses. The French poetry of the classical age had, accordingly, a historical value which the history of literature must recognize. A new epoch dawned with the French Revolution. A new world age, whose dark, ominous outlines are beginning to emerge, 240 can be characterized by the following basic traits: the transformation of life through science, a world-industrial system based on machines, work, or labor as the exclusive foundation of the social order, war against social parasites for whose idle pleasure others pay the cost, a new, proud feeling of mastery by man, who, having subordinated nature, will now lessen even the blind effects of passions in society. Yet over against such a rationalistic regulation of all the affairs of what is ultimately an irrational and unreasonable planet, society has also developed a historical consciousness that preserves what has been achieved already. Various nations have developed a feeling of their own identity through the workings of their parliament and press. The heroism of our century is rooted in the struggles generated there.

Slowly, poetry has begun the difficult task of finding the forms in which such a colossal content can be expressed. The drama of Shakespeare has been transformed by Schiller and Goethe. Goethe invented the hero who confidently lives out his life expressing his entire powerful being. Schiller's artistic genius captured the world-historical conflicts between absolute monarchy and freedom, between the Catholic Church and the spirit of Protestantism: thus he developed the tragedy of equally justified historical forces. To this day, German tragedy follows in the footsteps of Shakespeare and Schiller. Who can tell when and how a genius will discover a new drama, based on the foundations laid by Goethe and Schiller, in which a hero of our time will address us directly from the stage to both rouse us and reconcile us?

The emotionally impoverished technological factors in our life have undermined the metrical form of epic poetry. The novel has assumed the dominant role. Given the conditions of our age, the novel alone can fulfill the old task of epic literature, that is, furnish a free, contemplative view of the nexus of the real world. Simple circumstances close to nature, as selected by Goethe in his *Hermann and Dorothea*, can be produced by a pure nexus of completely poetic situations, whose appropriate form is metrical. However, today we are expected to understand the major centers of life in their essence and significance. Thus, the French novel has attempted to capture the soul of Paris, and Dickens has portrayed London as a single, colossal creature despite all its contrasts. Since we Germans now have a capital city, a new task exists for the German novel; and whoever solves it will be the most widely read author in our nation. Here too, the focus will be on struggling with the reality of contemporary life as it is. Of course, the insight that there can be an art form for prose which is just as rigorous as the metrical form will have to be accepted first. It was the great service of Friedrich Schlegel that he first made prose aesthetically respectable, partic- 241 ularly through his studies of Boccaccio and Lessing. The theory of the novel is the most immediate, and by far the most pressing and important task of contemporary poetics. The naturalistic novel of the school of the *Comédie humaine*, Flaubert and Zola, gives us poetry without a victorious hero, crises without actual reconciliation. Only from the heart of the masterful Dickens—who could share the feelings of children, the feeble-minded, and the poor—did the socially conscious novel develop. And only from the depths of the German historical consciousness was the first genuine historical novel created in Arnim's *Kronenwächtern* (Keepers of the Crown). Conrad Ferdinand Meyer is creative in finding ways to allow historical men to emerge clearly from the obscurity of time. Everything is in movement leading toward the unknown, like that society which the novel of the future will want to capture!

There is a core to the meaning of life, as the poet would like to portray it, which is the same for all ages. Thus, there is something eternal about a great poet. But man is simultaneously a historical creature. When a new social order has been instituted and the meaning of life has changed, the poets of the preceding epoch no longer move us as they once moved their contemporaries. This is our situation today. We are awaiting the poet who can speak to us about our sufferings, our joys, and our struggles with life!

# 2

# *The Three Epochs of Modern Aesthetics and Its Present Task (1892)*[1]

VI, 242

TRANSLATED BY MICHAEL NEVILLE

Would that the demand for beauty finally be given up and once and for all replaced by the demand for truth!

—*Schiller to Goethe, 7 July 1797*[2]

It is one of the most vital tasks of contemporary philosophy to re-establish, through the further development of aesthetics, the natural relationship among art, criticism, and an engaged public. This relationship has always been very difficult to maintain, but that is to be expected. We know how much attention and effort Goethe and Schiller devoted to this relationship, and how today it is particularly wanting. The creative artist has always been very sensitive about criticism that violates the lovingly formed organic unity of his work. But he is currently developing a special dislike of aesthetics for its abstract speculations about beauty which prevailed for so long at the universities.

In the days of Boileau, Lessing, or Wilhelm Schlegel, criticism found a fixed standard in the prevailing aesthetic theory. Today, however, in relation to his new tasks, the critic is too often forced to judge on the basis of his own *ad hoc* reflections. No consensus

[1] This is the translation of "Die drei Epochen der modernen Ästhetik und ihre heutige Aufgabe," first published in *Die Deutsche Rundschau*, vol. 18 (1892), pp. 267-303. Reprinted in *GS*, VI, 242-87, to which pagination in the margin refers.

[2] This is not a verbatim quotation.

exists among the public which can sustain the artist striving to attain higher goals. A lively exchange between aesthetic reflection and aesthetic culture is thus lacking in the leading circles of our society.

If the artist, the aesthetician, the critic, and the public are to influence one another and to learn from one another, aesthetics must proceed from an unbiased understanding of the vast artistic movement within which we live today. And a few displeasing works of art produced by this new movement should not make aesthetics blind or deaf to its legitimacy.

The beginnings of this artistic movement lie far back in the past. However, it seems to me that the generation directly influenced by 243 the July Revolution of 1830 was the first to break away completely from classicism and romanticism. Then, as in 1848, one could still clearly hear the rumble of the oncoming legions determined to bring about the transformation of European society in accordance with the principles of a thoroughly secular and earth-centered spiritual life. The soil of the old Europe trembled. The view of life which had been developing since the fifteenth century and which had found its expression in art from Leonardo da Vinci and Shakespeare through Goethe was disintegrating. The broad outlines of a new view, still indistinct, began to emerge on the horizon. The recognition of this European situation became the source of a new literature and art, which in turn provided evidence for the power of the suddenly changed life-mood that was setting in. I shall try to delineate this new trend in three theses.

In the first place, this literature has sought to express the oppressive feeling that the structures of life in society have become old, senile, and untenable. In Paris, this new literature developed side by side with socialism. These writers describe, and in describing they undermine. They both savor their worm-eaten civilization and hate it. They are enraptured with it, and then point their fingers at the sickness and death within it. However, analysis is only possible on the basis of an entirely correct, thorough, and precise presentation of the facts. Secondly, the new poetry seeks to be naturalistic. It wants to manifest reality, as it actually is, and to analyze it as do the sciences of anatomy and physiology. Whatever is alive and dynamic in human and social terms, whatever each of us experiences in his own life and in his own soul—if it has not already fallen under the knife of science—is placed under the dissecting knife of these new poets. Thus they prefer psychological depth to action. Their aim is to know. The center of this movement is Paris and its dominant ideas are shared equally by Balzac, Taine, and Zola; their strongest literary impulse is to bring out the physiological, indeed the bestial, aspects of human nature, i.e., the irresistible instincts for which the intellect merely lights the way.

The same tendencies assert themselves in the artistic character of contemporary poets, painters, and composers. These qualities of contemporary art and literature have become ever more prominent since the 1830s. I shall attempt to state this development in a third thesis. The basic trait of the new art is the tendency to move from the bottom up, to ground each art more firmly and solidly in reality and in the nature of its particular medium. Thus Balzac sought to give, in a methodical way, the physiology of the French society of his time in an interconnected cycle of novels; he was primarily concerned with the connection between human passions and the social sphere in which they develop and with the pathological limitation of persons in whom these passions arise. French social drama followed him in this. Similarly, Richard Wagner went back to the fundamental elements of music. For him, music, along with speech and mime, was the expression of feeling; more especially, music, in its rhythm and intonation, shared such expressiveness with speech. Wagner sought to give this kind of expression its ideal presentation in melody. On the basis of his view of music he developed its intimate connection with poetry and mime in his *Gesamtkunstwerk* (total work of art), the opera. But at the same time this produced a more powerful and intensified effectiveness for music itself. Semper, Richard Wagner's colleague during the flourishing of the arts in Dresden as well as in the violent days of May 1849, wanted to renew architecture from the bottom up, just as Wagner was revitalizing music by basing both theoretical observations and actual creation on vital impulses. More consistently and profoundly than anyone before him, Semper recognized and made use of architecture's dependence on its materials, and saw the source of its language of forms in skilled crafts—workmanship with textiles, ceramics, metal, carpentry, and primitive stone construction. He, too, developed a *Gesamtkunstwerk*, in which architectural masses are enlivened, as it were, with ornaments, color and a host of figures, painted and sculpted forms. He saw in the Renaissance the true continuation of Roman architecture and the foundation for today's architecture. Yet according to him Renaissance art "did not attain even half of its potential, since, owing to the uncongenial spirit of modern times, it has been overtaken and left behind hopelessly by its macrocosmic sister art, music."[3] From the

244

[3] Semper, *Stil*, vol. 2, p. 457. He describes this architecture stemming from the Renaissance as "the unfolding of a grand symphony of masses and spaces." (*Ibid.*, p. 371.) (D)

few extant *Gesamtkunstwerken* of the Gothic, Romanesque, and Renaissance periods, Semper derived the real task of the spatial and visual arts and a more complete ideal of their function. What still exists of such artworks is in part unfinished, and has subsequently become discolored, dismantled, and altered owing to [modern] taste which isolated the artwork in order to enhance it. However, Semper understood that styles usually arise from this unifying art of architecture which articulates and animates space, and that they must still arise there today.

245 We find ourselves today in the midst of this new movement. The strength of its stylistic principles is shown by the fact that even opposing tendencies are obliged to conform to them. Thus even such a classical author as Gottfried Keller, in his *Leute von Seldwyla* (The People of Seldwyla), has employed stark realism to make apparent the social soil from which his characters, their passions, and destinies grow. Our age is no longer acquainted with ideal characters such as Iphigenia, Wilhelm Meister, and Lothario, who transcend time and place. Painting has returned to color as its fundamental means of expression. It is seeking to do away with all traditional schemata of perception and composition, and to look at the world as though with new eyes. Everywhere the natural tendency to elevate the ideally beautiful above common reality—that is, the traditional well-ordered delineation of form—is being sacrificed to the need for uncurtailed, untrammeled reality and truth. What our age finds most important is to see reality, or at least the desire to see it—the striving to subordinate all of our thought, production and action to it, and to submit our deepest wishes and ideals to its laws. Donatello, Verrocchio, Masaccio, the old Dutch and Southern German masters, and the creators of the old English theater, most especially Marlowe, also wanted to see reality with new eyes. With this impulse, they created a major new style of European art, whose period of prominence has just now elapsed. Today we are experiencing a similar turning point; but for each new epoch of art the tasks become more difficult. An artist of the fifteenth and sixteenth centuries apprehended human reality in terms of the powers of individuals, the destiny implicit in their character, contrasts and relations among them, and their relation to a higher context. Today's artist would have us see in the artwork the actual relations in which men stand to one another and to nature, and the laws of reality to which we are subject. This is the driving force of the application of the biological law of heredity already to be found in George Sand, and in the preference given by

Balzac and Musset to abnormal psychic states and complexes, but above all in the derivation of characters and passions from social conditions. A colossal task!

Certainly, success has also been achieved recently along the usual well-trodden paths, as has been shown by Peter Cornelius, Anselm Feuerbach,[4] Gottfried Keller, Neo-Gothic architecture, and a number of important composers. Moreover, historical consciousness and historical learning have facilitated the appreciation, utilization, and remembrance of the existing major forms of art. However, our sympathy is with those venturesome artists who are not only able to see into the soul of our society—a society whose outlook is undergoing a tremendous upheaval unknown since the last days of the Greco-Roman world—but who are also capable of articulating something of the liberating vision for which our society yearns. From them we hope for new modes of artistic expression appropriate to us. And we shall follow them all the more confidently, the better they command the traditional modes of expression, the more ready they are to make use of what is sound and is still valid for us in these forms, and the more they avoid the danger of allowing the basic expressive powers of their art to degrade into base sensuality and brutality, and the graphic reproduction of vulgar reality.

246

We do not need to build up aesthetics anew in order for it to enter into a healthy relationship to these vital artistic endeavors of the present. For the artists themselves have already found it necessary to inquire into the true nature and means of the particular arts; they have had to create aesthetic principles for themselves. The aesthetics of our century must be sought elsewhere than in compendia and thick textbooks. In their times, Leonardo da Vinci and Dürer thought and wrote about their art; Lessing, Schiller, and Goethe created a new technique of drama and epic poetry by combining theoretical reflection with artistic practice. In our day Semper, Schumann, Richard Wagner, and the modern poets have similarly coupled artistic speculation with artistic creation. In Germany, Otto Ludwig especially, and Hebbel as well, are perceptive guides to the new directions; in France, it is the whole new generation of poets from the Goncourts on. Moreover, contemporary anthropology and art history can teach us, through the comparison of forms and their development, to transcend every historically limited mode of taste and to return to the nature of art itself. They furnish

[4] Anselm Feuerbach (1829-80). Painter noted for his cool coloring and clearly delineated classical style.

the means for considering aesthetic questions in an unbiased, scientific way, free from traditional speculative aesthetics.

We shall attempt, first of all, to elucidate the resources and methods which the work of the last two centuries makes available to a contemporary aesthetician and to evaluate their significance.

247

## I. THE THREE PRECEDING METHODS OF AESTHETICS

The development of aesthetics in modern times is similar to that through which jurisprudence, theology, and moral philosophy have passed. These have similar histories in that each of them is addressed to a certain sphere of culture and is aimed at deriving, from the knowledge thus attained, principles for the further evolution of that same sphere.

The arts and sciences began among us with a renewal and a free, brilliant development of that which had been discovered by the ancients. We still possess no account of the highly remarkable aesthetics of the *Renaissance*; up until the work of Stein, the history of aesthetics has stuck to the smooth highway that connects the great systems. No one has yet investigated to what extent aesthetic reflection accompanied and influenced the great creative period of art in the era from the Renaissance to the middle of the seventeenth century. At that time, aesthetic thought constituted a renaissance itself—except that one did not merely comment on Aristotle's *Poetics*, but also read what was preserved from his successors. This later aesthetic literature, as represented for us in Cicero, Horace, Plutarch, Plotinus, Philostratus, Callistratus, and Pseudo-Longinus, contained tendencies and principles in aesthetic matters which were much closer to the sixteenth century than Aristotle was. In particular, this literature laid stronger emphasis on the imagination which spontaneously produces the extraordinary. These contemporaries of the Pergamene School or of Roman artistic practices must have had a different way of thinking about aesthetic matters than the contemporaries of Phidias and of Polycletus. They stressed the sublime, the picturesque, the individual and moving expression, especially in the painterly treatment of the eye. They elevated the imagination to the sphere of aesthetic phenomena, in accordance with the insight of the aesthetically inspired Plotinus that the imagination continues the creative activity of nature. The aesthetics as well as the art of the sixteenth century combine an intensely exuberant sense of life and a naive delight in what is monstrous, as in baroque humor, with the sense of form and rules of the ancient world. In poetics, the rhetorical literature of the Roman empire formed the connecting link between the aesthetic tradition of the ancients and the spirit of the sixteenth century. Scaliger's influential *Poetics* (1561) drew less from Aristotle and Horace than from Hermogenes, Alexander, Menander and Diomedes, and his ideal was not Homer but Virgil.

## The Natural System of Aesthetic Laws and the Aesthetic Methods of the Seventeenth Century

248

The second half of the seventeenth century brought a great change in art and in aesthetics. In the political life of the absolute states that were on the rise, above all in France, the forces of regularity, rationality, and fiscal and administrative control gained the upper hand. In the conventions of courtly life as well, regular, restrained form gained predominance over the passions, and the sovereign intellect shaped the public demeanor of prominent personalities. Thus art encountered new types of men, new ideals. At the same time, and not unrelated to this, mathematical abstraction and deduction began their triumphant advance and provided the foundation for the natural science which prevails in Europe. Thus there arose alongside the theory of natural law and natural theology, as it culminated in Deism, a natural system of aesthetics as well. France was its homeland. It arose there at the time when the poetics of Ronsard was being displaced by that of Boileau and d'Aubignac. Heinrich von Stein has shown how the new aesthetics gained ground and influence in connection with Descartes and with the development of his philosophical rationalism, especially at Port-Royal.[5] However, Stein has not yet really solved the next problem, which is to demonstrate how, despite several precursors, among whom Kepler stands out, this rationalist aesthetics first attained its height in Leibniz and his school; from there its dominating influence extended to Baumgarten, Meier, Euler, Sulzer, Mendelssohn, and Lessing.

The source of this period of solid theoretical work in rationalist aesthetics lies in Leibniz's profound intuition about how the main

[5] See his *Die Entstehung der neueren Ästhetik* (1886).

components of psychical life relate to one another and in his inspired hypothesis about the causality of mental life.

This intuition was shared by him and other philosophers of the seventeenth century. Spinoza had said "will and intellect are one and the same (*voluntas et intellectus unum et idem sunt*)."[6] Leibniz derived from this a more precisely formulated *relationship of power, desire, and perception.* Perceptions are inner activities in the monadic unity of the soul; they arise because the soul is a power; the effort (*conatus*) contained in this power to pass from one condition to another is appetition, and accordingly a volitional process.[7] We 249 are inclined to say that Leibniz is right about the nature of psychical life as regards its creative and spontaneous character, including its relevance for the arts; but the significance of this profound psychological insight was diminished by its connection with the metaphysical fairy tale about monads. In accordance with this latter view, he derived the overall mirroring of the universe in representation not from real interactions between the monad and its objects, but only on the basis of an ideal connection between the whole world and the soul embedded in it. In this way, causal considerations were excluded from the explanation of the occurrence of aesthetic images. And when, in subsequent aesthetic thought, lesser minds corrected him, much of the inspired power with which Leibniz had articulated the harmony of the universe and thus established the aesthetic viewpoint was lost.

The second source was Leibniz's hypothesis of *minute* or *dull perceptions.* Cicero had appropriated this doctrine from philosophical works of his own time—principally from Stoic texts. He needed it for the foundation of the doctrine of innate ideas. Writers in the seventeenth century then made use of it for solving different problems; Montaigne, for example, utilized it in order to be able to provide an account of the basis of our decision between motives of equal strength. By means of this hypothesis, Leibniz supplemented Locke's analysis of intellect into its components of sensations and residual ideas; Locke's own brilliant explanation of perception in terms of the cooperation of imperceptible, almost unconscious judgments[8] paved the way for him to do this. Now for the first time a *real explanation of the most important psychical*

[6] Baruch Spinoza, *Ethics*, Part II, proposition 49, corollary.

[7] See Gottfried Wilhelm Leibniz, *Opera Philosophica*, ed. by J. E. Erdmann (Berlin: Eichler, 1840), pp. 464, 714. (D)

[8] See John Locke, *An Essay Concerning Human Understanding*, Book 2, chapter 9.

*phenomena* became possible. Thus a *rationalist aesthetics* could now also be created by connecting Leibniz's intuition with his hypothesis.[9]

Descartes, in his text on music (completed in 1618),[10] had already indicated the principle of such a rationalist aesthetic theory, which made it possible to move from the rules of poetics back to more fundamental aesthetic relationships. According to this principle, the satisfaction bound up with sensory perceptions arises from the ease of distinguishing and conjoining impressions. Consequently, the basis of our aesthetic satisfaction in sensory impressions is rational or logical.

This principle was made psychologically comprehensible by Leibniz. He began by agreeing with the French classicists that the logical character of poetic form, especially unity in multiplicity, is the basis of aesthetic satisfaction in such form. And in his main discussion of minute, unnoticed or dull perceptions,[11] he reduces taste to this rational factor. By means of his hypothesis he then shows how sensuous pleasure also derives from a hidden intelligibility in sensory perception. He provides the best grounding of his aesthetics in the short essay, "Über die Glückseligkeit" (On Happiness), which I shall now consider.[12] Power, perfection, order, and beauty are "interconnected." "The greater a thing's power, the more noble and free it is." "All elevation of being I call perfection." "The greater a power is, the more it is possible for plurality to emerge *from unity* and to reemerge *in unity*, where a unity regulates a plurality outside itself and represents it in itself."[13] In our own words: the activity of an undivided psychical power is at all times a unifying of the

250

[9] What Dilthey calls "Leibniz's intuition" is the realization that perception participates in the dynamism of psychic life. His hypothesis of minute or unconscious perceptions allows him to claim that perceptions continue in the mind even when they fail to meet the two conditions established for their retention by Locke. These Lockean conditions were: (1) keeping the perceptions actually in view by "contemplation," and (2) reviving them through "memory." See Leibniz, *New Essays on Human Understanding*, trans. by P. Remnant and J. Bennett (Cambridge: Cambridge University Press, 1982), p. 140. Leibniz responds that the faculty of memory presupposes a disposition in perceptions to persist even when we do not actively attend to them. Thus perceptions have an implicit power to preserve themselves, and any changes that we find in perceptions must be accounted for by the more explicit power of appetition.

[10] René Descartes, *Compendium Musicae*, in *Oeuvres de Descartes*, vol. 10, ed. by Charles Adams and Paul Tannery (Paris: Leopold Clef, 1908), pp. 79-141.

[11] Leibniz, *Opera*, p. 197. (D)

[12] *Ibid.*, pp. 671-673. This is Leibniz's most important treatise for aesthetics. (D)

[13] *Ibid.*, p. 672.

many in the one, and such psychical power enjoys the degree of its own perfection whenever it thus subjects multiplicity to its unity. Leibniz's exposition continues: the degree of this "unity" appears as "harmony" or "*order*." "All beauty originates from order, and beauty awakens love."[14] Let us again interpret. Delight in beauty is thus the result of a consciousness of the augmented activity of psychical power in accord with its inherent law, which requires it to produce unity in plurality. Thus it happens that "the beauty of another person, of an animal, or even of a nonliving creation, painting, or artwork," in "impressing its image on us," "implants and awakens" in us an elevated and perfect existence and a corresponding delight. Then "our heart senses" a perfection which the intellect does not yet comprehend but which nevertheless is entirely rational.[15]

From this the aesthetic impression of *music* can be explained, according to Leibniz, and this explanation of it, which was then further developed by Euler, was the touchstone, as it were, of the entire rationalist aesthetic. "Everything which makes a sound has in it an oscillation or a back-and-forth motion. Everything which makes a sound has an invisible beat. Whenever such a beat proceeds not confusedly but regularly and works together with a certain alternation, it is pleasant."[16] Leibniz illustrated this by the aesthetic impression of rhythm, of regular motion in dance, of regular succession of long and short syllables, and of conjunction of rhymes. The principle of pleasure is here always the same. "Motions in conformity with proportion and order attain their pleasantness from that order; for all order proves useful to the mind."[17] Let us apply 251 this principle to music. "A regular, although imperceptible, order occurs also in the artfully produced beats or motions of vibrating or quivering strings, pipes, or bells, indeed, even of the air which is thereby brought into regular agitation: this air then further produces a resonance in us by means of our sense of hearing, in accord with which our animating spirits are active. For that reason music is so suitable for moving our hearts."[18] In his view, pleasure in proportion within the visual realm also rests on this principle.

[14] *Ibid.*

[15] *Ibid.*, p. 671.

[16] *Ibid.*

[17] *Ibid.*

[18] *Ibid.* See also pp. 717ff. on music, and the following: "Les plaisirs que la vue trouve dans les proportions, sont de la même nature; et ceux que causent les autres sens reviendront à quelque chose de semblable, quoique nous ne puissons pas l'expliquer si distinctement." (*Ibid.*, p. 718.) (D)

*Artistic creation*, too, can be accounted for in this way. "Each soul knows the infinite, knows all, but confusedly; as in walking on the seashore and hearing the great noise which it makes, I hear the particular sounds of each wave, of which the total sound is composed, but without distinguishing them. Our confused perceptions are the result of the impressions which the whole universe makes upon us."[19] These dim representations and their connections present themselves also in feelings (*sentiments*), and thus taste (*goût*) further arises out of them. On this basis he then explains delight in the beauty of objects or in the harmony of the universe, i.e., in the beauty of nature. We see how an aesthetic frame of mind was dominant in Leibniz. "The beauty of nature is so vast, its contemplation contains such sweetness—as does the illumination and the good emotion that results from it—and it is so splendidly advantageous, that whoever has tasted it regards all other delights as trifling in comparison."[20] Now since this frame of mind operates as an impetus in the soul, an architectonic process of formation arises from it in powerful monads. This tendency of our soul to shape architectonically is most apparent in dreams, where we effortlessly and unintentionally invent things to which we would have to devote considerable thought when awake. The same tendency also operates in intentional actions.[21] Thus, alongside the capacity for grasping the harmony of the universe through the architectonic unity of thought, there appears the other capacity to architectonically imitate an object and to create something in virtually the same way as God would.[22]

Leibniz himself gave no more specific applications of his principles to the particular problems of aesthetics. Although in several passages he showed a lively interest in the direction taken by the French art of his day, he nevertheless did not involve himself in the debates concerning poetics. His utterances about musical harmony and about proportion in visual images are mere formulae. Here, too, this highly inventive genius discovered only an instrument for solving the problems, a key, as it were; but the particular solutions themselves were left to his successors. Precisely this approach provided a powerful stimulus for his disciples to continue this work. To be sure, as this younger generation developed, it at the same time came under the influence of the English empiricist school. 252

[19] *Ibid.*, p. 717; trans. in Leibniz, *Selections*, ed. by Philip P. Wiener (New York: Charles Scribner's Sons, 1951), p. 530.

[20] *Ibid.*, p. 673. (D)

[21] *Ibid.*, p. 717. (D)

[22] *Ibid.*, p. 712. (D)

Thus the first system of aesthetics was created by Baumgarten and Meier, based on Leibniz's principles, but also influenced by the English theory of feelings. And of no less importance were the particular explanations that were arrived at on the basis of Leibniz's principles. They were used by Euler to account for the impression of harmony and by Hogarth and other artists to account for the effect of the line of beauty. Thus specific *concrete questions of aesthetics* could now be treated with real competence. In his *Essay on a New Theory of Music*,[23] Leonhard Euler (1707-83) proceeded from the view that consonance is explicable through an acoustical understanding of the relation of tonal vibrations. This understanding is based on an additional metaphysical principle, which is: "Two or more tones are pleasing when a numerical proportion of the simultaneously occurring vibrations is apprehended; when, by contrast, no order is sensed or the necessary receptive order is suddenly interrupted, the tones become displeasing."[24] Hogarth introduced his copper etchings with the symbol of the serpentine line and entitled it "the line of beauty." In the *Analysis of Beauty* he then worked out how the beauty of lines consists of "the special quality of the combination of lines which furnish the eye a pleasant way of following them."[25] In the effect of framing, he showed still more clearly the value which each means of uniting a multiplicity of elements can have for an aesthetic impression. In their writing about 253 painting and sculpture, the Richardsons,[26] who were themselves painters, showed sensitivity in characterizing the effects of multiplicity, contrast, and unity in paintings. In his *Letter on Sculpture*,[27]

[23] *Tentamen novae theoriae musicae ex certissimis harmoniae principiis dilucide expositae* (Petropoli: Ex typographia Academiae scientiarum, 1739).

[24] Dilthey gives what seems to be his own German translation from the Latin and quotes the original in a footnote: "Binos pluresve sonos tum placere, cum ratio, quam numeri vibrationum eodem tempore editarum inter se tenent, percipiatur: contra vero displicentiam in hoc consistere, quando vel nullus ordo sentiatur, vel is qui adesse debere videatur, subito perturbetur."

[25] We have translated Dilthey's German, but it departs somewhat from Hogarth's text: "The serpentine line, by its waving and winding at the same time different ways, leads the eye in a pleasing manner along the continuity of its variety. . . ." Hogarth, *Analysis of Beauty* (Hildesheim: Georg Olms Verlag, 1974; reprint of the 1753 ed.), pp. 38-39. Hogarth actually distinguishes between a waving line which he calls the "line of beauty" and a serpentine line which he calls the "line of grace."

[26] Jonathan Richardson (1665-1745) and his son, also Jonathan (1694-1771), collaborated in writing *An Account of Some of the Statues, Bas-Reliefs, Drawings, and Pictures in Italy* (1722), which was used extensively as a guidebook by young Englishmen.

[27] Frans Hemsterhuis (1721-90), a Dutch philosopher, published the *Lettre sur la sculpture* in 1765.

Hemsterhuis used reproductions of two vases, one of which produces an effect by means of unity in ornament and painting, while the colorful richness of the other fails to make an impression. And Lessing proclaimed in a completely Leibnizian manner: "Everything in the mortal creator [the poet], should be an outline of everything in the eternal creator, and should accustom us to the idea that just as in Him all is resolved for the best, it will in him also."[28] Thus Lessing's doctrine of the true unity of dramatic action was also based on this rationalist aesthetic.

### *The Value of Rationalist Aesthetics*

Rationalist aesthetics conceives of beauty as a *manifestation of the logical in the sensuous* and of art as a visible presentation of the harmonious nexus of the world. In his sensuous intuition, the artist obtains an obscure but intensely felt awareness of this nexus. As there is but a single world-nexus, the sensuous relationships that exist within it must ultimately be formulated in one principle. Natural beauty and artistic beauty express this nexus in their respective languages. Even the most spontaneous expression of imagination is subject to rules. Such rules are found in harmonics and metrics; they are operative in the flow of a line, in the formation of a figure, and in the ornamentation produced by the architect and the artist. The taste of a poet is developed as an embodiment of such rules. Unity of action and the precepts deriving from it govern drama. And all these rules are grounded ultimately in the rational order of the universe.

This rationalist aesthetics is, first of all, an expression of significant tendencies of an age. Its history provides a first major example of the way in which the attitude of an age as it arises from the general structure of society simultaneously dominates the art, the taste, and the aesthetic theory of that time. Thus it is that aesthetic theories arise alongside artistic movements and influence them, just as they are, for their part, influenced by these movements.

At the same time, however, this rationalist aesthetics has a valuable core whose validity endures independently of the age of classicism. The problem will be to extricate what is valid from what is erroneous. There are universally valid artistic rules which derive from the nature of the artistic enterprise, and the problem will be merely one of separating them from historical variations in taste.

[28] Gottfried Ephraim Lessing, *Hamburgische Dramaturgie* (1767-69), 2 vols., in *Werke*, vol. 4 (Munich: Hanser, 1973), p. 598. Phrase in brackets added by Dilthey.

254 That requires, however, a difficult transformation of Leibniz's metaphysical aesthetics into a psychological aesthetics. One reason why perceptual images and artworks please us is that the activity through which we unify the multiplicity in them (which may therefore be called a cognitive activity), produces an aesthetic effect on the totality of our psychical life. Of course, none of the rationalist aestheticians formulated this thesis and the problem contained within it at this level of generality. But as we saw, Leibniz, the most profound among them, possessed in his system the presupposition for posing the problem in this way. And the individual works of those aestheticians influenced by the rationalist school already contained evidence for the above thesis. Similarly, the Leibnizian theory of the *harmony of the universe* implies the further thesis that a metaphysical connection obtains between our aesthetic capacity and its external objects, and Kant developed this thesis to some extent. The relation between the unifying activities of our intelligence and the unified and intelligible order of reality, especially sensory reality, will always constitute the condition—or, if one prefers, the postulate—by means of which alone we can make comprehensible to ourselves our aesthetic apprehension of the world. Admittedly, however, this condition of aesthetic intuition points to something unfathomable, a primal source of harmony, which is inaccessible to our thought.

## The Analysis of Aesthetic Impressions and the Aesthetic Methods of the Eighteenth Century

During the first half of the eighteenth century a change took place in the conditions governing the arts and aesthetic reflection. The aesthetics of the Renaissance had moved from Italy to France, where the system of natural aesthetic laws was then established and subsequently completed in Germany; but now England was taking the lead. Here, too, a transformation of the social order—accomplished through the English revolution of 1688—was the basis of an altered attitude among people, and this attitude then simultaneously influenced the arts and aesthetic reflection. In this land of industry, commerce, and political freedom, the power of autocrats, princes, and courtiers—a power bound by form, and inwardly motivated by aristocratic and feudal impulses—gradually lost its authority over the will and imagination of the people; the independent, cultured gentleman began to be conscious of his worth. Locke's ed-

ucational plan already aimed at producing this sort of cultured man. 255
Poetry formed the ideals and the types of this cultured bourgeois society alongside those of the aristocratic classes.

In the Dutch Republic, the birthplace of European freedom, Rembrandt showed people in all their vitality. He was unconcerned with the idealizing power of the line in painting and unimpressed by the postures and forms of social rank. The Dutch genre-painters of the seventeenth century had let plain human everydayness show through. Now in England this new spirit—partly through the political ties of that country with the Netherlands—also took hold in literature, which is the clearest and most effective expression of the aesthetic consciousness of an age and which stands in closest connection with literary criticism and aesthetic theory. The new English society required an art which would cultivate independent education and foster a moral attitude. Addison, on one occasion, looking out on London, declared touchingly that of all those who thronged the streets, most had only a pseudo-existence; he wanted to make them into real people. What was new here was that he intended to do so not by means of religion, but by means of aesthetic and moral culture. These two kinds of culture were inseparable from the new way of thinking.

Another remarkable change was also taking place. From the time of the Renaissance, the visual arts and architecture had maintained a predominance alongside poetry. The formal beauty in the depiction of personalities in the aristocratic sixteenth and seventeenth centuries still speaks to us today from the walls of museums and palaces in an abundance of portraits and in the glorification of a stately magnificence. Royal power was given sumptuous and confident expression in grand architecture, in the vast structures of palaces, in the flowing lines of their ornamentation, and in the formal arrangement and restrained natural abundance of their gardens. Now, however, music, the art of inwardness which is accessible to anyone in a quiet chamber or at the spinet, gained a dominance—alongside poetry—which it has maintained up to our day.

At the same time a vague, deep-seated appreciation of nature became prominent. This had the most far-reaching significance for the aesthetic outlook of this new age. Together with the rise of the scientific and philosophical conception of the autonomy of nature, we witness the emancipation of landscape from figure painting. It was in the age of Spinoza, Leibniz, and Shaftesbury that Claude Lorrain, Ruysdael, and Hobbema made landscape painting an art in itself. This appreciation of nature produced a heightened sense of intimacy and also a greater sensitivity for detail under the influence of the observations of nature by a Buffon and a Linnaeus. This is also what we find in the literature of the eighteenth century: the first great poet of this sense of nature, Rousseau, was a passionate botanist.

256

These changes of taste during the eighteenth century were also accompanied by the liveliest discussion about aesthetics. Art criticism showed itself to be a guiding force first in the English periodicals, then in the handwritten reports of painting exhibits circulated by Diderot, and further in Lessing's dramatic theory. Much of the extensive journalistic literature of the eighteenth century was filled with aesthetic debates and with art criticism. The novel of the middle class, the comedy of manners, the operas of Gluck, and the dramas of Lessing and Schiller arose amidst the liveliest aesthetic reflection and amidst debates about art criticism.

Historians of aesthetics have been unable to articulate these vital relationships which provide the context for the abundant aesthetic writings they study. However useful the work of Zimmerman, Lotze, and Hartmann may be, they are caught up in an unfruitful dispute about Herbart's formalism. This formalism was an idle and merely academic speculation, contributing little either to the prevalent analysis of the beautiful into its effective elements, or to the knowledge of the aesthetic value of forms, which was already familiar to those who wrote about technique. It was without any influence on the arts. To be sure, its theoretical one-sidedness made it stimulating; nevertheless, after causing a temporary stir in the universities it proved to be nothing more. Another error stands out even more strongly among these historians. They overestimate the value of aesthetic speculation. They consider only secondarily or incidentally those authors who have analyzed the material medium and formal expressive means available to each of the arts, and who have begun on the basis of such analysis to discern the developmental laws of those arts. The neglect of Semper in these historical works is indicative of the one-sidedness of these historians, since in our century aesthetics owes more to him than to anyone. Thus despite their thorough and intellectually rich studies, it still remains necessary to determine the development and significance of the two methods which the eighteenth and nineteenth centuries have added to the system of natural aesthetic laws of the seventeenth century, and which have provided aesthetics with its positive results.

The first of these methods is the *analysis of the impression* which an aesthetic object calls forth—an analysis of the effective elements that arouse such an impression.

This method arose from the progress of the analytic tendency in the human sciences since Locke and Hume. In England and Scotland, it was then applied simultaneously to ethical theory, theology, aesthetics, and political economy. It attained its first major triumph in Adam Smith's theory of the productive factors of economic life and their interconnections. Hutcheson[29] paved the way for aesthetic analysis by introducing the sense of beauty which marked out the terrain for the philosophy of art and established its problems. Many works analyzing the arts appeared in the period from the 1740s through the 1760s:[30] Harris' *Three Treatises*[31] and Batteux's *Les beaux arts*;[32] Mendelssohn's essay on the feelings[33] appeared independently of Burke's *Enquiry*,[34] and that on the sublime and the naive was already written in 1757.[35] Besides the writings of Young,[36] Webb,[37] and Kames[38] we must consider those of Diderot and Lessing.[39] Already in these first decades of the analytic method, description and analysis extended from the basic psychophysical analyses of Rameau and d'Alembert to the description of genius by Dubos, Young, and Wood, to the tracing of the distinguishing principles of the particular arts in Dubos, Harris, Webb, and finally in Lessing's *Laocoön* and his celebrated analysis of tragic effects. Dubos, Burke, and Kames wrote the most important texts that were being read by our German aestheticians through the 1780s. The

257

[29] Francis Hutcheson, *An Inquiry into the Original of our Ideas of Beauty and Virtue*, 2nd ed. (London, 1726).

[30] This sentence and the following titles have been interpolated. Dilthey merely lists authors and dates.

[31] James Harris, *Three Treatises, the First Concerning Art, the Second Concerning Music, Painting, and Poetry, the Third Concerning Happiness* (1744).

[32] Abbé Charles Batteux, *Les beaux arts réduits à un même principe* (1746).

[33] Moses Mendelssohn, *Briefe über die Empfindungen* (1755).

[34] Edmund Burke, *A Philosophical Enquiry into the Origin of Our Ideas of the Sublime and the Beautiful* (1756).

[35] Mendelssohn, *Betrachtungen über die Quellen und die Verbindungen der schönen Künste und Wissenschaften* (1757).

[36] Edward Young, *Conjectures on Original Composition* (1759).

[37] Daniel Webb, *Remarks on the Beauties of Poetry* (1762).

[38] Kames, Henry Home, Lord, *Elements of Criticism*, 3 vols. (1762).

[39] Beardsley notes that Diderot's *Lettre sur les sourds et muets* (1751) anticipates Lessing's attempt to define the distinctiveness of the medium in each art in his *Laokoon, oder über die Grenzen der Malerei und Poesie* (1766). See Monroe Beardsley, *Aesthetics from Classical Greece to the Present* (New York: Macmillan Co., 1966), p. 161n.

extent of the extraordinary progress made by means of this method can be roughly measured by comparing two works, one of which shows such analysis in its beginning, the other at its current level of maturity. The first is the *Elements of Criticism* by Kames, which appeared in 1762. The other is the *Vorschule der Ästhetik* by Gustav Fechner, a set of essays collected and printed in 1876, although some of them had already appeared earlier.

Kames was writing during the greatest epoch of Scottish intellectual activity. Born in 1696 as Henry Home, he led a long, extremely happy life in Edinburgh as a student, a lawyer, and finally as a judge and as Lord Kames. Edinburgh was at that time a center of intellectual activity. Kames was a friend of Hume, Adam Smith, Reid, and Franklin. Not only was he a multifaceted, prolific writer with the moral dynamism and practical bent characteristic of the Scots, but he also showed a delight in the senses and a power of aesthetic reflection which was unique. A sense of beauty accompanied him until he finally was able to satisfy it completely by building and landscaping his estate. His main work was an analysis of beauty and art, *Elements of Criticism* (1762).

This work was in its time highly esteemed on account of the 258 completeness of its analyses and of its definition of aesthetic concepts, in which it surpassed Burke's more inspired but uneven work. It gave evidence of a natural capacity for feeling aesthetic impressions intensely and correctly, and for reflecting on them. It was an outstanding work due to a rare familiarity with the poets and, at the same time, an extremely skilled use of the results of the Scottish psychology of the day. It already had before it extensive analytic material in the works of Dubos, Hutcheson, Gerard, Rameau, Hogarth, Harris, Batteaux, d'Alembert, Rousseau, Montesquieu, and Diderot; it was, however, especially Burke's analysis of the sublime and the beautiful that served as its model. Thus the *Elements* was the most mature and thorough eighteenth-century investigation of the beautiful. In spite of some logical and systematic weaknesses, it enables us to comprehend Adam Smith's designation of Lord Kames as the "master" of the Scottish analytic method of the time. Lessing, Herder, Kant, and Schiller made much use of it. It laid the foundations for Schiller by being expressly dedicated to the aesthetic education of a nation, and it anticipated Lessing and Goethe by recognizing the unique dramatic greatness of Shakespeare and by taking primarily his works as the basis for its analyses.

Kames' analysis focused on the *impression* made by *aesthetic objects*. It was decisive for the aesthetic analysis of this epoch, as well as for its ethical analysis, that they were devoted exclusively to aesthetic pleasure and moral judgment. Psychology was not yet capable of a description of genius. Kames found a simple natural correlation between the *emotion involved in an aesthetic impression* and a *specific property of an aesthetic object or process.* This kind of aesthetic analysis led to a delineation of the feelings as the true locus of aesthetic apprehension.

It was the nature of aesthetic experience that gave the decisive impulse to separate the capacity to feel from the will. Burke had already laid great stress on his important insight that aesthetic contemplation and the volitional attitude are completely different. The simplest interpretation of this insight was psychological, namely, to derive aesthetic pleasure from disinterested feelings—those from which no desire proceeds. Thus gradually there arose the theory that feeling is an independent province of psychical life—a theory which was then systematized by Tetens[40] and Kant. On this point Kames assumed a superior position. He did not fall into the error of positing the life of feeling as an independent province in the sphere of the soul. And yet *emotions* that constitute aesthetic pleasure in an object and do not pass over into desire—which in Kantian terms would make them "disinterested"—are sharply distinguished from *passions* that do pass over into desires and strive to produce actions. For example, a beautiful building or a beautiful stretch of countryside evokes a quiet, nonappetitive pleasure. We first entirely grasp the nature of an aesthetic impression, however, when we distinguish that emotion which is stimulated by the real presence of an object from the emotion which is evoked by its mere *ideal presence.*[41] Ideal presence relates to reality as an idea of memory relates to the object which it represents. It is more vivid in painting than in words, in theatrical performance than in painting. All art is based on the fact that the same emotion is evoked by the ideal presence of an object as by its actual presence—it is only the intensity of the emotion that diminishes as the vivacity of the imagery fades. This concept of the ideal presence discovered by Kames is the source of the theory of aesthetic semblance.[42] Even today, Kames' positive formulation of this concept remains superior to the negative formulation of it in modern theory.

259

It is with this empirical approach of describing and analyzing

[40] Johann Nicolaus Tetens (1736[38]-1807) is sometimes considered to be the source of Kant's three-faculty division of knowing, feeling, and willing.

[41] See Kames, *Elements of Criticism*, 11th ed. (London: B. Blake, 1839), p. 34.

[42] See Friedrich Schiller, *On the Aesthetic Education of Man*, 26th letter.

impressions of feeling that we first become aware of the full dimension of a problem which did not yet exist for rationalism: is it possible to universalize aesthetic impressions? How and to what extent can aesthetics and taste be *universally valid*? Hume first sketched the concept of the *standard of taste* as a solution to this problem in one of his essays.[43] Kames then developed this important concept in the last chapter of his work.

He holds that there is to be a discipline of aesthetics which is the authority in the realm of taste. Its basic principles are derived from the analysis of the human feelings and established alongside the principles of morality—they are related but independent. An impression of an aesthetic object contains a multiplicity of feelings which are connected with properties and relations of that object. It is thus possible for aesthetic criticism to be universally valid because specific *aesthetic impressions* are, in accordance with the nature of our mind, regularly *connected* with certain *properties of the aesthetic object*. The proof for this lies in the general consensus of aesthetic judgment among cultured people. To discover these stable connections by means of psychological analysis is thus to provide a foundation for aesthetic criticism as a discipline.

260 Such a regular connection is in each instance a stable element on which aesthetic criticism can count. And from the union of these stable elements arises the "standard of taste," i.e., the pattern or the model of taste, which develops in a decisive minority through education, reflection, and experience. Its ultimate condition is, however, a *sympathy* among humans and with things. Each aesthetically sensitive person is governed in these feelings by what is constant in human nature. And the psychical or physical processes which affect him produce emotions which are always similar to their causes. A contorted posture, a crooked column, a languid or vigorous motion will evoke a similar change or emotion in us. We notice how, in this theory of the universal validity of taste, the ideas of the Roman Stoic philosophers are developed further. These ideas had also strongly influenced Kames' teacher Shaftesbury.

Finally, what gave Kames' work its lasting worth was that his brilliant aesthetic analysis disclosed and displayed a *large number of aesthetic elements*, i.e., constant relationships between objects and impressions. To a great extent, Kames anticipated Fechner, who mentions him, yet apparently has not made use of him. The degree of agreement between them is most instructive just for this

[43] David Hume, "Of the Standard of Taste" (1757).

reason. The method which actually analyzes an impression has led, for Fechner just as for Kames, to the uncovering of a variety of such stable connections between impressions of feeling and the external properties which evoke them. Specifically, Kames had first shown how aesthetic feelings are fixed on the properties of a particular object, and then how further aesthetic effects proceed from the relations of objects to one another.

Kames designates as *beauty* the impression of "sweetness and gaiety"[44] that we find in objects of sight. This is a *complex* impression. The *sensory* beauty of a visible object is composed of impressions of the colors, the regularity and simplicity of the shape, and the uniformity, proportion, and intrinsic orderliness of its parts. But there is also a beauty of the visual image that derives from the *associations* it has for us. Especially important in this regard are the relations of the object—its purposiveness, its utility. One of Kames' finest analytic achievements is the distinction which he introduced here between the "intrinsic beauty" which the beautiful object by itself excites in sensory apprehension and the beauty which arises from the relations of the object added by thought.[45] In different ways, Kant as well as Fechner followed him in this distinction, the latter without really knowing his work. And what insight into particulars Kames displays! He was already experimenting with the aesthetic effects of the circle, the square, the rectangle, and the triangle. It is interesting to note that for him, as for others, the square seemed more pleasing than the rectangle, while Fechner favors the rectangle in which—according to the rule of the golden section—the smaller side relates to the larger as the larger does to the sum of both. In his discussion of beauty, Kames makes much use of Hutcheson and Gerard.

261

Kames then sought out the properties whereby an object creates the *impression of "grandeur and sublimity."*[46] He found that in sublimity a magnitude or greatness, which completely occupies our vision and attention, is connected with properties of beauty. He appealed to the following experience to make apparent the relationship of grandeur and sublimity to beauty. When we approach a small conical hill, we look closely at each part and notice the

[44] Kames, *Elements*, p. 83.

[45] *Ibid.* The latter is called "relative beauty."

[46] Kames, *Elements*, p. 90. Dilthey uses the single word *Erhabenheit* where Kames used the phrase "grandeur and sublimity." In what follows we have added quotes to indicate which particular term is actually used by Kames.

"slightest deviation from regularity and proportion."[47] Supposing that the hill is now considerably enlarged so that its regularity becomes less conspicuous to us, then it will appear less beautiful. It will, however, on that account make just as agreeable an impression, because a "slight emotion of grandeur comes in place of what is lost in beauty."[48] Finally, if the hill is enlarged into a great mountain, then "the small degree of beauty that is left is sunk in its grandeur."[49] Such sentences were written as part of a tacit dialogue with Burke, against whom Kames rightly stressed the transitional stages which lead from the beautiful to the sublime and the positive character of the impression of sublimity which makes itself felt in the expansion and the elevation of the soul.

He then offered an excellent analysis of the impressions produced by the various forms of *motion* and the *force* which manifests itself in them. Simple motion has a calming and pleasing effect, for instance, when I see smoke rising on a quiet morning. By contrast, the exertion of force manifested by water rising in a fountain "rouses and enlivens the mind"[50] because this force is constantly overcoming gravity. In the next chapter he analyzed *novelty* and the *unexpected appearance* of objects and their unfailing effects on the masses. Finally, he analyzed what makes an object "risible" or capable of causing "laughter that is altogether pleasant"[51]—such 262 an object must always appear "slight, little, or trivial."[52] The ease with which he assigned the various aesthetic feeling-states their characteristic value is admirable.

From here Kames proceeded to the *relations* in which several objects stand to one another and showed how further aesthetic effects result from their apprehension.[53] In the striking examples, especially from Shakespeare, which he adduced, he showed with great aesthetic sensitivity the aesthetic effects of "resemblance and dissimilitude"[54] and of "uniformity and variety."[55] He also identified in the feeling of "congruity and propriety"[56] an effect stemming from the relation of agreement of connected objects. And

[47] *Ibid.*, p. 92.
[48] *Ibid.*
[49] *Ibid.*
[50] *Ibid.*, p. 110.
[51] *Ibid.*, p. 119.
[52] *Ibid.*, p. 118.
[53] See the beginning of chapters 3 and 8. (D)
[54] *Ibid.*, p. 120.
[55] *Ibid.*, p. 132.
[56] *Ibid.*, p. 145.

finally he examined the role of connection and comparison in the impressions caused by what is dignified and what is ridiculous, respectively—in the latter the laughable is mixed with the "improper."[57] Thus he discerningly derived a multitude of aesthetic feelings from the impressions of the relations among various objects, in the course of which, to be sure, the lack of a foundation for aesthetic analysis in the theory of perception as we possess it today becomes conspicuous.

I shall not go into Kames' application of these results to literature, architecture, and landscape gardening; rather, I shall sum up the *common* findings of Kames and Fechner, these two great analysts of aesthetic effects. Contents of sense, as such, evoke pleasure. The various ways we can attend to these contents, as well as the formal relations within the sequence of our representations, all provide sources of amusement, boredom, or delight in apprehension. If, moreover, aesthetic values are combined in a whole, then these elements are supplemented by a principle of intensification which derives from the relationships based on their connections. Unity in multiplicity, symmetry, proportion, composition from parts with similar structure, and then again a wealth of impressions, and contrast—these are all elements of aesthetic effect. In addition, however, there is the relationship of such external phenomena to what is inner, of an image to the life projected into it, of external movement to the inner process evoked by it and corresponding to it—everything that Fechner includes under "aesthetic association." Thus each aesthetic impression is found to be composed from elements. In each, connective mental processes are seen to be operative. All aesthetic effects are composed of simple elements.

## *An Evaluation of the Analysis of Aesthetic Impressions*

263

More than a century separates Kames' *Elements* from Fechner's *Vorschule der Ästhetik*, a work which I will not discuss here, since it is so widely read today.[58] In the meantime, the physiological study of sense impressions and sensory perception had provided a much firmer foundation for aesthetic analysis. Nevertheless, one notices that certain limitations, which Fechner also has not been able to transcend, are inherent in the method itself.

[57] *Ibid.*, p. 160.

[58] See Dilthey's use of Fechner in "The Imagination of the Poet," esp. pp. 87-90.

When aesthetics is based on the analysis of impressions, it moves in a *circle* from which it cannot entirely free itself. In striving to locate the properties of beauty, it takes as the criterion of those properties their capacity to influence our feelings. However, not every effect on the feelings is aesthetic; rather, there exists here a distinction between crude effects on the feelings which occur due to their personal appeal, and an aesthetically moving effect. Thus analysis must *already presuppose* a certain concept of *what is aesthetically effective*. Definitions of beauty developed slowly in aesthetics; then Kant, in an exceedingly effective manner, placed certain distinguishing features at the forefront of his investigation. He sharply separated crude, sensuous, or material feeling-effects from the "territory" of beauty. But Kant offered no proof for his conceptual determination of the distinction between the sensuous and beautiful, nor did he draw the boundary correctly. Here lies the immediate fundamental problem for aesthetic analysis. It needs to bring about, by some method or other, a consensus about the nature of aesthetic effects. Aesthetics and art criticism have no more important or sacred duty than to identify and guard against those crude feelings and sensuous effects which appeal directly to the whims of the audience. The mere method of analyzing impressions of feeling cannot, however, perform this guardian task of the aesthetician and the art critic.

Moreover, the *execution of the method* encounters an inherent *difficulty* which makes it questionable whether the method by itself can attain objectively certain and universally valid results. Its procedure is determined by the following technical consideration: I can only recognize the feeling aroused by an aesthetic content as a relatively general effect if I submit myself and others to repeated experiments, and if I find changes in myself corresponding to changed conditions—as required by the familiar rules of induction. In this way, analysis turns into experiment. Aesthetics becomes an experimental science. And the more it can vary the conditions and test the effects in many cases and on very different persons, the more universally and securely its principles can be formulated. Since this method seeks a causal relationship between a pleasure and a property which evokes the pleasure as its effect, it can also be called inductive. The discovered causal relationship itself can be called a law. Insofar as that relationship expresses a rule to which effects are subject, it can be called a principle.

This method by and for itself cannot overcome the following difficulty. The aesthetic impression produced by a property of ob-

264

jects can be tested on only a limited circle of persons and only for a given time. Even when I experimentally isolate a particular component such as a line or a shape, a chord or a sequence of tones, the effects I experience are conditioned by acquired habits. At first I experiment with myself. As a person educated and historically conditioned in a certain context, something affects me aesthetically in a particular way. The impression embodies the results of a considerable amount of cognitive sense experience. The immediacy and simplicity of the impression is a psychological illusion. It stands in relation to the dim mass of representations, drives, and feelings of my acquired psychic nexus; it is oriented and conditioned by this nexus. Thus even if all my experiments disclose that some state of affairs has a thoroughly uniform effect on my feelings, the real cause of the effect will still be difficult to determine. Now I extend my procedure; I test the aesthetic impression of the state of affairs on other persons as well. But here too, the range of the experiment remains geographically and temporally limited, and it remains so of necessity. Longstanding cognitive usages are embodied in our sense experience, and this can, over generations, produce judgments of taste which then appear to be simple and immediate. The sense of form in Pericles' generation is quite different from that in the Baroque era, and it could be that their respective customs also influence their judgments of taste about simple lines. I do not know whether this difficulty can ever be resolved as such. But insofar as it can, this can only occur through a broadening of our horizon by means of historical considerations. For analysis by and for itself possesses no means of separating what is historically conditioned 265 in taste from what is universally valid. Thus analytic, inductive, experimental aesthetics turns out to be limited and conditioned also in this respect.

If one then surveys the results of this method, a new difficulty comes to the fore. The analysis of aesthetic impressions arrives at an indeterminate number of regular relations between the contents capable of producing impressions and the impressions themselves. From this perspective, the effect of an artwork or a landscape seems extremely complex, that is, compounded from very disparate impressional elements. However, the effect itself is unified. *An artwork is not a mere aggregate of properties capable of arousing us.*

Furthermore, it remains an open question whether these specific lawful relationships do not point to a deeper connection, already presupposed by analysis, between our capacity for aesthetic apprehension and the aesthetic properties of reality (so-called natural beauty). It could be that beauty is rooted in such a *comprehensive lawful* connection, which then manifests itself through analysis in particular relations between properties of aesthetic objects and their corresponding impressions. If such a universal connection exists, then historical changes of taste could also ultimately be related to it. Thus it is that speculative principles for the explanation of beauty have been developed in all ages. Theories about the latent rationality of reality, which can nevertheless be felt, first became prevalent in the seventeenth century as a metaphysics of beauty and still had widespread currency in the eighteenth. Goethe's philosophy of nature is characteristic of its time in assuming a unity between an organizing impulse of nature, which functions unconsciously but purposefully, and the creative capacity of the artist. And some of the most insightful aestheticians—such as Goethe himself, Oersted,[59] and Semper—tested this idea with great success in particular cases. Related to it is another idea of much more current influence, namely, that beauty, artistic impressions and artistic creation always consist in a relation between outwardly perceptible forms and an inner meaning expressed by them.

Finally, the mere analysis of impressions cannot account for the most important, universal human interest in art, an interest which 266 motivates artists and the public alike. This interest concerns the question of the *cultural function of art* in human life. If this question can have a rigorous answer, it must come from combining the analysis of impressions with a historical-sociological consideration of art. Here, too, there is a point at which the efforts to analyze impressions can easily become circular. Some implicit attitude toward art, an idea of its inner meaning, will guide the labors of such analysts, even where they are not conscious of such presuppositions.

## The Historical Method and Nineteenth-Century Aesthetics

A third, *historical* method has evolved and is suitable for supplementing the other two. It deals primarily with creative minds and with powerful works of art. If it uses psychology for its interpretation of the facts, then another kind of analysis can be developed from it, namely, an *analysis of the creative aesthetic capacity*. I have

[59] Hans Christian Oersted (1777-1851). Danish physicist and chemist who also wrote aesthetic essays such as "Two Dialogues on the Fundamental Principles of Beauty, and on the Physical Effects of Tones" and "Two Chapters on the Natural Philosophy of the Beautiful."

attempted to show the limitations of the experimental method. On the basis of my earlier studies of the history of literature and poetics I would like to explain why such an analysis of creativity is a necessary condition for the further development of aesthetics into an experiential science which can gradually resolve the questions raised by aesthetic speculation and thus serve the practical demands of art criticism and the public which appreciates art. Artists mistakenly suspect aesthetics of being primarily aimed at them and at influencing their work. We are too modest for that—and also too well aware of the sensitivity of artists. Instead, aesthetic reflection contributes to the study of art, to art criticism (which is by no means adequately appreciated), and to the debates of the public by creating a vital milieu for the participation in and evaluation of art, together with an appreciation of its higher significance. Such a milieu is important for the artist and can considerably influence progress in the arts. Indeed, it is precisely our German aesthetics which has maintained that art fulfills a crucial and immortal function in human history. German aesthetics has interpreted and defended genuinely great art over against the crude or sentimental instincts of the masses.

The historical method in aesthetics, together with the description of genius and the creative capacity, stems from the middle of the eighteenth century, following on the heels of the analysis of aesthetic impressions. Two approaches were decisive. Montesquieu and Dubos indicated how artistic talents are produced by a given milieu in society. When Dubos astutely derived the origin of art from man's need for a vivid sense of his existence, the connection between social conditions and art became quite obvious. Then Winckelmann successfully applied a hermeneutic technique which, by adapting itself to its object, actually brought a whole sphere of great artistic accomplishment within the scope of our historical understanding. An aesthetic domain thus came to life again and was understood in its essence. It was not merely represented but was relived. Winckelmann's approach demands an affinity between the interpreter and the object interpreted. His revival of Greek art was possible only because we had retained an inner relationship to Plato, and through this to the aesthetic world-view of the Greeks. Plato could thus serve as a tool for understanding ancient art. Thus a conception of classical Greece was developed which became the starting point for all of our interpretations of art history and art theory. According to this conception, the value of Greek sculpture is absolute; its object is ideal, a "spiritual nature projected purely by the understanding";

267

this ideal is an imitation of a beautiful body in its overall form or contour; the specific content of this ideal is a noble simplicity and calm grandeur in both posture and expression.[60] German aesthetics had made beauty central and ultimate for the arts by interpreting its function as the presentation of the ideal, and this is due largely to Winckelmann's influence. Indeed, even the relation of beauty to a metaphysical system, which is so prevalent in our speculative aesthetics, was already implicit in Winckelmann's Platonism. Thus art came to be conceived by us through reference to classical Greece, as religion through reference to Christianity and law through Roman civil law. In contrast to Winckelmann, Herder proceeded from language and poetry. His genius was his capacity to recapture the feelings of the soul from what is expressed in sounds. Thus for him that which is basic and truly living in the realm of art is to be found in nature poetry. Following Winckelmann, Lessing investigated the relation of visual beauty to the conditions of representation in space. In contrast to such spatial art, he designated literature as a temporal art and its subject matter as action. Thus he supplemented Winckelmann's method by investigating the relation of artistic practice to the means of representation of the particular arts and thereby de-

268 riving rules for the artist and for the style of the particular arts. In this investigation Lessing's eminent skill in differentiating pure, indisputable conclusions from what is uncertain was overpowering, and his rules gained great influence over artistic practice.

In the development of German aesthetics which followed Winckelmann and Lessing, four factors seem to me to have worked together. The gradual development of the historical method in the study of art rests on their conjunction.

German transcendental philosophy rediscovered the *creative capacity of human nature* in all domains. This philosophy provides the great impulse to consult one's own experience about human nature, which was initiated by Kant and which dignified and enlivened everything around him. Genius is, according to Kant, an innate, creative capacity which gives the rule to art. According to Fichte, genius transforms the transcendental viewpoint into the common viewpoint. Then Schelling emphasized the unconscious element in genius which accounts for the unfathomable nature of its creations. The conceptions developed by Solger, Schleiermacher,

[60] See Johann J. Winckelmann, *Gedanken über die Nachahmung der griechischen Werke in der Malerei und Bildhauerkunst* (1755), trans. as *Reflections on the Painting and Sculpture of the Greeks* by J. H. Fuseli in 1765.

Hegel, and Vischer take their point of departure here. Admittedly, however, they all stopped short of the decisive point, namely, the psychological analysis of the creative process in a particular art.

The second factor involves the *relation* of this creative capacity *to the objects of natural beauty* which it imitates. This relationship constitutes one of the most difficult problems of aesthetics. Schelling, in the spirit of Plato, offered a fundamental solution through his doctrine of the aesthetic character of the world system. But even all the debates of the Hegelian school about this relation and the place of natural beauty in the system could not move beyond a most highly problematic solution to produce reliable and fruitful concrete insights. These could only result from a psychological analysis of the processes in the individual arts.

The third factor involves the relation of artistic effects to the *artistic medium and means of representation.* Artists who were also aestheticians have always had a predilection for this relation. Lessing's investigations inspired many similar seminal works by painters, poets, and architects. Their special investigations have been successful in deriving a great multiplicity of artistic forms and rules on the basis of the differences between the arts.

And now a fourth factor must be added, which increases this multiplicity beyond all limits and seems to make insoluble the task of establishing rules. Winckelmann had distinguished stages in the law of the development of Greek sculpture. In doing so he made use of a statement by Jos. Just. Scaliger about the stages of Greek literature.[61] Schlegel then transposed Winckelmann's characterization of the four epochs of sculpture back to the history of Greek literature. Thus Greek art was first perceived as an organism whose development followed a lawful sequence. Taking note of the sharp difference between the Greek artistic vision and modern consciousness, Schiller, Friedrich Schlegel, and Hegel carefully distinguished and defined the main *epochs of art* in human history as a sequence of artistic attitudes toward reality. Thus for the first time it was possible to discern the inner connection by which the development of the arts is woven into the larger fabric of cultural and spiritual development.

269

This historicity of artistic content[62] was the last of the four factors which the historical method came to take into consideration in

[61] *Opusc.* (1612), p. 323; see the *Poetics* VI, 1, of the elder Scaliger about the epochs of Roman literature. (D)

[62] The content of a work is its meaning, which should be distinguished from the object or subject matter that is represented.

studying the work of art. Yet in accord with the German turn of mind and, above all, the interests of the speculative epoch, this standpoint which considered the historical content of the artwork predominated over the other factors, which were equally legitimate. The progress of the historical method in aesthetics was limited accordingly. The historical-philosophical method of Hegel prevailed. It neglected those factors in a particular art which derive from its relation to the object imitated, its medium, and means of representation. Questions about forms of expression and sensuous material, style and technique were passed over. Yet through them alone could the creative capacity of the artist have been grasped. Even the significant aesthetic writings of Gervinus[63] and Schnaase[64] manifest this one-sidedness.

Slowly and almost unnoticed by the German public, a well-balanced approach to art which also encompasses the sensuous and technical aspects, as advocated by Goethe and Rumohr,[65] attained methodological success. At the same time as volume after volume of Vischer's aesthetics appeared with the purpose of summing up speculative aesthetics, Semper was writing about style in technical and tectonic art. He gave the first example of the empirical historical method, which explores the inner structure of what has been achieved historically within a particular art, while taking into account its decisive constitutive moments. In spite of several important errors, he made a significant contribution. He was able to designate his work as practical aesthetics, in obvious contrast to speculative 270 and general aesthetics. The way he proceeded from the laws of spatial imagination, traced their effects in simple artistic achievements, and then moved up to the great creations is an enlightening model for how an important historical problem is to be solved in aesthetics. In his approach to art, he was the real successor to Goethe, everywhere following the latter's reflections about imagination, artistic creation, and style. There is also another work, though admittedly not of the same stature and consisting only of fragments, in which Otto Ludwig adopts Goethe's approach to probe the technique of dramatic art, especially that of Shakespeare,

[63] Georg G. Gervinus (1805-71). German historian and literary critic; one of his main works is *Geschichte der deutschen Dichtung* (History of German Literature), 5 vols. (1835-42).

[64] Karl Schnaase (1798-1875). German art historian, who sought to represent the development of art against a broad sociohistorical backdrop.

[65] Carl Friedrich Rumohr (1785-1843). One of the founders of German art criticism as a historical discipline.

with the eyes of a seer.[66] Through such works an empirical and well-balanced historical method has gained more and more ground.

We must now ask to what extent the methods which describe and analyze creative artistic activities empirically and historically are able to fill the gaps left by the two earlier approaches. Given the conflicting artistic tendencies that exist today, the vital task of aesthetics is to make itself heard and to foster a mutual understanding among artists, art critics, and an interested public. What are the means and the perspectives available for such a task?

## II. IDEAS CONCERNING THE SOLUTION OF THE PRESENT TASK OF AESTHETICS

Experimental aesthetics is unable to explain how the work of art is more than a heap of impressions. By means of the analysis of aesthetic impressions, it arrives at only an aggregate of elements that arouse us. The unity of the artwork is for it merely one operative factor alongside others. Should this unity be lacking, then there is just one less pleasure-inducing element, which can, it is assumed, be replaced by adding others. Consequently the style of an artwork and of its particular effects cannot really be made comprehensible by this experimental aesthetics.

Rationalist aesthetics, for its part, perceives beauty only as an intelligible unity. This unity is distinguished from logical unity merely by its lower degree of distinctness. Therefore, according to the principles of this aesthetic theory, beauty must produce a weaker effect than truth. Aesthetic sense impressions are themselves regarded as reducible to relations among ideas. The theory of music put forth by Leibniz and Euler is the necessary consequence of this approach. Every attempt to reduce harmony, tonal affinities and color effects to relations among ideas has failed. Yet if the attempt at such a reduction is abandoned, all that is left is a faint pleasure in an intelligible relation accompanying the elementary sense effects, but foreign and external to them; the unified and powerful effect of a great work of art remains unintelligible, since the unity of the artwork, i.e., its style, pervades and enlivens the whole and inheres in each line, in each melody.

271

Consequently, both methods are insufficient. We must supplement the analysis of impressions by means of an analysis of creation.

[66] See Otto Ludwig, *Dramaturgische Aphorismen.*

And we must replace abstract theorems about unity and order in multiplicity with ideas acquired from an analysis of the living historical nature of art.

## Creation and Appreciation

For the expert even a few notes from a melody by Mozart suffice to distinguish it from all other music. A fragment of a marble statue from the classical Greek period can be dated by the archeologist. Raphael's use of line cannot be mistaken by the expert for that of any other painter. Thus for any particular genius, the mental activity by which he combines sensuous elements has the same fundamental character in each recurring combination. Accordingly, there is in each artwork a mode of unified activity—an inner delineation, as it were—proceeding from the articulation of the basic shapes down to the smallest ornamentation. This we call the *style* of the artwork.

The style of an artwork produces an impression which is not adequately characterized as pleasure, satisfaction, or a delightful feeling. Rather, a definite form of activity is imparted to the psychic life of the perceiver, and in this activity the psyche is broadened, intensified, or expanded, as it were. Style exudes an energy which enhances the vitality of the perceiver and his feeling of life. The attempt to re-create the activity of a great soul, as embodied in a fresco of Michelangelo or in a fugue of Bach, calls up in me a corresponding energy and thus, in a very specific manner firmly established by the object, heightens my own vitality. Thus feeling here is only the reflex of the exertion of psychic energy and activity by which I appropriate the artwork. Through feeling I obtain a reflexive awareness of this inner activity. Consequently the processes involved in the *aesthetic apprehension* of reality, in artistic *creation*, and, finally, artistic *appreciation* are closely *akin* to one another. The appreciation of an artwork is also an activity of the 272 psyche, though more relaxed and tranquil. Its phases take place imperceptibly, but that heightening of spontaneous vitality which is so characteristic of aesthetic pleasure results directly from the form of this activity. We can go further. The enhancement and expansion of one's existence in aesthetic creation or appreciation is akin to the delight that arises from the mode of volitional activity involved in bold and consistent thinking or in courageous actions. In both cases, the psyche, by its *delight in the inner form of its own activity*, assumes a superiority over the crude satisfaction of impulses. This delight alone, among all feelings of pleasure, is independent of what is external and can always give lasting fulfillment to the psyche. The history of our moral development consists of the progressive triumph of this highest vitality which manifests itself in our inner and outer struggles as well as in that mode of spiritual existence which constantly operates independently of external influences.

If I want to glimpse reality through the eyes of a great creator, if I want to comprehend a great spatial magnitude, or the dynamical, moral sublime, then an even greater exertion of energy is required. All of my sensory, emotional, and intellectual powers will be summoned up, enlivened, and intensified, without being overstrained, since I am only re-creating something. When I follow a dramatic action by Schiller, in which the noble spirit of a powerful will is at work, I must elevate and raise myself into an analogous state of mind. But as I assimilate the work in this manner, the particular components of aesthetic delight, which were distinguished in the analysis of aesthetic impressions, also enter the process. These components as analyzed by Burke, Kames, and Fechner blend into the more encompassing process of reception just described. They not only enhance my delight through an addition of new pleasure elements; they do still more in that they satisfy all aspects of my psychic life equally and completely, and impart an awareness of a fullness which is unfathomable because it flows from many sources, like a mountain stream swelling up from countless rivulets.

The meaning of an artwork does not, therefore, lie in an aggregate of pleasurable feelings; on the contrary, the enjoyment of that work fulfills us completely because it increases the vitality of our mind and leaves no striving which has been awakened in us unfulfilled. It satisfies our senses and expands our psyche at one and the same time. An artwork which produces such persistent and total satisfaction in people of different nationalities and times is a *classic*. In this effect alone, and not in some abstract concept of beauty which the work should realize, lies the criterion for the authenticity and value of an artwork. For all too long, aestheticians and art critics have put this barren concept of beauty at the basis of the theory of art. Similarly, an isolated consideration of impressions of pleasure which are produced by the artwork is utterly incapable of making the meaning of the work comprehensible. The immense and sacred importance of art for humanity can only be understood if one starts with the natural power and scope of the artist's psyche and the way in which it encompasses reality significantly, thus impressing a public, which, despite the fact that it consists of people from all walks

273

of life, can be carried away by greatness. In this way, it is possible to grasp the intensification of the powers of apprehension, the expansion of the psyche, its discharge, and its purification as it produces a great artwork.

Admittedly, psychology, given its current level of development, can derive only a few general truths about the creative imagination. The aesthetician must proceed from the creative processes in the particular realms of art. His task is to describe, identify, and analyze these processes. He must present them in all their singularity and with all the riddles which they still contain for our psychology. The spatial imagination, the imagination that plays with tones, and, finally, the imagination that fashions poetic images of human beings and their actions manifest respectively different traits. Each must be subjected to a separate and detailed study. I have given this kind of description and analysis of the poetic imagination in an attempt to provide poetics with a more firm foundation. Statements by poets themselves about the workings of their imagination proved to be a very important resource for this work. Since I published my first observations on this more than a quarter of a century ago,[67] even since my essay dedicated to Zeller in 1887,[68] the available materials about this have grown to such an extent that I would now be able to offer a much more extended and detailed description of the poetic imagination. All the evidence manifests a basic agreement about the most prominent features of the poetic imagination. The same path must be traversed for the other arts. Although the artist may be more reticent here and his own statements scantier, architecture and music can nevertheless find a second mode of support from accounts of the lawlike processes of visual and tonal imagination in their simplest forms as provided by Goethe, Purkinje,[69] Johannes Müller, Semper, and others. The study of the imagination of the sculptor can likewise approach the intentions of the artist from another perspective by means of anatomical considerations such as undertaken by Henle.[70] However, one must above all be receptive to the facts, describe and analyze them without attempting to reduce them to the level of our currently prevailing psychology. On the

274

[67] "Phantastische Gesichtserscheinungen von Goethe, Tieck und Otto Ludwig" (1866), in *GS*, XV, 93-101.

[68] "The Imagination of the Poet," in this volume.

[69] Johannes E. Purkinje (1787-1869). Czech physiologist who investigated the functions of the eye and studied subjective visual figures and recurrent images.

[70] Jacob Henle (1809-85). German anatomist and pathologist; student of Johannes Müller.

contrary, I am convinced that this psychology will be forced to transform itself when it confronts the concrete analyses of specific regions of spiritual and cultural life. Who would be able to understand a Socrates or a Pestalozzi[71] or any other pedagogical genius by means of our current psychology? Pestalozzi in his classroom and Fröbel[72] among his children in the Thuringian mountains inventing children's games and songs: psychology stands perplexed before their loving attempts to enter the obscure recesses and the innocence of the child's psyche. Not only are these phenomena inexhaustible and very complex, but also they contain more than can be explained by our current psychology. The ethical genius who charts new paths for man's ethical life and brings about new ideals of life proves to be even more great and powerful. As psychology develops it will gradually be able to appropriate more of the powerful reality of a pedagogical or ethical genius. Today, however, the most immediate requirement is the *description and analysis* of such great manifestations of human nature, without appealing to those hypotheses that are necessary when psychology seeks to derive all of its findings from a finite number of analyzed phenomena. The same holds also for the description and analysis of the creative artistic capacity.

In light of all this, it is clear that there is within art no right or wrong path, no absolute beauty, and no final authority. Rather, a genius comes upon the scene and compels men to see through his eyes. Then other artists learn to perceive and to represent in the same way, and a movement or a school is formed. These are questions of influence and power, not of what is right or justified. For it is merely a question of whether the style of Marlowe and Shakespeare can dominate the stage and move their most distinguished contemporaries—above all the great queen—whether Michelangelo can build palaces and churches and fill them with human forms so that even competing contemporary and later artists will fall under the spell of his forms. All great battles of art criticism involve the evaluation of something already existing or established, and the claim of a pretender to mount the throne or to overthrow an artistic dynasty which has become stultified. These critical battles have been very useful and effective, and I will show that aesthetics has accumulated sufficient criteria for resolving such struggles, provided

275

[71] Johann H. Pestalozzi (1746-1827). Swiss educational reformer.

[72] Friedrich W. Fröbel (1782-1852). German educator and founder of the kindergarten system.

that the critic learns to understand art in relation to its time, the secret of which the artist is striving to articulate. For "We, we live! The day is ours and the living are in the right."[73] Thus art criticism in our day must above all face up to one important reality, that of naturalism, which is asserting itself in all the arts and in all culturally developed nations. And when our present-day pundits prophesy that sacred religious art, visions, and symbolic poetry are about to supplant naturalism, this merely shows that they do not understand the character of our times and that they confuse its caprices with its enduring character.[74]

## The Language of Forms and the Rules of Art

The all-powerful impulse which drives an artist to embody in sensory images what is within him is, first and foremost, what gives a common stamp to all true works of art.

The way in which we become conscious of the external world—namely, as resistance to our will[75]—explains the basic sense in which we spontaneously and inevitably attribute something inner to what is given to sense as outer. The essence of aesthetic apprehension and creation, i.e., the *relation of feeling and image*, meaning and appearance, inner and outer, is based on this. Thus stable symbolic relations between sensuous, outer forms and psychical contents develop. It is mainly the relations of our emotions to our reflex mechanism which provide the basis for the fact that those emotions discharge themselves in expressions, gestures, and tonal relationships, and that we can then always read back something inner in such outer manifestations. The schematic correlations found in speech between intensity, pitch, tempo, rhythm, and the emotions are especially effective in music. These relations can be observed when a child plays with its voice, for the child's moods are manifested in the pitch and intensity of its sounds and in their rate of succession. In music such relations become detached, as it were, from their foundation. Another source of such musical schemata is movement in dance, for such movement also renders psychical processes visible to the senses. In all these cases stable connections be-

[73] Friedrich Schiller, "An die Freunde," lines 9-10, in *Sämtliche Werke*, vol. 1 (Munich: Hanser, 1962), p. 419.

[74] Symbolism did in fact replace naturalism.

[75] See "Origin and Justification of Our Belief in the Reality of the External World," in *SW*, vol. 2.

tween what is inner and what is outer arise from linking emotions and bodily movements. Secondly, there exist processes of apprehension in which we conceive the external sensuous properties of an object as held together by means of a power analogous to the will. This is the source of the animism of primitive peoples, as well as of mythic thought and the ineradicable tendency of poetry to constantly regenerate the vital force of nature from the vital activities of a well-rounded human being. Nature always is and remains alive to the poet, insofar as he relates to it as a whole person. From this cooperation of the will in aesthetic apprehension there arise many particular relations between inner states and outer processes—especially the impression of the sublime. Here, too, we find a multitude of schemata for aesthetic apprehension.

276

In this way the matrix of a *language of forms* for the particular arts develops. Important here are the deep-seated relations which arise among the languages of form in visual art, ornamentation and architecture, and among the languages of form in music and literature. For these relations make possible the architectural *Gesamtkunstwerk* as well as the musical-poetic *Gesamtkunstwerk*. The realm of the language of forms also extends beyond the arts. Customs, religion, and law, especially in their early stages, use the language of forms to impress us and are thereby related to the arts.

On the basis of our investigation of artistic genius, we can now broaden the practical conclusions which we derived from our consideration of creation and appreciation. We have recognized a personal element in the noblest effects of art, and yet it is precisely the personality of the genius which bears within it something universally valid and necessary which links him to his public. By means of it we understand the language of sensuous manifestations and read the gestures and actions of men; by means of it the inner meaning of everything outer, and ultimately of the entire phenomenal world, is opened up for other men. We learn to see through the eyes of the great painters. Through Shakespeare we learn to understand what happens on the stage of the world and through Goethe what comes to pass in the quiet depths of a human soul. Art helps us interpret destruction as a parable.[76] For that reason the only real artist is one who can advance our ability to interpret reality. Those who merely copy reality teach us nothing which a bright person and good observer would not know without them. They are no better than the idealists, who simply repeat what has long ago

[76] Allusion to the final chorus of Goethe's *Faust II*.

already been said within the language of art. Both derive their *raison d'être* from a boredom that desires temporary diversion. We, however, call for aesthetic impressions whose energy and power will be able to do justice to the enormous enlargement of the human horizon. Never was an artist so free to exercise his genius as today.

277 On this basis the *individual arts* develop—apparently from three quite different roots. The first is the aim to beautify or give significant form to that which nature has produced or to that which serves human purposes. This decorative impulse can already be found in the adornment of warriors and women, tattooing, masks, and wall coverings. According to Semper, the imaginative patterns used in weaving textiles and embellishing metal and wooden artifacts can even be found in the highest form of art which adorns what is useful—namely, architecture. Another root of art, entirely separate from this, is the irresistible human impulse to imitate. "The drawings and carvings of the ancient cave dwellers in Europe show such a high level of perfection that some have suspected that they were forgeries." Bushmen and Australian aborigines cover the walls of their caves, American Indians their cliffs, with drawings. Here we see the basis for the mimetic arts, i.e., painting and sculpture, but also epic poetry and drama. A third distinct root of art lies in the impulse to discharge and communicate emotional states through expression. Here we see the basis for dance, lyric poetry, and music. Accordingly, the arts evolve from separate, deeply rooted, and strong impulses, which then condition their particular development. The individual arts have only a few paltry laws in common with one another. On the basis of the differences in their media—the particular conditions governing the development of the individual arts—we obtain artistic laws of ever more limited scope.

The most general features of comprehensive consciousness, as found in spatial perception and temporal connection, involve *forms and rules* that are binding for both artistic creation and aesthetic appreciation alike. The system of natural aesthetics, i.e., the first method which we discussed, established these forms and rules. They are seen to accompany aesthetic creation and apprehension themselves, for in the production and perception of images in space or of processes in time, these forms and rules derive from the demand for any aesthetically satisfying comprehensive consciousness. Here the great rule of the system of natural aesthetic laws assumes its place: *unity in multiplicity* is the first condition of an aesthetic impression. The sensuous power and dominant energy of the artist only finds adequate expression through connecting an abundance of sensuous impressions, and only a unity in multiplicity which fills our field of consciousness and satisfies its full potential is able to captivate us. To this is added a second rule, which has not yet 278 received such a universal formulation, although it is surely implied by the principle of association already advanced by Kames. The first rule referred only to sensory impressions and their unity. But such a sensory whole stands at the same time in relation to the entire acquired nexus of psychic life. Although this nexus functions without being raised to clear consciousness in its individual constituents, and can only be partially reproduced to supplement and complete certain images, it nevertheless constitutes the hidden background of all our images. The *more encompassing and normal* this *acquired psychic nexus* is and the *more completely* it enters into relation with the images to fulfill and saturate them, the more the artistic product takes shape as a representation of reality in its true meaning. The same holds for the extent to which receptive consciousness is stimulated and satisfied.

To this we must add the special nature of forming and apprehending images in *spatial relations* or in *temporal sequences*. Accordingly, there are an *indeterminate number of further conditions* to which the arts are subject and *further rules* of artistic creation and impression. Lessing, in his *Laocoön,* derived such rules from the difference between space and time as media. The rules are then differentiated more finely according to the relation of the subject matter to the *nature of the medium* in which it is represented. Important laws exist here, although they are today being disregarded to the great detriment of art. The rejection of rules and the acceptance of formlessness are always signs that the time has run out for one style, without a new one having developed yet. Then the timeless laws of art are repudiated along with the rules of a historically conditioned technique.

One law of painting which has the advantage of being easily tested is that outer reality assumes an ideal distance by being framed. The foot with which I tread the soil, the hand with which I touch the stone, are separated from a landscape by its frame. This landscape is now only there for the sense of sight; its reality is thus reduced. We can now go one step further. The fresco which is integrated into an architecturally articulated space must also—no matter how much life and spirit it may possess—display a certain architectural distribution of masses and conform in mood and attitude to the given architectural space. The integration of this fresco into the articulation of space, into what might be called the im-

279 mutable realm of architecture, requires a rhythmic flow of line and a concentration on what is enduring in the characters and in the events depicted. Mere atmosphere as it predominates in contemporary framed landscape paintings must be avoided even when landscape serves as background. The immutable forms and great developmental laws of nature, which stand in fixed relations to our lives, must be made visible. Similarly, the distribution of colors in an architectural whole and in painted sculpture must serve to integrate the architecturally articulated space, the frescoes, and sculptural works into one living whole. A painting on canvas, by contrast, is free to depict all kinds of things. And yet even here the scope and intensity with which reality can be brought to life must be commensurate with its subject matter. Who would tolerate a caricature having the colored splendor of a great painting? And indeed, the German artists of the sixteenth century showed a genuine sense of form in choosing to banish into the shadow-world of chiaroscuro everything which would strike us as improbable if it were physically near or would be intensely repulsive on account of its ugliness.

At this point the dispute over the spatial *Gesamtkunstwerk* can also be resolved. Such an artwork is rooted in the principle of an affinity among the languages of form found in architecture, in ornaments and furnishings, and in sculpture and painting. Here spatial art produces something powerful and vital in which one spirit expresses itself in the languages of different arts and uses walls, columns, statues, and pictures for its living embodiment; it projects an *ens sui generis*. Such an ideal hovered before Raphael and Michelangelo when they found themselves drawn to architectural projects. It was the key idea underlying both the artistic achievements and the aesthetic writings of the great Semper. If only he were still alive today, since such great tasks confront us now without any artist his equal. And this ideal, I am convinced, has the power to produce unsuspected effects and developments in all the spatial arts. But a consideration of the laws of art teaches us that in a *Gesamtkunstwerk* the independent efficacy of the particular arts must be limited. At the same time, the individual arts can retain their autonomy outside the *Gesamtkunstwerk*. The independent vitality of a painting which is intended to be taken in and for itself has its own validity. Similarly, Wagner's *Gesamtkunstwerk,* which is based on the particular character of music, will be successfully developed. But it must allow the single arts united in it to have their independent efficacy alongside it.

A large measure of the discomforting effect that much of the undeniably important naturalistic literature has on today's cultured reader derives from its *disregard for valid aesthetic laws*. The crav- 280 ing to let reality be seen demands freedom from the fetters prescribed by old-fashioned rules of style. That which is new strives to move about under its own power. This is especially so in drama, as in the case of Marlowe, Lope de Vega, and Goethe. One may dispense with some of the rules handed down by tradition. But this will only make it more evident that other rules are necessary for obtaining theatrical effects. Thus the time required for the apprehension of the unfolding of action and the proximity in which that process is brought to us through direct theatrical representation must stand in a fixed and proper relation to the subject matter of each work. When during the course of a whole evening, I—along with many others—witness a theatrical performance, the experience should be enjoyable throughout its duration, and even afterwards should leave behind a feeling of corresponding fulfillment; to that end, the treatment and the subject matter must meet certain requirements, which aesthetics does not invent, but which proceed from the nature of the undertaking. The fact that drama is composed in terms of scenes and that the process is interrupted by means of intermissions already shows that drama must have a much higher degree of unity, a more thorough simplicity, than epic narrative. Further, the sensory power and vitality of theatrical imagery demands a more cohesive and intense development than is necessary in fiction; otherwise confusion and fatigue set in. Many important plays show especially clearly that however much is gained by depicting the full scope of life through a loosely connected series of images, it still cannot compensate for the loss of forcefulness which stems from the disintegration of the action into such images. Efforts to find a substitute for the traditional simple resolutions of drama are in all events worthy of consideration. But an artwork should not end implausibly. Death alone provides a definite conclusion, while life itself—if it is allowed to go on—always remains highly problematic.

If we then consider the subject matter of drama, we see that whatever is small, lowly, and ugly can play a role only insofar as it is set in relation to that which is valuable and great in human nature. Artists are currently striving to broaden the range of their material. We have seen that aesthetics must not attempt to limit this striving by establishing an idea of beauty as the criterion of art. Thus the attempts by speculative aesthetics to define the place of the ugly within a dialectic of the beautiful have been invalidated.

281 There is no inherent limit to the capacity of the artist to shape reality. The artistic laws to which even the greatest genius is subject simply follow from the purpose of art, namely, to provide lasting satisfaction and to enhance life, and from the relation of this purpose to the material and the means of representation. These laws are grounded in the nature of art itself.

When material is treated in accordance with indigenous artistic laws there emerges a style or inner form of the artwork. On the other hand, we find an infinite and unfathomable meaning-content that derives from the relation of the specific subject matter to the entire consciousness of the artist. Understood properly, speculative aesthetics is correct. Each genuine artwork does have an infinite meaning-content, for it orients its subject matter toward the entire universe as reflected in the spirit of the artist. It bestows inner meaning on its subject matter by making its relations to this universe visible. And it does this in a naive manner, without design, merely through the way in which the artist sees and teaches us to see.

## Naturalism

I shall attempt finally, by means of a combination of the methods as well as of their results, to answer the question about the sense in which within the mimetic arts—especially painting and literature—we can speak of re-creating reality.

On the slope of a mountain in the Black Forest there stand farm houses whose roofs beckon to the passerby. Their appearance evokes a melancholy, sweet mood of domestic peace. The natural beauty which presents itself so simply there is woven together into a unity—by means of many thought processes or processes equivalent to them—from subjective conditions of the observer and objective elements of impression. I supplement the outer image with all my representations of inner states of quiet constancy in work and pleasure, year in, year out. This image is pervaded and permeated, as it were, both by the severe monotony of such a life and by the serenity with which it is blessed. And my own momentary condition then determines the particular coloring of the image. I may either give in to a protective impulse which yearns for quiet security, a need for rest; or I may be stirred by desire for simple activity, in which case a sadness about the monotony and seclusion from the world prevails. Thus the sensory impression, even when it seems to affect us by itself, that is, to appear without reference to anything else, is intertwined with a dim nexus of representations, drives, and feelings in the background of my psychic life. An aesthetic impression, like a sensory perception, is not only composite, but is conditioned and unified by innumerable intellectual processes. The way in which we think today about music or architecture has evolved slowly from experiences and intellectual processes! There is an intellectual aspect inherent in aesthetic feeling just as there is in sense perception. If I differentiate a musical interval, its impression rests on its relation to the tonal system. When I play a melody, countless associations arise which give way to others, as the melody progresses, and become connected with each other. The sublimity which can accompany a few soft tones lies not in what I hear but in the undulating sea of representations that comprises the background. 282

What is given as reality here?

I perceive a face and impress it on my memory as an aggregate of colors and three-dimensional spatial relations. But the unity of my consciousness is active in the perception of all this by means of a great number of imperceptible acts that elapse quickly. Thus image components are united and completed by my inner life. My own psychic life is in resonance. The structure of what is perceived is acquired from one especially noticeable point, which I will call the aesthetic point of impression. Every carefully observed face is understood on the basis of such a dominant impression. The overall features are derived from it as a starting point. On the basis of this impression and repeated memory, indifferent features are excluded, while telling features are stressed and refractory ones de-emphasized. The remaining whole is unified ever more decisively. For when memory is attentive and revitalizing, it is not a stagnant repetition of that which has been, but rather a complex of new processes similar to those of perception. We can confirm this through our own experience. When we perceive a familiar face we see the structure thus created in the data of sense.

The genius of the portrait painter consists above all in the normal but powerful grasping of the dominant point and in the structuring of the overall composition by means of exclusion, emphasis and de-emphasis. Thus the portrait does not approximate the original—which only a photograph can—but rather the image apprehended by those who know the original and know it well. And just therein lies its superiority over photography. A portrait gives that familiar image in which all our knowledge of the original is stored up, as it were. Therefore it exhibits not the momentary, but, as in every genuine work of art, something elevated to permanence. For only 283 something like this can bear constantly repeated observation while remaining inexhaustible. If the portrait has turned out well, nothing is missing in it nor does anything foreign obtrude. If it has turned out extremely well, then the portrait discloses the face even more profoundly to those who have known the original subject for a long time. This then is the highest triumph of portraiture.

Thus it becomes evident in the simple case of a portrait that mimetic art is not a copy of reality, but rather a guide to its more profound understanding made possible by the transformation of images through genius. This copy of reality is not to be found within consciousness; that would be a *contradictio in adjecto*. Rather, mankind is indebted to the artist for something completely different. This can no more be grasped by an aesthetics of feeling than by a formalistic or speculative aesthetics. It is instead a matter of understanding how in a work of art, image, form, feeling, thought, and spirit are all connected from within. All mimetic art presents a nexus of life; we saw how nature, which is dead for abstract thought, is alive for an impressionable subject. But wherever there is life, its functions and parts are held together by something pivotal for the energy and feeling of a specific existing being. The artist seizes upon this in what I call the point of impression. And on this basis, structure and form become understandable and significant, capable of being represented and of impressing us. We are fortunate to have in Lenbach[77] a portrait artist who confirms all of this through his example. If we can go further back in time, the great author Dickens is especially instructive precisely for his mastery of the point of impression. It is from this kind of nexus of life that at least some of the effective elements isolated by analytic aesthetics draw their power. And in this respect, the historian does not differ from the artist. Here the gift of being able to perceive a historical personality in focus is one with the capacity to portray this artistically and induce others to also see it. If the imagination does not seek to copy a particular given reality, then its processes of excluding, intensifying, and diminishing in the service of producing a powerful image are bound only to those conditions which result from the total order of reality within which the freely created image is possible. If the artist works predominantly by means of abstraction, then we are left with an empty, faded ideality. If he especially

[77] Franz von Lenbach (1836-1904). Germany's foremost portrait painter of his time.

uses intensification and diminution, then the art characteristic of Thackeray and Rembrandt results. 284

Once these insights have been established, what do the claims of naturalism amount to? Can they signify more than opposition to a way of apprehending and presenting reality which is now exhausted and worn out? Although naturalism arises each time that an epoch of art has run its course, in our day it is the protest of truthfulness against the traditional language of forms created in the fifteenth and sixteenth centuries for people who were quite different—people with different eyes and different mental capacities. Naturalism strives, albeit unknowingly, for the creation of a new inner form of the artwork, a new style, a new technique in the individual arts. For this is what it means for naturalism to compel people to see through its eyes.

A style is a persistent mode of apprehension and representation which is conditioned by the goal, means, and laws of an art, and created by an artistic genius. The power to fashion such a style is the measure of creative capacity. Shakespeare, Leonardo, and Dürer show how remote an enduring style is from so-called idealization: precisely that which is most brittle, factual, and particular is used in the greatest of styles as a moment in the process of producing an impression of reality.

## Contemporary Art

We have seen how a mode of apprehension and a style are determined by the spirit of an artist. This spirit is, however, historically conditioned and shared by a large number of the artists of an epoch. The appreciative public of an age learns to favor the same mode of apprehension, and this, in turn, has an influence on the artists. Thus I have earlier been able to show[78] that the *technique* of a poet is always just the *expression of a historically limited epoch.* There are artistic laws for literature, but there is no universally valid literary technique. Attempts such as Freytag's to project a general technique of drama cannot succeed. Form and technique are historically conditioned in their very substance. And it is the task of art history to trace the successive types of technique.

The style and the technique of Raphael, Michelangelo, Shakespeare, Cervantes, and Corneille are no longer ours. That style was the greatest since the days of the Greeks. Just as it appropriated

[78] "The Imagination of the Poet," in this volume.

universally valid elements from the ancients and turned them to good account, it will itself continue to have a further influence. But 285 it was also merely the expression of an age. It may appear audacious to single out its main characteristics by means of those mimetic arts whose subject matter is man; yet such an approach is enlightening precisely for our present age and its concerns. The individual power of human beings, their autonomy, yet at the same time their connection with a pure ideal system of order and other individuals participating in it: this was the secret which all great artworks of that epoch articulated in a variety of ways. As a result, this style shows a propensity for ideal relations between persons, contrasts, parallels, gradations, and harmonious arrangements of groups. Its figures are all constructed within an ideal space, as it were. This was the style not only of Raphael, Michelangelo, and Corneille, but also of Shakespeare, Lope de Vega, and Cervantes. The parallel plots, the analogous and contrasting figures found in Shakespeare are ultimately oriented toward a point in an ideal space. Schiller's drama *Wallenstein* derives its enormous meaning from the circumstance that here opposing political forces, confronting one another with equal justification, really do provide a basis for the structure of the actions. The political preconditions underlying the action are already displayed in the camp of Wallenstein's army.

Science has taught us to always seek lawful relations in reality. Today even man can only be understood by the systems that condition him—the systems of natural laws, of society, and of history. Every artistic work reflects this striving to understand. We seek to articulate the lawful relations existing in any sphere of phenomena, even in an individual formation. With an unlimited concern for truthfulness, the artist seeks to express the character and value of the real system of natural laws in which man is placed. The arts point to real relations everywhere: the relation of the worker to the machine and the farmer to his soil, the bond of persons working together for a common end, genealogical lines of descent and heredity, the confrontation of the sexes, the relation of passion to its social and pathological basis and of the hero to masses of unnamed people who make him possible. In the present upheaval surrounding the arts, we await men of genius who will create a new style for the particular mimetic arts.

In every such time of crisis, naturalism appears. It destroys the worn-out language of forms; it attaches itself to reality, seeking to obtain something new from it. This was the case with Donatello,

Verrocchio, Masaccio, and Marlowe. They prepared for the style and technique of great creative geniuses.

Today, too, new means are being sought to produce new effects. 286

Who could turn a deaf ear to the power of this progressive movement? It will continue to transform our literature and produce a new style in all the arts, for it manifests the power of a new mode of thinking gained from science. From a sense of affinity between literature and science, which has grown steadily since Voltaire, Diderot, and Rousseau, this new school has provided a blend of both. Zola especially advocates this blend. We have shown how an estimable feeling for truth here nevertheless leads literature astray. To be sure, the poet also makes real life—and, as such, truth—his theme. However, for him everything that exists becomes understandable through that point on which all actions and feelings ultimately turn, never through the abstractions of the conceptual attitude. With all the resources of his vitality he appropriates life, encompassing and grasping it. A literary work claiming to be scientific goes even more radically astray than one that preaches morality. The poet must suspend the easy answers offered by an uncritical scientific attitude to the great question, What is life? He must learn from science and will not want to contradict any real truth. However, he should not allow himself to be misled by popular natural science journalism. When an artistic genius looks life in the face in his own way—patiently, seriously and persistently—he will, like Dante, Shakespeare, and Goethe, apprehend it more profoundly than he ever could from all the books on physiology and psychology. Then we will be able to move beyond the theory of the animality of human nature, the gloomy specter that haunts our literature and makes it so dismal. On the one hand, it has led an idealist like Tolstoy, moved by a half barbaric, half French dread of human bestiality, to negate life. On the other hand, it has encouraged others to find a dismal delight in animalism.

It is a profound and honest trait of our new literature that it strives to portray current society as it is, with relentless truthfulness, and thereby subject it to criticism. But how much more fortunate were Cervantes, Erasmus, and Rabelais as they fought their battles against a feudal, priestly society. They did so in the name of a middle-class common sense. They were convinced of the ultimate triumph of their cause. Consequently a radiant sense of humor emanates from their works. But our middle class dramas have no heroes. Our sharply etched images of society as it is lack the feeling that even in social crises human nature has latent within it the 287 power to triumph and that man can overcome all the dislocations from which he suffers today. Our writers are at times impressed by the Latin ideal of the destruction of family and property in the interest of political tyranny, at times by the backward Nordic cult of the rights of unbridled individuality, or then again by a barbaric Slavic wallowing in the bestial sphere of human life. The depth of the Germanic character must become our poetic source for a consciousness appropriate to our time of what life is and what society should be. Such a consciousness must do justice to the present and no more. For every generation of poets and thinkers attempts to make sense of the enigmatic, unfathomable face of life, with its laughing mouth and mournful eyes. This will remain an unending task.

# 3

# *Fragments for a Poetics (1907-1908)*[1]

VI, 313

TRANSLATED BY RUDOLF A. MAKKREEL

## PRELIMINARY CONSIDERATION

Lived experience provides the basis for religion, art, anthropology, and metaphysics. We must not only accept these experiences as they come, but generate and multiply them. Then we must designate them and compare them, etc. . . .[2]

## LIVED EXPERIENCE

A lived experience is a distinctive and characteristic mode in which reality is there-for-me. A lived experience does not confront me as something perceived or represented; it is not given to me, but the reality of lived experience is there-for-me because I have a reflexive awareness of it, because I possess it immediately as belonging to me in some sense. Only in thought does it become objective.

Everything that I experience or could experience constitutes ⟨a nexus or system⟩. Life is a process which is connected into a whole through a structural system which begins and ends in time. For a spectator this presents itself as a closed identity because of the sameness of the phenomenal body in which this process takes place. At the same time, it must be contrasted to the emergence, growth, decline, and death of an organic body by noting the peculiar fact

[1] These fragments were taken from Dilthey's literary remains and constitute notes from 1907-1908 that were to be used for a revised *Poetics*. Printed in *GS*, VI, 313-20, to which pagination in the left margin refers.

[2] There follow several phrases which serve as a shorthand for ideas to be developed.

that every part of it is ⟨connected⟩ with the other parts in one consciousness by means of some kind of lived experience[3] of continuity, connectedness and self-sameness. In the human sciences, I restrict the expression "life" to the human world; it is thus determined by the domain in which it is used and is not subject to any misunderstanding.

314

This life is localized temporally, spatially, and through interaction in conjunction with a general sense of process as found in our experience. These spatial, temporal relations that consist of interactions are, however, different from the relations that occur in natural processes, etc. In the human sciences, interaction does not designate that relation in nature established by thought, according to which causes and effects can be recognized as being determined by the principle of *causa aequat effectum*. Rather, it denotes a lived experience. This can be designated by expressions such as the relation between impulse and resistance, pressure, reflexive awareness of being furthered, joy about other persons, etc. Naturally the term "impulse" in this context does not designate a power, spontaneity, or causality posited by some explanative psychological theory, but merely the lived state of affairs (somehow grounded in the psychophysical life-unit) through which we experience the intention to execute movements aimed at an external effect. Thus lived experiences arise which can be generally expressed as involving the interaction of different persons.

The expression "lived experience" designates a part of this course of life. As such it is a reality that manifests itself immediately, that we are reflexively aware of in its entirety, that is not given and not thought. The death of a loved one involves a special structural relation to grief. This structural relation of grief to a perception or a representation, referring to an object about which I feel grief, is a lived experience. This structural nexus appears in me as a reality, and everything that it contains of reality is lived experience. This lived experience is delimited from other lived experiences by the fact that as a structural nexus of grief, of perceiving or representing what the grief is about, and of an object to which the perception refers, it constitutes a separable immanent teleological whole. It can be isolated within the household of my life because it belongs to it structurally as a function.

As it is with the above lived experience, so it is with a cognitive experience, with every volitional experience that realizes a purpose,

[3] German text reads: "*Bewußtsein (Erlebnis?)*"

every aesthetic experience: lived experience designates a part of the course of life in its total reality—a concrete part which from a teleological point of view possesses a unity in itself. Because the concept of the present does not ascribe any dimensions to it, the concrete consciousness of the present must include the past and the future. Therefore lived experience is not merely something present, but already contains past and future within its consciousness of the present.

The religious thinker, the artist, and the philosopher create on the basis of lived experience. 315

In the ceaseless advance whereby the future always becomes something present and this in turn something past in the constant and continuous stream which we call time, the present is a cross-section which as such has no extension. If we conceive of time apart from what fills it as a line, then its parts are of equal value. Even the smallest part of this continuum is linear, a sequence that e-lapses, and therefore not ⟨a point on the time line⟩. The moment in which the future becomes present, it is already sinking into the past. The present is a cross-section in this stream. This cross-section as such could not be experienced. How then is the present really experienced?

It is the nature of the present to be filled or ful-filled[4] with reality in contrast to the representation of reality and its peculiar modifications either in memory or in the anticipation of reality and the will to realize it. This being ful-filled with reality is what remains constant in the advance of time, whereas the content of lived experience is subject to change. This advancing process of being ful-filled with reality can be a living experience in contrast to a representation of a past or future lived experience. Thus we say that we always live in the present. The present as experienceable is not this cross-section, but the continuously advancing being ful-filled with reality in the course of time. Because this advance is continuous, and because the nature of the present in it is always to be ful-filled with reality, the present always exists as the same and without any break or gap. Everything that is there for us as the fulfilling of time and thus as the fullness of life is such only in this present. As lived experience recedes into the past and our memory, more of it is drawn into a continuum whose temporal moments are mere determinations of its meaning in the nexus of life. On this basis, the modifications of our intuition of time, such as duration,

[4] *Erfüllung* can mean both filling and fulfilling, but we will stress the latter.

succession, change, and the measurement of stretches of time, arise from the determinations of the ful-filling of time.

The qualitatively determined reality that constitutes lived experience is a structural nexus. To be sure, it runs its course in time; it is experienced as a sequence that e-lapses; its temporal relations can be apprehended. But in the structural nexus of this temporal course, that which, although past, endures as a force in the present receives a peculiar character of *presence*. Although lived experience is a process, it is a dynamic unity—and this not only objectively, but in our consciousness. This word "presence" indicates that when a component of the structural nexus of lived experience recedes into the past—but is experienced as a force reaching into the present, it obtains a peculiar relation to the present in our lived experience, namely, that of being drawn or incorporated into it. This is a different relation than when something stands over against the experienced state of the present or when something separated by other lived experiences nevertheless is experienced as exerting an influence on the present. But this presence, this character of a dynamic unity, even this consciousness of it, is after all only the consequence of a property of the structural nexus which constitutes lived experience. And what is this property?

316

I experience the death of a person; an intense grief wells up in me; it leads to an expression of it in words to others, or to a volition which somehow refers to this death. In the structural nexus of these processes the successive parts are connected through the unity of the object. Although this is a condition for the unity of the lived experience, it does not yet delimit it over against other lived experiences. Again we ask: on what does this delimitation of the lived experience rest?

Lived experience is determined by presence and by qualitatively determinate reality. The qualitative aspect of lived experience is something totally different from that of a natural object. In the latter the quality is apprehended in relation to that whose quality it is. In lived experience there is only this qualitatively determinate reality and nothing exists for us behind it. That is indeed the whole reality of the lived experience. Take, for example, how Dürer's painting of *The Four Apostles* in Munich first becomes a lived experience for me. All other male figures, etc.[5] I cannot claim,

[5] The meaning of this phrase is not clear. Perhaps Dilthey wants to suggest that the lived experience of this painting with four male figures recalls all other paintings with male figures that he has seen.

however, that this whole lived experience lies in the picture or even in that which I focus on as meaningful. Rather it includes its context or milieu, etc., in short, the whole reality that constitutes the lived experience. What I focus on in the apperception of lived experience is a partial selection; it may already be an interpretation. Grief about my friend: was it really that? The lived experience ends when I leave the room. I lose my ability to hold the painting in consciousness when I meet someone, etc. However, I can return to it. It is merely an extension of this lived experience when I revisit it. Here a peculiar relation is formed. The lived experience of the latest visit contains the fullness of the earlier visits. Past lived experiences have come together in a more powerful unity. They stand in a special relation to the present lived experience. When I see a person again, I can feel as if we had never been separated. That is how intimate and special the relation is. Lived experiences are related to each other like motifs in the andante of a symphony: they are unfolded (explication) and what has been unfolded is then recapitulated or taken together (implication). Here music expresses the form of a rich lived experience. However far apart the individual experiences of visiting the museum may be, something is explicated in them, and finally we obtain the total fullness of the last lived experience in which an implication or recapitulation is realized—a complete lived experience is constituted.

## The Lived Experience of the Poet

317

He has a great capacity for suffering. He becomes engrossed in this suffering and fashions it into a lasting mood. Precisely because of this he is able to liberate others by allowing suffering to be resolved in tranquility.—Musical experiences. The music of Beethoven, etc. On the other hand, the joy of creating.

It is important to approach lived experiences *disinterestedly*. This is as much the case in philosophy, etc., as in poetry. Disinterested means impersonal. Christ on the Cross, who is conscious that death is involved in his divine mission, acts impersonally. Disinterestedness is thus not only a property of the aesthetic impression, but also of the lived experience of the creative artist. Thus Kant stands corrected.

The liberation of the imaginative process from contingency is also its liberation from the personal.

## STRUCTURAL PSYCHOLOGY

### Localization of Psychic Processes within the Structural Nexus in Terms of the Relation of Whole to Parts

We naturally gather lived experiences that have been fixed by their expressions into a system, which is then completed as a memory system, as conduct of life and totality of life. Illusion and its dissolution, passage from passion to reason, etc.: this kind of completing process takes place in poetry, in conversations about our experience of life, in a philosophy of life.

This [gathering together and completing of lived experience] is more basic and more natural than the move to psychology. Lived experience obtains an expression, which represents it in its fullness. It brings out something new. It neither utilizes nor in any way requires psychological concepts.

When the subject stands in a positive relation to an object, the correlate of the lived experience is a value; when the state of the subject also tends toward that object, the value becomes a purpose. Thus a terminology arises which has nothing to do with sensation and feeling.[6] It is through the process of interpreting objectifications of lived experience that things ⟨receive⟩ a positive determination. We move not in the sphere of sensations, but that of objects; not in the sphere of feelings, but that of value, meaning, etc.

I experience that something obtrudes itself on my consciousness because of its intensity. What occurs at any point of our psychic life is also there for consciousness. I am grieved about the death of my nephew; I remain localized in space and retain my temporal orientation. Through introspection I make all this the object of my observation. Can I base a science on this? If I want to express these observations in words, then they become part of a linguistic usage that has been conditioned in many ways. Observation itself is conditioned by the questions that I pose. Merely to ask myself or others whether the aesthetic impression of a mountain involves empathy is to induce such empathy. Observation has shown us how states such as feelings, which can be expressed in some way, merge into each other. Furthermore: I can't make clear distinctions among

318

[6] Dilthey intended to revise his *Poetics* to replace the subjective language of feeling and pleasure with the object-oriented language of lived experience, value, purpose, and meaning.

classes of lived experiences. For example, is it the case that a sensation is a determinate feeling and a feeling always merely an indeterminate sensation? For this and other reasons the boundaries between our lived states are uncertain. Are there feelings that exist without reference to any content? Is hate a feeling or does it also already contain some kind of impulse or desire? Accordingly, only a different method can lead us further. It must proceed through an intermediary.[7] (It aims at a fundamental classification for more general purposes.)

Lived experience generates its own expressions. The latter are found in literature, etc. These expressions always contain a relation of subject and object. In language, this relation manifests itself as an intuition or concept (judgment) *of* objects, a feeling *about*, an intention *to*, etc.

In each of these expressions there is a relation which exists between a state of a subject and an object. This in turn makes possible the objectification process, which then gives us objects designated by a positive value, a positive judgment, or a direction of will. On the other hand, modes of relation arise which I designate as reality, law, etc., value, action, etc. When I then correlate similarly designated objects and the expressions and modes of relation which arise from these objects, I discover a peculiar relationship. These modes of relation exhibited by different objects are the same for large groups of them; in every case ⟨we can⟩ order these groups around a type, this type and what is correlated with it is clearly delimited from every other type. Thus, *whereas a fixed delimitation was not possible for lived experiences, this can be found for expressions and objectifications.*

I designate as structure the relation that exists among the components of a lived experience. Type is the most simple mode in which a lived experience is constituted in a group. What is structured in this way then enters into more general structural relationships, and these finally form a schematism, a context located in the course of a psychological development that shapes the unity of the life-unit.

This indirect procedure that uses expressions has to some extent been applied by Brentano and Husserl. Brentano goes back to Mill, who in turn refers back to Comte, the great critic of the introspective method. But its pure execution depends on insight into the follow-

[7] The intermediary meant here is the intermediary between lived experience and understanding, namely, expression.

ing: expression, understanding, structure, function, attitude (relation).

The three groupings[8] are first clearly distinguished through the categories that emerge in them. These categories are abstract concepts that refer to something living that is incontestably a *relation*, which can then be designated as a *function*, insofar as together with 319 other basic relations it is referred to the whole. . . . Kant's antithesis of form and content can be ruled out here. . . .

## Meaning as a Category of Life

The meaning of life is the unity of the totality of the parts and the value of the individual parts. This unity lies in the nature of life. Thus meaning is a category obtained from life itself. It is thus not an aesthetic category, even though art is based on it. Proof: no one can avoid this perspective.

The meaning of things is already inherent in them. The meaning of relations of life. Natural attitude. How could Goethe have proceeded differently?

If we step aside from our chasing after goals and calmly turn in upon ourselves, then the moments of our life appear in their significance.[9] *This is the natural view of life*. In the poet this manifests itself more intensely. He apprehends the significance of life. Since the poet is not incited to action by what he perceives, the human world becomes significant to him. The meaning of an event lies in the fact that its causal nexus at the same time produces a value. For the man of action, value lies in a goal; for the poetically inclined, value lies in every moment of life. In youth, life and poetic attitude coincide—life can still be spontaneous. Deliberate action forces life and poetic attitude to diverge. It is then that our poetic powers usually disappear. In Goethe, however, they were intensified as a mode of contemplation separate from action. Therefore he needed to withdraw from life in order to write poetry. Then the significance of every moment of life manifested itself all the more forcefully in contemplation. He who only writes poetry remains a dreamer, but the man of action restricts the poetic within himself.

[8] Dilthey seems to mean the three kinds of relations in lived experience: type, general structures, and schematism.

[9] The word *blicken*, which was inserted into this sentence by Misch (see *GS*, VI, 319), is omitted in Misch's later text, *Lebensphilosophie und Phänomenologie* (Darmstadt: Wissenschaftliche Buchgesellschaft, 1967), p. 73. The omission is explained in note 1.

## Poetics Considered from the Perspective of the Theory of Meaning

When we deal with the problem of the tragic or the comic, we see how useless every abstract value theory is for understanding the poet. It is not a question of differentiating values, but of their inner (structural) relations to each other and to the individual as a totality and to life as such a totality; not evaluations, not relations of subordination, but rather relations which lie in the real inner qualitative relations of parts to the whole. The main concept here is the qualitative relation as based on the qualitative determinateness of lived experience.

It is especially important that lived experience be comprehended as a unity in memory, and that it be related to other lived experiences 320 in the totality of life = meaning. The meaning of life provides an inner bond between poetry, religion, and philosophy, and refutes the theory of *l'art pour l'art.*

# II

# POETRY AND LIVED EXPERIENCE

# 4

# *Goethe and the Poetic Imagination (1910)*[1]

ED, 124

TRANSLATED BY CHRISTOPHER RODIE

To which of the immortal goddesses
Shall we award the highest praise?
I seek no dispute,
But I myself will give it
To the perpetually moving,
Ever new,
Strange daughter of Jove,
His darling child
Imagination.

—*Goethe, "Meine Göttin"*[2]

The poet's imagination, considered in its relations to the material of lived reality, tradition, and what earlier poets have created, is central to all literary history. From these relations spring the characteristic basic forms of the creative imagination and its poetic products. No modern German poet demonstrates this centrality of the imagination in literary creativity as clearly as Goethe, and none demands as much insight into the nature of imagination in order to be understood. This derives from the position that Goethe occupies in European literature.

In the introduction to this volume[3] I described how the course of European literature was determined by the emergence of modern

[1] Earlier versions of this essay were published in 1877 and 1905. This translation is based on Dilthey's final reworkings for the second and third editions of *Das Erlebnis und die Dichtung* (hereafter *ED*), 3rd ed. (1910). Pagination in the margin is in accordance with the 15th ed. (Göttingen: Vandenhoeck, 1970).

[2] In *WA*, 2:53. The translation follows that in *Goethe*, intro. and trans. by David Luke (Harmondsworth: Penguin, 1964), p. 63.

[3] "Gang der neueren Europäischen Literatur" (The Course of Modern European Literature), which was added to the 3rd ed. of *ED* . See 15th ed., pp. 7-17.

science. This literary movement had endured for almost a century and a half when Goethe was born. He grew up under its influence, and the sum of its accomplishments was preserved by him. He was also surrounded by the German Enlightenment; when he began to write poetry, Lessing was at the pinnacle of his influence. Goethe adopted as his own the most characteristic tendency of this German Enlightenment—which was determined by our entire history—that of man's immersion in himself and in the ideal of his universal nature. But the historical mission of Goethe, building on the great achievements of the Enlightenment, was to introduce a new era of poetry. It was in Germany that this new era arose. Goethe and the Romantics were linked inseparably in their efforts to further the emancipation of the poetic imagination from the domination of abstract thought and "good taste" which knew nothing of the power of life. We all know how this emancipation was initiated in various countries, in the English doctrine of genius, in Rousseau, Hamann, Herder, *Sturm und Drang*. Goethe was carried forward by this movement. But the new poetry itself was his creation. And the struggle of his poetic imagination with the Enlightenment—even with the spirit of the science of that time itself—is a spectacle unparalleled in the history of literature.

125

This is the reason that despite a multitude of significant attempts to understand Goethe, I am perhaps not unjustified in proceeding from a general perspective to try to fathom the power and particular character of Goethe's poetic imagination, and only then, from the insights obtained in this manner, to examine his life's work.

Scientific work, philosophical meditation, and government service took up a large portion of Goethe's life's work. These activities did not merely occupy him during the long periods in which he produced no poetry; they were indispensable to him for that engagement with life and with the world which he needed in order to fulfill his poetic mission; and only an intellectual mastery of the Enlightenment could clear the way to his poetic world.

His versatile creativity was centered in his imagination. He often expressed this himself—most plainly when he had attained a clear self-consciousness through his sojourn in Italy and his contact with Schiller. In 1788 he said of himself, concerning the substance of his Roman experiences: "In these eighteen months of solitariness I have found my true self again, and that self is the self of an artist. . . ."[4] And in a noteworthy self-characterization originating from the pe-

[4] Goethe to Karl August, Duke of Sachsen-Weimar, 17 March 1788, *WA*, IV, 8:357; trans. in Ludwig Lewisohn, *Goethe: The Story of a Man* (hereafter *GSM*) (New York: Farrar, Straus, 1949), p. 348.

riod of his collaboration with Schiller, he said of himself that "the focus and base of my existence consists in an ever more active drive toward poetic creation, operating continuously, directed both inward and outward. When this has been grasped, all the other apparent contradictions are resolved. Since this drive is restless, it must turn outward in order not to consume itself for lack of material."[5] This self-characterization accounts for his interests in the fine arts and his contributions to public life and science through this outwardly directed striving of his creativity. Since at the time he believed that he was finally sure about his true calling, he considered these other interests and pursuits "false tendencies."[6] But the objective observer will be more inclined to agree with Schiller that they were the broad foundation for a poetic life-work of an entirely new kind which was inseparably bound up with the formation of his personality. Thus Goethe's place is not among the great natural scientists, philosophers, or statesmen, but with Aeschylus, Dante, and Shakespeare. 126

## LIFE

Poetry is the representation and expression of life. It expresses lived experience and represents the external reality of life. I will try to evoke the main aspects of life in the memory of my reader. In life, my own self and its milieu are given to me; also a feeling of my existence, a mode of conduct, and an attitude toward the people and things around me; these exert pressure on me or offer me strength and pleasure, make demands on me, and occupy a place in my existence. Thus each thing or each person receives a particular force and coloring from its relations to my life. The finitude of existence, bounded by birth and death and restricted by the pressure of reality, awakens in me the longing for something enduring, changeless, and withdrawn from the pressure of things, and when I look up to the stars, they become for me the symbol of such an external untouchable world. In everything surrounding me, I re-experience that which I myself have experienced. At dusk I look down upon a quiet town at my feet; the lights appearing one after another in the houses below are to me the expression of a secure, tranquil existence. The life I find in my own self, my situations, and the people and things around me constitutes their life-value, in

[5] *WA*, I, 42(2):506.
[6] *Ibid.*

contrast to the values they receive through their effects. It is this life-value that the literary work shows first of all. Its object is not reality as discerned by the intellect, but rather my own state and the state of things as manifested in life-relations. What a lyric poem or a story shows us—and what it fails to show us—can be explained on this basis. But life-values are related on the basis of the totality of life itself, and these relations give meaning to persons, things, situations, and events. Thus the poet addresses himself to what is significant. When memory, life-experience,[7] and its intellectual content are used to raise the relations of life, value, and significance to the level of the typical; when an event is made the bearer and symbol of something universal; and when ends or values become ideals, what is expressed in this universal content of the literary work is 127 not knowledge of reality, but the most vivid experience of the interconnectedness of our existential relations in the meaning of life. Beyond this there is no idea of a poetic work and no special aesthetic value which poetry should realize.

This is the fundamental relation between life and literature upon which every historical form of poetry depends.

Surely the primary and most decisive feature of Goethe's poetic work is that it grows out of an extraordinary energy of lived experience. His creations are utterly foreign to the literature of the Enlightenment, and for this reason even Lessing was unable to appreciate him. His moods transform everything real, his passions intensify the meaning and form of situations and things beyond the realm of the usual, and his restless creative drive changes everything around him into form and image. In this respect there is no distinction between his life and his literary work. His letters demonstrate these qualities just as much as his poems; and this peculiarity must become evident to anyone who compares these letters with those of Schiller. Even here, Goethe's poetry is already completely different from the literature of the Enlightenment.

Life already contains the forces operative in the imagination.

## THE POETIC IMAGINATION

### I

The imagination strikes us as wondrous, as a phenomenon wholly different from the everyday doings of men; yet it is only a more

[7] *Lebenserfahrung* (life-experience) is more encompassing than *Erlebnis* (lived experience). It also incorporates understanding.

powerful disposition which some people possess, grounded in the unusual strength of certain elementary processes. Beginning with these processes, human life develops in accordance with its universal laws into a concrete form which deviates completely from the ordinary.

The specific characteristic of the poet already asserts itself when his perception fashions simultaneous sensations into spatial forms or sequences of sensations into rhythms, melodies, and phonic patterns. His life-relations, moods, and passions exert a primordial force on the constitution of his perceptions.

Memory images have quite different degrees of clarity and intensity, of power and distinctness, in different individuals under otherwise similar circumstances. From shadowlike representations stripped of color and sound to shapes of things and persons which some can project onto the visual field when they close their eyes, we find a spectrum of wholly different forms of reproduction. With the talent for descriptive poetry we can connect the extraordinary capacity to preserve the visual sharpness of reproduced representations and to bestow conspicuousness on those that are freely produced. The poet's ability to think concretely demands as its basis a dynamic sequence of sharply defined images. Likewise, it presupposes a plenitude of acquired impressions and a completeness of memory images: this is why poets are for the most part also marvelous storytellers.

128

What then is the relation between accumulated experience and a freely creative imagination, between the reproduction of forms, situations, and destinies, and their creation? Association, which recalls given elements in a given combination in a reproductive representation, and the imagination, which produces new combinations from the given elements, appear to be separated from one another by a very clear boundary. But in investigating the real relation of these two major psychic functions, we must employ the descriptive method without any explanatory hypotheses. Only in this way can the literary historian acquire the confidence to avail himself of more refined psychological insights, rather than of the crude conceptions of everyday life in his interpretation of literature.

In the observable course of psychic life, the same representation can no more return within one consciousness than it can recur identically in a second consciousness. Just as the new spring does not allow me to see last year's leaves back on a tree, so I can't resurrect—even obscurely and indistinctly—yesterday's representations. When, after having perceived an object, we close our eyes and do not otherwise alter our position, the representation into which the perception has passed over still possesses its greatest intensity and conspicuousness. Yet only a part of those elements which were contained in the perceptual process are represented in the after-image of memory. Even here—where, after all, only a mechanical mode of memory is involved—a concern to recall the whole image unmistakably requires an attempt at re-creation.

But when other images have insinuated themselves between the perception and the representation, and we then strive to recall the perception completely, the remembered representation is constructed on the basis of a definite inner perspective; it incorporates, 129 as materials, only as many elements of the object of the original perception as are occasioned by the conditions now present. These elements impart an affective coloring to the image through the relation of similarity or contrast to the present state of mind. This is how, in times of the most painful unrest, the image of a previously calm, though joyless, state of affairs can suddenly appear before us as a blissful island of sunlit peace. Indeed, not infrequently a wholly false representation is constituted.

Finally, when we strive to recall to ourselves not single impressions, the memory of which refers to a specific act of perception as a momentary image, but—as is usually the case—representations or combinations of representations, each of which represents the object in all its perceived states, then the formation of such a representation is still further removed from mechanical reproduction and approximates much more closely that of artistic re-creation.

In short, just as there is no imagining which does not depend on memory, there is no recollection which does not already contain within itself one aspect of the imagination. Recollecting is at the same time metamorphosis. This allows us to see the connection between the most elementary processes of psychic life and the highest accomplishments of our creative capacities. It allows us a glimpse into the origins of the vitality and variety of the human spirit, wholly individual and unique at every point, of which the immortal creations of artistic imagination are the best expression. Reproduction is itself a formative process.

Thus, the disposition of the poet already manifests itself in the power of the simple processes of perception, recollection, and reproduction, by means of which all sorts of images, including those of characters, destinies, and situations, are activated in consciousness. In memory itself, we then discover an aspect through which it is linked to the imagination; metamorphosis permeates all our images. This is also true for the remarkable phenomenon of hypnagogic imagery. Is there anyone who, with eyes closed prior to falling asleep, has not taken delight in simple phenomena which appear then? Stimuli stemming from inner organs appear to a dormant, yet receptive, visual sense as rays and mists. From these, without any design or intention being involved—for we are submerged in the purest and calmest state of contemplation—luminous and colorful fantasy images unfold with constant variations.

The transformation in memory of images and their interconnections is, however, only the simplest and, accordingly, the most instructive case of the formative processes which are typical of the imagination. These processes of intensification, diminution, arrangement, generalization, typification, formation, and transformation, which are sometimes unconscious and sometimes conscious and intentional, produce innumerable new intuitive forms. Certain aspects of images are excluded, others are intensified, and intuitions are completed through memories.[8] And this transformation into something new that transcends what is contained in, or derivable from, lived experience and perception, also affects the connections of representational images. A thinking in images emerges, and in it the imagination attains a new freedom. We attempt to rethink the past. We project future possibilities, invent free happenings and lose ourselves in them, empathize with inanimate objects and endow them with unexpected living processes. And all this is intensified when these spontaneous activities become purposive through conscious design. The forces which produce this series of formative processes originate in the depths of the psyche as it is moved by life in various ways toward pleasure, pain, mood, passion, and striving.

130

In all this we see a basic predisposition in certain persons whereby everything, from the most basic processes of psychic life upward, aims at poetic creativity. It operates with the greatest strength in children, in primitive people, in individuals with passions and dreams, and in artists. Thus it is distinguished from the regulated imagination of the political thinker, the inventor, or the scientist whose professional discipline serves to regulate the formative processes in accordance with the standard of reality.

2

How then does poetic imagination itself arise from this imaginative predisposition which leads toward poetic creation, and what are its distinguishing marks?

[8] Cf. "The Imagination of the Poet," in this volume.

As we have seen, the imagination is inseparable from the whole psychic nexus. Every communication which occurs in daily life automatically transforms lived experience; wishes, fears, and dreams of the future transcend reality; every action is determined by an image of something which does not yet exist: ideals of life project ahead of man—indeed, ahead of the human race—and lead both toward higher goals. The great moments of existence, birth, love, and death are transfigured through customs and institutions which adorn reality and point beyond it.

131 From the function of the imagination in the world of daily life I now distinguish that *productive activity* of imagination through which a *second world* distinct from that of our practical activity is formed. This mode of imagination expresses itself spontaneously in the production of the dream—the most ancient of all poetry. Furthermore, this imagination deliberately fashions such a second world whenever someone strives to liberate himself from the bonds of reality; this occurs in play, but most especially wherever the festive intensification of existence through costume, masquerade, or solemn procession brings forth a world separated from that of everyday life. The age of chivalry and the courtly culture of the Renaissance show how a poetic world completely detached from life can already be predelineated in this life. Likewise, the religious imagination produces a world distinct from experienced reality. Here intuitions of divine beings arise through contact with invisible forces. These intuitions are interwoven with life, its suffering, and activity. Thus this religious imagination which produces myths and belief in the gods is at first bound up with the needs of life. With the development of culture, the imagination separates itself from the purposive relations of religion and attributes an independent significance to that second world, as is shown by Homer, the Greek tragedians, Dante, and Wolfram von Eschenbach. Accordingly, it is poetry that first fully liberates the supersensible religious world from the constraints of our vital needs and purposive relations.

Only now can we grasp the nature of the *poetic imagination*. Up to this point we have merely discussed the general conditions of the poetic imagination, which integrates all the psychic processes whereby the poetic world is given shape. These psychic processes are always rooted in lived experiences and the substratum of perception fashioned by them. Lived relations govern the poetic imagination and come to expression in it, just as they have already influenced the perceptions in the poet. Here, involuntary and imperceptible processes prevail. These processes constantly affect the color and form of the world in which the poet lives. This is the point at which the connection between lived experience and imagination in the poet begins to reveal itself. The poetic world is there before any particular event inspires the poet with the conception of a work and before he writes down its first line. The *process* in which the *poetic world arises* and a particular *literary work is constituted* derives its law from an attitude to the reality of life which is completely different from the relation of elements of experience to a system of knowledge. The poet lives in a wealth of experiences of the human world as he finds it in himself and discovers it outside himself; for him these experiential facts are not data from which he extracts generalizations, nor are they used to satisfy his system of needs. The poet's eye concentrates on them calmly and reflectively; they are *significant* to him; they arouse his feelings, sometimes gently, sometimes powerfully. However distant in the past or remote from his own interests these facts may be, they are a part of himself.

132

All the powers of the whole person cooperate in weaving together the colorful tapestry of poetic representation and its figures. *Feeling* is the vital source of all poetry. But poetry is at the same time permeated by *thought*. After all, mature persons form very few images which do not include general universal elements; and, owing to the effects of general social circumstances and psychological attitudes, there is no individual in the human world who would not at the same time also be representative from various perspectives. There is no personal fate which is not also a particular case of some more general form of life. Under the influence of the poet's reflective contemplation, images of men and destinies are shaped in such a way that, while they directly represent only single states of affairs, they are nevertheless wholly saturated by the universal and in this way become representative of it. General remarks that can be found scattered throughout literary works are in no way necessary for this; their primary function is rather to liberate the reader temporarily from the spell of feelings, tensions, and overpowering sympathies, thus elevating him to a contemplative mood. Finally, all poetry bears the stamp of the *will* from which it sprang. Thus Schiller saw in beauty a reflection of the moral. Goethe said, "Generally, the personal character of the writer influences the public rather than his talents as an artist."[9] The form of the will operative

[9] Eckermann, *Gespräche*, 30 March 1824; *CE*, p. 77.

in the production of the work of art is manifested in the author's handling of the plot.

The imagination produces figures or characters which are, within certain limits, like real persons. Thus Dickens lived with his characters as with people like himself, suffered with them as catastrophe befell them, and feared the moment of their demise. Balzac spoke of the *personae* of his *Comédie humaine* as if they lived; he analyzed, praised, and blamed them as if they belonged together with him to 133 the same respectable society. He could conduct long debates about what they ought to do in a particular situation. The way in which Goethe was moved by the tragic emotions of his poetry as he composed it can be inferred from his statement to Schiller that he did not know whether he could write a true tragedy, but that he was frightened at even the prospect of attempting it, and was almost convinced that he could destroy himself by the mere attempt.

Thus the poet deviates from all other classes of men to a far greater degree than we might be inclined to assume. In contrast to philistine interpretations based on everyday conceptions about composing poems, we will have to become accustomed to grasping the inner drive and the outwardly directed processes of a poet's demonic nature on the basis his psychic constitution. The poet is not to be measured by some average standard for the normal man. Indeed, it is on the basis of this powerful and wholly instinctive creative drive that Goethe's life and work is to be understood.

## GOETHE'S POETIC IMAGINATION

Goethe's imagination offers a classic instance of the powerful inner nexus described above, through which poetic creations arise from elementary processes. Everything in the conversations and works of the young Goethe was permeated by the strongest sense of life; every state of mind was expressed with concerted energy; images appeared which embodied this sense of life symbolically. Whatever Goethe said or wrote during his youth was fertile with the seeds of literary works waiting to come into being.

His incomparable verbal imagination emerges from this power of expressing states of mind. Language is the poet's medium. But it is more than that, for the sensuous beauty of poetry—rhythm, rhyme, and the melody of speech—constitutes a special realm of the greatest effects, which are separable from what the words mean. Who can be fully aware of the meanings of the words while reciting

Goethe's poem "To the Moon"? Their meanings are only a faint and mysterious accompaniment. Indeed, the linguistic imagination of the poet is based on the fact that he creates and forms so as to fix our attention on these effects, just as the painter does on the effects of his lines and colors. Goethe rules supreme in this realm of language. This derives from the fact that in him lived experience is always and immediately connected with an expressive drive. In his youthful conversation, he often switched over into recitation of his verses. And during his walks he sang to himself "strange hymns and dithyrambics"[10] in which the rhythms of his inner stirrings found their tonal expression. The great free rhythmical measures of his art in their natural course and vitality stemmed from within: never has such a will to power over life been expressed in such rhythms! In his youth he broke with the whole tradition of our language. He created a new poetic style on the foundation provided by Klopstock. In this, he made use of his native dialect. He exploited the living energy of verbs. He worked with unprecedented word constructions in which he added new prefixes to verbs, connected nouns with particles, verbs with their objects, strengthened the sensuous energy of the verb by dropping the particle. He combined nouns into new and larger word formations; he intensified expressiveness through the repetition of significant words; he ran through question, answer, and exclamation in order to re-create an inner movement. Every inner state is expressed in a particular melody of language. Then, in the first years at Weimar, he gradually tones down this utilization of his native dialect. He tempers the vehemence of his expression; he gives a more complete representation of psychic movement; through new means, such as the increased use of significant adjectives, he allows us to intuit reality. Just as Luther had first established literary German through his translations of the Scriptures, so Goethe together with Schiller instituted the classical mode of literary German. The greatness of Goethe's style developed on the basis of these innovations. His unique verbal imagination manifests itself in such accomplishments. Its power is so pervasive that all our subsequent poetry is dominated by it; even today his poetic language is able to call forth any mood in the reader.

134

This verbal imagination of Goethe's, which develops from the drive and talent to express lived experience, is combined with an

[10] *WA*, I, 28:119; *The Autobiography of Goethe. Truth and Fiction: Relating to My Life* (hereafter *TF*), 2 vols., trans. by John Oxenford (New York: John D. Williams, 1882), vol. 2, p. 112.

astonishing power of imagining the visual appearances of things. Thus, from the dynamic states of the psyche we ascend to the visual beauty of the objective world.

The following words by Goethe throw light on the natural basis of such a talent for providing visual forms:

> I had the gift of imagining a flower in the center of my visual field when I closed my eyes and lowered my head. It did not remain in its first shape for even one moment. But it immediately disintegrated, and from its inner core new flowers would unfold composed of both colored and green petals. They were not natural flowers, but rather fantastical ones, which nevertheless were regular like a sculptor's rosettes. It was impossible to stop this spontaneous creation; rather, it would last as long as I pleased, neither weakening nor strengthening. I could produce the same effect if I imagined the patterns on a stained glass window which would then similarly display continual changes proceeding from the center toward the periphery, just like the recently invented kaleidoscope.[11]

135

I myself have found it to be the case that, if conditions are favorable, at the moment before falling asleep an observer can see colored mists rise from the dark visual field and take on various forms: in this manner we catch a glimpse of what must have been, for Goethe, utterly effortless and beautiful creations of an involuntary creative imagination. In the *Elective Affinities*, which is pervaded by the idea of our physiological dependence even in the most lofty manifestations of emotional life, he transfers this talent to Ottilie, a character very dear to him. In a state between sleep and wakefulness, Ottilie discerned a dimly lit space in which she saw Edward, who was away at war. The account reminds us of what Cardano said about himself.[12] Several passages in *Tasso* give profound testimony to the power which the creations of the imagination exercise over the poet himself: "It is in vain that I repress that impulse which surges day and night within my bosom."[13] Then consider also how

[11] *WA*, II, 11:282.

[12] Girolamo Cardano (1501-76). A contemporary of Benvenuto Cellini, he held chairs of mathematics and medicine at Milan, Pavia, and Bologna. During sleepless nights he would observe images arising from the right-hand corner of his bed. See Cardano, *The Book of My Life*, trans. by Jean Stone (New York: Dover Publications, 1962) p. 147.

[13] *Torquato Tasso*, in *WA*, I, 10:229; trans. by Charles E. Passage in *Goethe's Plays* (New York: Frederick Ungar, 1980), p. 581.

Tasso describes to Leonore how he anticipates his exile to Naples: "I will go in disguise. I will assume the poor cloak of a pilgrim or a shepherd."[14] We share in Leonore's terror as she interrupts him in order to undo the dismal spell with which this image surrounds him. And Goethe presents the most general and powerful poetic image of this kind in *Pandora.*

Goethe also generalized the insight into the poet's nature which he had acquired from such experiences: "One now sees more clearly what is meant when it is said that poets and all genuine artists are born. The poet's inner productive force must bring back vividly those after-images, those phantoms remaining behind in his sense organs, memory, and imagination, and must do so spontaneously, without design or will. They must unfold themselves, grow, expand and draw together in order that from fleeting schemata images with true presence can come about."[15] He told Kanzler Müller that:

136

> My sensory receptivity happens to be so peculiarly constituted that I can remember all outlines and shapes with extreme clarity and distinctness, but am on the other hand very acutely affected by anything misshapen or imperfect. . . . For after all, if I did not have such keen receptivity and impressionability, the characters in my works could not be so vividly depicted and sharply individualised. When I was younger this ease and precision of perception deluded me for many years into thinking that I had a vocation and talent for drawing and painting.[16]

In his aphorisms, Goethe conceives the aim of poetry in the same way: "The poet is dependent on representation. The highest representations are those which rival reality, i.e., when their delineations by the spirit are so lively that anyone can take them to be real."[17]

In Goethe these two types of poetic imagination cooperate powerfully to produce a universality of poetic genius without equal in the modern age. He himself described the power and special character of his creative talent in his account of his last years in Frankfurt. "For many years I had never known it to fail me for a moment. What, waking, I had seen by day, often shaped itself into regular

[14] *Ibid.*, p. 232; *Goethe's Plays*, p. 583.

[15] *WA*, II, 11:283.

[16] *Goethes Unterhaltungen mit dem Kanzler Friedrich von Müller*, 17 May 1826, p. 107; trans. in *Goethe: Conversations and Encounters* (hereafter *GCE*), ed. and trans. by David Luke and Robert Pick (London: Oswald Wolff, 1966), p. 143.

[17] From "Betrachtungen im Sinne der Wanderer," in *WA*, I, 42/2:176.

dreams at night; and, when I opened my eyes, there appeared to me either a wonderful new whole, or a part of one already commenced."[18] This natural talent was operative in him both when alone and when among company. During this period, he gave expression to the self-assured consciousness of such a creative force in *Prometheus*. He had to regard this "talent altogether as Nature." It appeared as something "spontaneous—nay, even involuntary."[19] Sometimes it was idle for a long while, and he could then accomplish nothing even through design; then again there would be times when his pen could hardly keep up with his "somnambular poetizing."[20] Even the greater works of this period were composed as in a moment of inspiration, although Goethe had carried them within him and molded them for a long time. He wrote *Werther* in four weeks, "rather unconsciously,"[21] as if guided by a dream, and without having first put on paper either a sketch of the whole or the execution of any of the parts. He afterwards found hardly anything in it which needed to be changed. This was, then, the way in which his most perfect and unified work of art prior to *Hermann and Dorothea* originated. In all of this the properties of the poetic imagination strike us in their most extreme intensity: an involuntary, lawlike creativity, freed from ordinary life and its purposes, but rooted in the fullness of psychic powers.

137 This peculiar feature of Goethe's youthful writing persisted into his late years, though it was modified by equanimity and diminishing imaginative power. Long periods of preparation alternate with periods of the most intense creativity. In 1795, while at work on *Wilhelm Meister*, he wrote that the firewood, gradually gathered and prepared, "is finally catching fire."[22] In order to preserve a poetic mood and the inner creative drive, he would seek solitude, preferably at the castle in Jena. Yet deliberate efforts of this sort could never assure success; his best always came to him spontaneously. His creations developed over long stretches of time:

> Certain great themes, legends, things handed down from the remotest past were impressed so deeply in my mind that they remained alive and operative within me for forty to fifty years. My greatest treasure seemed to be the capacity to see such

[18] *WA*, I, 28:311; *TF*, vol. 2, p. 211.
[19] *WA*, I, 29:14; *TF*, vol. 2, p. 237.
[20] *WA*, I, 29:15; *TF*, vol. 2, p. 238.
[21] *WA*, I, 28:224.
[22] Goethe to Schiller, 15 December 1795, *WA*, IV, 10:348.

> valued images often renewed in imagination, for they were, to be sure, always transformed, yet they matured toward a purer form, a more definitive representation, without undergoing essential change.[23]

In other poets, such as Schiller, tremendous conscious effort went into the creation of every narrative work. It seems that the impulsive power of the will is even communicated in the plot, and gives it that powerful movement which we admire in Schiller's dramas, whereas Goethe's works—even his greatest—do not exhibit this characteristic. Furthermore, Goethe would not ignore the judgments of his friends about what he had begun. He was decisively influenced, especially by Schiller, in working out the plots of *Wilhelm Meister* and *Faust*. In other cases, the judgments of friends led him to abandon the plan for a poetic work. Like other great authors, he could also be deeply moved and distressed by merely visualizing the figures of his imagination. When he visualized to himself a situation in *Wilhelm Meister* in complete detail, "he finally began to weep bitterly."[24] The same thing occurred when he read aloud a just completed portion of *Hermann and Dorothea*: "You see how one can be melted by one's own fire,"[25] he said as he wiped his eyes.

But an adequate conception of the power and peculiarity of Goethe's imagination emerges only when one perceives how its effects permeated every part of his being. Its influence pervaded his life, his world-view, and his ideals. When he was still a youth, his imagination ruled over a plenitude of as yet unregulated forces. It intensified enormously the joys and sorrows he experienced in those years of youthful energy, it enveloped everything real in a veil of beauty and conferred on him the gift to enchant both men and women and sweep them along with him. His imagination sometimes idealized his present situation, but then again it sometimes exaggerated beyond endurance what was restrictive in every circumstance of his life and drove him, by means of novel images, into limitless distances. Thus his imagination intensified both his genius and the restlessness and dissatisfaction of his youth to the point that he toyed with suicide, and became inconstant in his friendship, love, work, and life goals; it led him to the demonic of the superhuman as expressed in the *Urfaust*. At that time he appeared to

138

[23] *WA*, II, 11:60.

[24] Goethe to Charlotte von Stein, *WA*, IV, 4:231.

[25] Caroline von Wolzogen, September 1796, trans. in *GCE*, p. 53.

Jacobi as one possessed, one who found it almost impossible to act voluntarily. His poetic imagination offered him time and again a temporary escape from the troubles of his life by raising this life to a world of illusion or semblance. He unburdened his soul by expressing what moved him. He separated himself from his own situation by placing himself outside it and viewing it as something alien to him which then could take its place in the realm of poetic imagination; and there, such a situation, liberated from its roots in his own life, could be allowed to unfold according to its inherent consequences. This same imagination was also helpful when he took command of himself and developed the ideal of his maturity. For this ideal was based on extracting the greatest possible meaning from life in its totality. In contrast to the actualization of abstract ethical rules, the meaning of life was actualized imaginatively and grasped through images of the past, of the future, and of the possible as such. For the life contained in these images lies at the basis of every ideal conception of the individual self. Finally, Goethe's poetic imagination unlocked the mystery of nature and of art. Because Goethe's efforts to intuit nature were akin to the processes of artistic productivity, his experience of the creative power of his own imagination was at the same time a disclosure of the power of nature itself. He regarded nature as a purposive power, governed by laws, which expresses itself in metamorphosis, intensification, an architectonic of typical forms, and the harmony of the whole. Consequently, art was for him the highest manifestation of the workings of nature.

## POETRY AND LIVED EXPERIENCE

All the general characteristics of poetry derive from the relation of life, imagination, and the formation of the work. Every poetic work 139 presents an individual event. It provides the mere appearance of something real through words and their combinations. Accordingly, it must utilize all the means provided by language for producing the impression and illusion of reality; its primary and most significant aesthetic value lies in this artistic treatment of language. The work does not aim at being an expression or representation of our actual life. It isolates its object from the actual context of life and treats it as a totality in itself. In this way, it transports the reader into a sphere of freedom, in that he finds himself in a world of appearance not subject to the necessities of his actual existence

(*Existenz*). But the work heightens the reader's feeling of his human existence (*Daseinsgefühl*). For the person confined by the course of his life, it satisfies the longing to experience possibilities which he himself cannot realize. It opens up to him a view into a higher and more powerful world. When re-experiencing such a world, his whole being is caught up in a sequence of psychic processes appropriate to it, ranging from pleasure in sound, rhythm, and visual clarity to a genuine understanding of an event on the basis of its relations to the whole scope of life. For by representing some part of reality, every genuine poetic work accentuates some characteristic of life which has not been seen in this way before. At the same time that it makes a causal chain of processes or actions visible, it allows us to re-experience the values that belong to an event and its individual parts through their relation to the context of life. The event is thus raised into something significant. There is no great naturalistic poetry which does not express such significant features of life, however bleak, bizarre, or dominated by blind natural forces they may be. It is characteristic of the greatest poets to present events in such a way that they illuminate the context of life itself and its sense. Thus poetry opens up our understanding of life. Through the eyes of the great poets we perceive the value and connectedness of things human.

The subsoil of poetic creation contains personal lived experience, the understanding of alien circumstances, and the broadening and deepening of experience through ideas. The point of departure for poetic creation always is life-experience, whether as personal lived experience or as understanding of others in the present or from the past, and of the events in which they interact. Each of the countless states of life which the poet lives through can be designated, in psychological terms, as lived experience; but a more fundamental relation to his poetry can only be assigned to those aspects of human existence which disclose to him a *basic trait of life*. If the poet also draws upon the world of ideas—and the influence of ideas upon Dante, Shakespeare, and Schiller was very great—then we should note that all religious, metaphysical, and historical ideas are, in the final analysis, models or representations distilled from the great lived experiences of the past. Only insofar as these ideas make the poet's own experiences intelligible to him do they help him to see something new in life. Thus the idealism of freedom,[26] which Schiller adopted from Kant, merely served to elucidate Schiller's great inner

140

[26] See Dilthey's sketch of a typology of metaphysical systems in *SW*, vol. 6.

experience, in which his noble nature became aware of its dignity and sovereignty through its conflict with the world.

Innumerable modifications of the poetic experience have developed on the basis of lived experience! By giving the inner religious world a dramatic visibility, the Greek tragedians produced an expression of a deeply felt lived experience. But this expression was at the same time a representation of a powerful external state of affairs and must have had an incomparable effect. We still experience something of these effects in the Oberammergau passion play and in our great oratorios. A different kind of modification of experience can be found in Shakespeare, who allowed his understanding to be fully absorbed by externally given events, and then imbued them with his own sense of life. Thus his characters were as diverse as they are in nature and as complex as lived experience can make them. Goethe gives expression to his own lived experience, to the formative process at work within himself. From this relation between lived experience and its expression, there emerges the full course and depth of psychic life which is not available to introspection. In each case, a relation between personal lived experience and expression is interwoven with a relation between what is given externally and understanding—but always in a different proportion. For a psychic state is given in personal lived experience simultaneously with, and in relation to, the objectivity of the surrounding world. The psychic life of the other is grasped through understanding and re-creation; yet I see it there only because I project myself into it. In the various modifications of the poetic experience, it is only the intensity and the connection of these moments which differ. The visionary talent of the poet, which teaches us about ourselves and the world, about the ultimate attainable scope of human nature, and about the fullness of individuality, develops on this foundation. Countless forms of this visionary aptitude exist.

When on this basis an event is endowed with significance, a poetic creation arises. Just as we distinguish the chemical composition, weight, and temperature of natural objects, and study them for 141 themselves, so we can take a narrative poetic work, whether it be an epic, romance or ballad, drama or novel and distinguish within it subject matter, poetic mood, motif, plot, characters, and means of representation. The most important of these concepts is that of motif, for it is here that the poet's experience is grasped in its significance: it is through the motif that this experience is connected with the plot, the characters, and the poetic form. The motif contains within itself the creative force which determines the form of the work. These particular moments which can be distinguished in the poem develop out of life-experience as if by organic growth; each of them performs a function relative to the work as a whole. Thus every poem is a living creation of a special kind. A full appreciation of a poet would require us to define all the conditions, both within him and external to him, which influence the modifications of lived experience and understanding characteristic of his creativity, and to comprehend the productive nexus in which the motif, plot, characters, and means of representation are then formed.

As I now try to express the relation between Goethe's life, life-experience, imagination, and poetic works, what strikes me again above all is the wonderful unity and harmony of his existence. There is hardly an incongruity or dissonance in it. His life is a development according to an inner law, and how simple this law is, how regularly and steadily it operates! On the basis of his intuition of the creative force of nature, Goethe proceeds to re-create life as the object of poetry. He shapes his poetic world and his own life in one indivisible context according to the inner lawfulness he finds there.

The condition for this extraordinary phenomenon can be found in German history; since Luther and Leibniz, the Germans have tried to develop an inner bond between religion, learning, and literature based on the immersion of the German spirit within itself and its self-formative powers. Thus a world-historical force came into being whose influence was spread, both during and after the eighteenth century, from Germany throughout Europe. This force inspired all the creations of Goethe's age. Goethe can be linked to the transcendental philosophy of Kant, Fichte, and Hegel and to Beethoven's instrumental music; he strove to elicit something universally human from the unconscious depths of our existence. He shared with these philosophers and with Schiller, Humboldt, and Schleiermacher the ideal of the formation of man from the inner law of his being. On the basis of this culture there arose a poetic world created by Goethe, Schiller, and Jean Paul, which has been developed further through Novalis and Hölderlin. 142

The entire spiritual development of Europe was influenced by this new world-historical force. It was from this standpoint that Goethe accomplished the greatest poetic task of understanding life in terms of itself, and thus representing it in its significance and beauty. His poetic talent was only the highest manifestation of a creative power which was already operative in his own life. In Goethe, the processes of living, forming, and producing poetry (*Le-*

*ben, Bilden und Dichten*) achieve a new unity based on the scientific study of nature. This unity has established a model of truthfulness, of pure naturalness, of clear vision, and of unprejudiced interpretation of our existence—a model which has influenced all subsequent thinkers, poets, and writers.

I will now make use of a comparative procedure in order to further illuminate the nature of this poetry by means of likenesses and contrasts. For us today, Shakespeare and Goethe stand out as the two greatest forces of modern world literature. And, as we have seen, precisely these two represent particularly important modifications of the poetic experience and consequently of the portrayal of humanity. These two great Germanic seers, who have focused their penetrating gaze on the unfathomable visage of life, complement one another; and kindred natures stand at their sides.

## SHAKESPEARE

Dickens' letters and accounts of his life allow us an insight into the workshop of a poet. He appears as a genius whose whole life is spent experiencing reality in the most detailed, spontaneous observation of that which new spheres of experience continually offered him. He saw so much through his various occupations and life situations—as apprentice, legal secretary, reporter in Parliament and in the country—he was able to observe so many facts, and to study thoroughly not only the prisons and asylums in most European countries but also respectable society, that no German poet's life is comparable to his. However, this must be connected with his impetuosity, his monstrous blunders due to his feverishly energetic nature, and his indifference to the further refinement of his own personality and to any higher intellectual pursuits. All these are the external circumstances of a life full of bliss and sorrow, shared with
143 the characters that were fashioned from this experiential material. He yields himself completely to that which he perceives outside himself.

By studying such detailed accounts of the poetic activity of this contemporary of John Stuart Mill, we obtain knowledge which also sheds light on the inner life and constitution of Lord Bacon's contemporary, who seems wholly incomprehensible to us.

Shakespeare seems enveloped by impenetrable mysteries. The most zealous research has produced only a few really authentic primary sources: a number of documents of church records and legal transactions, and several polemical passages by contemporary authors. It seems that he did not attract the attention of his contemporaries to any great degree. Only with great caution can inferences about his way of thinking, his religious or philosophical convictions, and his character be drawn from his dramas. His sonnets are a mystery, inasmuch as we do not dare to take them literally on account of their enormously paradoxical emotional tone. But neither can we afford to dismiss the assumption that they contain a core of the most intensely subjective and personal feeling.

We take as our point of departure a few indubitable facts about his creative disposition given in his works. Shakespeare displays a range of accurate, profound, and wholly positive perceptual images, with which no other poet's fund of exact images can even be compared. One must suppose him to have had a perceptual energy and memory far exceeding even that of Goethe and Dickens. He had a sovereign command of the signs for things; Max Müller has calculated that he had approximately fifteen thousand words at his disposal, almost twice as many as Milton. Experts have shown his knowledge of plants and animals to be amazingly exact and extensive. He speaks of falcons and falconry as someone who had spent his life as a hunter, and some of these passages have been rendered intelligible only through specialized investigation by experts. He speaks of hounds as if, like Walter Scott, he always had a few favorite dogs lying at his feet. In a time when medical ideas about insanity were still full of superstitions, he appears as such an acute observer of pathological psychic states that prominent psychiatrists of our day have studied his *personae* in the way that one studies real cases. His knowledge of law cases and legal procedures is such that prominent English jurists can account for it only with the supposition that he had the opportunity to acquire expertise as the apprentice of a lawyer. The scope and depth of his characterizations indicate to us the utmost bounds of poetic creativity.

144

All this presupposes, as its cause, not merely the greatest perceptual energy and memory; we must also conceive of a genius who utterly devotes himself to reality—noticing, observing, forgetting himself completely, and transforming himself into that which he grasps. I cannot help thinking of Ranke's phrases: "I would like to efface my self"[27] and "show only what actually happened."[28] Shake-

[27] Leopold von Ranke, *Englische Geschichte*, vol. 2 (Leipzig: Duncker und Humblot, 1870), in *Sämtliche Werke*, vol. 15, p. 103.

[28] Ranke, *Geschichten der romanischen und germanischen Völker von 1494-1514*, in *Fürsten und Völker*, ed. by Willy Andreas (Wiesbaden, 1957), p. 4.

speare lived not within himself, but in that which stimulated him from without. He was a great human observer. He felt no need to develop a system of strong convictions or to create an imposing, powerful self. Like Raphael, he is depicted as a mild and gracious being; and yet at the same time it was characteristic of him to pursue every human disposition and passion to its ultimate consequences and its most secret hiding place. This corresponds to his manner of representation, which depicts men as they appear to the external observer in real life; their physical presence is fully distinct, but their volitional processes, their ultimate motives, often remain obscure.

The accounts of his life are in agreement with this view. The brisk, almost feverish pulse of his protagonists beats in him, too, as is the case with Marlowe and Ben Jonson. He married at the age of eighteen, and in the following year was burdened with the care of a family. (He was born in 1564, married in 1582, had a daughter, Susanne, on May 26, 1583, and two other children, Hamnet and Judith in 1585.) Between 1585 and 1587, when he was in his early twenties, he appeared in London to establish a livelihood for himself. By 1592, at the age of twenty-eight, he had already achieved fame and prosperity. As a consequence, Greene could characterize him in a pamphlet of that period as "being an absolute *Johannes Factotum,* [who] is in his own conceit the only Shake-scene in a country."[29] By 1598 he had begun to be fully recognized, and from then on his name appeared on the title pages of his dramas. Even then he began making gradual preparations for his secluded retirement in Stratford. By 1602, at the age of thirty-eight, he was already a well-to-do country gentleman in Stratford, although he was still active in London. Then we find him, in his forties (a more precise dating cannot be determined from sources now available), at home in his stately house surrounded by his gardens, relaxing from the turbulent haste of his life. His career was at an end. He died in [145] Stratford at the age of fifty-three on April 23, 1616, immediately after the wedding of his youngest daughter.

In the two matters which are usually said to be decisive for life—marriage and career—rash, hasty decision seems to have been followed by great difficulties and disappointments. A harsh experience of life and a resolute, clear handling of it filled Shakespeare's mature years, and, strange to say, the overriding concern of his life was not merely his poetry, but just as much his determination to raise

[29] Robert Greene, a fellow dramatist, wrote this in 1592.

himself and his family into the ranks of the well-to-do landed gentry. Like Dickens, he became acquainted with life and men not as a chattering and gawking onlooker, but as a participant in the most exuberant comedies as well as in tragedies. He had that dynamic disposition which would rather do the wrong thing than nothing at all. Cervantes, the one poet comparable to Shakespeare in his knowledge of life, also rushed restlessly through his life as a secretary of a papal legate, as a soldier in the most varied campaigns, in the chains of captivity, and as an author. And it was precisely these colorful experiences of restless youth wrestling with realities which gave such poets the main material of their experiential horizon. Aeschylus and Sophocles, too, acquired their understanding of the world in their active lives as citizens and soldiers, and it was only Euripides who lived out his life in his library as a man of letters.

How the course of Shakespeare's life brought him the vast experience of the world which his dramas exhibit can still be reconstructed. The landscape around Stratford recurs again and again in his writings; he grew up in that landscape, with its gently rolling hills, lush green meadows, and the groves and fruit orchards in which the villages lie concealed and through which the Avon winds. This is the backdrop for *A Midsummer Night's Dream* and *The Winter's Tale*. Folk poetry, country fairs, and *merrie olde England* still cast their cheerful brightness over the land. The introduction of *The Taming of the Shrew* and much of *The Merry Wives of Windsor* recall for us persons and scenes from these days of his youth. In addition, folk songs and legends surrounded Shakespeare during his wanderings. At that time, too, the receptive psyche of this landowner's son—who must also have been a passionate hunter, judging from the story about his poaching on the land of a neighboring nobleman—appropriated innumerable images from the world of plants and animals through which he moved joyfully. The area also provided material for the countless jests about narrow-minded small farmers and villagers in his dramas. And it was here, too, that the great and bloody past of his country left its marks. A road led from Stratford to Warwick Castle, eight miles away. In the castle courtyard surrounded by massive turrets, and among tombstones, one could still feel the presence of shades out of the past, including that of the great kingmaker. A few miles further lay Kenilworth, which at that time belonged to Leicester, who employed one of Shakespeare's relatives; and biographers have

146

enjoyed imagining the eleven-year-old boy present at the great festivals given there for the queen by her favorite.[30]

However that may have been, life as reflected in his writings must surely have become familiar to the boy early, in Stratford itself. Between 1569 and 1587, during Shakespeare's boyhood and youth, the merry life of the town—in whose financial accounts champagne, claret, and muscatel played no small role—was punctuated by no fewer than twenty-four visits by theatrical troupes between 1569 and 1587, the years of Shakespeare's boyhood and youth. Goethe and Dickens also tell how, from early childhood on, characters from poetry were woven into their real lives. "It is curious to me," says Dickens,

> how I could ever have consoled myself under my small troubles (which were great troubles to me), by impersonating my favorite characters in them. . . . I have been Tom Jones (a child's Tom Jones, a harmless creature) for a week together. I have sustained my own idea of Roderick Random for a month at a stretch, I verily believe. . . . Every barn in the neighborhood, every stone in the church, and every foot of the churchyard, had some association of its own, in my mind, connected with these books, and stood for some locality made famous in them.[31]

These recollections express, better than any of us could, how the figures from legends and the stage must have impressed themselves on the youthful Shakespeare, and how personages out of the past began to come to life before him in the historic setting of Warwickshire.

There are good grounds for assuming that he became acquainted with the complexities of life early, while still living in Stratford, and his father's business difficulties gave him an early taste of harsh reality. This was to be true for Dickens as well. Still a youth, Shakespeare had the passionate experiences of love and marriage behind him. Then came London. In these youthful years he never looked back; he preferred to do something questionable rather than merely to be a bystander. What a contrast this makes to the personality of the young Goethe, who was cautious, deliberate, and at bottom fully in control of himself even when he appeared to abandon him-

[30] Lord Robert Dudley, Earl of Leicester.

[31] From *David Copperfield*, quoted by John Forster in his *Life of Charles Dickens*, vol. 1 (London: Chapman & Hall, 1874), pp. 9-10.

self utterly to passion. When Shakespeare arrived in London, perhaps with several manuscripts in his baggage, he based his life on his profession of dramatist and actor. He joined the Globe Theater troupe, which had close connections to the queen's household and became the King's Players by royal charter during the reign of James I. Shakespeare's sonnets give moving expression to the new shadows which this step cast over his life. What attracted him becomes apparent when one considers Goethe's and Dickens' passion for the theater, and thinks of Molière and Sophocles. The actor and the truly creative poet—especially one such as Shakespeare—have, at the basis of their genius, the same imaginative capacity for transforming themselves into various characters; what is intended in the poet's words first becomes completely real in the actor's performance.

147

And what an effect Shakespeare's profession must have had on him at that time! It not only gave him stage experience, but also—as was the case with Molière—it appears to have fully developed, to the level of highest virtuosity, his capacity to transform himself completely into the most diverse characters. One discerns in the actor that he is always someone other than himself, thinking and feeling himself into different roles; Shakespeare's profession as an actor must have been strengthened by his natural tendency to be a collection of individuals and thus to view the world and life in manifold ways, to feel himself in various ways. The free and easy style of life in London of that day allowed for contact with the highest social circles on the one hand, and with vagabonds on the other. This offered Shakespeare an incomparable opportunity for absorbing the shifting scenes of human life and the most varied characters; and his position as dramatist pressed him to take pen in hand and write what he saw.

In one of his conversations with Eckermann, Goethe once remarked that as regards the material of life itself he was at a disadvantage compared to Sir Walter Scott; in *Wilhelm Meister* he had to turn to the landed nobility and actors in order to bring a breath of life into the novel; and in general, the more he reflected on the nature of writing poetry, the more painfully did he sense how difficult were the conditions under which he worked. Shakespeare wrote when historical conditions were uniquely favorable. What he had read about Rome in his Plutarch, what surrounded him in the ruins of England's past and in the Elizabethan age, with its violent characters, its dramatic political life and its bloody climaxes: all this necessarily presented itself to the eye of a genius

148 looking for the core of things as a nexus of active heroic characters and violent catastrophes. All this was, as it were, observable in London, where one could see the queen either riding through the streets to the Tower or in her barge on the Thames. Shakespeare saw everyone then making history immediately in front of him on the stage. In Shakespeare we thus find not only the fresh colors of life as unfolded in the Middle Ages, but also what is personal and striking in different destinies, as seen through a modern perspective instructed by humanists, natural scientists, and politicians.

To this we must now connect the little that we know of his education. Shakespeare scholars have completely abandoned the view that he was a pure natural genius; but we can only speculate about the sort of education he did have. Ben Jonson claims that he had "little Latin and less Greek," but that claim must be understood as coming from a rival revelling in his classical education. It was enough for Shakespeare to have a general sense of antiquity through its languages and the linguistic coloring of its literature; he did, to be sure, read Plutarch (whom he loved best among the ancients) and Ovid in translation. In this respect he was like Schiller. He undoubtedly read Rabelais' *Gargantua,* but there appears to have been an English translation of this novel at that time. He also read Montaigne in the translation by Florio, with whom he was personally acquainted. Perhaps he made use of Italian writings in the original. But nothing is more certain than that Shakespeare entertained no scholarly interests in the strict sense, and that he had no urge to formulate any consistent conception of the natural world. And by what right do we interrogate a poet concerning his convictions about God, the immortality of man, or any other cardinal point of metaphysics? The essence of genius is penetration and concentration. Shakespeare, who viewed the world through the eyes of all kinds of people, was so free in the way his powerful spirit could enter into different mentalities and personalities that he could hardly confine himself to *one* intellectual standpoint; to do so would have seemed to him like being in prison. The subtleties of dialectical thinking clearly interested him, but only as intellectual coloring of characters, as intellectual material for the play of feelings, or as possibilities to be explored. Metaphysical doctrines are present here and there in the sonnets and dramas, yet we do not know to what 149 extent they can be regarded as his abiding convictions. The philosophy for which he shares an inclination is that Roman practical wisdom which comforts us and teaches us to bear the blows of fate—the philosophy of the humanists and of Montaigne. Occasionally he is raised above the tragic aspect of life by the awareness that all life is appearance and dream—and this, too, was frequently expressed in the literature of his time.

There is another consideration that allows us to assume a significant link between this great poet and the literature of his time. This link is already suggested by the discovery of his intimate acquaintance with Montaigne's work, which is indeed decisive for a historical understanding of Shakespeare. Our consideration concerns the analysis of human characters and emotions. Can one believe that the exemplifications of the primary human emotions present in his great dramas were merely free gifts of his natural genius? He felt the need to submit to intellectual analysis the facts he experienced and lived through with a penetration peculiar to genius: the nature of man, the diversity of human character types and ways of thinking, human emotions and the destinies produced by them. He was undoubtedly influenced by the new literature of his time which aimed at teaching the art of seeing into the subtle complexities of man's psychic structure. Unfettered princely power and life at the court promoted the scrutiny of human nature. It was essential to be attentive in order to hold one's own at court. Everything there was personal, and depended on the way one sized up others and represented oneself in accordance with his own interests. Innumerable treatises were written to serve this need. In them, physiognomy, stature, and gesture were studied as signs of character traits and inner dispositions. Human passions were described and analyzed. Through innumerable channels, these reflections about life reached everyone; and Shakespeare constantly associated with men who were imbued with and guided by this literature. On this basis we understand his capacity to make the structure of individuals transparent, even to the point where we seem to see the blood coursing through them. Finally, his sustained reflection was directed to the basic connections among character, passion, and destiny in human life. In this, he is influenced by certain ideas of humanism which originated in Roman literature and harmonize with the essence of Protestantism. These ideas received a new depth from his lived experience. Shakespeare's dramas are the mirror of life itself. They do not comfort us, but teach us about human existence like no other creation of European literature. 150

Whenever he develops subject matter into a poetic motif, he tends to preserve the peculiarities of, and seeming contradictions in, his traditional sources. Thus his subject matter retains the earthiness of reality. By interpreting his subject matter, he gives it an inwardness. Yet there often remains something intangible about his characters. The observer should regard them as he does persons in real life—looking into them from the outside.

Nowhere in his works do we find projections toward an ideal, future man or state. He accepts the social world around him as an unalterable natural order. He lives in complete harmony with the monarchical-aristocratic world of the England of his time. The life-problems of his dramas spring from that particular world. His characters are heightened likenesses of the people he came upon there—and they are heightened precisely in the direction of the sense of value which existed in this society. It is without any hint of criticism, but with positive satisfaction, that he observes the contrast between those fortunate and powerful individuals who live above everyone else, and a conceited gentry, ridiculous scholars, adventurers, and soldiers of fortune. The double plot—indeed, the double world of his dramas—is based on this contrast.

To be sure, Hamlet speaks strongly and bitterly about the arrogance of those who, in the security of their positions and offices, look down upon the unfortunate, about the sluggish course of justice, and about the neglect of poverty. And from his sonnets one sees how much Shakespeare himself suffered from the pressure of this aristocratic society—in the uncertain position of an actor, favored by the world of the court, and yet having no fixed place or status in its order. But he accepts all that as a fate which flows from this social order, which at the same time made possible all the power and beauty of life which he represented in his dramas.

This aristocratic order of things determines the feeling of life of Shakespeare's characters. His tragic heroes live with a sense of their power, and the bright and noble characters of his comedies play with life in the proud awareness that its misery does not even graze their toes. All these *personae* have the highest, most sensitive feeling of themselves; also, they respect those who lead a similar genteel existence. And the surface brilliance which envelops them and their surroundings, without which the effect of these dramas is inconceivable, also stems from this aristocratic order. Macbeth's mighty, gloomy castle filled with weapons, the streets of Verona lined with the fortified houses of the feuding nobles, the solemn castle of the Danish king, in whose halls pomp and circumstance and the smell of death were curiously mixed, the clanking armor, the pomp of the kings, the ceremonial vestments of the bishops—all this enhances his characters and the events. It would be futile to imagine the crimes of Claudius, King of Denmark, of Macbeth, or of Richard

III taking place in the rooms of a modern royal palace, and it would be pathetic to shift such crimes to the confines of the large cities where they take place today. For in our day, there is something attenuated, artificial, and restricted about the deeds and destinies of kings—as necessitated by modern life.

The hierarchy of aristocratic society provided Shakespeare with a multitude of artistic effects of the highest order. I will point out only one of them here. In the music of the opera it is possible to combine a variety of moods and characters into a unity of life and to embrace the wealth of existence in a single moment; for several persons can give musical expression to their individuality simultaneously. The playwright is denied such an effect. But what is musical in his work originates not only from an inner music of its lyrical figures, but also from the total effect of the whole, as it arises in the memory of the spectator. As the drama progresses, contrasts in the feeling of life and peculiarities of the characters manifest themselves successively. But in the memory of the spectator this manifold is gathered into dissonances and harmonies, like tone sequences blending into one another. This blending produces a feeling of the richness and the mixed character of life. Since Shakespeare had available to him such an intricate hierarchy of society and such pronounced contrasts within it, he was able to produce these effects with particular intensity.

Finally, we must note a relation between a general characteristic of the English spirit and the nature of Shakespeare's poetry, although it is incapable of being exactly defined or grounded. Empiricism and the bent for induction corresponding to it developed in England with the same consistency which this nation displayed in the development of its constitution. Ever since Bacon's time, Plato and Aristotle have had no authoritative influence whatever on English attitudes and inclinations. Both the simple observer and the methodical scientist show an incomparable and refreshing impartiality in their perceptions and in the study of the natural and social realities surrounding them. Other modes of thought may have prevailed among philosophers and theologians, and may even have influenced the intellectual life of wider circles; during Shakespeare's time it was, after all, precisely Platonism that exerted the greatest influence; but these tendencies did not alter the empirical bent of the English spirit. Clearly, something corresponding to this bent is operative in the poetic attitude toward the world characteristic of Shakespeare and Ben Jonson, Smollett, Fielding and Richardson, Dickens, Thackeray, and Walter Scott. Opposing tendencies in po-

152

etry, as represented by Byron, Shelley, and Coleridge, who were especially influenced by the Germans, were never in conformity with the English spirit and accordingly never acquired a leading and lasting influence on it.

When we sum up all the characteristics of Shakespeare's poetic creativity, they throw light on Goethe's fundamental poetic orientation by contrast. In my introduction,[32] I have described the place of each of these two orientations in European literature; the differences discussed here supplement that account. Shakespeare lived predominantly in the experience of the world: all the powers of his mind reached out toward that which was happening around him in the world and in life. Goethe's peculiar gift is to express the states of his own soul, the world of ideas and ideals within him. All the senses and powers of the former aim at cultivating, enjoying, and giving form to lives of every sort and characters of every class. The latter looks ever into himself, and he ultimately wants to use what the world teaches him in order to heighten and deepen his sense of self. To the one, producing artistic creations outside himself is the highest spiritual concern of his life; to the other, however, the ultimate thing remains to form his own life, his own personality, into a work of art.

## ROUSSEAU

In the *Nouvelle Héloïse,* Jean-Jacques Rousseau was the first modern European to create a triumphantly effective work of art by developing characters from a wealth of personal inner experience and thought, without having any outstanding gift for or habit of perceiving or observing other people and their circumstances. The wretched life of this powerful man was characterized by a total inability to grasp any person in his true nature. This was immensely unfortunate in the complicated circumstances of the Paris of his day, abounding with problematical types and sophisticated knowledge of human nature. For him, other men were what his passionate spirit led him to believe they were; he lived wholly within himself. Thus it is of extraordinary interest for the investigation of the imagination to trace the development of his great novel, and we are enabled to do so through his *Confessions* and his letters.

153

He was forty-four when, on the ninth of April 1756, he moved

[32] Introduction to *ED*, pp. 7-17.

to the Hermitage in La Chevrette Park. "Today for the first time," he said, "I have begun to live." Here, with his mind utterly calm, surrounded by the magic of nature and solitude, he saw his imagination bring forth characters with irresistible force—and this in opposition to both his principles and his will, for novel writing brought him into contradiction with himself and his deepest convictions. The fundamental process went like this: from swirling mists of dreams, he condensed and formed into palpable figures whatever hovering images he had of happiness, of pleasing situations and characters corresponding to his feelings and his deep passionate nature. This process is at work in all great poets, and even Shakespeare's Miranda[33] and Hermione[34] are embodied dreams of longing. But in Rousseau it was dominant; it governed his whole novel in its earliest form. His imagination had worked in this way since his youth. In the fourth book of his *Confessions* he tells how, when surrounded by nature, he always found himself stimulated to such dreamlike poetic activity:

> I then ruled with a free hand over all of nature; my heart, hurrying from object to object, gathered magnificent images about itself and became enraptured in feelings of delight. When I then for my own amusement realized them in thoughts, what force of the brush, what vividness of color, what strength of expression I imparted to them! It is said that something of all this is to be met with in my works which, after all, were written towards the wane of my years.[35]

The epoch of life in which he found himself gave such dreams an enormous power. "I saw myself in the decline of life, prey to a painful sickness. I supposed I was near the end of my way without having fully relished even one of the joys which my heart craved, without once having poured forth the lively feelings which slept in this heart, without having savored, but only sampled, that intoxicating bliss which filled my soul but was always choked back for lack of an object and could vent itself only in my sighs."[36] "To die without having lived"—an idea which is unnervingly sad. 154

In such a state of feeling he enlivened the lonely, enchanting nature around him with his images—majestic trees and lawns, and

[33] Prospero's daughter in *The Tempest*.

[34] Queen of Sicilia in *The Winter's Tale*.

[35] *The Confessions*, trans. by J. M. Cohen (Baltimore: Penguin Books, 1973), p. 158.

[36] *Ibid.*, p. 396.

purple heather, which seemed to have been created for the realization of all his dreams of happiness:

> I filled them with being in accordance with my heart; I created myself a golden age, in accordance with my taste, in which I recalled to myself the experiences of earlier times to which sweet memories were tied, and painted with lively colors the images of happiness which I could still desire.[37]

This was it exactly; images of experiences from his youth gave his imagination the material for projecting a painting that encompassed all the happiness for which he could still yearn. He even expressed how this happened:

> I envisaged love and friendship, the two idols of my heart, in the most captivating images and ornamented them with all the charms of the female sex, which I had always revered. I preferred to imagine two women rather than two men as friends because while they are found more seldom, they are for that very reason all the more worthy of love. . . . I provided this painting with characters . . . which were admittedly not complete, but were to my taste. . . . I gave the one a beloved to whom the other was a fond friend and even something more besides. However, I permitted neither jealousy nor quarrels, because it is hard for me to represent any sort of painful feeling. . . . Enchanted by my two lovely models, I identified myself as much as possible with the beloved and friend. But I made him young and worthy of being loved, and besides that I gave him all the virtues and failings which I knew myself to possess.[38]

He moved the scene to the Lake of Geneva, which had long been bound up with all his dreams of happiness; "whenever the ardent wish for the happy and sweet life, which escaped me and for which I felt myself born, inflamed my imagination, it always took the Canton of Vaud, the lake, this enchanting landscape, for the scene of action."[39] Like the characters in Homer's underworld, his figures drank life from "a few memories of youth." They acquired other traits from Richardson's novels, in which all the sensitive souls of that time lived as if in a higher, more noble reality. And, finally, a historical subject matter influenced these images—the story of Abe-

[37] See *ibid.*, p. 398. The passage cited by Dilthey in German seems to be a paraphrase of the one cited here.

[38] *Ibid.*, pp. 400-401.

[39] *Ibid.*, p. 148.

lard and Héloïse, which had taken place long ago in this very Paris and its environs. Rousseau began by jotting down a variety of letters, without any sequence or connection:

> When I set about putting them together I often got into serious difficulty; it is not very credible, but true, that the first two parts were written almost entirely in this manner, without my having had a deliberate plan, indeed without my having yet foreseen that I would feel tempted to make a proper work of them.[40]

155

In the winter of 1756-57, when the weather confined him to his room, he began to order these pages into a sequence for the purpose of making a kind of novel of them. Then the Countess d'Houdetot entered his life as the fulfillment of his dreams, as the reality of the shadow which he had named Julie, and with this event in the spring of 1757 began the second stage of the development of his novel, which lasted until its completion and publication. This stage no longer has the same interest for us, since we are no longer able to recognize the transformations which the novel underwent, at least in their particulars. The main change was that now the relationship to a married woman, which accorded with his lived experience—or rather with what, because of a lack of worldly experience, he had constructed in his imagination—took the place in his life once occupied by the ideal he had projected of maidenhood. In addition, there seems to take place in Rousseau a shaping of several characters by splitting up certain aspects he found in himself and felt to be incommensurable; the same process can also be clearly observed later in Goethe.

In Germany's heroic age we already find two works which bear the same stamp of personal creation. Through the study of romance narrative poetry[41] from which our romances of chivalry developed, we acquire a deeper insight into the latter. Although no consensus has yet been reached about the sources of the two most brilliant of our epic poets of chivalry, Wolfram von Eschenbach[42] and Gottfried von Strassburg,[43] their relation to their sources have been sufficiently clarified to permit highly probable inferences about their creative processes.

[40] *Ibid.*, p. 401.

[41] Dilthey has in mind poets such as Chrétien de Troyes (1160-90), who wrote some of the earliest Arthurian romances.

[42] Circa 1170-circa 1220, author of the epic poem *Parzival.*

[43] His primary work, *Tristan und Isolde*, was written about 1210.

Gottfried's subjectivity permeates his entire poem. In the magnificent words with which he acclaims the lyric and epic poets of chivalry (except the greatest of them)[44] he extols poetry—in a manner similar to Goethe—for renewing youth and arousing the courage to exist and joy in life. This was his poetic ideal in contrast to Wolfram's wilder and darker tales. The world of chivalry was not native to him; one might well think that he seized upon it because it was capable of being the medium for his cheerful sense of life, perhaps even for personal circumstances and experiences. In two passages of his *Tristan* I find suggestions of the manner in which the poet himself experienced the pleasure and pain of love—in the beginning and in the well-known canto which describes the life of love in the solitude of nature; a different and contrasting expression appears in this context to be the poet's playful jesting with his readers. A secure feeling of the abundant pleasures of life; a clear preference for living life cleverly, even cunningly; contempt for women's character and an enraptured devotion to their charms—all these give his works the imprint of the romance novella: "For as long as life's light shines, he shall live with the living." With these words, Gottfried unites—on the basis of the richest experience—uncommon psychological depth with the depiction of emotional states. And the fundamental emotional thrust, which is proclaimed in the introduction and recurs meaningfully throughout, is truly Germanic in insisting that even the suffering of love is bliss. This mixed sentiment gives the poem an enigmatic and altogether individual quality. On the basis of this emotional thrust or attitude toward life, the whole is then shaped in a transparently simple plot. Like Rousseau's work, it is founded wholly on an interest in the lovers and their fate.

156

However, Gottfried's work also exudes traits which manifest a subjective sovereignty of feeling and personality: a playful charm, pleasure in deceitful tricks, a most liberal philosophy of life, a strong interest in the legal aspects of human relations and in the complexities of juridical dialectics. Finally, it manifests two barely concealed attitudes: a hatred of ecclesiastical power and its interference in the legal system, and a ridiculing of the ideals of chivalry which anticipates that of Cervantes and Ariosto. The more sovereign the sense of the world with which these two critical attitudes are conveyed, the more effective they become.

Wolfram's incomparably greater poetic ability is shown by his

[44] Wolfram von Eschenbach.

poems also to have been far more flexible. We discern his personality more clearly than we do that of Gottfried. It is the proud, manly, powerful personality of a not so well-to-do knight in a quiet Franconian castle, who did not bow to princes, and who wanted to be loved by his lady not because of his songs alone, but rather—like his heroes—because of his courage, chivalry, and eagerness for battle. The introduction of *Parzival* already announces that an ideal is to be placed before the reader; it is the ideal of the most beautiful life of chivalry glowing in the lonely soul of one passed over by fortune. And this ideal is represented in a development which, in certain measure, must be regarded as the reflection of the inner struggles of its author. This epic harbors within it the seeds of a *Bildungsroman*: other characters are placed beside its central character to produce a sense of contrast and completeness, just as in 157 *Wilhelm Meister*. Wolfram depicts a unity of life, extending from youthful torpor, through doubt and aimless adventure, to a manly and sensible devotion to the highest of life's callings—that of the knight striving for God. As far as we know, this characterization of development is unique in the entire literature of the Middle Ages; and without deep personal experience and reflection on lived experience it is utterly inconceivable. In this manner, our two great epic poets of chivalry worked their personal lived experience and their independently acquired views of life into the material of the Arthurian romances.

We now return to Goethe.

## GOETHE

### I

Nature endowed Goethe with the fullness of its gifts: beauty, robust constitution, and creative genius. His development came at a time when economic life, the legal safeguards of bourgeois affairs, and religious freedom were steadily expanding in Germany. The tight bonds of family life and of social organization which had been handed down from early Protestant times were beginning to loosen; individuals secured room in which to move more freely, and their emotions led them to chart their own course. This liberation of personality was supported by the influence of French and English authors.

Our poetic literature arose in this setting. Its ideals were those of personal existence—love, friendship, and humanity—as reflected in the German temperament, sense of homeland, and delight in nature. Goethe was surrounded by the springtime of this poetry. From his Franconian background, nurtured amidst the free cities and benign ecclesiastical rule of the upper Rhine and Main valleys, he received the gift of rejoicing in his own individuality while being open to the individuality of others, and seizing the pleasure of the hour. The status of his family, patricians in the old free city of Frankfurt, gave him a sense of self, security, and unimpeded mobility. An easygoing upbringing, without the restriction and discipline of ordinary school life, permitted the free development of his mental powers and his imagination, but also of his inclination to give way entirely to his feelings. His constitution was such that his 158 primary need was to revel in life, to immerse himself in what it offered, and then to express this. A singular sensitivity of feeling made him capable of infinite happiness, but also of boundless sorrow. There were times in his youth when his passion completely overpowered him. Some of these episodes are well known, such as the time when, still a boy and confined to the house, he became so distressed by the fate of Gretchen that he threw himself to the ground, wet the floor with his tears, and refused to leave his room; he allowed his imagination to become obsessed with the poor girl's misery to the point that he became violently ill.[45] Later, in Leipzig, he burst from his sickroom to catch a glimpse of his beloved in the theater and was there gripped by such a fever that he "thought his death was imminent."[46] A lung infection was the result of the passionate way he behaved during this period. And yet a few days after this episode, when his passion reached its peak, he wrote to an intimate friend: "I'm telling you what I feel, everything I'm thinking about—and if I am at my end, then I pray that God not give her to me."

Even in the most extreme passion, he is always conscious that no single life-situation can satisfy him; he desires lived experience in all its fullness and with all its freedom. An almost feminine sympathy with human beings of every sort and an imagination

[45] At age fourteen Goethe fell in love with Gretchen, the daughter of a Frankfurt shopkeeper. When some of their friends became involved in a serious forgery case, Gretchen and Goethe were interrogated. After his innocence had been established, Goethe did not know what was happening to Gretchen; he imagined her in the hands of the police. She is generally thought to have been the model for the Gretchen of *Faust*. The original account of this episode may be read at the end of Book V, *Dichtung und Wahrheit*; *WA*, I, 26:331-42; *TF*, vol. 1, pp. 173-78.

[46] The girl was Katherine Schoenkopf. Goethe's account of this episode is to be found in a letter to his friend Behrisch of 10 November 1767.

which intensifies it in re-creation, allow him to feel his way into every life-situation. He fully comprehends the felicity inherent in each situation and the value each has for the enhancement of human existence. Goethe embraces all individuals whom he finds congenial, idealizes them, and heightens his own sense of existence by pursuing these relations for their full meaning and beauty; and yet no single one of them can bind him. Every love is accompanied by the latent consciousness that it must not become a fetter. Every friendship produces in him the demonic sense of his superiority. And when such a friendship is severed, producing a sense of guilt, his imagination allows him to feel most painfully the other's suffering. His capacity to fully assimilate the various life-situations and his joy in doing so is so great that he has no need of any spiritual freedom that transcends these situations. This is the main trait of his character which, like nature, sometimes brings forth good and sometimes evil—and he wants nothing beyond this. He is completely passionate, but at the same time, completely rational in the consciousness of what he needs. Controlling his situation and thereby dominating others, he develops powers of every sort, with the exception of the abstract moral strength that militantly opposes life-situations and the world. This explains his pure admiration of Schiller's moral greatness. It was pure precisely because he himself had no need for such moral strength. Similarly, we can understand why Schiller the artist admired this man, who is nature and who acts like nature herself. 159

Those close to him in his youth experienced something unpredictable and demonic. For them he became a force of destiny which affected their lives deeply. This was the experience not only of the women in his life, but also of Kestner[47] when Goethe suddenly published his *Werther*; of Wieland[48] when the "shameful and outrageous" *Götter, Helden und Wieland* (Gods, Heroes, and Wieland) was published, which turned the younger generation against him; then of Lavater;[49] and much later of Herder, who languished in the gloomy rectory in Weimar because of his opposition to Goethe's

[47] Johann Christian Kestner (1741-1800) was befriended by Goethe in Wetzlar. Kestner married Charlotte Buff, the model for Lotte in *Werther*.

[48] Christoph Martin Wieland (1733-1813). German poet and novelist. Wieland's claim that his own version of *Alcestis* was superior to that of Euripides is ridiculed in Goethe's farce, *Götter, Helden und Wieland*.

[49] Johann Kaspar Lavater (1741-1801), a preacher, writer and physiognomist, corresponded with Goethe from 1773. In 1774 he visited Goethe in Frankfurt and traveled with him along the Lahn and the Rhine. Goethe twice (in 1775 and again in 1779) visited him in Zurich. Toward 1780 Lavater's exaggerated religious zeal began to interfere with the friendship, which was broken off by Goethe.

preeminence. Goethe himself also suffered deeply from life and from himself. A need for strong emotional impulses was inherent in his powerful poetic disposition; they were, so to speak, a regular expense in the budget of his physiological economy and did not cost him any sleep. But, psychically, this same disposition made him extraordinarily subject to melancholy. It was by no means mere play of the imagination for the young Goethe to consider suicide. A frightful restlessness sometimes drove him: "People say of me that I carry the curse of Cain."[50] Thus two basic moods permeate his youth and his early works. First, he commits himself neither to any place nor to any relationship. The demonic in him, which seeks all of life and is not content with this or that part of it, breaks loose again and again. "It is just when they are happily joined together that souls made for one another most often misunderstand each other."[51] And then the other mood arises repeatedly: the longing for a quiet place where he would find peace, the desire to forget the limitless demands within him in an intimate relationship. Then every limited existence seems enviable to him and he feels a desperate need for something calm and fixed in his existence. This is the metaphysical aspect of his spirit which is expressed first in religious, and subsequently in scientific and philosophical terms. Full satisfaction of this longing was attained only through his devotion to the whole and the one—a devotion which silences the clamor of the will as it inheres in individual human existence.

To a man having such a nature, every life-situation must have seemed too narrow. His father's house oppressed him. Then, too, the society of Leipzig was regulated and dominated by court life. When he subsequently tried, within the context of the younger generation, to free himself from this oppression through the bold ideal of a new strong humanity, he came to be regarded by this generation as the poet of the superhuman; then the personal narrowness of his existence was felt even more painfully by contrast. The stagnation and restrictiveness of backward Frankfurt and his 160 unfulfilling role as an idle solicitor in his father's house were unbearable to him. In Weimar he finds for the first time a sphere of action which his striving for scope demands. As a friend, advisor, and minister of the duke, he worked to administer the area and participated in the political affairs of the League of Princes, which

[50] Goethe to Kestner, 12 June 1773, *WA*, IV, 2:92; *GSM*, p. 86.

[51] Goethe to Sophie v. La Roche, 12 May 1773, *WA*, IV, 2:87-88. Text altered by Dilthey.

was concerned with the relations of the Duchy to the other German states and was connected ultimately with the general situation in Europe. Here for the first time he acquired that grand and unhindered freedom of movement—in both the good and the bad sense—which at that time existed only in the world of the court. He came to feel at home with nature on his own piece of land. And he experienced a love which calmed his soul for the first time.[52] For a considerable time, his letters expressed a feeling of pure, complete happiness. But with time a restrictedness manifested itself here as well. How few of his hopes for great accomplishments had been realized! He had neglected his poetical works. As leader of the young generation of poets, he found himself being displaced by Schiller. His renown was already becoming a thing of the past. Thus once more he broadened the scope of his activity, accomplishment, and enjoyment. His work in Italy, the friendship with Schiller, and a great new creative period first gave his existence in Weimar its real impact on the world at large. From this humble ducal residence he came to dominate the literature of his nation, and in the course of his incessantly active life he was able to see how his achievements affected world literature.

But however much his life expands—with all the changes produced by the transition to an active existence and all that happened in the course of his life—Goethe's relation to life remains essentially the same. During his first ten years as an official in Weimar, his striving to come to terms with life, to make use of everything for his self-development, is ever the focal point of his existence. His letters to Frau von Stein show that at no other time of his life was his ear as sensitive to the stirrings of his inner life, and his striving for the further development of his being as strong. It is through action that he develops and discovers his nature. He enjoys the new wealth of images provided by his journeys to various courts. He observes the inner states which his new circumstances produce in him, and it is only when he enjoys and reflects on the meaning of what he has experienced—in the company of a worldly and sophisticated woman who fills his entire soul—that it acquires its ultimate and highest value for him. Similarly, when in Italy, every object is perceived by him with the enjoyment of intuiting it, and with the consciousness of his own enhancement through it. Even

[52] Goethe became aquainted with Charlotte von Stein, lady-in-waiting to Anna Amalia, the duke's mother, shortly after his arrival in Weimar in 1775. In the course of his first ten years in Weimar he became increasingly attached to this married woman, seven years his senior.

161 there, his self-development and the expression of his self in poetry remain the focal points of his existence. There is nothing in Italy which cannot be of use to him. In his accounts of himself, he sums up the meaning of his existence, a meaning which it will continue to have from the turn of the century on. The practice and enjoyment of the visual arts, the participation in public affairs, and the study of the natural sciences continue to occupy an extensive part of his life. But he pursued these matters in connection with his interest in universal development, and consistently devoted himself to poetry in all its aspects as his true calling. His struggles with himself came to an end, and he lived in the consciousness of his personality, in the full certainty of its value, in devotion to encompassing life-experiences which he enjoyed fully in association with the great men of all ages, with a timeless sense of the relation of his fully developed personal existence to what is eternal.

2

His penchant for continual *reflection on life* took root very early and did not involve the curiosity of a spectator. With his unlimited impressionability, he had to learn to come to terms with his life, to endure it calmly—to endure not only its fullness of joy and significance, but also its limitations and suffering. Thus a stratum of reflection which becomes ever deeper and more encompassing is formed on the basis of his existence. The manner in which it arises from his life may be seen in his letters. The letters to Frau von Stein are unique for the way in which they show a person expressing how he experiences himself, other people, the world, and destiny. To him, every aspect of the world which he sees expresses something of the power and sense of life. To him, every exceptional person becomes an expression of human nature in a particular embodiment. To him, every lived experience becomes a lesson about a trait of life itself. With incomparable sensitivity he feels his relation to nature in the changes of the seasons, in the sunrise, and in the evening twilight. He heeds the stirrings in the secret depths of his soul and through them he comprehends human existence and human development. Relations of the most universal sort, which pervade our whole existence, are present to him at every moment: relations between the restlessness of human existence and what is calm and constant; between the power and freedom of individuality and the whole that determines it; between what is unchanging in us and what develops; between the originality of the person and external influences. Finally, the relation which determines the temper of our existence most deeply and universally—that of life to death; for the boundedness of our existence by death is always decisive for our understanding and evaluation of life. It is characteristic of Goethe that this relation which tragically overshadows all human existence in the poetry of Sophocles, Dante, and Shakespeare is pushed to the horizon, as it were, in his view of life. 162

This reflection on life constantly flows from life itself; hence it grasps the experienced life-nexus together with the value and significance of every state of affairs, every personality, and every situation in life. It is an interpretation of existence on its own terms, independent of all religion and metaphysics.

This stratum of reflection about existence is the soil from which his poetry springs. And the inexhaustible appeal of his works, especially of *Wilhelm Meister, Elective Affinities*, and *Truth and Fiction*, is due to the wisdom and artistry of life which so thoroughly permeates them.

Personality, the circumstances surrounding it, and its formation are central to Goethe's view of life. His conception of things human always remained dependent on what he was able to attain in his own experience of life. When, from this point of view, he examined the historical past, life seemed to him to remain the same throughout the course of time. Everywhere he found the same modifications of human nature, the same curious turns in character development, and the same psychic states which he himself had experienced. Thus every personality and lived experience from the past acquired meaning for him through something falling within the scope of his own experience. In "The Eternal Jew,"[53] Christ descends into the world a second time. When he saw the world for the first time it seemed to him "all wondrous confusion" yet "filled with the spirit of order"; he trembled, striving to free himself from it, and having succeeded in doing so, he once again became entangled in it. And now when he returns it seems "still to lie there going round and round in that sauce, just as it lay in that hour when, in the bright light of day, the Spirit of Darkness, Lord of the Old World, splendid in the sunshine, produced it."[54] Prometheus, Mohammed, and Faust attract him, and the essence of these characters is for him a timeless variant of human nature. His "Neueröffnetes moralisch-politisches

[53] See *WA*, I, 38:55-64.

[54] *Ibid*., p. 60.

Puppenspiel" (Newly Opened Moral-Political Puppet Play)[55] and the fragments related to it represent not a present state of affairs, but unchanging human strivings. And everyone is familiar with Faust's response to Wagner, who expresses his joy at "entering into the spirit of the time":

163

> My friend, the times that antecede
> Our own are books safely protected
> By seven seals. What spirit of the time you call,
> Is but the scholars' spirit, after all,
> In which times past are now reflected.[56]

*Götz* and *Egmont* let us see more deeply into Goethe's historical thinking. Both works portray historical situations in detail. They illuminate the life of the past with the greatest vividness. But Goethe projects his own lived experience into his protagonists, and the historical relations which affect them are represented in the mood of an observer who recognizes with satisfaction that human strivings are always the same, even in past ages. And precisely this is the source of the undying appeal of *Götz*: the adventures once chronicled by the old man with the iron hand are transmitted to the audience as in a genre painting; they are portrayed with that feeling of overflowing Germanic power and vitality from which they sprang. This is why objective knowledge of their context as such and of the historical forces surrounding them is unnecessary. *Egmont* was written when this mode of historical awareness was well developed; scenes such as the protagonist's conversation with William of Orange and the regent's conversation with her secretary Machiavelli clearly show Goethe at his historical best; they are extracts from his experiences of court life and government service. But the protagonist himself is a freely shaped human personality and is for that reason implausible in his historical context—he is at bottom unhistorical. The power of Protestant and free middle-class ideas that surrounded Egmont and was so prominent in the Dutch Revolution is not made evident enough. The great current of historical life does not flow through this play. It was, in fact, Schiller who created modern historical drama, for it was he who always captured the world-historical aspect of his subject matter in his plays.

Let us now examine Goethe's historical writings. In them we see

[55] *Ibid.*, 16:1-55.

[56] *F*, p. 109.

him abandoning the pragmatic method, with the knowledge that only the totality of our psychic powers can comprehend the historical object. He thus approaches it as an artist. But history as a science has another side as well; the historical object can be understood only in terms of the whole in which it is contained; its causal relations and its meaning can only be grasped if the historian is always conscious of the nexus of universal history. He must set his object at a distance from himself, as a world for itself, toward which he strives to maintain an unprejudiced attitude. Only then do the historical impulses surging through every part of history become visible. But instead of detaching the historical world from the observer, Goethe clings to the natural relation between man and history. He puts all his life-experience directly into it and thus makes it something present. He is full of admiration and lets himself be instructed. And since personality is the center of his view of life, he seeks it above all in the past. If human progress can be demonstrated anywhere, it is in the natural sciences, but Goethe's *Zur Farbenlehre* (Theory of Color) sees in its course only "rising and falling, progress and regress, in a straight line or in a spiral."[57] He is a brilliant observer of the changing relation of man to objects in nature, and of the power of personality in the formation of theories, but he has no sense of the necessity which determines the stages of progress in natural science. Likewise, in his treatment of current history, he is not interested in the wider context in which a new order of things influenced events, although he could not overlook it completely. Here again he attends to the ever constant forms of life-relations and feelings that he finds in the wars and all the social developments around him. The French Revolution does not evoke in him any intense joy over the liberation of humanity, and the Napoleonic occupation does not evoke any deep and abiding sorrow about the collapse of everything which had constituted Germany's political strength. On the other hand, a spirit such as Goethe's had to have the greatest capacity for biographical representations. *Truth and Fiction* is epoch-making in the history of man's biographical reflections upon himself and his relations to the world. On the whole, historical vision is for Goethe basically the extension of his reflection about life into the past, the apprehension of abiding forms of humanity and their relations, and ultimately a completely universal interpretation of life itself. The apprehension of perpetually recurring forms of individual existence and development so dom-

164

[57] *WA*, II, 3:148.

inated his mind that humanity, its progress, and the state as an intrinsic value and locus of power seemed to him to be empty abstractions and phantoms.

3

It is from this stratum of reflection that Goethe's poetic works emerge. Their foundation is life and its interpretation; their focus is personality. The *relation of lived experience to poetry*, which is decisive for Goethe's poetic creativity, is determined by this reflection.

165 The human world exists for the poet insofar as he experiences human existence in himself and tries to understand it as it confronts him from outside. In understanding, the visionary eye of the true poet is raised toward the infinite. For in understanding he projects all his inner experience into other human beings, and yet at the same time the unfathomable alien depths of another great being or a powerful destiny lead him beyond the limits of his own; he understands and gives shape to what he would never be able to experience personally. It is for this reason that the characters of Coriolanus, Caesar, and Marc Antony attain a comprehensible, coherent realization in Shakespeare's imagination which is beyond any historian's reach. Goethe, too, had an ample share of this gift, as his characters Götz and William of Orange demonstrate. Coupled with this was his genius for depicting the bustle of the world, ranging from the impudent dramatic jests of his youth to *Faust, Part II,* or for circumscribing a sphere of existence in terms of typical characters and relationships, as he did in *Hermann and Dorothea* and *Die natürliche Tochter* (The Natural Daughter). Yet what characterizes these creations, especially his prose fiction, is a mode of representation filled with a total feeling of life which stems from the depths of his soul: sometimes as a strong delight in life, sometimes as sovereign irony, or even, as is the case in *Wilhelm Meister*, a feeling which accompanies the course of events like the melody of life itself. But what is truly distinctive about him first fully shows itself when he uses a legend, history, or event as a vehicle, a symbol, for his personal lived experience. With *Werther, Prometheus, Faust, Tasso*, and *Iphigenia* his subjects provided him possibilities for intensifying his own lived experience. The effect of such characters as Faust and Mephisto is further intensified when, with irony and delight, the poet sets them in opposition to the bustle of the world; but despite all this, that which is novel and profound in what he

tells the world flows directly from his life and runs in the veins of Werther, Faust, Tasso, and so many other characters. This has nothing at all to do with observing inner processes and representing what has been observed. What we experience through self-observation is everywhere confined within narrow limits, and even scientific reflection on psychic life acquires much less in this way than is generally assumed. For when we turn our attention to our own states, they all too often vanish. The approach of the poet who expresses personal lived experience is completely different. It is based on the structural nexus connecting lived experience and its expression. Here, what is experienced enters fully and completely into the expression. No self-conscious reflections separate the depths of lived experience from its expression in words. All the modulations of his psychic life, the gradual transitions in it, and the continuity in its course are thus made accessible to the understanding through expression. Herein lies the visionary meaning of lyric poetry—this expression being used in the widest sense. The fact that instrumental music opens depths of the psyche to us which cannot be observed rests on this same relation between lived experience and expression. Goethe's most characteristic talent lies in his ability to express the full content of his personal lived experience. His linguistic imagination as described above provided him with all the means for doing so. His poetry of the inner life, which has taught us all to grasp the inwardness of human life more deeply, more purely, and more truly, came into being as his incomparably rich, dynamic psychic life found exhaustive expression in lyric poetry, drama, and prose fiction. And when one considers his place in the context of European literature, compares him with its most prominent poets, and looks at his accomplishments, a further aspect of the peculiar significance of our greatest poet emerges. He is the greatest lyric poet of all time; his *Faust* arose from this lyricism and all his more important epic or dramatic works are filled with the sound and rhythm of psychic life.

166

Indeed, how encompassing is the personal lived experience which this universal spirit brought to expression!

He always lived with an intense consciousness of himself. He never lost himself so completely in an object that he did not at the same time feel himself and his relation to it. Every note from his youth pictures a state of mind which shows him, restless with energy, in some situation or other. Thus the poems of his youth also are the natural and straightforward expressions of his sense of existence at a given moment. When in *Die italienische Reise* (Journey to Italy), or in his works on natural science and history, he is concerned with important matters, as a rule he represents them in such a way that we can sympathetically experience his relations to them and feel again the joyous energy with which he submits to the objectivity of things.

His striving to give his personality the highest development stemmed from his historical situation. All contemporary literature was directed at the intensification of human existence. The theological disputes, through which Lessing had had to work his way toward his ideal of life, were now past. The new generation broke through the confines within which this great man had been forced to apprehend life and the world. Goethe's young contemporaries, 167 most especially Herder, lived free from the burden of tradition. The determination to unfold all their faculties in action and in enjoyment sustained them. The individual wanted what life has to offer, wanted to experience it himself, think it, and savor it all in pleasure and sorrow, without any limits.

But what completely distinguished Goethe's personal poetry from that of his contemporaries—from that of a Lenz[58] or a Klinger,[59] for example—and elevated it above theirs was a striving toward the fulfillment of his own existence, toward the realization of everything human in his person and in his life. This made him insatiable to assimilate in intuition, understanding, and lived experience all the spiritual forces, significant men, and great movements which surrounded him. With a quickness of mind peculiar to him he took from books what suited him, and left everything else alone. Next to Voltaire he was the most universal man of the eighteenth century. But Voltaire's universality derived from his application of *raisonnement* to all objects and tasks, while Goethe's derived from understanding through re-experiencing everything human. All understanding is grounded in lived experience, but in Goethe's case understanding enriches his own experience in turn to expand his existence. He once said that the cornerstone of his moral and literary development was the fact that he always traced each spiritual expression back to something primordial, godly, and imperishable. He was able to understand whenever he placed something alien into relation with his own life, and what was understood became a moment of his own development. His being was so rich, and his

[58] Jakob M. R. Lenz (1751-92). German poet and friend of Goethe.

[59] Friedrich M. von Klinger (1752-1831). German dramatist and a friend of the young Goethe.

need to give unbounded scope to his existence and objectivity to his insights so strong, that he also incorporated the religious, scientific, and philosophical tendencies of his time into his lived experience. These tendencies included the liberating power of the Enlightenment and biblical criticism, the religious sentiment of the Zinzendorf[60] circle, Jung-Stilling[61] and Lavater, Winckelmann's Greece, the rediscovery of Spinoza, and Herder's new conception of nationalities. Also included are Kant's doctrine of the spontaneity of human reason, his stress on self-reflection, his separation of the knowable from the unknowable, his insight into the relation between organic nature and artistic creation; and, finally, the new discoveries of natural science and Schiller's concept of the aesthetic education of man for practical life. Goethe was like a river which grows wider and more powerful as ever more tributaries flow into it. Self-development and knowledge of the world were the same for him. Thus the peculiar greatness of his personal poetry lay ultimately in the fact that what was most personal was bound up most intimately with those aspects of universal movements which became part of his being. It was precisely because the greatest spiritual phenomena had become part of his lived experience that they could be linked to his own personal destiny and could move and affect him deeply. This and this alone made possible the greatest poetic work produced by anyone since Shakespeare: *Faust*. 168

There can be no doubt that the foundation of Goethe's poetry lay in personal lived experience, understood in this comprehensive sense. Goethe's autobiography expresses this clearly. There one sees the poet situated in a social order which accommodated only personal destinies and private passions; the wretchedness of this social order is only intimated; at the same time, one sees a rising recognition in the young generation that only significant subject matter treated as true to life makes genuine poetry possible. But Goethe writes that in order to find this,

> I was compelled to seek for every thing within myself. Whenever I desired a true basis in feeling or reflection for my poems, I was forced to grasp into my own bosom. . . .

[60] Nikolaus Ludwig, Count of Zinzendorf (1700-60), was the patron and subsequently the bishop of the Moravians.

[61] Jung-Stilling (properly Johann Heinrich Jung) (1740-1817) became acquainted with Goethe during his medical studies in Strassburg. The first part of his autobiography was reworked by Goethe and appeared as *Heinrich Stillings Jugend*. He came from a strongly pietistic background.

> And thus began that tendency from which I could not deviate my whole life through; namely, the tendency to turn into an image, into a poem, every thing that delighted or troubled me, or otherwise occupied me, and to come to some certain understanding with myself upon it, that I might both rectify my conceptions of external things, and set my mind at rest about them. The faculty of doing this was necessary to no one more than to me, for my natural disposition whirled me constantly from one extreme to the other. All, therefore, that has been confessed by me, consists of fragments of a great confession.[62]

As the ninth book of *Truth and Fiction* makes clear, this tendency was then reinforced by current empirical psychology and the poetry of Wieland. Both recommended "insight into the hidden recesses of the human heart"[63] and "knowledge of the passions which we partly sensed and partly divined in our breast, and which, from then on, we had to treat as something important and worthy, though they would otherwise be condemned."[64] A passage of the greatest importance! It shows how deeply Goethe himself, looking back on his life, sensed the power of the historical situation which pushed him into personal poetry. But one cannot let Goethe's own view stand without some qualification. Who can say how personal talent, the disposition of the people in the Rhine and Main regions, and the isolation of Goethe's native city from the political struggles of the period interacted with the general historical situation? Schiller, in contrast to Goethe, captured another aspect of the age—the power struggles of the great states, and the vehement desire for a more liberal structuring of society which was bound up with these struggles—the world of practical action. And what exultant acclamation greeted Schiller! Goethe's way was more quiet; he entered 169 those ultimate depths that our music and philosophy had already laid claim to.

Goethe's fundamental poetic orientation underwent noteworthy variations. Up until 1796, when he completed *Wilhelm Meister's Apprenticeship,* all his poetic works originated from his personal lived experience. He expresses himself on this subject while working on them, and his retrospective reflections put this still more clearly into relief. The poetic process is the same in the majority and most important of the creations of this period. A psychic state is expe-

[62] *WA*, I, 27:109-10; *TF*, vol. 1, pp. 234-35.

[63] *WA*, I, 27:225.

[64] *Ibid*., pp. 226-227.

rienced in all its potency, together with its external context or all its associated representations, states, and forms; and whenever an external process which is suited to become a vehicle for these experiences of the heart presents itself to this inwardly motivated poet, a fusion occurs in which the nucleus of a poetic work is produced that contains all the characteristic traits, the total mood, and the contours of the whole. Hence he could say that for him every poem had been a confession, an unburdening, by means of which he liberated himself inwardly from the states of mind which weighed upon him. Thus in every creation of this type, Goethe himself is there among his own characters. This resembles the mysterious manner in which he beholds and speaks to himself in the poem "Ilmenau." His themes are generated from his own existence. In his letters and poems, we find a psychic state which only lasts as long as the situation which called it forth; in the larger works we find a more manifold kind of life, which is for the most part referred to a person who received his life from the heart-blood of the poet. This relationship of Goethe's poetic works to life is gradually modified, particularly from the time in which he, along with Schiller, begins to dominate German literature from Weimar. By this time his life has become more calm. The fullness and strength of his lived experience has diminished while the sum total of his objective experience has grown extraordinarily. Ideals for the future are superseded by a recapitulation of the results of the past. Scientific research strengthens the objectivity of his perception. Although the effect of his personal circumstances on his poetry is still powerful, it is rooted in the sum of what he has experienced and in a general attitude to the world which developed from these experiences. This wisdom—which is the attitude of a mature mind toward life—animates and spiritualizes the great epic poetry of the second half of Goethe's life. The collected, enduring power of this wisdom is the subject of his didactic lyric poetry, and it even makes *Faust, Part II*, into an image of the world itself.

## 4

From his youth on, Goethe strove to fix lived experience, the experience of life, and life-ideals in a world-view; but this project required a philosophical foundation.[65] This was due to the fact that 170

[65] Here Dilthey uses the term *wissenschaftlich* to designate the concerns of philosophy.

our poetry developed in a philosophical epoch. Lessing, Schiller, and the Romantics gave their world-views a philosophical grounding. This need for a grounding must have been felt especially by Goethe who possessed the most powerful imagination of the modern world! Insofar as his imagination viewed the world poetically, he fell into conflict with the science around him; he was obliged to defend the nature of his imagination, and that could be done only in a universally valid manner, i.e., through a philosophically grounded world-view. Here we see a new aspect of the circumstances that conditioned Goethe.

Ours was the latest of the European literatures to develop, and it did so in the midst of a powerful spiritual movement which embraced all the civilized countries. Modern science arose in the seventeenth century, and in the eighteenth century it laid the foundations for the liberation of humanity from the oppression of religious tradition, for the knowledge of the system of causal laws in nature and the domination of nature which this knowledge makes possible, for the recognition of the deeper nexus of spiritual phenomena which constitute the historical world, and for theories which were able to guide the transformation of society. Thus humanity came of age through science. The educated classes strove enthusiastically to increase the individuating power of personality and to liberate it from the strictures of the old aristocratic-monarchical order. Our great German poetry emerged under the influence of this movement. Consequently, with regard both to its course of development and to its character, it was necessarily quite different from the national literatures which other modern peoples had already created during the flowering of the European imagination[66] and at the beginning of the scientific age. As our poetry began to develop, an intellectual conception of reality existed, and ordinary language reflected the prose of science. Our literature could create its means of poetic representation only slowly and with difficulty. In Lessing it achieved a new, strikingly realistic dramatic art based on a strict unity of action; in Klopstock it achieved the poetic energy and force of expression which enabled it to affect even the deepest levels of the psyche; and in Wieland it acquired grace, a smooth epic flow, and the language to express subtle changes at the surface of life. Because of its painstakingly slow progress compared to the literatures of Italy, England, and France in the sixteenth and sev-

171

[66] Dilthey is here referring to the Renaissance literature of Petrarch, Lope de Vega, Cervantes, and Shakespeare. See *ED*, p. 8.

enteenth centuries, our poetry stands out for its greatness of content. An immense scientific and philosophical effort had preceded it, and it was itself bound up in the most intimate way with the intellectual efforts of Winckelmann, Lessing, Möser, Herder, and Kant. These men created a new conception of the spiritual world. And in Goethe's time these studies were given a foundation in a constellation of astronomical, geological, and biological insights which has placed man, ever since Buffon, in the evolutionary nexus of the universe; and in Germany, Herder—taking his point of departure from Kant, but at the same time being in diametrical opposition to him—worked in this direction.

Goethe brought his unlimited capacity for assimilation to bear on all these intellectual achievements. He absorbed whatever in them was congenial to him. He intensified and unified what he appropriated. Moreover, he had the good fortune to participate in the development of the German spirit toward its highest attainments in poetry, philosophy, and science; and he embraced the moments of this development within himself—just as Sophocles, Michelangelo, and Johann Sebastian Bach before him had been able to do in their more restricted spheres.

The manner in which he unified these moments was determined by his own distinctive outlook. For his intellectual approach was as simple and thoroughly penetrating as his capacity for assimilation was unlimited. Intuition, imagination, and poetic talent comprised the core of his mental powers. His aim was everywhere and always to become aware, to live, and to understand reality. His approach is dominated by the intuitive process which proceeds by relating parts to the whole. It appears in his scientific pursuits as objective thinking and in his poetry as the intensification of a reality according to its inherent law. He never had much of an inclination for abstracting from what is living and for theories which explicate partial aspects of life, or for the long-winded argumentation of philosophers and their thinking about thinking; he had little confidence in all that and little gift for it. He always lived in the unity of things and in the structural relation of parts to whole.

For Goethe nature was an all-living being whose formative power he experienced in himself as creative imagination. Nature had this meaning for him ever since his youth; but only in the course of time was his initially vague conception of nature thought out methodically and given scientific form. For, in the same way as his "objective thinking" and his artistic activity were most intimately

172 related,[67] he saw everywhere and in various ways that God, nature, human beings, and their re-creation of the divine world constituted one vital system. At first this intuition was enveloped, as it were, in a dim, mystical, pantheistic feeling; and it was subsequently clarified in his studies of philosophy and natural science. He was around twenty when, having returned home from Leipzig because of sickness, he came under the influence of the religious teachings of Zinzendorf, immersed himself in Paracelsus,[68] Helmont,[69] and Arnold's history of Church heresies,[70] and in this way fell under the influence of a gnostic system of the evolution of the universe. Even then he was already possessed by the intuition of an emanating universal life-force unfolding in a multiplicity of forms. In Strassburg, he gradually abandoned the religious form in which he had grasped this universal life-force and through which his restless temperament had found tranquility. But this same intuition of a universally operative life-force—an intuition grounded in his own contemplative imagination and only influenced by others, such as Spinoza, by way of receiving clarification—reappears in *Prometheus*, *Mahomet* (Mohammed), *Werther*, and *Faust, Part I* in different moods. This genius of the imagination saw the world poetically from childhood on. He sensed life in rocks, in rushing waters, and in plants—all movement and form was to him its expression. A poetic world surrounded him even before he wrote his first verse. Then, as the boy began to write reams of verses, this world began to grow. What magic there is in the poems of his Leipzig period—the magic of a nature filled with life, of his own personal vision of this nature and his capacity to sympathetically feel every force active in the world! Then, as he moved beyond the scope of the poetry

[67] See especially *WA*, II, 11:60. "Bedeutende Förderniß durch ein einziges geistreiches Wort."

[68] Pseudonym of Philippus A.T.B. von Hohenheim (1493?-1541). Swiss-born physician, alchemist, and philosopher, who challenged the existing humoral theory of disease and developed a theory of medicine based on the harmony of the patient with the universe.

[69] Jan Baptista van Helmont (1577-1644) was a Belgian chemist, physician, and theosophist who is best known today as the discoverer of carbon dioxide gas. He attempted to explain physiological processes from a combination of chemical and metaphysical principles.

[70] Gottfried Arnold (1666-1714) was a Lutheran theologian and church historian. The work to which Dilthey refers is the *Unparteische Kirchen- und Ketzer-Historie* (first published in 1699-70 in four volumes). Arnold based this "impartial history," on his extensive knowledge of the original writings of heretics and separatists of every period of Church history, rather than on the accounts of their beliefs and practices given by orthodox writers.

of the Enlightenment, and the notion of a single universal life engrossed him, both the pastoral setting and the gods which, up to that point, had played their roles within his poetic vision of nature, vanished; now the system of nature emerged clear, pure and full—always changing, in accordance with this most agile, active mind, and yet always the same.

However, Goethe's world-view was even more deeply determined by his poetic conception of the human world. This conception was natural and necessary for a mind which took its point of departure from an undogmatic interpretation of life on its own terms. The enduring appeal of this conception is due chiefly to this fact. Whoever looks back contemplatively on his own life sees its most important events as either facilitating or obstructing the development of his power, his joy in life, the value of his individuality; it is precisely in this way that he grasps the meanings which accrue to the particular moments in the course of his life. This is the natural attitude with respect to the course of one's own life. It constitutes 173 the basis of the poetic representation of life. No one has adopted and pursued it in a purer form than Goethe; he allowed no metaphysical or religious presuppositions about the value of life to interfere with it. Every personality appeared to him as the realization of an individual value through a causal nexus. Shaftesbury and Herder reinforced him in this approach. He lived completely within this perspective, and it operated unconsciously and spontaneously in his lived experience of nature. It made itself felt in each of his experiences of the overall nexus of nature. Accordingly, nature appeared to him as the realization of an inherent vital force and significance in a causal nexus. Something fraught with meaning is active in nature and is fulfilled in her. "Is not the core of nature in men's hearts?"[71]

Thus from his youth on he found himself attracted to pantheism; *Werther*, *Prometheus*, and *Faust* proclaim "the inner, fervent, and holy life of nature." The essay "Die Natur" (Nature) of 1782, however it may have originated,[72] gives expression to the world-view common to Shaftesbury, Herder, and Goethe. Nature is animated by an inherent divine power. She is *one* and uniform throughout. Nature appears as the most perfect artist, working with unique techniques. And then Goethe provides the formula of the new

[71] *WA*, I, 3:106. "Ultimatum," lines 12-13.

[72] It is now generally accepted that the fragment "Die Natur" was not written by Goethe himself, but by Georg Christoph Tobler (1757-1812), a Swiss theologian who belonged to Goethe's circle in Weimar in 1780-81.

pantheism: "Nature has differentiated herself in order to enjoy herself. She is always giving birth to new forms of life that can enjoy her and is insatiable in imparting herself."[73] The same standpoint is adopted in his comments on Spinoza, written in the winter of 1784-85 while Goethe was reading this great thinker. Being, force, and perfection are one and the same. This is the philosophy of affirming the world, established by Giordano Bruno in opposition to the medieval attitude of contempt for the world, and then formulated in precise concepts by Spinoza.

But Goethe did not need the abstract proofs of these thinkers; his response to nature was intuitive-reflective; he attributed validity to thought only insofar as it was supported by perception. Thus it was necessary for him to distinguish between what could be investigated concretely and what could not; and this distinction already occurs in his Spinoza essay. According to Goethe, the infinite power itself cannot be apprehended by the finite human mind. He directs his investigations only toward its intuitable products.

His eye-oriented imagination, focusing on what was visible—"born to see, created to behold"[74]—had, since his student days, led him to do research in the natural sciences. Through this he obtained insight into the technique of nature, a concept central to his world-view. This technique operates through the formative laws of constancy, intensification, and polarity. It produces typical forms in nature and allows these forms to develop. His well-known biological discoveries grew out of his constant preoccupation with these natural principles. To him it seemed self-evident that the forms of nature emerge in a progressive development from the divine force inherent in the world. Yet his real interest lay in what was accessible to intuition: the typical forms into which nature differentiates its content and the laws according to which the types are realized. By pursuing his objective thinking in this direction he attained an insight into the meaning of the world as a whole, since this manifests itself in the structural forms of life. Thus for him there is no inner and outer in nature, no separation between an event and its sense, no bifurcation of nature and spirit. Everything is One—"a sea . . . that surges with heightened forms."[75]

This view of nature illuminated the essence of the visual arts for him in a great flash of insight which Schelling subsequently elab-

[73] *WA*, II, 11:7.

[74] *WA*, I, 15(1):302. *Faust, Part II*, lines 11288-89.

[75] *WA*, I, 3:93. *Gott und Welt*: "Im ernsten Beinhaus," verse 24.

orated. In art the imagination articulates what is typical in the forms of nature, and in this way it continues nature's unconscious creativity in the sphere of consciousness. This insight also provided Goethe a solution to the riddle of the possibility of a kind of knowledge[76] which at that time embroiled the philosophers in endless debates. Nature, a totality which realizes itself in parts, is one with the activity of an intuitive mode of thought, which proceeds on the basis of this relation of the whole to its parts. Insofar as this relationship prevails, thought is one with its object.

While Goethe's intuitive mode of thought, sustained at all times by a feeling of the unity of the universe, proved to be extremely inventive and fertile for the scientific study of organic nature, the mathematical natural sciences were necessarily wholly alien and inaccessible to him. In these sciences, the intellect analyzes the intuitive content of phenomena and, on the basis of mathematical relations, constructs objects which are not encountered directly in experience. It was Goethe's historical destiny to despise and struggle against the mechanistic sciences of nature, without his being able to delay their irresistible progress. Even though the physics of his *Farbenlehre* is untenable, its physiology provided the foundation for Johannes Müller's physiological optics. Goethe, this visual genius, took delight in the phenomena of light and color of his optical experiments; he treated this most pure of the elements of this world like a believer treats a divine being; and he tenaciously maintained 175 the legitimacy of intuition and the poetic beauty of the world over against the colorless abstractions of science.

The spiritual world and the human actions in it are for Goethe the inner side of human nature and thus inseparable from nature. But here sensible intuition can no longer guide him. Furthermore, he made no use of the attempts of his contemporaries to comprehend the system of the social-historical world—neither of pragmatic psychology, of Hegel's system, nor of the new science of history. He allowed men and things to affect him, and taught himself about himself and the world through his practical activity. The objectivity of his view of this spiritual world was grounded only in the purity, impartiality, and universality with which he went about this. It is in this way that the diversity of individually disposed personalities became apparent to him. The natural forms of human existence extend through these personalities—the sexes, age groups, character types, and the forms of development and decline. Society is struc-

[76] The problem of an intuitive intellect raised by Kant.

tured similarly in terms of classes, types of occupation, and political roles, and propagates itself through various situations in life. Everywhere he sees what is invariable and necessary. Major systems of relationships, on which the social-historical world depends, become apparent. Nature has provided us with a wealth and harmony of powers; each of these, even an instinctive drive, has its own particular value; and each is articulated in a particular way in each individual. "Follow the law which is appointed for you. You must be as you are, you cannot escape yourself."[77] On this basis man is able to shape his personality through consistent and unbroken activity. Personality is the highest intrinsic value in the world. "Every age has its peoples, its slaves and masters; but they all say the same: the greatest happiness of the children of the earth lies in personality."[78] And all social organization has the task of promoting free activity in persons which will further the common good. Thus the class-bound socialism of *Wilhelm Meister's Travels* finds in the free-guild association the means to provide a stabilizing framework to the restless mobility of modern economic life. Caught up in this play of forces, man can still attain a sense of certainty and tranquility from within, even in the midst of his activities, by devoting and subsuming them to the unity of the All-One. In summary, man's task lies in consistent, joyous action, in accordance with this intuition of the meaning of life.

However, even these vague intimations of a system are themselves 176 too abstract, too inflexible, and too bare to disclose Goethe's wisdom of life. And every attempt to capture the airy soaring spirit of this view of life in concepts or systems strips it of its luster and light; it leaves behind only miserable shadows. Here a precept cannot be separated from the process in which it emerges, nor can advice on how to live be separated from him who gives it. The multiplicity of meaning in individual life-relations—manifold and infinitely nuanced like life itself—was discerned by Goethe and accounts for his visionary power, his wisdom. It transcends morality and the aesthetic attitude. For from the totality of life's tasks, morality abstracts a mere end or rule whose realization constitutes value for us. And the aesthetic attitude presupposes that we already understand the significance of life. Goethe's wisdom involves the art of living, but it is more than that. An indescribable energy for joyful activity proceeds from it, an affirmation of the meaning of

[77] *WA*, I, 3:95. *Urworte Orphisch.*

[78] *WA*, I, 6:162. *West-östlicher Divan*, VIII, Buch Suleika.

our finite existence, an understanding of life in terms of itself. And he acquired this outlook just as much from the sad deaths of his characters Mignon[79] and Ottilie[80] as from the bright sunlight of his own life.

The sphere of the knowable runs over into the sphere of the unknowable. For in his mind nothing is rigid or detached. Man refers his life task to an intuition of ultimate things, which assures him the realization of his task. Here lies the origin of religion and of every sort of faith or belief in ultimate realities. But a clear line separates the interpretation of life and the determination of the human task from any mode of belief which transcends what can be experienced. Such belief is subjective and relative in its origin and its value; it varies with stages of our life-development, it varies even at one and the same time for a specific person, depending on the kind of mental activity it concerns. Goethe found that as an artist he was a pantheist, as a natural scientist, a polytheist, and that as a moral man he inclined toward a belief in a divine personality. Moreover, inasmuch as we "become mystics in old age,"[81] he comes at last to adopt and be comfortable with articles of faith which, in accordance with his optimistic expectation that our needs and the state of the world can be harmonized, affirm the guidance of human life from above, mental entelechies, and the immortality of the ceaseless activity of life.

For us today, Goethe's significance lies in this understanding of life in terms of itself and in the joyful affirmation of this life. He pursues the sense and significance not only of his own life, but also of the world. He considers every event and every fact in relation to the world as a harmonious whole. His poetry reconciles us with the world and transfigures it. In conversations which have been preserved and are occasionally suggestive of Luther's table talk we are struck by the patriarchal enjoyment and humor with which he affirms an unshakable and happy belief in the world as a valuable and meaningful system. He expands in all directions from this central core of his world-view. The older he gets, the stronger becomes his need to subsume more and more facts under the living whole which stands before him; his immense capacity for intuition appears to have come into the world in order to subject everything in it to his consideration; and his death is merely the cessation, decreed by

177

[79] From *Wilhelm Meister's Apprenticeship*.

[80] From *The Elective Affinities*.

[81] Conversation with F. Förster (1828), in Biedermann, *Goethes Gespräche*, vol. 3, p. 516.

nature, of an operation which was nevertheless destined to continue forever. His vision is always clear, true, and pure. Yet even in this respect he differs enormously from Voltaire, who was the greatest master of the European spirit in the eighteenth century before Goethe! Voltaire was a wondrous being who would one day appropriate Newton in order to understand nature, while the next he would turn to Bolingbroke in order to revolutionize historical study; he seemed to see things from all sides and to perceive and utilize every movement around him; he was a Proteus, always someone different, never himself, for he was always able to hide himself cleverly behind someone greater than himself, who saw more deeply and thought more elegantly and nobly; Voltaire speaking to himself was not the same Voltaire who spoke to his European public. By contrast, the eyes of Goethe the poet always meet ours with the same purity and unfathomable depth whenever we examine anything he discovered or thought. His most private thoughts are one and the same as those he expresses in *Iphigenia*. His experiential reflection about life, his scientific work, and his poetry fully accord with each other in what they teach. He was still surrounded by simple circumstances which made possible a universal development of his personality and a natural, serene conception of existence.

5

This mode of thinking, which operates in experience, provides the foundation of Goethe's poetry; it determines the genesis of poetic themes, the formation of plots and characters, and the inner form of this poetry; the development of his poetry is based on it.

His imagination must have been constantly striving to elevate experienced reality into the poetic. In the years of his youth his conversation was full of images and similes; he dramatized "every thing of importance which occurred in actual life."[82] When he 178 adopted world-historical symbols for his lived experiences or projected them into historical and contemporary events, this was only an intensification of the constant process of symbolizing and typifying his lived experience. The highly effective themes of *Prometheus*, *Faust*, *Werther*, *Wilhelm Meister*, *Iphigenia*, and *Tasso* emerged from his efforts to integrate his personal destiny with the great movements surrounding him. It was this that determined the *inner form of his poetry*. The hard, jagged raw material of events

[82] *WA*, I, 28:235; *TF*, vol. 2, p. 173.

is wholly recast and purified in the process of being formed by the imagination. This process retains nothing except what is requisite for the straightforward expression of lived experience and its meaning. It excludes all irrelevant facts from the plot, all contingency in the composition of the characters. And as a result the simple embodiment of human significance stands before us. From the depths of the consciousness of the time, Goethe's poetry articulates a new world of human awareness ranging from a new titanic defiance to a new intimate empathy[83] with nature. He is the first modern poet to represent not only the fearful phenomena of the passions, but also the whole man in his relation to the eternal forces around him and in the way he secretly suffers from life and other people; in this respect all modern poets are his students. Moreover, the powerful originality of his imagination gives people and things a visibility without being obtrusive—it gives them the clearest possible existence in a distant ideal world. His singular genius for language, coupled with a naive power of expression rooted in his Franconian homeland, was developed through incessant practice, and by assimilating both the literature of an age of aesthetic reflection and the great poetry of the past which was then being rediscovered; this genius for language provided the means for representing all the nuances of human awareness. It was supplemented in a very special way by his constant and varied efforts in the visual arts and by the most intimate familiarity with specific works. Goethe strove from an early age "to observe with precision the visible characteristics of objects."[84] "The eye was, above all others, the organ by which I seized the world. I had, from childhood, lived among painters. . . . Wherever I looked, I saw a picture. . . ."[85] Earlier schools of painting stimulated him to see the scenes of life in a painterly manner—painterly in the sense of transforming the external world to produce effects in accordance with the laws of the visual arts. Cervantes was Goethe's greatest modern predecessor in this respect, for he must have been influenced by the great paintings of Italy and of his native country. From the garden scene in *Faust, Part I,* to *Hermann and Dorothea* and Faust's transfiguration, this innate, yet cultivated capacity elevates the whole external world into the sphere of beauty. And how wonderfully it does this for everything from the inner world as well! His joyful participation in everything living, 179

[83] This is one of the relatively rare occasions that Dilthey uses the word "Einfühlung."

[84] *WA*, I, 26:314.

[85] *WA*, I, 27:16; *TF*, vol. 1, p. 185.

his deep understanding and his humane tolerance are responsible for the fact that in his work every being manifests its inherent value and, at the same time, its determinate limits. Moreover, his artistic skill of articulation and of fashioning a style imparts a final beauty to these inner and outer worlds. It gives each work a form of its own, often an entirely new one, as is the case in *Faust*, *Wilhelm Meister*, and *Hermann and Dorothea*. In these works this skill functions just as it does in the author's own life; it connects the self-sufficiency and persistence of individual states with the progress of the whole. The procedure of this imagination combines with the poetic rule prescribed by Lessing to impart movement to objects and dissolve rigid characterization into inner life, thus allowing people to appear differently in different situations. Goethe does not show the unity of human life in fixed traits, but rather in an inner law which binds together its living moments—like a melody of human existence. He is the poet of the beautiful, just as Raphael is its painter and Mozart its composer.

Goethe's poetic development is like the growth of a plant. He takes from the soil that for which he has an affinity; he assimilates it according to the law of his being; and the seasons of life flow by. The poetic works of his youth are free and easy in their use of the conventions of the period; but the material for his pastoral play *Die Mitschuldigen* (The Accomplices) and for the light, playful songs of his Leipzig period was taken entirely from his experiences of life. In these genres he was already moving beyond his German predecessors. Then he enters a second period, clearly distinguishable from the first, which extends from his time in Strassburg on into the first years at Weimar. During this period Goethe gave the new generation's vague striving for greatness its highest expression. He left behind the kings and vassals of Shakespeare and Corneille; his concern became the man of genius, whose importance was recognized in the eighteenth century: Prometheus, the creative artist; Mohammed, the religious genius; Faust, with his boundless striving for knowledge, power, and happiness; and Werther, in whom a life of feeling of the utmost intensity consumed itself in its solitary opposition to reality. This new poetic world found expression in a specific style, which articulated and connected the most intense and most significant moments of life. Could anyone then have predicted what possibilities of development lay in this profusely endowed individual? When he had made up his mind to settle in Weimar, he moved gradually into a new phase of poetic activity. The beginning of this phase was an important life-experience which came about as Goethe decided to exert his influence on the world. Action which aims to encompass everything and strives to overcome the limitations of a given situation brings with it ceaseless changes in one's state of mind and a feeling of insufficiency. The disappointments of the life-impulse produce the most profound human experience, according to which only steady, pure, and consistent action, pursued with a consciousness of one's own limits, can bring about an enduring inner freedom of the soul. Because Goethe experienced this more intensely, more consciously, and with fewer presuppositions than any other man of his time, he was in a position to apprehend psychic development in its inherent, almost imperceptible growth. It was unlike both Lavater's conception of psychic development, which was confined by its Christian heritage, and Wieland's shallow conception influenced by the French spirit of the age. For Goethe's psychic development had a typical character which issues directly from sheer experience of life. This was to be the theme of his narrative poem "Die Geheimnisse" (The Mysteries). Here the religiosity of Lessing and Herder attains its final consummation in the idea that every positive belief is only a symbol for inner experience, and the same lived experience which is central to Lessing's *Nathan the Wise* is consummated in the pious and wise Humanus of "Die Geheimnisse." 180

> For all our powers press onward and outward
> To live and strive and act, here as there.
> But we are pressed and bound from every side
> And the forces of the world carry us along with them.
> But in this inner turmoil and external struggle
> Our spirit hears the words, faint and dark:
> From the powers that bind all creatures,
> He frees himself who can overcome himself.[86]

*Iphigenia*, the representation of a pure soul for whom self-mastery leads to self-redemption, is rooted in the same experiences. It is self-abnegation, then, which opens the way to contributing to the common good. The work of self-abnegation consists in steadfastness, purity, forbearance, love, and tranquility. It places limits on indeterminate strivings which lack specific aims. From the time he attained maturity, Goethe tended more and more to locate the value of life in this kind of steady, consistent activity. Not only did his own administrative activity aim at this ideal; it was also furthered

[86] *WA*, I, 16:178.

by the philosophies of Kant and Fichte, and above all by Schiller in whose great life poetry became action, since other sorts of activity were denied him on account of the wretched political situation. Moreover, the threat posed by the French Revolution to the whole prevailing order directed even poets of the soul, love, and beauty to the world of action. Thus, like Schiller, Goethe recognized in all enjoyment, all knowledge, and all inwardness only a preparation for contributing to the common good, and this awareness was exemplary for the course of our nation. Thus *Faust* and *Wilhelm* 181 *Meister* end by moving into the world of action. In *Wilhelm Meister,* Goethe portrayed a developmental history in its typical stages. The conception of *Faust* required that self-limitation through resignation be deemphasized: his existence develops in typical stages of a different sort, and even at the end, he has not attained consciousness of his limitations; but here, action for the common good is set forth more forcefully than anywhere else as the highest value of life.

Both works portray life as a developmental process which realizes an ideal through a series of stages. They do not extract a particular aspect or a limited time span from life; rather, they aim to encompass the whole man: an infinite and never completely soluble task! European poetry was raised to a higher level in these works, when Goethe connected that which is most personal with the most encompassing relations of our existence, and when he set the bustle of the world and a robust joy in life over against mature ironic reflections about the depths of the soul. Wonderful new means for poetic impression were fashioned here, and they had a tremendous effect on the nation and, through *Faust,* on world literature. Then, in his autobiography, Goethe undertook once more to narrate a developmental history as it emerges from talents which he revealed only through their products and from the effects of the world on them.

*Faust* and *Wilhelm Meister* accompanied Goethe throughout his entire life, and yet they remained unfinished, like life itself. The artist in Goethe needed a comparatively simple subject matter in order to realize perfect beauty. And Goethe's lived experience was so universal, his mind so active, that unlike any other artist before him he took moods of life and aspects of psychic reality which appear to exclude one another completely, and fashioned their isolated significance into distinct worlds—the robust joys of love and the wealth of beauty in the *Roman Elegies*, the psychic depths of *Pandora* and the *Trilogie der Leidenschaft* (Trilogy of Passion), and the contemplative quality of *The West-Eastern Divan.*

It would be impossible to delineate further periods of his poetic development. Ever more series of processes determining this development, each of them initiated at a different time, finally came together. The study of the laws of organic development led to the simplification of his poetic portrayal of nature, and suitable poetic forms then emerged, such as his didactic poems. Then, when he searched for such laws of development and enduring forms in human life with its chaotic multitude of phenomena, he was able to order them in terms of basic types of individuals, their circumstances, and society. The power that Greek art, with its typifying tendencies, exerted on him grew accordingly. These were the presuppositions of an objective poetry which transfigured the truth of life into beauty. Goethe was the first to consciously make poetry an organ for the objective understanding of the world. His mind was purified to such an extent by his continual scientific study of nature, and was so much at one with its processes, that in *Hermann and Dorothea* he was able to show how nature's lawfulness is disclosed in spontaneous creation—and how it shines through figures and destinies which are at the same time unrepeatable, unique, and individual! Homer's objective poetry was, according to the belief of the time, a gift of nature; Goethe's objective poetry was produced on the foundation of a scientific attitude toward reality, which refined his mind and thus enabled him to perceive things instinctively, purely, and without reasoning. Before him, Leonardo and Dürer aspired to do the same in their domain—they provided models for every higher representation of the human form in the future. And then, as the awesome specter of the French Revolution moved closer and closer to life in Germany, Goethe made use of the same typical form to describe—in a great trilogy of which only the first part, *Die natürliche Tochter* was completed—the structure of French society as displayed through representative persons. He also showed the factors which would necessarily bring about its destruction. He became increasingly observant and reflective. In the *Elective Affinities* we are stirred magically by his treatment of the problem of marriage through the combination of an almost theoretical attitude with the deepest emotional sympathy. This combination is represented in a symmetrical arrangement of carefully balanced relationships of typical characters, which plainly has a musical effect. With increasing frequency he moves away from typical representation and glides into symbolic representation; for as an old man he allows the moment and its emotive power to dissolve into the nexus of distant memories: life itself must be expressed,

182

and that is possible only in symbolic representation. In his late lyric poetry each moment is filled and saturated, as it were, by the past. Only exuberant expressions can be adequate to such fullness of experience. His attitude becomes increasingly serene and contemplative; world literature, which he follows attentively, offers him new forms for this, as can be seen in *The West-Eastern Divan*. His creativity ends with a final expression of his wisdom of life in philosophical poems and aphorisms. The sublime style of his old age draws together enigmatically the dissonances and harmonies of 183 life and lets things be seen more powerfully and solemnly—the way mountains appear at the onset of night—in a last, impressive effort of old age to complete for posterity those inherently incomplete works, *Wilhelm Meister* and *Faust*.

6

All Goethe's poetry is fundamentally lyrical. Lyric poetry, the poetic form of inwardness, is, along with music, the special domain of the German-speaking nations. What a variety of syntactical means for expressing feeling, desire, and volition, and what a wealth of words for the nuances of emotional life our language provides! This inwardness and its linguistic means of expression have developed slowly, and come into play in lyric poetry.

Obligations prescribed by an institutional order grounded in a Divine Being governed the lives of the Germans of the sixteenth and seventeenth centuries. Protestant religious thought traced these obligations back to the unifying ground of consciousness. The composed and collected character of the significant personalities of this period was rooted in this Protestantism. Then this ideal of character received further definition through the secular scientific culture of the seventeenth century and was given expression in the lyric poetry of Paul Gerhardt,[87] Gryphius,[88] and Fleming.[89] The variety of life brought out different aspects of the essence of lyric poetry, but the individual who expressed himself in this way was a fixed quantity—religiously, metaphysically, and morally. Slowly these constraints on the expression of personality were relaxed; our lyric poetry passed through the stylistic forms of the Enlightenment, of Klopstock, and of its flowering in the following years. Goethe grew up

[87] Paul Gerhardt (1607-76), German poet, well-known for his Protestant hymns.

[88] Andreas Gryphius (1616-64), a leading representative of German Baroque poetry.

[89] Paul Fleming (1609-40) was another German poet of the Baroque period.

in the midst of these changes. He was the first to abandon completely the notion that character is something fixed, solid, and indissoluble as established by religious-moral obligation, by the intellect, by a religiosity which is really a longing for happiness combined with fear of it, or by a premature connection of a new freedom with tradition. There was a musical energy in his soul which responded to every impression made on it by the world with a tonal pattern of its own. And his psychic life was so finely tuned, so quick of response, so active and sensitive, that it seemed to express his relation to the world in its entirety and with complete objectivity. Each of his poems has a soul of its own, shaped in the form of an ethereal body that appears this way but once and then vanishes. He gives the simplest and most comprehensive expression to the lawfulness of psychic life. Every phase of life speaks of life in its own language and with its own rhythm of psychic movement. The typical relations of life seem here to be felt in accordance with their full value for the first time. And although each poem communicates only as many aspects of nature as can be experienced in a particular state of mind, it still appears that no one had ever before lived in such intimate communion with nature.

184

This lyrical element pervades Goethe's entire body of poetry. But above all he overcame the rigidity of character portrayal found in previous German poetry. His characters exude a new freedom and inner dynamism. What is constant in them is a law governing the development of their individual existence, a rule governing the course of their life. Everything substantial or fixed is dissolved in the melody of life.

Starting with this, we must now seek to penetrate into Goethe's art of character portrayal. As always, the first task is to determine what a poet takes from life as material for the formation of his characters, and literary history has recently developed very precise methods for doing this. To be sure, it has not always been conscious of the limits of this approach. A person's life is intertwined with the destinies of many others in surprising ways; he has sudden encounters with others who confront him with arresting presence, but who then generally disappear again in the bustle of the world; others touch him even more fleetingly, perhaps only through the utterance of someone to whom he is otherwise indifferent, or perhaps merely through a notice that stands out among the facts crammed into a newspaper article. All this, in turn, is so interwoven with what we have seen, read, or heard about lived experience, and the seeds of motifs, characters, and plots are always so much in the air that it seems to us impossible to establish with certainty the connection between the given data about the life of a poet and the products of his imagination. Mephisto, Gretchen, and the motif of the *Elective Affinities* might have flashed before Goethe in fleeting encounters in life, which had practically no significance within the framework of his own life. But they had precisely that quality which prompted his imagination to engage in the delicate formative activity of producing characters.

The other task is to indicate the moments of the poet's life-experience which determine the process of forming characters from the material given by life. Goethe fashioned the motifs of his works from his own inner life, his pains and struggles. For him struggle, which is the mainspring not only of every representative poetic work but also of life itself, originates in man's own inner life. It is characteristic of Goethe, that after the reorientation of his life in Weimar, the resolution of this struggle is also almost always accomplished in the inner life of man himself. According to Goethe, a deep, loving look at the nexus of nature, in which man is situated and his destiny fulfilled, makes it possible for anyone to become reconciled with life; or if, through a kind of blindness, he is himself unable to find such a reconciliation, he can still attain it through the mind of the poet. This is the Tyrtaic[90] element in Goethe's poetry, which he proudly asserted over against the "hospital poets."

185

At this point, we can now also understand the limits of Goethe's poetry, without which it would lack its wondrous power. Some extol and envy Goethe as one favored by fortune, while others cite his famous statement that he had known pure happiness only very few days of his life. Some complain that he shows no feeling for real suffering in his poems; to others he appears to have shared every pain. Goethe made poetry out of the struggles which he had experienced—and that he experienced them deeply is expressed in both his letters and his poems. If he once said that he wanted Iphigenia to speak just as if no stocking weaver were starving in Apolda,[91] this must be interpreted to mean that he excluded from his poetry suffering of the most natural kind which derives from the bare struggle for existence and power, from conflicts of wills in society: he lived and made into poetry those struggles which originate, are fought out, and are concluded in the inner life of

[90] Tyrtaios, a lame schoolmaster and elegiac poet of the seventh century B.C., who inspired the Spartans to fight and fulfill their destiny.

[91] A small place near Weimar.

man. He could not do otherwise; once he defended himself by saying that he had never put into poetry anything he had not lived.

The peculiarities of his poetic technique follow from this fact. Shakespeare constructs a person and his actions from a few dominant motives and passions; Goethe juxtaposes many living elements. The imagination of even the greatest poets is limited. The danger of the first technique is artificiality, something comparable to an abstract model or to a machine; the danger of the second is incoherence. The characters of the former poet lack the fullness of life; they often seem to be constructed only of muscles, bones, and ligaments; the characters of the latter are sensitively true to life, but there is not always a plausible connection between their inner states and the actions required of them for the progress of the poem—although they do not disclose the unbearable discrepancies between feelings and actions of Rousseau's characters.

As regards their external form, *Werther, Prometheus, Mahomet,* and *Faust* were also fashioned in this way, although predominantly from lyrical moments (this term being taken in the widest possible sense). While they lack a coherent direction of their actions, they compensate by showing inner life with impressionistic intensity. *Faust* is the apotheosis of this art form. Goethe's wonderful ability to give the most delicate expression to states of mind and their actual backgrounds, and to render them in images, appears in his most hastily written notes as well as in his lyrical poems. In *Faust* he now represents what moves him through the great trope of an action which lets even the deepest lived experience be expressed in a beautiful exterior. He describes all this with the transparency and purity of nature herself; never has anyone been more true. As he shows himself through this, Goethe becomes the embodied ideal of an age, and *Faust* is the comprehensive symbol in which he reveals his whole life. Then in *Tasso* and *Iphigenia* he provided himself with another wholly new form of the drama of the inner self for which *Die Geschwister* (The Siblings) and *Stella* had paved the way. Here one soul acts on another, and what happens in the external world is like a mere garment or cloak. An inner process is represented with such constancy that we can follow it almost from hour to hour. It involves a small number of persons for a short duration, and without much change of place. All theatrical brilliance and all external dramatic devices are rejected so that our interest will focus completely on the inner life. Thus Goethe's poems always lead us back to the great man who speaks to us in them. Each of his works draws attention to his personality, which is present in all of them.

186

He teaches us to allow men and things to act upon us naturally, purely, and independently of their relations to our person; to understand life in its fullness and harmony, in terms of itself; to appreciate its value, and to face every setback and difficulty with renewed, joyful, and consistent action. His power to overcome, to forget, and to renew himself is communicated to us not only in his writings; it is also evident from everything that we know about his life. And no critique which attempts to devalue the letters and biographical accounts in favor of the poetic work will be able to invert the relation [established here between the life of the author and his works] and to reduce Goethe's life, nature, and development to mere means of understanding his works. For what a man ultimately intended in his life's work is also what attracts us to him and ultimately holds our attention after his life has ended.

# 5

## *Friedrich Hölderlin (1910)*[1]

ED, 242

TRANSLATED BY JOSEPH ROSS

There is an old belief that the gods manifest themselves and reveal the future of things in innocent souls. Hölderlin lived in such pious, innocent purity and in translucent beauty of being. When as a youth he passed among his comrades of the Tübingen *Stift*, it was as if Apollo strode through the room. His image was impressed for life upon one boy who saw him there at musical performances, standing with his violin in his hand: the regular form of his face and the gentle features of his countenance, his handsome figure, his meticulous, immaculate attire, and the expression of sublimity in his overall appearance were striking. Hölderlin's noble nature was deeply offended by every vulgar sentiment. Ordinary sensual happiness and all worldly ambition were far beneath him. For himself he longed for nothing other than a simple destiny so that he could live his art contentedly. He wanted to preserve the simple purity of his soul. His visionary power derived from this purity of his being.

At that great moment of German literature when our poetry reached its peak, when the subjective idealism that champions personality and freedom inspired the youth, and when the French Revolution opened prospects for a more perfect society, Hölderlin and his friends strode forward to meet the challenge of this new world. They were expecting a new, higher humanity and strove to bring it about. Among his comrades, Hölderlin was like the embodiment of a more pure, harmonious form of human personality. In this he resembles Schiller, who was like an older brother inspiring an infinite longing for heroic existence in this gentle, enthusiastic soul. But how could this enthusiasm among the German youth have maintained itself as the Revolution degenerated more and more, as

[1] This essay was originally published in the 1906 edition of *ED*. Dilthey added several paragraphs to the 1910 edition. These have also been included in the translation. See *ED*, 15th ed., pp. 326-327. Pagination in the margin is in accordance with the 15th ed.

its wars produced the conflict between love of freedom and patriotism, as the European reaction asserted itself? Authoritarian forces prevailed. There was no place in the German states where the young generation could work for a more liberal social order. Autocracy, the social pressure of nobility and wealth, religious narrow-mindedness proved victorious in this society. Resignation was inevitable.

243 No practical career was available for this quiet, musing, lyrical genius. Since Hölderlin was without any means, the privations of life had their effect on him. Everything drove him from the world of action and enjoyment to turn inward, into the depths of things, into a total solitude. Unrelentingly and intensely he listened to the voices within himself and in nature, to see if they would communicate to him the divine mystery that slumbers in all things. Thus there came to him the prophetic tidings of possibilities for a higher form of humanity, of a future heroism of the German nation, of a new beauty of life which would accomplish through us the will of divine nature and of a poetry expressing the eternal rhythm of life itself, which surrounds us inaudibly. At the same time, however, there arose in him a deep experience most peculiarly his own, the lived experience that all greatness and beauty deriving from the divine order of things is for us always accompanied by suffering in life; that every revelation of divine unity in love and human friendship brings with it a painful separation, and that the joy of inner power also involves the burdening pressure of difficult things.

Hölderlin's helpless soul probed ever more deeply into the experiences of the mixed and ambiguous character of human existence. The nobility of his nature allowed him to withdraw into a quiet, composed self-resignation. The heroic poem that he wanted to live and write became a tragedy of sacrifice. In all that he composed, he wanted to express the character of life itself as it had manifested itself to him in his lived experience. This was a constant presence for him. Every present was replete with memories. He found a language of new simplicity for all that. A new melody unfolded in this musical genius. It was a prophetic creation. It anticipated the rhythmic style of Nietzsche, the lyric poetry of Verlaine, Baudelaire, Swinburne, and that which our contemporary poetry is striving for. While musing by placid brooks whose soft babbling accompanied the song of his soul, and internalizing the peaceful, gentle lines of the south German hills and streams in his rhythms, he gradually found this new form. "As Jupiter's eagle listened to the song of the muses, I hear the wonderful, infinite harmony in me"—"the melody of the heart."

## HOMELAND AND FIRST PLAYFUL POETIC EFFORTS

Hölderlin is from the town of Lauffen on the Neckar. There he was surrounded by the quiet charm of the Swabian landscape. On the bank of the pleasant river was the old church of Saint Regiswindis. From a craggy island in the river protruded the gray tower of an old castle, and against the vine-covered slopes on the other shore rose the crumbling wall of an old monastery. Close by was the house of his father, the warden. Friedrich Hölderlin was born in this house on March 20, 1770. His parents were steadfast, patient, cheerful people. His father lived only a few more years, and although his young mother married the mayor of Nürtingen, the child soon lost this second loving guardian as well. Hölderlin was then nine years old. The precociousness and sensitivity of his feelings were shown by his later declaration that the impression of this death attuned his soul to a seriousness that thereafter never left him entirely. His mother stayed in Nürtingen, and Friedrich attended grammar school there until the age of fifteen. Here he was surrounded by the same impressions of the Swabian countryside: the Neckar flowing among gentle hills and surrounded by poplars, with the Alb mountains in the background. The boy would sit and muse on the quiet banks or in the nearby forest. It must have been there that he read (and who knows how often?) the lyric poets who filled the youth of the 1780s with enthusiasm. Once on a cliff in the forest he recited Klopstock's *Hermannsschlacht* to his brother.

244

His feeling for nature was informed by the impressions of these landscapes. The boundless sea and wide plains, whose infinite horizons permit one to look and move in all directions, have the effect of liberating the soul and imparting to it a sovereign sense of life. But where someone finds himself surrounded, but not confined, by gentle hills and soft valleys, where the fine distant lines of blue mountains draw him outwards while the valley protects and shelters him, here the effect is a gentle, congenial relationship to nature. It is a feeling of being sheltered and of comfortable intimacy with valleys, streams, and hills, but also a longing for the shimmering distance. The Swabian poets—Hölderlin, Uhland,[2] Mörike[3]—are imbued with such a feeling for nature: a sense of union with the

[2] Ludwig Uhland (1787-1862). Romantic poet known for his folk ballads.

[3] Eduard Mörike (1804-75). His poetry combines classical form with a deep feeling for his Swabian homeland.

soft contours of the hills, with the peaceful, habitable valleys, and with the past that we dreamingly project into the crumbling monasteries and castles.

> "In my boyhood days
> . . .
> Safe and good then I played
> With the orchard flowers
> . . .
> And learned to love
> Amid the flowers"[4]

At the age of fourteen, Friedrich entered the lower secondary school at Denkendorf located in one of the former monasteries, and two years later the morc advanced school at Maulbronn. The inevitable prospect for gifted children of moderate means in Württemberg was to go into the ministry, and Hölderlin's loving, pious mother looked forward to seeing her son a pastor some day. In these schools the foundation was laid for his solid knowledge of the Greek language and its literature. Later he liked to recall how,

245

> From the death of the hero
> My heart first perceived the grand, golden words
> With a shudder of anticipation.[5]

However, the artistic ideals of antiquity which suited his noble poetic nature so well came into more and more direct conflict with the prevailing orthodox Christian views and with a religious vocation. Spoiled by the kind hand of his loving mother, the boy also found himself repulsed by the hard, monastic discipline that was still common in institutions meant to train future ministers. This was the source of an inner conflict between his ideals and the reality of his actual life and his future. This conflict, which came to define his sensitive and defenseless soul, would give his poetry its intensity and his life a tragic course. He learned to withdraw into himself with his ideals, to be alone with himself, with nature, and with a few similarly attuned souls; early on he experienced the melancholy feeling of having great eccentric gifts, being different from the up-

[4] "Da ich ein Knabe war," in Hölderlin, *Sämtliche Werke*, Grosse Stuttgarter Ausgabe (hereafter *GSA*), ed. by Friedrich Beissner (Stuttgart: J. G. Cottasche Buchhandlung Nachfolger, 1943-77), 1(1):266, 267; trans. by Michael Hamburger in *Hölderlin: Poems and Fragments* (hereafter *HPF*) (New York: Cambridge University Press, 1980), pp. 81, 83.

[5] *GSA*, 1(2):607.

right and industrious people around him, having no share in their comfortable pleasures, and yet renouncing all these aspects of everyday human existence.

Such as he was, he had to love Homer and Ossian, Klopstock and Schubart, at times to hate Wieland intensely—and to worship Schiller. Writing verse was a part of school work, and he did it with passion even in Denkendorf. Among his poems from this time are found childlike poems of gratitude to his teachers of a ceremonious nature, some religious poems which in no way rise above the triviality of pious verses used by country preachers to adorn the end of their sermons, and a very sentimental and rambling poem that pleads for God's mercy for his mother, sister, brother Karl, each in turn. His poetry received its initial impetus from his first love. This was a harmless student love with a secret engagement, the devotion of a good, loving girl to an intellectually superior youth, secret meetings, farewells and reunions according to the rhythm of the semesters, and finally a breakup after three years of uncertainty. His Luise cherished the exalted feelings of these tear-filled years. She most of all loved to walk in the cemetery. In her room she thought "of God and of him." She read his favorite poets and wrote somewhat clumsily in his style. Werther and Ferdinand could not have been more sincerely and more innocently enthusiastic, but finally he had to confess to his love that he suffered from an ambition that would perhaps never be fulfilled, but which separated his path from hers.

246

With this love, a personal tone entered his verses: "On my walks I am constantly rhyming on my tablet—about what? can you guess?—of you! of you! and then I erase it again."[6] Here were definite feelings which lent themselves to being put in meter and rhyme. Thus he came to understand the personal poetry of Klopstock, and followed him in the use of ancient meters—something which would become very significant for him. Yet, he first found a natural and strong expression for the unruly course of his feelings in the prose of his letters. This prose was completely influenced by *Werther, Fiesko,*[7] and *Kabale und Liebe.*[8] He felt the impetuous beat of his own heart in the manner of the *Sturm und Drang* period of Goethe and Schiller. While he wrote, he wept like the heroes of these novels and dramas. Like Werther, he felt himself elevated

[6] See Carl Litzmann, *Friedrich Hölderlins Leben* (Berlin: Hertz, 1890), p. 19.

[7] Friedrich von Schiller, *Die Verschwörung des Fiesko* (1783).

[8] Schiller (1794).

above the comrades around him. His unfulfilled ambition devoured his heart. He longed to weep tears of joy on the shoulder of a friend.

## HÖLDERLIN AS A YOUNG MAN: HYMNS TO THE IDEALS OF HUMANITY

Then came his student years. In the fall of 1788, at the age of eighteen, he entered the University of Tübingen. But these years did not bring him the usual carefree, joyous life. He felt as though he had only changed prisons. He was crowded into the cramped old *Stift*, the former Augustinian monastery, together with other young theologians to be educated at public expense, and he was under the supervision of assistants and tutors who still wore the cowl formerly worn by monks. But what especially oppressed this soul thirsting for beauty was that he himself had to wear a black gown with white clerical bands, and, though from the first he made an effort to wear this clerical garb with elegance, the feeling of being so marked and therefore disdained by many still distressed him. Theological studies as conducted in the *Stift* could not satisfy him. Tübingen, once the stronghold of Protestant faith, had not withstood the inroads of the Enlightenment. Here, and at the same time in Halle, a compromise between orthodoxy and the Enlightenment had been made. 247 Man's primeval faith in miracles, divine punishment, prophecy, and revelation could not be maintained in the face of knowledge of the immutable laws of nature and of pragmatic psychology. Theological apologists sought to salvage some of what was essential to the Church's position from this situation by means of an artificial and spurious system of abstract concepts. The result was a repulsive combination of ancient intuitions and modern philosophical reflection. The better students attending the lectures only reluctantly swallowed the sorry mishmash handed down to them in Tübingen and Halle by Nösselt, Knapp, Storr, and Tieftrunk. Hölderlin yearned to escape this monastic "cell." He would gladly have studied law and only his mother's pleas held him back. Besides, his secret engagement weighed like a chain upon him. It was only in Tübingen that he painfully freed himself from this engagement. From all this he fled again into the ideal world, into the sacred realm of the Greek poets, to Ossian, Klopstock, and Schiller.

Since versification was a widespread malady of the time, he found comrades in his longing for poetic laurels even in the *Stift*. His great need to live with exalted friends, shut off from the world, was satisfied completely by two young poets, Neuffer and Magenau. A poetic fellowship was formed, with an album into which the friends copied their verses. In Stuttgart, he visited Schubart, the patriarch of Swabian poets, and who naturally received him with paternal kindness. Stäudlin, a gifted, kindhearted poetic soul, became intimately involved, as Gleim had earlier and Schwab would later, in this poetic fellowship, and the young poets first found a place for their verses in his *Schwäbischer Musenalmanach* (Swabian Almanac of the Muses).

Hölderlin's poetic style developed steadily after these initial stages, which were influenced primarily by Klopstock and Schubart. From Klopstock, the young poet adopted forms of speech and ways of conjoining them which suited his sensibility, and he retained these until the end.

> Never will I endure it, ever,
> To take these childish steps,
> These halting half-steps like a prisoner,
> Never will I endure it, never.[9]

And in another poem:

> Farewell, you golden hours of a past time,
> you lovely child-dreams of greatness and fame.
> Farewell, farewell, you playmates![10]

Gradually Klopstock's odic tone and his classical meters disappeared. The influence of Schiller's lyric poetry exceeds that of all others. Hölderlin appropriated what was new in this poetry: the inner rhythm which expressed the course of mental processes by the ordering and combining of clauses. This was the beginning of his rhythmic style. The same influence of Schiller can be noted in Matthisson's lyricism, and this poet of gentle melancholy also influenced Hölderlin and his fellow poet, Neuffer, through the euphony of his verse and a natural, smooth flow of feeling. If one compares Neuffer's "Abendschwärmerei" (Evening Enthusiasm) with Hölderlin's "Gott der Jugend" (God of Youth), one sees the effect of this new form of lyric poetry on poets of such diverse ability, for Neuffer was a very mediocre talent indeed.

248

This new form first attained its full development in Hölderlin when the powerful content of Schiller's writing became the focus

[9] "Zornige Sehnsucht," *GSA*, 1(1):90.
[10] "Einst und Jezt," *GSA*, 1(1):96.

of his poetry in the hymns to the ideals of humanity. They were conceived as a whole and are the greatest artistic achievement of these early years.

Here, however, we must note a personal influence which determined Hölderlin's world-view and the substance of his poetry more powerfully than anything else. It stems from his friendship in his youthful years with the two Swabian leaders of the new philosophical movement, Hegel and Schelling. Hegel had entered the *Stift* with Hölderlin in the fall of 1788, but Hölderlin mentioned him for the first time in 1790. At that time they both lived in the same room in the *Stift*. The young poet's first dream of love and happiness had just come to an end. The impulse to develop his potential freely had triumphed. At this important moment in his development a fortunate providence led him to Hegel. Schelling entered the *Stift* in the fall of 1790 and became acquainted with the poet through Hegel. Schelling was not yet sixteen years old at that time, but he was a precocious genius, which made him the object of great admiration in the *Stift*. But Hölderlin could not establish a very close relationship to Schelling, who was proud and confident of success.

Hölderlin and Hegel formed an immediate and sincere friendship rooted in their shared Swabian background. They both felt the need to organize their lives around the family and the constant ethical relationships of their Swabian homeland, and they also shared a tendency to speculate, recognizing no limits for thought. With other friends they read Plato, Kant, and Jacobi's letters on Spinoza,[11] the second edition of which appeared in 1789. This book contained Lessing's creed of the "One and All." This ancient Greek phrase for the presence of the divine in the universe was entered by Hölderlin in Hegel's album in February 1791.[12]

249

At this point in our account we must look beyond the confined monastic atmosphere of the *Stift* to the extremely active intellectual life of Germany at that time. Three forces were especially influential: a revival of interest in ancient Greece, a philosophical and poetic movement which transformed the whole inner life of our nation, and the French Revolution which influenced that same inner life from without. The effect of this lively activity spread even to the

[11] Friedrich Heinrich Jacobi, "Über die Lehren des Spinozas," in *Briefen an Herrn Moses Mendelssohn* (Breslau, 1785).

[12] Recent scholarship has shown this to be an addition to Hölderlin's entry by someone else, possibly Hegel himself. See Friedhelm Nicolin, ed., *Briefe von und an Hegel*, 2/1 (Hamburg: Meiner, 1977), p. 136.

quiet rooms where the students of the *Stift* sat at their desks studying the notes of their philosophical and theological teachers.

What had, for the most part, already been done for young people elsewhere, still needed to be done here. The students at the *Stift* had to liberate themselves from the internal and external authority of theological doctrines. In Hölderlin, the simple piety of his parental home and of his good mother triumphed repeatedly over philosophic doubts and Greek ideals. Around 1790 or 1791, the time of his first contacts with Hegel, he was still striving to justify positive Christianity. He began with Kant's refutation of all proofs for a supersensible world and with Jacobi's doctrine that reason left to itself must ultimately deny God. The certainty of immortality and the existence of a personal God which could not be guaranteed by reason could be found, according to him, in the well-attested tradition of Christ, his testimony, and its confirmation by miracles. This reflected the worn-out apologetics of contemporary theology in Tübingen. A more intensive study of Kant moved Hölderlin away from this watered-down faith of his teachers, just as it had already freed his fellow students Schelling and Hegel. From this point on he retained only the inner humanistic value of Christianity and acknowledged that the divine was communicated through Christ but only in the same way as through the founders of other religions. Subsequent comments by the older, weary Hölderlin, when he had already succumbed to insanity, change nothing on this point.

Foremost among the forces determining our cultural life was the revival of interest in ancient Greece. While Hölderlin was strongly attracted to Greek studies even in his early schooling, he now received an important new stimulus from his tutor Philipp Conz, who had been influenced by Winckelmann and Heyne.[13] Conz combined the study of the ancients with an enthusiasm for the new German poetry. A philologist, translator, poet, philosopher, and inspiring teacher, he had been a friend of Schiller's since his youth. His influence naturally intensified the power which the poets of the gods of Greece had over Hölderlin. "Die Geschichte der schönen Künste Griechenlands" (The History of the Fine Arts in Greece) was the subject of the thesis for which the young student received his Master's degree.

250

The basic idea of this new humanism—that humanity and beauty had obtained their exemplary embodiment in the Greeks—became

[13] Christian Gottlob Heyne (1729-1812). Classical philologist, whose writings dealt with all aspects of antiquity, including mythology, art, and cultural history.

decisive for the two friends in the *Stift*, the poet Hölderlin and the philosopher Hegel. Plato was for them the interpreter of Greek humanity as he had previously been for Winckelmann. This greatest genius of the Greeks fulfilled this role over and over again. As each of these youths developed different aspects of this conception of the Greeks, they actively stimulated each other. Hegel's point of departure was the profound sense of fate in the Greek tragedians; Schelling's lay in the myths of the Greeks and their pantheistic view of nature. Hölderlin grasped the most profound aspect of the Greek conception of the world—an awareness of the affinity of nature, men, heroes, and gods. For him, the Greeks exemplify the lived experience of our inner affinity with nature; they exemplify an art which glorifies the beauty of the world based on such a unity of life and which honors great passions as sacred; they represent the cult of friendship, of heroism and of the yearning for great, heroic existence fraught with danger. The longing for this vanished world never left him in the misery of contemporary German life.

The other cultural force which laid hold of the youths came from philosophy. These writers, born in the 1770s, appropriated the idealism of freedom as expounded by Kant, Schiller, and Humboldt and combined it with a view of the universe which was derived from poetry and adequate to the imagination. Here Hölderlin, the poet, influenced his friend Hegel. From Shaftesbury through Schiller's early poems and *Philosophische Briefe* (Philosophical Letters),[14] there is an effort to grasp the universe as a totality filled with a power that can be understood by the imagination and the heart. Hölderlin struggles to find poetic symbols to express the inner relation between divinity, a nature that is fully alive, and the divine nobility of man.

The last of the cultural forces that determined this generation was the French Revolution. It opened the gates of a new era for 251 the Germans as well. It was impossible for the youths in the *Stift*, oppressed by the great tyrant in Stuttgart and the lesser ones in Tübingen, not to be stirred by the great abstract ideas of this movement! The students established a political club, and Schelling, Hegel, and Hölderlin belonged to it. In 1793, the same year in which France abolished Christianity and introduced the Cult of Reason, the students placed a liberty tree in the marketplace and danced around

[14] Published in *Thalia*, 3rd issue (Leipzig: Georg Joachim Göschen, 1786), pp. 100-139. Not to be confused with the famous *Letters Concerning the Aesthetic Education of Man.*

it in noisy jubilation. When the duke heard about the revolutionary speeches, the songs of liberation and the singing of the *Marseillaise* by his theologians in the *Stift*, he suddenly appeared in the dining hall of the institution and delivered a reprimand. There was no way of reconciling him to the idealism of the superior students in the *Stift*. It was at this time that Hölderlin sang of the harvest when the league of heroes would triumph, in his "Hymne an die Freiheit" (Hymn to Freedom): "When tyrants' thrones are toppled, and when tyrants' henchmen turn to dust." He thought that the moment of the birth of freedom had arrived and that the heroism of ancient Greece had been revived by the heroes of the French Revolution.

The young generation expected that human existence would be enhanced by the French Revolution, the Kantian philosophy so congenial to it, and German poetry. This expectation manifested itself in various ways during those years. It became a new phase in the development of that ideal of life which first took form in Lessing. It then assumed an altered form in Herder, the young Goethe, and in their colleagues. In *Iphigenia* and *Don Carlos* it appeared in a new, more profound shape. This ideal contained the conscious, philosophically grounded aim of the improvement of humanity, the freedom of the human spirit, and the greatness of the German nation. In Jena, a circle of youths gathered around Reinhold and then Fichte, who considered the goal of the new philosophy to be the advancement of the German people and German society. In Berlin, Friedrich Schlegel acclaimed the new philosophy and the French Revolution as the greatest tendencies of the age, and Schleiermacher's *Soliloquies*[15] proclaimed an enhanced mode of personal life. In Tübingen, we find Schelling, Hegel, and Hölderlin gripped by these same ideas.

Hölderlin's hymns and the first draft of his *Hyperion* originated amidst this ferment.

Lyric poetry in its simplest and most moving form gives voice to the feeling of existence as it is evoked by lived experience. This is intensified when emotion culminates in general contemplation. Various kinds of transition lead from the personal poem to that great lyrical form which is based upon contents that transcend the personal fate of an individual, take possession of him, and completely determine his frame of mind. This kind of lyric poetry comes into being when the feeling of the poet is stirred by great objective realities, by deeds of strong personalities, of peoples or of mankind

252

[15] *Monologen* (1800); English trans. by Horace Friess (Chicago, 1926).

itself, by ideas directed to the major concerns of the human race, finally and most of all by the totality of things. Feeling for great objects is enthusiasm, and the form in which it is expressed is the conscious, great art which strives to give voice to sublime feelings. Klopstock and Schiller were the exemplars of this lyric poetry in Germany. And it is the lead of Schiller that Hölderlin follows in the epoch when the new, universal ideas moved him.

The hymns which came into being in this way form a cycle intended to proclaim the ideal values of mankind as felt by the new generation. Each of these hymns bears one of the great names, which the French revolutionary spirit also made the objects of its cult. Thus, Hölderlin dedicated a hymn to humanity. "I am no longer so much concerned about individual men," he wrote at this time. "My love is for the human race."[16] The time had finally come when mankind could work on its perfection with full awareness of itself. The "god in us"[17] has liberated himself. We feel "the divine happiness of rejoicing in our own power";[18] the "tinsel barriers"[19] which separated the classes in the old class-state collapse. The new man lives in inner unity with kindred spirits.

> His greatest pride and his warmest love,
> His death, his heaven is the Fatherland.[20]

Other hymns extol beauty, freedom, the genius of those who are youthful and daring, the genius of love and friendship.

> Climb up on the vine-covered hill,
> Look down into the broad valley!
> Everywhere love's wings,
> Gracious and splendid everywhere.[21]

They all point back to the most significant hymn, the hymn to truth, or as it is put in the corrected version for print: "Hymne an die Göttin der Harmonie" (Hymn to the Goddess of Harmony).[22] This hymn contains his basic creed as grounded in Shaftesbury and Schiller.

Like the young Schiller, Hölderlin saw in love the cosmic power

[16] Letter to his brother (no. 65), *GSA*, 6(1):92.
[17] "Hymne an die Menschheit," *GSA*, 1(1):148, line 80.
[18] *Ibid.*, line 66.
[19] *Ibid.*, p. 146, line 22.
[20] *Ibid.*, p. 148, lines 71-72.
[21] "Hymne an die Liebe," *GSA*, 1(1):166, lines 13-16.
[22] *GSA*, 1(1):130-134.

whose manifestation in the universe, in the human mind, and in society is harmony. Love is the metaphysical or mystical nexus that pervades reality, enlivens nature, and binds everything human. Even the choice of words in the hymn is influenced by Schiller's *Philosophische Briefe* and his philosophical lyric poetry. At the same time, Hölderlin, according to his own report, drew from Leibniz. 253
The divine power of love "flows from the cup of life;"[23]

> Warmly and softly blow the winds,
> Lovingly fair spring descends into the vale.[24]

Man is the "Son" and "manifest mirror"[25] of this divine power. This world conception of Hölderlin's is panentheism: a divine power, separate from the elements of finite reality, creates the universe in time, and similarly the human spirit in its immortal development reaches beyond its finitely determined earthly existence.

This hymn marks an important point in the development of the world-view of the three Tübingen friends. According to one of the poet's letters, its plan and the work on it probably date from the year 1790, at the latest 1791; it was printed in 1792. Hence, it originated during the beginning of his association with Hegel. But, judging from what has survived of Hegel's writings from the Tübingen period and the subsequent period in Switzerland, Hegel still adhered to Kant's moral law as the highest rule of morality; at first, in his student years, he recognized love only as an empirical ethical principle utilized by popular religion: love merely prepared the way for philosophical knowledge of the moral law. In later notes written before his stay in Frankfurt, the viewpoint that finds its ethical principle in love is subjected to harsh criticism. Thus, Hegel's evaluation of love as the motivating principle of ethical life was completely different from Hölderlin's view as expressed in the "Hymne an die Göttin der Harmonie" and related poems. Here love is the universal bond that unites men with each other in a higher life. Whereas Hölderlin proceeds to regard love as the principle that holds the world together and to see beauty and harmony as the manifestations of love, the entire structure of Hegel's thought at this time flatly precludes acceptance of a panentheistic or pantheistic view such as Hölderlin's. From Schelling also there is no statement from the time before 1795 which gives expression to a principle of unity in the universe.

[23] *Ibid.*, p. 131, line 33.
[24] *Ibid.*, lines 41-42.
[25] Dilthey is not really quoting, but paraphrasing. See *Ibid.*, p. 132, lines 61-64.

A poet's enthusiasm speaks in Hölderlin—the same enthusiasm which then found its greatest expression in the world-view of the novel *Hyperion*. In the hymns, Hölderlin surpasses Kant's idealism by means of the awareness of man's kinship with the divine. It is this awareness that characterizes his basic intuition from the beginning. The Greek tragedians had early filled him with the consciousness of the proximity of men and the gods. Conjoined with 254 this was his unique feeling for nature and his intuitions of the cosmic power of love, of the character of the universe, which is harmony. Perhaps even then he was already acquainted with Spinoza through Jacobi's letters, and influenced by Schiller's *Philosophische Briefe*. If we ask to what extent his poetical prophecy of a future monism influenced Hegel and Schelling, we must imagine the impression of his whole personality. A special sort of influence passes from a significant person to his friends. Hölderlin possessed a poetic enthusiasm for the beauty and harmony of the universe, a pure devotion to the divine ground of things from which they flow, and a peculiar ability to transfigure reality into something beautiful, to revere and enjoy every appearance as embodying the divine. All this had to be constantly present to his philosophical friends whenever consequences could be drawn from their principles, which resembled Hölderlin's intuitions. No one can say when and how often this occurred. But that it did occur cannot be doubted.

Insofar as the form of Hölderlin's hymns had been influenced by Schiller, it must be understood on the basis of the latter's philosophical poems. Schiller found his own unique lyrical expression for the time's great pathos, which aimed at the realization of ideal values in a new humanity. The lyrical style that he discovered was completely different from that which Pindar, Klopstock, and Goethe had found for the reactions produced in the soul by sublime subjects. Schiller fulfilled his task by a use of rhyme appropriate to philosophical lyrical verse. He conjoined powerfully moving phrases into an integral, broadly sweeping whole. Thereby he utilized every resource of language to render visible the articulation of inner activity by means of some external process. The powerful but obscure feeling evoked by a great object or event is allowed to unfold in terms of its parts until all of its moments have been elevated to consciousness and are thus held together in the mind. Particularly effective is the crescendo of feeling, whereby the parts of an ideal intuition are connected in simple parallel sentences until our emotional response ebbs again in accordance with the nature of feeling. Thus, the poem "Die Götter Griechenlands" (The Gods of Greece) initially runs through all the aspects of the divine world; with each our sense of its beauty is enhanced; repeatedly this feeling is fulfilled and confirmed by new aspects of the intuition, until suddenly an infinite longing and a boundless feeling of loss overwhelms us and we dwell on every fact that serves to illustrate this loss. Then a new, broad rhythm arises, expressing the growth of the feeling that results from having probed the parts of this ideal world, and being passionately pulled along[26] from part to part. This rhythmical structure demands a kind of verse which does not restrain the onward movement of feeling by a definite ending. And how marvelously the rhythmic structure of "Die Götter Griechenlands" fulfills this demand, with its five-beat trochaic lines. Eight such sweeping lines in crossing rhymed couplets form a verse. The two last lines have no closing rhyme to hinder the forward movement from verse to verse, which is given an especially masculine power through the firmly established trochaic beat. In the "Künstler" (Artists) there is a similar, although freer, treatment of iambic verses which are given a softer coloring through the use of rising accentuation. Full, powerful words are set into rhyme; the choice of dignified expressions matches the nobility of thought; the images are as bold as the subject demands.

255

Hölderlin also makes use of all these artistic resources in his hymns by virtue of his innate sense for the melody of language. Phrases beginning with the same key words follow one another uniformly; they express a deliberate ascending movement; then slowly this tide ebbs in broad waves of extended sentences. Strong, resounding end-rhymes enhance the melody of the verses, and some of the words affect us with a peculiar immediacy. We hear the melodic resonance of the stormy, youthful poems of Schiller.

> Love brings to young roses
> The dew from lofty air,
> Love teaches warm breezes to mingle
> Amidst the fragrance of May flowers;
> She leads the faithful Earth
> Around Orion;
> And every stream at her beckoning
> Glides into the wide sea.[27]

[26] *Fortgezogenwerden* (being pulled along) is a term that is also used in "Toward the Foundation of the Human Sciences" (see vol. 3) to describe the way the meaning of one lived experience leads to that of others. See Makkreel, *Dilthey*, pp. 286, 289.

[27] "Hymne an die Liebe," *GSA*, 1(1):166, lines 17-24.

No contemporary of Hölderlin nor anyone after him measured up so well to Schiller's form. But from the quiet corner occupied by Hölderlin it was only with difficulty that any influence could be exerted upon the great world of our literature. A few of the hymns appeared in Stäudlin's *Schwäbischer Musenalmanach*. Matthisson embraced the young poet for his "Dem Genius der Kühnheit" (To the Genius of Boldness).[28] And Schiller accepted this ode and the poem on fate, which marked the end of this period, for his new journal *Thalia*. The grandly conceived series of hymns did not gain recognition. What an influence it could have exercised upon the youth! How it would have facilitated the public's understanding of Hölderlin's further poetic development! It was his first failure.

256

The lived experience expressed in Hölderlin's hymns was the heroic striving of the youth of those years to realize a higher humanity in themselves and in the society around them. Accordingly, he had to create figures within himself to represent this heroism. They sprang from his inner depths with irresistible force and led to his *Hyperion*. He had already begun work on it in Tübingen. The plan is first mentioned in June 1792. A friend characterized the poet's Hyperion at this time as "a freedom-loving hero . . . full of strong principles."[29] The young philhellene chose modern Greece as his stage. The ardent memory of what once happened on this soil could be interwoven with the new Greek heroism—which, to be sure, was of a somewhat dubious nature. In 1770 a war of liberation began in Greece, in which Russian military operations supported the Greek uprising. These events formed the background of the novel. Against this background, Hyperion was to be presented as the hero striving to bring about a life of freedom and beauty—the embodiment of all the dreams of the new youth. During the latter part of his time in Tübingen (1793), Hölderlin once wrote to his brother: "My love is for the human race. . . . I love its great and beautiful potential even in depraved human beings. I love the generations of the coming centuries. For this is my most blessed hope and the faith that keeps me strong and active: freedom must come some day. We live in a time when everything is leading toward better days."[30] "I want to have an effect on the world in general."[31] Similarly, Hyperion says: "They will come, your humans, O Na-

[28] *GSA*, 1(1):176-178.

[29] Magenau to Neuffer, November 1792, *GSA*, 7(1):435.

[30] Hölderlin to his brother (no. 65), *GSA*, 6(1):92.

[31] *Ibid.*, p. 93.

ture."[32] Hölderlin being constituted as he was, the inner story of the hero had to become the focal point of the novel—despite all the available material for a historical spectacle. Because he had still experienced so little, the novel developed only gradually in conjunction with his own personal destiny.

The university years came to an end. In the first days of December 1793, Hölderlin completed his examinations in Stuttgart, and he could now have fulfilled his loving mother's wish that he enter the Swabian ministry, as Mörike would later. But Hegel, Schelling, and Hölderlin did not consider doing this; they had sworn themselves to the service of humanity. But where in the Germany of the time was there a way for them to achieve greater influence? They had no means of earning a living other than being a private tutor and no greater prospect than a professorial chair. But Hölderlin's future seemed to be in the hands of a benevolent fate. Schiller was staying 257 in Swabia about this time, and he had been asked to find a private tutor for the son of Frau von Kalb. He met with the young poet for half an hour, and his impression was not unfavorable. Even before Hölderlin had completed his examinations, the next phase of his life was thus decided. Just before Christmas he made his way to Thüringen, where Charlotte von Kalb lived on her estate, Waltershausen, near Meiningen. He was to teach her son. Thus his fate led Hölderlin directly into the circle of his compatriot, Schiller, who had influenced him very strongly through his ideas. And his new situation gained him access to a circle of men who dominated German literature at that time. But even here existed that unique mixture of material wretchedness and lofty striving that characterized his life. Frau von Kalb, as was her nature, approached him with her entire wealth of motherly feelings, which she always showered on gifted young people. She sought to place the shy Swabian in touch with the surrounding literary world. The poet repaid her by the most conscientious execution of his duties to her son. But he wore himself out in vain in this business. Frau von Kalb finally had to admit that herself. In Jena and then in Weimar he tried again. Then she acceded to his wish to leave the child and settle in Jena. She wrote to Hölderlin's mother herself to reassure her about her son's daring step. She provided him with funds, conveyed a sympathetic appreciation for his poetry, and facilitated the contacts that he sought in Jena.

Kant and the Greeks occupied him primarily in Waltershausen.

[32] *GSA*, 3:90.

Schiller's treatise on "Grace and Dignity," which had just appeared, stimulated his own aesthetic studies. He believed that one could venture a step further than Schiller in going beyond the bounds set by Kant. Undoubtedly he wanted to proceed to the reality of the beautiful in the universe. This was probably the context for an essay on aesthetic ideas composed during this time period. Most of all, however, the novel *Hyperion*, begun in Tübingen, occupied the poet in Waltershausen. It was in the fall of 1794 at the latest that the fragment was completed, which Schiller then published in *Thalia.*

In this fragment Hölderlin projected *Hyperion* as a *Bildungsroman* such as had become common in our literature since Wieland's

258 *Agathon*. He conceived the *Bildungsroman* from Schiller's point of view: it begins with naive perfection, deriving from one's nature alone, and it aims at the ideal to which we can elevate ourselves through a rigorous education. In between we observe highlights of the eccentric development of his heroes.

After the disappointments of traditional school philosophy and of insignificant personal relationships—Hölderlin himself had just broken off a shallow love affair with the flirtatious daughter of a Tübingen professor—Hyperion returns to the soil of his Ionian homeland again. "His old friend, spring"[33] surprises Hyperion and evokes feelings of approaching happiness. In the midst of this spring, Melite, a pure soul imbued with the self-sufficiency of a heavenly being, appears to him. This is a truly Germanic motif that connects spring, the feelings it awakens, and their fulfillment in the beloved. This motif has been used by him in his later writings as well. The Hölderlin tragedy now begins to unfold between the two lovers: it involves the secret sorrows of a passionate youth who cannot satisfy himself and cannot be satisfied by others. The quiet, saintlike girl is stirred by him and deeply moved in her innermost being. Here we encounter for the first time the poet's own confessions about his ill-fated propensity for melancholy. "I have often wondered," Melite says, "what it could be that makes you so peculiar. It's a painful mystery that a soul like yours should be oppressed by such sorrows."[34] "Tell your heart that one seeks in vain for peace outside oneself."[35] Then there are also moments of great happiness granted only to rare, noble men, with their coexisting boundless capacity for suffering. In the magical twilight of the grotto of Homer, friends

[33] *Ibid.*, p. 166.
[34] *Ibid.*, pp. 174-75.
[35] *Ibid.*, p. 175.

sat around a statue of the blind poet—funeral rites for everything great that had once been; this motif, too, was revived in the later novel.

Misunderstandings lead to separation. Hyperion takes refuge in "the hidden power of nature which reveals itself to us wherever light and earth, heaven and sea surround us."[36] Here we find a third motif of the later novel: nature calms the heart that is everywhere impinged upon, that suffers and cannot understand. Nature is holy, mysterious, incomprehensible, and seems to ask us, "Why do you not love me?"[37] In the twilight of this love we feel at ease. The beauty of life, heroism, the kindness of women, and poetry are all manifestations of divine power. This power is here understood pantheistically, in contradistinction to the hymns. It is that "which endures, which survives beneath a thousand varied shapes, which was and is and will be."[38] Awareness of this unfathomable power produces a love for it, which first provides our thought and action their true and lasting foundation. These expressions of a poetic pantheism were written down before Schelling's advance to monism, before Schleiermacher's *On Religion*,[39] with which they have so much in common, and long before the monistic turn in Hegel.

259

The fragment resembles an overture which indicates the motifs of a musical drama before the drama itself begins. The rhythmic style of his prose is intimated tentatively and gropingly.

## MATURITY

At the beginning of 1795, Hölderlin settled down in Jena to devote his life to his literary work. He also was considering lecturing at the university there. A time of extreme activity begins in which he was concerned to establish himself in the literary world.

After years of diffuse activity, he found himself compelled to make a coherent effect upon the world. The man who more than anyone else in Germany stirred people to do so also lived in Jena then. In November of 1794, while Hölderlin was staying in Jena with his pupil, he had heard Fichte's lectures daily and spoke with him occasionally. Like all the strongest, most gifted young men in

[36] *Ibid.*, p. 181.

[37] *Ibid.*, p. 183.

[38] *Ibid.*, p. 180.

[39] Friedrich Schleiermacher, *Reden über die Religion*, trans. by John Oman, *On Religion: Speeches to its Cultural Despisers* (London, 1893).

Jena, he followed him enthusiastically. "Fichte is now the soul of Jena. And God be praised for that! I know no other man of such intellectual depth and energy."[40] Here he found an awareness of the ultimate principles of knowledge, with the most daring consequences drawn from them, combined with the courage "to write and lecture about them despite the power of darkness."[41] Since he could now work in total independence, he gave serious consideration to the problems which Fichte's philosophy posed for him. After he had quietly worked the entire day, he would go to hear Fichte lecture in the evening. His own philosophical standpoint was developed through the study of this philosophy. Like Schleiermacher later in his *On Religion*, Hölderlin learned that pure theory could not lead beyond the reality of consciousness. When Fichte 260 sought to go behind the facts of consciousness to an absolute ego, he seemed thereby to annihilate consciousness and hence every content of this ego. Even then Hölderlin apparently saw that a poetic intuition of the universe was the only basis for the objective understanding of the world as a coherent whole. The affinity of his position with Schleiermacher's holds also in this respect. For Schleiermacher this intuition was given in religion; for Hölderlin it was given in poetry. The ideas from the time of his hymns concerning love as the foundation of ethics began to waver under the influence of the unrelenting Fichte.

The impression of Fichte and his enthusiastic young disciples must have strengthened Hölderlin's expectation of a higher form of humanity and a new heroism—an expectation that he had shared with his friends in the *Stift*, Hegel and Schelling, and on the basis of which the plan of his *Hyperion* had been conceived. As soon as he could, he reported to his old friend Hegel about the "titan Fichte"[42] who fought for humanity and whose sphere of activity would surely not remain confined within the walls of the lecture hall. Hegel joyfully told Schelling that Hölderlin's interest for cosmopolitan ideas was steadily increasing. "May the Kingdom of God come and may our hands not lie idle in our laps!"[43]

The enthusiasm of Fichte's disciples was associated with a movement of the young generation, which manifested itself at various places in Germany. Because it had its roots in the French Revolution, the movement had a European character. At the same time, the

[40] Hölderlin to Neuffer, November 1794, *GSA*, 6(1):139.

[41] *Ibid.*, p. 140

[42] Hegel to Schelling, *GSA*, 7(2):19.

[43] *Ibid.*

*idéologistes* proclaimed, on the basis of the scientific theory of evolution, the idea of raising man to a state of strength and joy unknown until then: what science had predicted, the revolution was to actualize. While facing death, the outlawed Condorcet expressed his vigorous and cheerful faith in the development of human society toward a system of government assuring the cultivation of all our powers, in a book[44] which influenced the entire future generation, including the socialists and Comte. In England, the admirers of the French Revolution were working on a rational restructuring of the social order. It can be said that this was the first time that eighteenth-century ideas of solidarity and of the progress of humanity, which had still been linked to enlightened monarchy, came to have autonomous, effective power in Europe.

It was against this historical background that Fichte developed his ideas of the universal, creative faculty which contained the law 261 of a future, higher order of society and of the fulfillment of individuals. This same background strengthened the will to action in his disciples. Thus, also in Hölderlin's soul, the ideal of a higher form of humanity grew increasingly more distinct, determinate and great. "If it must be," he wrote at that time, "then we will break our unfortunate lyres, and do what artists have dreamt of."[45] From the psychological perspective, it is difficult to connect such intensely earnest words with Hölderlin's sensitive poetic nature. It is as if he had transcended his essence. This is the same mystery that we also encounter in Nietzsche. But whatever its basis—throughout his entire life, including the period of his insanity, the hero is the focal point of his poetry and assumes increasingly pensive and colossal shapes until the final version of his *Empedocles*—which again relates him to Nietzsche.

Such attitudes and ideas furthered the work now facing him with his novel *Hyperion*. The heroic element in it took on firmer features and greater scope. Schiller and Fichte provided the contrast on which the intricacies of the final version of the novel is based. The figure of Alabanda took its life and color from Fichte's impetuosity, from his disdain of empty doctrine, from his proud consciousness of the dignity, freedom, and immutability of the human person. We have notes from this Jena period which give us insight into the development of the novel. He is experimenting with a new beginning

[44] Marquis de Condorcet, *Sketch for a Historical Picture of the Progress of the Human Mind*, trans. by June Barraclough (London, 1955).

[45] Hölderlin to Neuffer, November 1794, *GSA*, 6(1):139.

and a new form. The poet meets Hyperion, whose mature personality and thought is depicted, and who then relates the story of his life. For a while Hölderlin also attempted to rework the novel in verse form. Nowhere could the plan of an aesthetic work be carried out better than in the atmosphere of Weimar and Jena. When Hölderlin wanted to lecture on this subject, he found a most receptive audience in the students at Jena.

Hölderlin was just twenty-four years old and in very difficult financial circumstances when he strove to bring to a hasty conclusion the poetic and aesthetic works he had begun. His philosophical ideas were still immature, and it was impossible for him to quickly work through the extremely difficult aesthetic problems with which he was grappling in a way that he could publish them. The novel could only creep forward slowly. This genius of a new lyrical form, who made every impression resound within himself, was not to be 262 hurried by external needs. His marvelous poems were not commodities. He brooded over his work in solitude for long days. His only recreation was an occasional conversation with Fichte and, even more importantly, his contact with Schiller, whom he visited as often as seemed proper and whose personality and discourse revived him again and again. His means of subsistence became increasingly sparse despite a most frugal life-style. He had but *one* scanty meal per day. Even more than the external poverty in which he lived, his inner situation depressed him. He couldn't focus on any particular work. Every lived experience, every piece of knowledge was reclaimed by the sad, dark depths of his being and became lost in it. Nothing could be extricated from these depths.

The experience of those years overwhelmed him gradually, slowly, and awesomely. Immediately after his arrival in Jena, he wrote: "The proximity of truly great minds and also the proximity of truly great, spontaneous, courageous hearts alternately disheartens and inspires me; I must pull myself out of my gloom and slumber, must gently but forcefully awaken and cultivate half-developed, half-dead powers if I am not finally to take refuge in a sad resignation." With time, the pressure arising from these surroundings increased. Bitterly, he felt himself slipping further and further away from these people—the pain of loneliness and of being misunderstood. These great figures somehow shared the same goals for poetry, for philosophy, and for the structuring of their lives. His soul alienated itself from one after the other. Who could live near Goethe without wishing for an affirmation of one's work by Goethe? It was during his stay in Jena as a tutor that Hölderlin first met him.

This took place when he visited Schiller there. He was greeted warmly by Schiller, and he hardly noticed a stranger in the background. Neither his appearance nor his subsequent words led Hölderlin to suspect anything unusual. He didn't catch Goethe's name when he was introduced. He greeted him coldly, almost without a glance. The stranger leafed through the *Thalia*, which contained Hölderlin's poem "Das Schicksal" (Fate) and his *Hyperion* fragment, but said nothing at all. This strange meeting went on for quite some time. Later on in Weimar, the young poet met Goethe again at the home of Frau von Kalb. This time Hölderlin sensed a kind of humane greatness through their conversation; he appeared "quiet, full of majesty in countenance and also full of love, extremely simple in conversation" that was enlivened "by the sparks of his genius, which is certainly by no means extinguished. . . . Often one thinks that one is in the presence of a truly kind-hearted father."[46] When Hölderlin then settled down permanently in Jena, he often met Goethe at Schiller's house. But Hölderlin was still so young, and personally very awkward and modest. His lyric poetry, which, in its own way, was to become one of the highest achievements next to Goethe's, was only just beginning to find its own proper tones. Goethe could not really grasp the marvelous, lyrical talent of the young poet on the basis of the few poems by Hölderlin that Schiller sent to him for possible publication in the *Horen*. He appraised them politely but very coolly. He sensed an orientation akin to Schiller's, but without his fullness, power and depth. [However,] Goethe did praise them for "a certain loveliness, intimacy and simplicity,"[47] for a serene view of nature but without any knowledge of her: "They express a gentle striving that resolves itself into a state of contentment."[48] From then on Hölderlin disappeared from Goethe's awareness, except for a brief encounter in Frankfurt. Hölderlin had already visited Herder during his first stay in Weimar, and Herder appeared to be interested in him, but only a very superficial contact was possible between Herder and this student of Schiller and Fichte. Soon nothing more is heard about his association with Fichte.

263

Schiller alone stuck by his Swabian friend and did whatever he could for him. Ever since Hölderlin had read Schiller's early dramas, he felt within himself a great love based on the kinship of a more

[46] Hölderlin to Neuffer, 19 January 1795, *GSA*, 6(1):151.

[47] Goethe to Schiller, 1 July 1797, *Der Briefwechsel zwischen Schiller und Goethe*, vol. 1, p. 355.

[48] Goethe to Schiller, 28 June 1797, *Briefwechsel*, p. 352.

gentle spirit with a strong one. Schiller repaid him with a firm, loyal devotion. He published the *Hyperion* fragment in his *Thalia*. He recommended that Cotta publish the entire novel under favorable conditions, and he encouraged the young poet to work for the journal *Horen*, because this would greatly help Hölderlin's financial situation. He sensed the very dangerous state of Hölderlin's mental condition. "Strong subjectivity," combined "with a certain philosophical mind and pensiveness"[49] are driving him more and more into himself. Schiller sympathetically felt how hard it was to gain the upper hand over such a disposition. And this sympathy was all the stronger because he recognized "much of his own peculiar character"[50] in the young poet. What was happening to Hölderlin himself is revealed in a letter written shortly after he left Jena. Its quiet tone is moving. Often he felt, within the limits of his understanding, Schiller's entire worth, and wished that he could mean something to him in turn. And now his confession! He says how much he misses being near to Schiller, but "with all my reasons to stay, I could hardly have persuaded myself to go if this proximity
264 had not, on the other hand, disquieted me so. I always felt the temptation to see you, but saw you only to feel that I could mean nothing to you. I recognize that I have atoned for my proud demands with the pain that I have borne with me so often; because I wanted to mean so much to you, I had to tell myself that I meant nothing to you. But, I reprimand myself only mildly, for I am all too well aware of my intentions."[51] And later again, when a kind letter from Schiller expressed the wish that Hölderlin could again live nearby, so that he would be able to communicate his views fully, Hölderlin writes: "To be close to you is not permitted me. . . . As long as I was in your presence, I felt too constrained and when I was gone, my heart overflowed."[52] Enormous deep sorrow was the outcome of this, his great love, the greatest that he felt in his life except for Diotima.

Imperceptibly, all this produced in him the painful awareness of loneliness, which at root everyone senses whether he lives amidst family and friends, or in isolation. It derives from the nature of our individual existence, but it is experienced most intensely by a genius who draws on his own resources.

Hölderlin's stay in Jena had barely lasted three quarters of a year.

[49] Schiller to Goethe, 30 June 1797, *Briefwechsel*, p. 353.

[50] *Ibid.*

[51] Hölderlin to Schiller, 23 July 1795, *GSA*, 6(1):175.

[52] Hölderlin to Schiller (no. 144), *GSA*, 6(1):250-251.

In early summer of 1795 he returned to Nürtingen. It was as if he had been shipwrecked. He suffered, his soul had been wounded, and he felt humbled that he was again a burden to his kind mother. Until the end of the year, he remained at home, and then he once again had to go back to his old line of service, this time in Frankfurt am Main. It is hard to determine what he produced during this period of free work while he was on his own in Jena. But one important development was Hölderlin's application of the poetic form first established in his hymns to his personal lyric poetry.

In the last days of 1795, Hölderlin arrived in Frankfurt, where he was to instruct four children in the family of the banker, Jacob Gontard. In the first fragments of his novel, he had described his Greek ideal of a serene, harmonious feminine spirit. Now he came face to face with it in reality in the lady of the house.[53] A relief portrait of her shows a countenance of consummate Greek beauty. It shows that combination of softness and refined composure which Hölderlin understood so well. She came from a respected Hamburg family. Her education had made her familiar with languages and literature. She knew how to enjoy the company of the intellectual elite, for not only the Frankfurt plutocracy frequented her house, but also the poet Heinse,[54] and Sömmering, the anatomist and doctor.[55] Hölderlin took a strong liking to the oldest of her sons, with that sensitive understanding which the childlike purity in him had for children's souls. As a result the mother also was inevitably drawn closer to him, since she took sole charge of the education of the children.

265

Hölderlin's relationship with Susette Gontard became the greatest happiness in his life, an essential content of his later poetry, and one of the calamities which destroyed him. Her noble soul understood the simple, melancholy young poet. She even understood the sorrow which burdened him, and she sought to give him a more free relationship to life. The poet, however, saw in her the very Muse of his poetry, and he looked back on the flirtations of his earlier years—especially on the most recent silly one—with a peculiar attitude: "I have passed in sorrow so many a day of the most beautiful time of my life because I had to endure levity and disdain as long as I was not the only one who courted a lady. Afterwards I found favor and offered it, but my first enjoyment of intimacy

[53] Susette Gontard, whom Hölderlin calls Diotima in his poems.

[54] Johann J. W. Heinse (1749-1803). Poet and novelist.

[55] Sömmering's "Über das Organ der Seele" was published with an appendix by Kant.

was cancelled by the undeserved suffering that I endured."[56] Now, however, he experienced an inner affinity that was timeless like divinity itself.

The love that grew up between these two speaks directly to us in a few moving pages, which have only now become available. There are four fragments of letters and drafts: they go back to the spring of 1799, thus half a year after he left Frankfurt, and they extend into November. We can only speculate whether they were mailed in the form in which we find them. But in these pages, other letters from him to her, and also a letter from her, are mentioned. The first of these drafts reveals all the inner and situational relations of the two during Hölderlin's three years in Frankfurt. He sends her the second volume of his novel, "the fruit of our soulful days," expresses some dissatisfaction with it and then continues:

> If I could have gradually developed as an artist at your feet in tranquility and freedom, I do think I would have quickly become that for which my heart in all its suffering has longed, whether in tears, in the brightness of day, or in silent desperation. It is certainly worth all the tears we have shed through the years because we are not to have the joy that we could give each other, but it is outrageous to think that both of us must perhaps pass away with our full potential because we lack each other. It is this that often makes me so taciturn, because I have to silence such thoughts. Your illness, your letter—they bring it so clearly to my mind once more, as much as I would like to blind myself to it, that you are always, always, suffering—and I, like a child, can only cry about it! Which is better, tell me—that we are silent about what is in our hearts or that we say it to each other!—Always I have played the coward in order to spare you—have always acted as if I could put up with anything, as if I were the plaything of men and circumstances and as if I had no steadfast heart in me beating faithfully and freely for its own rightful best interests; dearest life! I have often failed and denied my dearest love, even my thoughts of you, only to survive this fate for your sake and as smoothly as possible—You, too, have always struggled, peaceful one! To have peace, you have endured with heroic strength and kept silent about what could not be altered, have hidden and buried your heart's eternal choice within yourself and hence we live in a kind of twilight and we no longer know what we are and

266

[56] Hölderlin to his brother, 2 February 1798, *GSA*, 6(1):264.

> have; we hardly know ourselves anymore; this eternal struggle and tension within surely must kill you eventually; and, if no God can alleviate it, then I have no choice but to pine away about you and me, or else to consider nothing else but you and to seek a way with you which will end the struggle for us.[57]

This is how pure and self-controlled this love had been. Even now, when he finds the misery of separation no longer tolerable, he nonetheless adds immediately: "I had thought that we could live even on denial, that this perhaps also would make us strong so that we could definitively say farewell to hope. . . ."[58] The writing breaks off here in the middle of the page. One pictures the poet, his dejected head in his hands, brooding about a dilemma from which there is no escape. He probably did not send the letter. Later he wrote on the back:

> To be pure in heart
> That is the greatest
> Of what wise men conceived,
> Men still wiser achieved.[59]

What an unforgettable effect this love had on him! Diotima brought him the happiness that he had not had before. She seemed like a child of the sun to him. With her persistent help and sympathy, *Hyperion* finally was published. He often discussed the progress of the novel with her. Through her influence the new form of his lyric poetry was perfected, and the most beautiful of his poems from this time were inspired by his love for her. Hölderlin writes to her about the Diotima of the novel and about Hyperion's love for her: "Take everything said about her and us, about the living of our lives, as an expression of gratitude that often is all the more true the less elegantly it is expressed."[60] Thus, one may read in the novel how she reconciled him with life, how she became the norm for every judgment about the values of life—and how she suffered because of him: "Holy being! how oft' I have disturbed your golden divine peace, and how many of the hidden, deeper pains of life you have learned from me." The most beautiful monument to his love is the elegy "Menon's Lament for Diotima":

267

[57] Hölderlin to Susette Gontard (no. 198), *GSA*, 6(1):370-71.
[58] *Ibid.*, p. 371.
[59] *GSA*, 6(2):987.
[60] Hölderlin to Susette Gontard (no. 198), *GSA*, 6(1):370.

Meanwhile we—like the mated swans in their summer
contentment
When by the lake they rest or on the waves, lightly rocked,
Down they look at the water, and silvery clouds through
that mirror
Drift, and ethereal blue flows where the voyagers pass—
Moved and dwelled on this earth. And though the North Wind
was threatening
Hostile to lovers, he, gathering sorrows, and down
Came dead leaves from the boughs, and rain filled the
spluttering storm-gusts
Calmly we smiled, aware, sure of the tutelar god
Present in talk only ours, one song that our two souls were
singing,
Wholly at peace with ourselves, childishly, wraptly alone.[61]

This state of affairs lasted for almost three years. Slowly during this time the seeds were being sown for the conflict in which it ended. Already during the first months in Frankfurt, the self-esteem of the poet suffered from his situation in the midst of Frankfurt plutocrats. Then in July 1797, this situation forced him to exclaim: "Oh! give me my youth once more, I am being torn by love and hate."[62] Some time later he spoke to his sister with great bitterness about the men among whom he had to live. "Here you find, with the exception of a few genuine human beings, only monstrous caricatures. For most of them, their wealth affects them as wine affects peasants; for they are just as ill-bred, blatantly vulgar, and arrogant. But that is also good in a certain respect: one learns to keep silent among such people—and that is no small thing."[63] "The harsh judgments of men," he writes at another time, "will drive me about until in the end I will at last be gone from Germany." But the worst thing he had to suffer in the house were the insults from the banker Gontard himself. In Hölderlin's presence, he once remarked "that tutors were also servants, that they could claim no special status since they were paid for what they did."[64] The smooth mask of this easygoing, polite man of wealth concealed an inner brutality that aroused horror. One can understand what Hölderlin's proud, sensitive, and yet so defenseless spirit endured in this man's presence.

[61] *GSA*, 2(1):76; *HPF*, p. 235.

[62] Hölderlin to Neuffer, 10 July 1797, *GSA*, 6(1):243.

[63] Hölderlin to his sister (no. 156), *GSA*, 6(1):270.

[64] Hölderlin to his mother, 10 October 1798, *GSA*, 6(1):285.

This was why he left the house of Gontard and Frankfurt in the fall of 1798. This came about doubtlessly by his own decision; he reports to his mother that he discussed his reasons for leaving with Gontard and that they parted courteously. And while he did not tell the whole truth here—he always speaks shyly and discretely of his experiences to his mother—still the essence of the account is irrefutably confirmed by his poem "Der Abschied" (Farewell). 268

This was a new, difficult experience that cut him off from life and people. With a terrible intensity, he kept his gaze directed toward the holiness that had appeared to him in Diotima. No commonplace relationship had any value for him any longer. He went ever further on the perilous path of severing his ideal dream from his real life. A bitter hatred of vulgarity consumed his soul. "When I die with shame, when my soul doesn't avenge itself on the insolent, when I am buried, overcome by the foes of genius, in a coward's grave."[65] The features of suffering, of separation among the living, of the brutal power of the common and vulgar were etched still more deeply into his image of the divine world. His love for unsuffering nature took on a pathological aspect.

Here, still another relationship that lasted throughout his Frankfurt years and strongly affected his development must be considered. Goethe speaks of the demonic forces that are at work in our lives. A curious circumstance brought Hegel, Hölderlin's youthful comrade, to him at the time that Hölderlin's situation was stimulating his many ideas about life and the world.

The two friends had been corresponding with each other; how attached Hegel still was to his old friend, how close he now felt to his way of thinking, is documented in a unique way in the poem "Eleusis," which Hegel dedicated to his friend in the summer of 1796. It is evening,

"About and within me is tranquility
. . . . your image, beloved friend,
and the delight of vanished days move before me; but soon
she (remembrance) yields to sweet hope—
Already I yearn with pain, for the fiery embracing scene,
then for the questions, upon the mysteries of the observed
mutual presence, which by the attitudes, expressions, and
dispositions of a friend are changed since that time—
the known pleasure of old comradeship, which no oath seals, 269
only to live eternal truth—peace never, never penetrated by

[65] "Der Abschied," in *GSA*, 1(1):276.

the law which regulates opinions and impulse.[66]

At the beginning of the next year, the wish of the two friends was granted. For a long time, Hölderlin, concerned for Hegel's welfare, had been seeking a suitable position for him. After he had become acquainted with Frankfurt society, he was able to offer him a position as tutor in a home in the fall of 1796. "If you want to come here, someone will live not far from you who, despite rather extreme changes of condition and character, has remained loyal to you in heart and memory and spirit, and who lacks nothing but you."[67] Hegel accepted the proposal. "What role my longing for you played in my speedy decision—I won't speak about that"; "in every line of your letter I see your immutable friendship for me."[68] During their entire stay in Frankfurt, these friends were together. Hegel's composed intellect did Hölderlin much good. From this Frankfurt period there is a letter which shows what his friend, who led Hölderlin back to the realm of ideas, meant to him at the time.

> One has, with all the strength of youth, often hardly enough thought and patience for what is necessary, so disturbing and debilitating is life at times, and no time is worse in every respect than the transition from youth to manhood. In no other period of life do other people and one's own personality cause so much trouble. This is really the time of sweat and anger, sleeplessness, anxiety and tempest; it is the bitterest time in life. But man goes through turmoil, like everything else that must mature, and philosophy has only to make sure that the turmoil passes as harmlessly, tolerably, and briefly as possible.[69]

It was the time when Hegel's new philosophy was developing in a theological guise. He finally parted from the way of thinking found in Kant, Fichte, and Schiller. Their basic idea had been the creative power of personality: through our intuitive and conceptual activity this power produces the world which we then perceive as if given from outside; in the sphere of our will, it generates the ideal that the person is to actualize in the world thus given. This power, striving toward the infinite, was elevated in Schelling's writing from the ego to the absolute. The division that develops in this All-One,

[66] Hegel, "Eleusis"; trans. in Gustav E. Mueller, *Hegel: The Man, His Vision and Work* (New York: Pageant Press, 1968), p. 60.

[67] Cf. Hölderlin to Hegel, 24 October 1796, *GSA*, 6(1):220. Dilthey gives this quotation in somewhat altered form.

[68] Hegel to Hölderlin, November 1796, *GSA*, 7(1):43.

[69] Hölderlin to his brother, 4 July 1798, *GSA*, 6(1):277.

along with the tragic awareness of it and the reconciliation which annihilates and yet preserves the antitheses—this was Hegel's formula in which a new, pantheistic sense of life came to expression. In the midst of opposites, in which the divine alone can have reality, the divine possesses and asserts its unity. The profundity of Christianity lies in this knowledge of the divine, of the pain of separation, and the bliss of reconciliation. That is Hegel's fundamental feeling, too—the persistent heartbeat of his philosophy. 270

From Frankfurt, Hölderlin went to the nearby, beautifully situated town of Homburg. He had found a modest dwelling looking out onto a pleasant meadow. "I go there when I am tired from work; I climb on the hill and sit down in the sun, and look beyond Frankfurt into the distance."[70] With what memories and thoughts! The will to give voice to what lived within him kept him going. Looking beyond his *Hyperion*, he worked on a plan for his *Death of Empedocles*. He had saved enough money in Frankfurt that he hoped to be able to live from it for a year. And Sinclair, a friend with untiring kindness, began to take an interest in him from this time on. Because of his standing in the world and his financial means, he was able to be helpful to Hölderlin through the time of his insanity. Sinclair, a philosophical writer and poet with a talent for business as well, and in touch with the most influential writers, was entrusted with the important affairs of the Landgrave of Homburg. He had already become close to Hölderlin in Jena. Now he was able to interest the poetically gifted Landgrave in Hölderlin. At this time Hölderlin also began to be known in wider circles. A. W. Schlegel spoke very favorably of a few of his poems in the *Allgemeine Literaturzeitung*. And yet the painful experiences of Jena recurred: a plan for a journal proved impracticable; the tragedy *Empedocles*, which seemed to him to be his real life's work, was not completed. The poems that he did complete during that time were left in his desk or were scattered in insignificant publications. His meager funds ran out. He returned to his mother, went from there to Stuttgart, could not make a living there either, and attempted again the life of a private tutor in Hauptwyl in Switzerland: he was discharged after a few months, courteously but basically without consideration. At home, he thought of making another start in Jena; he wanted to lecture there on Greek literature. A longing for Schiller seemed to have seized him. He wrote to him but received no response; this omission is easily explained by Schiller's situation at the time. Moreover, Hölderlin's statements about poetics were 271

[70] Hölderlin to his sister, 1799, *GSA*, 6(1):316.

so extraordinarily vague that they must have aroused Schiller's reluctance to accept responsibility for the fate of the young poet. It was around Christmas 1801 that he began his last journey to serve among strangers; he returned insane.

Hölderlin was thus allotted only a brief decade for his life's work, from his first draft of *Hyperion* in Tübingen until the beginning of his winter trip to the south of France. His career plunged into the darkness of madness precisely in those years in which great successful poets reach the heights of creativity. That must be taken into account if his poetic power is to be correctly evaluated. His life's work comprises the novel *Hyperion*, the dramatic fragments of *Empedocles*, and the poems.

## THE NOVEL *HYPERION*

You walk above in the light,
Weightless tread a soft floor, blessed genii!
Radiant the gods' mild breezes
Gently play on you
As the girl artist's fingers
On holy strings.

Fateless the Heavenly breathe
Like an unweaned infant asleep;
Chastely preserved
In modest bud
Forever their minds
Are in flower
And their blissful eyes
Eternally tranquil gaze,
Eternally clear.

But we are fated
To find no foothold, no rest,
And suffering mortals
Dwindle and fall
Headlong from one
Hour to the next,
Hurled like water
From ledge to ledge
Downward for years to the vague abyss.[71]

[71] "Hyperions Schicksalslied," *GSA*, 1(1):265; *HPF*, p. 79.

This is the song of fate that the child Hyperion hears resounding from the dark depths of life. What it reveals, placed as it is in the middle of the work, is the ultimate lived experience which gives the work its significance and power. 272

*Hyperion* is one of the *Bildungsromane* which reflect the interest in inner culture that Rousseau had inspired in Germany. Among the novels that have established their lasting literary value since Goethe and Jean Paul are Tieck's *Sternbald*, Novalis' *Ofterdingen*, and Hölderlin's *Hyperion*. Beginning with *Wilhelm Meister* and *Hesperus*,[72] they all portray a young man of their time: how he enters life in a happy state of naivete seeking kindred souls, finds friendship and love, how he comes into conflict with the hard realities of the world, how he grows to maturity through diverse life-experiences, finds himself, and attains certainty about his purpose in the world. Goethe's goal was the story of a person preparing himself for an active life; the theme of the two Romantic writers was the poet; Hölderlin's hero was a heroic person striving to change the world but finding himself in the end thrust back upon his own thought and poetry.

In this way, these *Bildungsromane* gave expression to the individualism of a culture whose sphere of interest was limited to private life. The governmental authority of the civil service and the military in the small and middle-sized German states confronted the young generation of writers as alien. But these young people were delighted and enraptured by what poets had discovered about the world of the individual and his self-development. Today's reader of Jean Paul's *Flegeljahre* (translated as *Walt and Vult, or the Twins*) or *Titan* in which everything about the contemporary German *Bildungsroman* is epitomized, will find the aura of a past world, the transfiguration of existence in the dawn of life, an infinite investment of feeling in a restricted existence, the obscure, wistful, power of ideals of German youths eager to declare war on an antiquated world in all its life forms and yet incapable of surviving such a war.

There had always been novels modeled on biography which followed the schooling of their heroes from the nursery onwards. Such glimpses into the inside of the course of a life led necessarily to an account focusing on significant moments of this life in their typical forms. The most perfect example of such an account is Fielding's *Tom Jones*. But the *Bildungsroman* is distinguished from all previous biographical compositions in that it intentionally and artistically depicts that which is universally human in such a life-course. 273

[72] Novel by Jean Paul.

The *Bildungsroman* is closely associated with the new developmental psychology established by Leibniz, with the idea of a natural education in conformity with the inner development of the psyche. This had its beginnings with Rousseau's *Emile* and swept over all of Germany. The *Bildungsroman* is also associated with the ideal of humanity with which Lessing and Herder inspired their contemporaries. A lawlike development is discerned in the individual's life; each of its levels has intrinsic value and is at the same time the basis for a higher level. Life's dissonances and conflicts appear as necessary transitions to be withstood by the individual on his way towards maturity and harmony. The "greatest happiness of earth's children" is "personality,"[73] as a unified and permanent form of human existence. This optimism of personal development, which illuminated even Lessing's difficult life-path, has never been expressed more joyously and confidently than in Goethe's *Wilhelm Meister*: an immortal radiance of enjoyment of life shines through this novel and those of the Romantics.

*Hyperion* grew in the same soil. The first fragment stressed explicitly that the path by which a man passes from a state of simplicity to that of perfect development is essentially the same in every individual. But Hölderlin was able to draw from his experience an insight into a new aspect of life—entirely foreign to the *Bildungsroman* up to then. Soon after publishing the fragment, he was no longer satisfied with it. He felt there was still undiscovered land in the realm of the novel. His lived experiences opened to him new possibilities for grasping and expressing the meaning of life.

*Hyperion* is not "an offshoot of Romantic poetry" as Haym has claimed;[74] if it lacks the cheerfulness of *Ofterdingen* this should not be taken as a weakness. The genuine significance of this work lies precisely in the fact that the poet for the first time makes manifest the darker features buried deep in life's countenance with a power that only lived experience can provide. He attempted to interpret life in terms of itself, to become aware of the values contained in life, both for their potential and their limits, just as Byron, Leopardi, Schopenhauer, and Nietzsche, who are akin to Hölderlin in essential features, did subsequently. All of this originated in this solitary man, who, far removed from the hustle and bustle of literary life, 274 contemplated the phenomena within and around him from day to

[73] Goethe, "West-östliche Divan," Buch Suleika. *WA*, I, 4:162.

[74] Rudolf Haym, *Die romantische Schule*, 4th ed. (Berlin: Weidmannliche Buchhandlung, 1920), pp. 341ff.

day. He was so alone that it was as if he lived in a desert or on an island remote from human society. But he was most lonely when he sought to communicate with family or friends. In embodying this interpretation of life, he developed a new form of the philosophical novel; all this achieved its greatest effect in Nietzsche's *Zarathustra*.

Voltaire and Diderot speak smilingly about the ambivalence of life, which they, as the children of Parisian culture, treat with their strong sensibility and sovereign intellect. With a relentless sense of reality and utterly without illusions, Swift analyzes the bundle of drives and passions that he finds in man, much in the way a pathologist dissects a malformed and degenerate body. The modern preoccupation with the bitter and wretched realities of life, especially in Schopenhauer, relates back in many respects to these predecessors. But the peculiar intensity with which the suffering of human existence has been felt since Rousseau was conditioned by new cultural circumstances. The conflict between nature and convention was intensified by the course of social development. European society was engulfed by a boundless devotion to ideals and happiness, by incredible demands on the order of society, indeed, on the order of nature itself, by a yearning that extended to infinity and to unprecedented conditions of happiness. "Infinity" is a word that the reader of fiction and of philosophical literature encounters everywhere at that time as an expression for the new attitudes about the mind, its states, and its objects.

> To those whom they love
> The gods who are infinite give all things wholly:
> All joys, which are infinite,
> All sorrows, which are infinite, wholly.[75]

A kinship of souls which can no longer be obstructed by conventions, a striving for the development of our full potential, which will no longer allow itself to be suppressed, the awareness of personal dignity—all this came into conflict with the social order and, in the end, with the very nature of things.

The backlash against the French Revolution that began after the execution of the king had a similar and equally important effect. The effort to bring about a new, more liberal order of society, which the French Revolution aroused throughout the civilized

[75] Goethe, from *Vermischte Gedichte*, in *WA*, I, 4:99, trans. by David Luke in *Goethe* (Harmondsworth: Penguin, 1964), p. 54.

world and which was kept alive by the finest youths of the age, found itself suddenly blocked everywhere by reactionary forces. It 275 was especially distressing that those who held fast to the ideas of the Revolution thereby came into conflict with their national consciousness, because the independence of many nations was threatened by the expansion of French power and the revolutionary army. These tensions were beginning to be felt at the time when Hölderlin was writing the final version of his *Hyperion*. And thereafter the military dictatorship of Napoleon, the repercussions of conditions in France on the individual states, and the justification of the forces of reaction in literature evoked an ever increasing pressure that suppressed every activity for the greater good. A general hopelessness spread. The more boundless the effort by which the young generation sought to develop itself in enjoyment and activity, the more deeply this miserable situation was felt.

These were the historical conditions for the appearance of men of genius—from Hölderlin to Leopardi—endowed with an almost pathological sensitivity for the harmonies and dissonances which the world evokes in our soul. Lord Byron lived at the limits of excess and madness; Leopardi was, on account of his physical deformity, in conflict with nature; Schopenhauer lived with a hereditary taint; and when Hölderlin's mental sensitivity collided with the adversity of his circumstances, he suffered the same fate that Nietzsche would subsequently. Thus, nature had destined these writers and poets to feel the dark shadows of life more intensely and to depict them more violently than had been done before. It is not that they spoke of imaginary evils or of suffering that they did not feel, as a vulgar optimism might suppose. Instead, they apportioned light and shadow differently than people with a life-embracing nature, and each of them did so in a way peculiar to him.

Hölderlin's *Hyperion* stands in this general historical context. It is a *Bildungsroman* in the course of which the protagonist's power seems to be destroyed rather than intensified. The novel, whose language flows like a lyric poem, proclaims an aesthetic pantheism that ends with an escape from life and its suffering. In this way the work transcended every previous form of pantheistic metaphysics and every rule of our classical poets. His work was as singular as his life was solitary. His efforts to move forward to new possibilities constitute the substance of Hölderlin's greatness. In this he prepared the way for modern times.

Slowly, with constant reworkings, this novel was completed. After the fragments from Waltershausen and Jena, a remarkable fragment appears from Frankfurt which reveals that Tieck's novel *William Lovell*[76] influenced the development of the plot. A letter dating from the summer of 1798, in which the poet cites important phrases from his characters Alabanda and Hyperion which remain practically unchanged in the concluding part of the novel, leads one to suspect that it was near completion around this time. *Hyperion* was finally published in two volumes: 1797 and 1799.

276

The scene is modern Greece. The possibility of blending the elegiac remembrance of past Greek greatness with the heroic will to renew such greatness must have appealed to Hölderlin. The events themselves were hardly a quarter of a century old. The poet had reason to hope that his protagonist would arouse greater interest than the "verbose and adventurous knights" that still delighted the German reading public in those days. The conspiracy which prepared for the Greek rebellion, and the dismal course of the revolution, filled with cowardice and violence, formed the right background for the tragedy of the new ideals of humanity as Hölderlin and his friends had experienced that tragedy during the course of the French Revolution. The inherent antagonism between the Greek masses oppressed by the Turks, and the heroic idealism of Alabanda, Hyperion and Diotima, reflects the overall political misfortunes of the times. And in the catastrophe which destroyed these noble characters, Hölderlin had a premonition of the fate of his own strivings.

Against the background of this military and political situation, Hölderlin depicts the inner development of Hyperion. A look back into the youthful years of his protagonist yields a story based on the nexus of his inner development: in this story, Hölderlin's own lived experiences are introduced one after another; his dreams of political activity were transformed into reality. Hyperion is Hölderlin himself. The characters with whom Hyperion comes into contact receive their inner life from the poet's memories. As Hölderlin reflects on his life's course, we see it once again in the mirror of poetry. Hyperion says at one point that in life, periods of expansiveness in action and the enjoyment of life alternate with periods of withdrawal into oneself. The novel also follows this rhythm of life.

Hölderlin always looked back at his childhood with nostalgia. Those were years of peace and freedom when "the compulsion of law and fate had not yet touched him."[77] A great teacher inspires

[76] 1795-96; published in three volumes.
[77] Paraphrase of *Hyperion, GSA*, 3:10.

Hyperion to devote his life to the realization of a higher humanity; this resonates with his memories of Schiller and Fichte. "May the spirit of man be great and pure and unyielding in its demands, may 277 it never bow to the force of nature!" He finds friendship in the form of the hero, Alabanda, and all memories of past Greek greatness seem to be revived in this character. Among the inspirations for the figure of Alabanda, the most significant in literature is Marquis Posa,[78] and the most significant in life is the philosopher Fichte. Like Posa, Alabanda protects his friend Hyperion, drives him into a life of action. When failure strikes Alabanda, the strong hero sacrifices himself for the weaker soul who had relied on him. And, like Fichte, Alabanda strives to make his mark upon the world; his creed is similar to Fichte's. "I feel a life in me that no god created and no moral begot. I believe that our existence is from ourselves. . . ."[79] Eduard Burton, a character from Tieck's *William Lovell*, also influenced the lively and colorful portrayal of Alabanda. The most painful misunderstandings and, finally, separation result from the unbounded devotion of Hyperion to Alabanda; Jean Paul's *Flegeljahre* subsequently adopted this motif. An early version of *Hyperion* relates these first fateful experiences still more directly in an emotionally charged narrative style, and the cheerful, childlike contours of its characters are reminiscent of the early chapters of Novalis' *Ofterdingen*.

For the first time Hyperion experiences the divisive element inherent in every personal relationship. A "long, morbid sadness"[80] envelops him. However, the healing power contained in life and youth also manifests itself. "Nothing is more beautiful than when the light dawns again in man after a long death, and when pain goes, like a brother, to meet joy, dawning from a distance."[81] Spring draws near. As if from a sickbed, Hyperion arises quietly and slowly; his breast quivers with hidden hopes; in his sleep even more beautiful dreams envelop him. Love takes possession of him on a spring day, and thereby he awakens to all the beauty of life. How often the poets of that time represented this experience as preparing one for productive activity! When Hölderlin wrote this chapter of his first volume, his own experience in Frankfurt filled his soul, and what he held back in silence even from his friends was allowed

[78] Character in Schiller's *Don Carlos* (1787).

[79] *Hyperion, GSA*, 3:141; trans. by Willard R. Trask (hereafter *H*) (New York: The New American Library, 1965), p. 152.

[80] *GSA*, 3:39; *H*, p. 52 (revised).

[81] *GSA*, 3:43; *H*, p. 55 (revised).

expression in the novel. Diotima raises Hyperion to a consciousness of his great destiny. By believing in him, she strengthens him. Her essence becomes a determinate norm for his thought and action; her presence moves the reserved Hyperion to reveal his entire existence in endless song. In her he sees the infinite in the midst of the finite, the divine in time: "The most beautiful is also the most sacred."[82] The light of the southern noontime sun is poured out over the scenes of this love story. They are moments in which life itself seems to stand still.

278

Can the unrest in this adolescent soul be quieted? According to Hölderlin, infinite striving cannot be satisfied by any finite object or finite situation. Longing for a higher humanity cannot find fulfillment in any individual. That is the new, melancholy feeling which Châteaubriand, de Staël, Constant,[83] and Byron express, though on the basis of a different mode of thinking. "Do you not know," Diotima says, "what you mourn for . . . ? It did not vanish years ago, it is impossible to say exactly when it was there, when it went, but it was, it is—it is in you! It is a better age, that is what you seek, a more beautiful world."[84] The very deep conflict felt everywhere in Germany as the result of attempts to realize ideal action in the world now confronts Hyperion. German idealism was then divided into two camps. The education of our aristocracy stood in conflict with our miserable political situation. Schiller wanted to solve this conflict by spreading intellectual culture in the nation; he saw this as the condition for the advance toward political freedom. Fichte and his disciples in Jena and Tübingen pressed for a complete change of conditions. The crisis of the novel is based on this opposition of tendencies. Hyperion, a person with a gentle and yet impulsive nature, with the inclination to become a poet as well as a hero, finds himself caught between these possibilities. Diotima acutely observes that he is destined to become the educator of his people. "From the root of humanity the new world shall spring!"[85] Since he had lost "the equipoise of beautiful humanity,"[86] since he "had been a man full of suffering and turmoil,"[87] he is capable of

[82] *GSA*, 3:56; *H*, p. 69.

[83] Benjamin Constant (1769-1830). Swiss-born French politician and journalist who attacked Napoleon; best known for his novel *Adolphe* and his liaison with Mme. de Staël.

[84] *GSA*, 3:66-67; *H*, p. 79 (revised).

[85] *GSA*, 3:89; *H*, p. 100.

[86] *GSA*, 3:88; *H*, p. 99.

[87] *GSA*, 3:88; *H*, p. 99 (revised).

bringing about a higher, stronger humanity at one with itself, for "a new divinity . . . a new future"[88] must come. He receives the call to support the struggle for freedom; Diotima cannot restrain her lover; he is swept up in the plans for the Greek rebellion and is torn by the conflict between an ideal goal and raw, undisciplined forces, between the demand made upon him as a hero to work with whatever is available and without any scruples, on the one hand, and his noble inwardness, on the other. Hence, a catastrophe is inevitable. Hyperion must abandon the cause of the Greeks. He is left only with the aristocratic knowledge that the man who acts powerfully in life enjoys the greatest happiness. In this hero of Fichte's idealism we find the origin of Nietzsche's experience that the exercise of power as such is the ultimate and greatest joy.

279 In the midst of the conflict of the strong and the noble with the commonplace world, a final aspect of human destiny asserts itself. This, too, comes to Hölderlin from his own life. If great opposites clash with each other in the world, if the duality of every situation that demands a decision reveals diverse possibilities and, further, reveals something questionable about each, then misunderstanding and dissension will arise even in the relationships among the most noble people. Hyperion, Diotima, Alabanda impose suffering on each other. They turn silent and thus individually become the helpless victims of fate. Psychological necessity is linked with contingencies of fate which are always ready at hand when life-situations become entangled to produce a catastrophe. This catastrophe leads to the inner destruction of Hyperion and to the death of his beloved Diotima and of his friend Alabanda. The development of the plot is masterful. It forces on the reader the metaphysical insight that a fearsome duality attaches to life itself. We possess life's beauty only in our relationships with human beings, and in each of these relationships there lies concealed something inviolable that separates us.

Only where our feeling, in reaching out, encounters no resistance—in the devotion to nature—is man rid of love's pain. The novel concludes with this, Hölderlin's ultimate, deepest experience. This devotion involves the renunciation of the futile effort to find happiness among men. Unity with nature presupposes separation from men. Hyperion thus surrenders himself in order to become one with nature, and he experiences with perilous intensity the

[88] *GSA*, 3:89; *H*, p. 100.

violence contained in her great forces. They live in his imagination as in the myths of the Greeks.

The German *Bildungsroman* of this time generally took its protagonist just to the point where he is about to act decisively in the world: even *Wilhelm Meister* ends in this way. The conclusion of *Hyperion* resembles that of Keller's *The Green Henry*.[89] But Keller felt the need to define his conclusion clearly; Hölderlin leaves it to the reader to interpret his obscure words. We tend to think of Hyperion's solitary, passive, and despairing immersion in nature as the end of his willing and acting, as the renunciation of worldly life for a hermit's existence of a peculiar sort. But a few passages suggest to me a different interpretation. At her death, Diotima predicts with prophetic power that Hyperion would emerge from the ruins of his dreams—"your days of poetry are already germinating."[90] The prologue of the novel announces its theme as "the resolution of dissonances in a particular character."[91] This can be understood as saying that the conflict in Hyperion based on the two tendencies of his nature is now resolved and that in the reestablished relation to an all-healing nature, the basis has been established for a still higher activity. "If the life of the world consists in the alternation of unfolding and enclosing, venturing out and returning to the self, then why is it not also so with the heart of man?"[92] This rhythm of life is underscored again by the final words of the novel; they point to a continuation of the protagonist's life which would bring him face to face with new circumstances. But the writer felt no need to give his readers a glimpse into such a future.

280

The novel leads us from the time of *Wilhelm Meister, Ofterdingen*, and *Sternbald* to that of Hegel, Schopenhauer, and Nietzsche. *Hyperion* is a philosophical novel, but not in the sense intended by the novels of Wieland and his school. Its concern is not the tedious conflict of fixed historical standpoints as the philosophical tradition has transmitted them. No pattern of any kind, no historically received system, no conventional assessment of the values of existence stands between Hölderlin and existence itself. In each of his characters, life fulfills the same function. Hölderlin wants to express what characterizes life at all times and in all places, not abstractly,

[89] Gottfried Keller's novel was written much later. First version appeared in 1854, second in 1879-80.

[90] *GSA*, 3:149; *H*, p. 159.

[91] *GSA*, 3:5; *H*, p. 171.

[92] *GSA*, 3:38; *H*, p. 50 (revised).

but by illustrating it through the destinies of the characters of his novel.

The existence of every individual exhibits a duality. Existence is, on the one hand, the appearance of a power present in nature, and as such it has an infinite value. Since, however, it manifests itself as something finite, individual, limited by other particulars, separated from every being that lives for itself, its happiness and its beauty are accompanied by finitude and suffering.

The All-One that differentiates itself within itself is proclaimed in *Hyperion*. This is not a metaphysical doctrine, but the experience of an artist who rejoices in beauty. In the radiance of nature, in the benevolent, strong inwardness of a person, in the joyous feeling of power, in every moment of greatest happiness, there is manifested a property of the ground of things that draws us to it in love and reverence. This experience is most intense when persons merge with each other—and the more completely they merge, the more profound it becomes. Hölderlin's old theory of the coherence of the world in love appears here in a pantheistic form. The verses of the great poets and the works of all the arts speak of this depth inherent 281 in all things. Every individual has a unique value. Some of the wording of Hölderlin's sentences can be found again in Schleiermacher's *Soliloquies*: "What is loss, if a man finds himself in his own world? In us is all. Why should a man be miserable when a hair falls from his head? Why does he strive to serve when he could be a god?"[93] Schelling subsequently saw art as the organ for the perception of the divine ground of the world: that is exactly what Hölderlin professed. Hölderlin also anticipates the pantheistic mysticism of Hegel.

Hölderlin speaks similarly of the finitude and suffering of the world: as a poet he draws on the intensity that inheres in such experiences. Because the eternal enters into the passage of time, its appearances are subjected to the pain of mortality. In the moment of greatest happiness when Hyperion first touches the lips of Diotima, he already knows this happiness will end. The first version of *Empedocles*, which is contemporaneous with his work on *Hyperion*, declares that everything subject to the law of succession must be unsatisfied, restless, and unhappy. It is significant that *Hyperion* traces the All-One doctrine to Heraclitus, who, in the midst of a life-affirming pantheism of the Ionian islands and coasts, gave powerful expression to the tragic feeling of transience which

[93] *GSA*, 3:16; *H*, p. 30 (revised).

is grounded in the passage of time. When the One disintegrates into multiplicity, the form of life becomes a conflict of particular forces. And in this struggle, the brutality of the masses predominates over the nobility of an ideal character. There are rare and good beings in the world who endure it because of what they are, but all too often barbarians around us pervert our best impulses even before they have been developed. It is dangerous "to expose one's whole soul, be it in love or in work, to destructive reality." The more pure a soul is, the more sensitive and vulnerable it is. This is the source of Hölderlin's aristocratic consciousness, through which he is akin to Nietzsche. He strives to produce a great work of art, not in order to influence his nation, but to satisfy his soul in its thirst for fulfillment. It would be futile to attempt to improve barbarians: they should merely get out of the way of the work of great men. Moreover, since each member of this multitude is an individual, he is intrinsically profoundly solitary, separate from others. "For man's wild heart no home is possible."[94] Something compels us to "fling ourselves into the night of the unknown, into the cold strangeness of some other world."[95] Indeed, there is in us even some hidden, perilous drive to kill "the joys of kinship and love."[96] Finally, the law of individuation itself is the source of a deep contradiction in us between the striving for the infinite and the happiness of a limited existence. 282

When we look at our whole being, we see that the fullness of life is tied to the power of suffering. "The more unfathomably a man suffers, the more unfathomable is his power." For Hölderlin it is an "old unchanging decree of Fate that a new bliss rises in the heart when it perseveres and suffers through the midnight of anguish, and that, like nightingale voices in the dark, the world's song of life first sounds divinely for us in deep affliction."[97]

How remarkable is the relationship of this novel to the philosophical work surrounding it!

In the essay "Of the I [Ego] as Principle of Philosophy"[98] (1795), Schelling advanced the first version of his pantheism. This turn in his thought thus became public only after the fragment of *Hyperion* containing Hölderlin's pantheism had appeared in the *Thalia*. The

[94] *GSA*, 3:16, *H*, p. 30.
[95] *GSA*, 3:16; *H*, p. 30 (revised).
[96] *GSA*, 3:16; *H*, p. 30.
[97] *GSA*, 3:157; *H*, p. 167.
[98] Trans. by F. Marti in F. W. Schelling, *The Unconditional in Human Knowledge* (Lewisburg, Pa.: Bucknell University Press, 1980).

basis for the philosopher's pantheism lay in the universally valid principle of the ego that extends beyond the individual. Hölderlin's pantheism was completely different in kind from Schelling's. The external conditions of the former lay in the general literary and poetic movement of the time in which Shaftesbury, Hemsterhuis, Herder, Goethe's *Werther* and *Faust* fragment of 1790, and Schiller's *Philosophische Briefe* constitute landmarks. From this movement there emerged a pantheistic world-view with which Hölderlin found himself in sympathy. Every phase of *Hyperion* shows the persistence of the All-One doctrine in Hölderlin's mind. After the *Thalia* fragment, the disappointments of Hölderlin's emotional life become the basis for the sublime experience of the soul's liberation through devotion to the Universe; even in the last version of the novel this is not changed at all. However, Kant and Fichte did force him for a while to attempt to justify this position. From his Jena period, in which Fichte had the strongest influence on him, there exists a remarkable record of three versions of his attempt to solve this problem. He accepts Fichte's basic idea: what exists for the ego is its phenomenon; but Plato's enthusiasm opens to him the intelligible world lying behind the finite ego. "Pure Spirit does not concern itself with matter, but is also not aware of things. There is no world for it, because apart from it there is nothing." Since consciousness first appears in the finite ego by virtue of its limitation, this ego would waste away if the beauty of the world did not reciprocate the soul's passionate longing. Here Hölderlin also asserts his All-One doctrine over against Fichte. What an impact it 283 must have had on him, when having returned home, he met Schelling and then studied his writings. Just at that time Schelling was finding a way for philosophy to move from the ego to the All-One.

But the affinity of ideas that united Hölderlin with Hegel went even deeper than his agreement with Schelling. This affinity is even more striking because an actual influence of Hegel on his poetic friend can only be demonstrated for the second volume of *Hyperion*. In Switzerland, Hegel added ideas to his theological studies which have a very striking affinity with those of our novel. He also took his point of departure from the opposition and division inherent in everything finite. Pain is attached to life as such. The aim of all higher development must be to overcome these separations. The attitude that works itself out in individual actions directed at objects is always restricted and limited by the fact that it only overcomes separation at a specific point. Love is a higher mode of unifying that which is separated, but even in it the separation of individuals from each other and from the world is not overcome. In vain does the beautiful soul seek its satisfaction through devotion, through tears of sympathy, through unceasing beneficent action. In even the most intimate and vital unification of people there is still separation—"this is the law of humanity." It is only religious consciousness of the unity of all life in love which overcomes all separateness. The agreement between the poet and the philosopher derives from the similarity of their approach. At that time, Hegel also began with life; he defined the Absolute by means of the categories contained in life. Consequently he regarded unity, opposition, self-reflection, the pain of opposition, and the intensification of consciousness in comprehension, as moments of the Absolute. But these and other thoughts similar to Hölderlin's remained among his papers. Their time together in Frankfurt cannot have influenced these ideas of Hölderlin, for Hegel came to Frankfurt in January 1797, while the first volume of *Hyperion*, which formulates all of them, would already appear at the Easter book fair. Hegel's poem "Eleusis" contained obscure pantheistic intimations.

> I gave myself to the infinite,
> I am in it, am all, am only it.
> Reappearing thought alienates,
> it is frightened before the infinite, and amazed by
> the deep view, which it does not comprehend.[99]

According to Hegel the divine could only be embodied and given shape in Greek myth. These intimations could reinforce the reflections of the poet—but they told him nothing new.

Hölderlin's inner development was the source of his All-One doctrine as it exists in the finished novel. Hölderlin defines the relation of understanding and reason to the intuition of the All-One as it is revealed to the poet in moments of enthusiasm for the beauty of the world. Understanding is only "knowledge of what is present at hand,"[100] that is, reflection upon that which is empirically given. Reason, according to him, is the mental activity that he had seen at work in the formation of Fichte's system, namely, the "demand for ever greater progress in the combination and differentiation of some particular material."[101] Both understanding and reason are as such incapable of comprehending the infinite. But when the

284

[99] Hegel, "Eleusis," pp. 60-61 (revised).
[100] *GSA*, 3:83; *H*, p. 95 (revised).
[101] *GSA*, 3:83; *H*, p. 95.

enthusiasm of the artist begets a lived experience of beauty, the essence of the divine is manifested to it. For the One that is manifested as a whole in the manifold of its differences is beauty, and in its content the essence of the divine is disclosed at the same time. Thus, philosophy first becomes possible through the lived experience of beauty in art. Philosophy elucidates the content of this experience, analyzes it, and reintegrates what has been analyzed by means of thought; in this way it penetrates reflectively into the depths of the All-One. Art relates to philosophy for Hölderlin and Schelling in the way religion relates to philosophy for Schleiermacher. "Poetry . . . is the beginning and the end of philosophical knowledge."[102] Only in enthusiasm is there creative power. Art is the source of religion, too.

Thus, philosophy could originate only in Greece. For the Egyptians the ultimate "is a veiled power, an awesome enigma; the dumb, dark Isis is . . . an empty infinity." The North, however, forces spirit back into itself prematurely: "The spirit begins to return into itself even before it is ready to travel."[103] Here, understanding and reason rule, hence reflection. These are ideas and phrases that will reappear in just this form in Hegel. Similarly, Hölderlin and Hegel shared a hope for a new Church which would bring about an inner harmony in the human race. According to Hölderlin, it would proclaim a religion of beauty which would be the beginning of a new world history.

The artistic form of a work of art derives from the task of portraying the meaning of life by means of concrete events. It is therefore proper that Hyperion, the subject of this *Bildungsroman*, who comes to understand the meaning of his lived experiences after they have run their course, tells his own story. He relates it to a friend in a series of letters which nevertheless assume the character of solitary confessions. Hölderlin fulfills the philosophical goal of this 285 work by uniting the succession of events as presented in the sequence of letters through a consciousness that integrates it in retrospect. When the struggle is over, Hyperion looks back in solitude, separated from people, but absorbed by the religious unity of nature. Still shaken by the recent events, he relives the past as if it were present. At the same time all this becomes associated for him with the feeling that has now taken possession of him: the total devotion of his ephemeral existence to an all-encompassing, eternal nature.

[102] *GSA*, 3:81; *H*, p. 93.
[103] *GSA*, 3:82; *H*, p. 94.

Nature is everywhere and has always existed as the witness to everything that has been. This is the keynote of each of these letters. The solitary hermit sees nature around him blossoming into lush greenness just as when he saw Diotima in the first spring. As nature's eternal harmony, into which life's every struggle is dissolved, permeates the nature scenes which accompanied both his best and his worst moments, a new narrative form is created, and it evokes a peculiar effect. It is a unique blend of feelings which produces the fundamental mood of the novel: an awareness of infinity in the midst of life's changes. Not only the first, but also the final words are about infinite nature. Appearance is a shimmering of light over the waters, a fleeting sunset upon the mountains, a play of the wind in the branches.

> O thou . . . with thy gods, Nature! I have dreamed it out, the dream of human things, and I say, only thou livest, and what they who know no peace have attempted and conceived melts away from thy flame like beads of wax![104]
>
> . . .
>
> O Soul! Soul! Beauty of the World! Indestructible, ravishing one! with thine eternal youth! thou art; what, then, is death and all the woe of men?—Ah! those strange creatures have spoken many empty words. Yet from delight all comes, and all ends in peace.
>
> Like lovers' quarrels are the dissonances of the world. Reconciliation is there, even in the midst of strife, and all things that are parted find one another again.[105]

The rhythms of this hymn, which concludes the novel, permeate all the central passages of *Hyperion*. Rhythm is Hölderlin's most characteristic artistic device. The rhythm of language in the structure of the tragedy is a symbol of the ultimate and supreme concept of his philosophy—the rhythm of life itself. In this rhythm the poet saw the expression of the lawfulness of the movement of life, just as Hegel had found this lawfulness in the dialectical progression of concepts. Although it was not until later that Hölderlin published his profound theory of the rhythm that governs everything even down to particular lines of verse, a sense of this relationship was already at work in him when he completed *Hyperion*, and he might 286

[104] *GSA*, 3:159; *H*, p. 169.
[105] *GSA*, 3:159; *H*, pp. 169-70.

already have developed it conceptually. The artistic form of *Hyperion* is symbolic through and through. In this it is akin to Nietzsche's *Zarathustra*.

Nietzsche felt Hölderlin's influence in the decisive years of his life. When, as a seventeen-year-old pupil in Schulpforta, he was to present a report about his favorite poet, he chose Hölderlin, and again later he came back to *Hyperion*. Hölderlin's philosophical novel exerted its influence on the poetic development of Nietzsche's view of life in *Zarathustra* from the basic idea to the form, indeed, down to the individual words. The style of both writers is musical. They both write for readers who read not "merely with the eyes." They coin new words for that which they want to express because they abhor worn-out figures of speech. And yet, they feel that what stirs them most profoundly remains forever unspoken. They both focus on the inner world, and they both seize the most audacious metaphors to make it visible. They live in the great antithesis between a higher, future humanity with its beauty, its heroes and their strength, and the vulgarity surrounding them and the hundred ways in which it has deformed the human psyche. Consequently, their style moves in antitheses. They work by means of a transition from dithyramb to irony. Their dithyrambs are poems in prose, and through their irony they play a sovereign artistic game with their enemies. Although, like Nietzsche, Hölderlin could make a psychic state fleetingly visible, as if by a flash of lightning, he could not depict a human being in the quiet light of day. The figures of his novel are all like shadows. They possess a mere momentary inner life. No external contour comes to the aid of the imagination to make them visible. In that highest sense, according to which being a poet means being a creator of figures and actions, Hölderlin turns out not to be a poet in *Hyperion*.

## THE TRAGEDY OF *EMPEDOCLES*

Hölderlin's *Empedocles* continues the drama of the soul developed by Sophocles, Racine, and Goethe. He goes beyond this toward an unknown goal, to new, supreme achievements that even today no 287 one has attained. When we approach the fragments of this tragedy, we must dismiss all memory of Shakespeare's plots, which incorporate a profusion of external details; all memory of the rules and artistic forms of Lessing and Schiller; and we must move beyond those critical judgments which refuse to consider Hölderlin's play dramatic by such standards. Hölderlin is not trying to portray extraordinary destinies, eccentric passions, or colorful scenes of life. He moves from the realm in which man is determined by his relationship to the external world, to consider what he desires from it or what depresses him about his external fate. He strives to represent the growing awareness of a reflective person when his private passions are stilled. It involves a coming to terms with our conditional existence, with the necessities of life that derive from our relationship to invisible forces. This process of coming to terms is the same in each of us: its presuppositions lie in what is the same in everyone and in that outside of us which determines the most general relation of human existence to the world. This process expresses something which must be grappled with in precisely the same way in the quiet dwellings of simple people as in the palaces of kings. It is something that is always present when man discovers the universal and ultimate relations of human existence to natural and supernatural forces in the things that affect him. This process of coming to terms does not just take place in a specific period of our life; it is constantly being aroused anew by what we enjoy, suffer, experience; it leads us gradually into new depths of life. It is the history of our psyche, which is more important than all our particular passions and achievements. When this process completes itself in a human being, he becomes sovereign and solitary, and the noise of the world reaches him only in terms of distant, indistinct sounds. And when this history is lived through as what is most powerful, strong, and great in a human being, it leads him somehow out of all the limitations of existence into the realm of freedom—even if this be through death.

In conceiving the idea of such a play, Hölderlin sought, like Goethe in *Iphigenia in Tauris*, a modern appropriation of what Attic drama had once been. With its origin in Greek religious life, Attic drama represented man in his ultimate relation to the divine forces. The challenge was to renew the splendor of ancient tragedy in its total religious depth! And, further, to do this while realizing that a literal belief in fate and atonement had given way to a religious view suitable to modern consciousness.

288

Hyperion shows the connection of the idea of heroism with a pantheistic religious outlook. This relation reflects the way Hölderlin came to terms with life, and his *Empedocles* builds on it as well. We cannot know how Hölderlin's innate potential and the historical forces which affected his development cooperated in the origination of his idea of heroism. All that we can see is the transition from this idea to his religious pantheism, and the new connection that he established between the two in his life-history. This was then elucidated in his *Hyperion*.

In ancient tragedy—especially in the Oedipus plays by Sophocles—Hölderlin recognized a similar history of the soul, which led up to the transfiguration of the hero in death and the blessing that derives from it. He saw here the possibility for a great religious tragedy in which he could give ultimate expression to his lived experience and perfectly represent the features of the world as he had first seen them. He had at one time planned a tragedy about Socrates which would end with Socrates' voluntary death: for this is how Socrates' end is presented in Plato's dialogues. But then he happened upon the story of Empedocles: here was a magnificent symbol for everything he had to say. Empedocles was a powerful man related to the Greek earth—he was basically a poet, a metaphysician, but thrust by the situation of his *polis* into reformative action. He storms through life in power and finally ends it in voluntary death by leaping into the crater of Mt. Etna.

The idea of this tragedy attracted Hölderlin's undivided attention even while he was working on *Hyperion*. The philosophical novel, *Hyperion*, unfolds within the constraints of modern life, of the protagonist's situation, and of the circumstances in which he was placed. Its effect is dissipated by an indeterminate conclusion. By contrast, the form and content of the new tragedy show the gripping progression of a powerful life to a tragic end. We find evidence in *Hyperion* itself that Hölderlin saw the inner relation of the two works in exactly this way:

> Yesterday I went up to the summit of Etna. There I remembered the great Sicilian who, weary of counting the hours, knowing the soul of the World, in his bold joy in life there flung himself down into the glorious flames . . . but one must think more highly of oneself than I do before, thus unbidden, one can flee to Nature's heart. . . .[106]

Being so intimately and temporally linked in the poet, *Hyperion* and *Empedocles* are dominated by the *one* basic mood in which 289 the urge to live and to have an effect merges with the desire for death. A few of Hölderlin's verses from the period of the tragedy's development express how he saw this connection as the basic feature in his hero's character:

[106] *GSA*, 3:151; *H*, p. 162.

You look for life, you look and from deeps of Earth
A fire, divinely gleaming wells up for you,
And quick, aquiver with desire, you
Hurl yourself down into Etna's furnace.

So did the Queen's exuberance once dissolve
Rare pearls in wine, and why should she not? But you,
If only you, O poet, had not
Offered your wealth to the seething chalice!

Yet you are holy to me as is the power
Of Earth that took you from us, the boldly killed!
And gladly, did not love restrain me,
Deep as the hero plunged down I'd follow.[107]

Hölderlin first mentions that he is working on the *Empedocles* tragedy at the end of the summer of 1797. At that time he already had a "complete, detailed plan"[108] for the tragedy. This plan still exists. Here, as in every later attempt to execute it, an external conflict is connected with discord in the hero's psyche, through which the voluntary death of Empedocles is explained. This genius is out of joint with the world because of his inability to bear "human inadequacy"[109] and because of man's inability to act in accord with his higher capacities. This is also the theme of Schopenhauer and, before him, of the Romantics. There is a conflict between Empedocles' ideal of the totality and harmony of existence on the one hand, and the necessity of losing himself in action in particular circumstances. He would like to live "in a grand harmony with all of life, with an omnipresent heart, intensely like a god, freely extended."[110] But his particular circumstances, as beautiful as they are, force him into a "one-sided existence,"[111] precisely because they are particular circumstances. Through his involvement with them, he becomes bound by the law of succession and hence he feels unsatisfied, inconstant, unhappy. As these afflictions of finitude oppress him more and more, he decides "to unite himself with infinite nature"[112] by voluntary death. External conflicts now lose

[107] *GSA*, 1(1):240; *HPF*, p. 31.

[108] Hölderlin to his brother, 1797, *GSA*, 6(1):247. Dilthey assumes this reference is to the "Frankfurter Plan," *GSA*, 4(1):145-48. In fact, it is doubtful that Hölderlin is referring to his *Empedocles* at all; see Beissner's discussion in *GSA*, 4(1):321.

[109] *GSA*, 4(1):147.

[110] *Ibid.*, p. 145.

[111] *Ibid.*

[112] *Ibid.*, p. 147.

all their significance for him, and he regards death as "an inner necessity,"[113] which follows him from his innermost essence. Although this plan places the chief emphasis of the drama in the inner 290 history of Empedocles, the projected dramatic execution of the play departs from it by unfolding a vivid series of familial, everyday social scenes and conversations. After all of Hölderlin's efforts to provide the motivation for his character, Empedocles' decision ultimately lacks inner necessity. Hence Hölderlin abandoned the plan.

It is only from after the time of his move to Homburg that we have any definite information about efforts to execute the tragedy. He pinned on this tragedy all the hopes that he still had for life. "It is to be my last effort to give value to myself in my own way."[114] From then on "he devoted most of his time" to the work. He was thinking of having the completed drama appear in the first issues of the journal he planned to found.

In the manuscripts of the tragedy that have survived, there is a continuous draft that extends from the beginning of the action to Empedocles' farewell to his favorite student, Pausanias; hence only the final scenes concerning his voluntary death are lacking. We can safely assume that we have here before us the version about which he wrote in June 1799 that he was finished with his tragedy up to the last act. There are also a few scenes of another draft, where a priest, elevated to the height of a man of power, becomes the worthy adversary of Empedocles, and where the freer poetic treatment approaches Goethe's *Prometheus*. Although they were written later, there is no doubt that these scenes belong to the same basic plan. I will not venture to say anything more specific about the historical origin and composition of the extant drafts. Instead, I will try to show the inner relation in the tragedy among material, lived experience, ideas, and poetic formation.

The historical Empedocles was one of those reformers who related science to a mystical form of faith, and, on its basis, proclaimed a religious order of life. Hence he is known as a philosopher, writer, priest, orator, statesman, and physician. He taught the power of love which holds the cosmos together in firm bonds of harmony, the inner affinity of all life, the transmigration of souls: these are views so akin to Hölderlin's religious sense that they, too, must have drawn him to the Greek seer and poet. A member of a noble family of his native city of Agrigent in Sicily, he took part in the

[113] *Ibid.*, p. 148.

[114] Hölderlin to his mother, 28 November 1798, *GSA*, 6(1):292.

overthrow of the short-lived aristocratic regime, became the political leader of the democratic forces, and helped them to victory; he is said to have declined the throne. But his opponents finally forced 291 him to leave his homeland. Another trait which is difficult to interpret, is shown to us in one of his songs of atonement, and must be added to our portrait of his powerful personality:

> I go about among you an immortal god, mortal no more,
> honored as is my due and crowned with garlands and verdant wreaths.
> When I enter the prosperous townships with these my followers,
> men and women both, I am revered; they follow me in countless
> numbers, asking where lies the path to gain, some seeking prophecies,
> while others, for many a day, stabbed by grievous pains,
> beg to hear the word that heals all manner of illness.[115]

He boasts of being greater than "mortal things . . . changing one baleful path of life for another."[116] Thus he appears to us, like Paracelsus, as a man in whom spiritual eminence, unbounded self-estimation, mystical ideas of power over nature, and charlatanism are oddly combined. The Greek tendency to spin fables caused him to be surrounded by pious legends and scornful tales. Diogenes Laertius, who collected all the gossip about him, reports of his presumptuous nature, his regal bearing, and the stately dignity of his gestures and words. And among the various reports of the sage's demise, there was also the malicious rumor that he had jumped into Etna.

This material provided the germ for Hölderlin's figure of a superhuman being (*Übermensch*), who dominated nature and life with tremendous power and turned them to his own use, who through thinking, acting, and enjoying discovered what life is. Empedocles had all the experiences of Hyperion, but in greater, more expansive proportions, and, being stronger than the latter, turned his back on the life that had become shallow and despicable to him. Hölderlin gathered together all the suffering of genius in his *Emped-*

[115] Empedocles, quoted by Diogenes Laertius (Fr. 112; VIII, 62) and Clement (*Strom.* VI, 30), in G. S. Kirk and J. E. Raven, *The Presocratic Philosophers* (Cambridge: The University Press, 1971), Fr. 478, p. 354.

[116] Empedocles, Fr. 115; Hippolytus, *Ref.* vii, 29; and Plutarch, *De exilio*, 17, 607c, in *ibid.*, Fr. 471, p. 352.

*ocles*, in a language whose simplicity touches the heart more deeply than the language of *Hyperion*. Only Goethe before him had found a voice like this for such suffering. The scenery that surrounds this figure is magnificent: lively scenes with Sicilian people, southern gardens with their blooming flora, the area near Etna, then the peak of this wondrous mountain. The atmosphere that surrounds this figure is reverential, even worshipful: two striking young people embody this attitude. One is an ideal maiden, modelled on the Panthea of tradition: she understands Empedocles' greatness through the sympathy bestowed by love—she is a Diotima who seems to come from Christ's side. The other is Pausanias, a favorite pupil of Empedocles. Embodied in him is all the magic of Plato's youth-figures—and Empedocles' relationship to him displays the 292 unique beauty of a personal relationship in which the teacher, with no jealousy whatsoever, sees his pupil actualize that which he himself could not. The gentle, measured relationship of these figures to each other produces a musical effect which harmonizes with the melody of Hölderlin's language.

The tragedy acquired its unity when Hölderlin grasped this traditional material as a symbol for the content of his own life. Hölderlin is true to the historical facts when he focuses on Empedocles' religiosity and reformative activity; and he used these two themes to project his own faith in a future religion of beauty, joy, and the free ordering of life. He also provided a background for Empedocles' actions by relating them to the chaos of the social and political setting, which allows us to discern the collapse of the Sicilian *polis*; and thereby Hölderlin could give expression to his own agonizing awareness of the political misfortunes around him. By going more deeply into the odd mixture of attributes which made Empedocles' character a riddle, he recognized the real problem of his tragic life. Goethe had touched upon this problem in his *Mahomet* fragment, which became known only many years later. In Voltaire's play, the riddle offered by the personality of the Arabic prophet was treated with the mere superficiality of the Enlightenment. But Goethe felt that only a powerful and completely true religious occurrence could have established the origin of this world religion. Hölderlin approaches the historical riddle presented by the reformative activity of Empedocles in the same way. Empedocles' religious consciousness proceeded from a living relationship to divine things. He can only be understood historically by grasping what transformed his original religious attitude into a belief in miracles, into dogma, into a rigid and external response to the most living reality. Here again,

Hölderlin is the predecessor of Schleiermacher. At that time, Hegel, too, had been persistently and extensively concerned with the transition from living religious consciousness to positive religion, with the externalization of inner faith, with the need to confirm eternal truths by tradition and miracles.

Hölderlin transposes his interpretation of Greek religious consciousness as derived from his poetic view of nature and as nourished by his familiarity with the Greek gods and myths onto Empedocles. The absolute ego that had at first been an abstract concept for Schelling became for Hölderlin a grand, comforting experience. 293 Through such a state of mind, Greek mythology gained a vitality that it had never had for Schiller or Goethe. Here we no longer see persons in mere personal relationships with one another, separate from nature and human life, but a transcendent world; here we see processes of interweaving, transformation, ascent and descent, germination and destruction, relating the bright ether and the sun that attracts it; they also relate mother earth, the ocean, and the rivers that it swallows up: this is the play of the divine forces themselves, of the more ominous ones that rule in the depths of the earth, of the somber sea god, and of the bright sun god, Apollo. It is only here that myth once again becomes a reality available to lived experience. A bond of affinity with nature pervades this living feeling for the interweaving processes of nature, for "the transformations and effects produced by the powers of her genius." When the gods abandoned Empedocles, he looks back to the days of his youth in which he first awoke to this divine world.

O heavenly light! men
Had not taught me—for a long time
When my longing heart could not find
The All-Living, then I turned to you,
Clung to you like the plant, trustingly
In pious joy blindly for a long time.
For a mortal knows purity with difficulty
But as my mind blossomed, as you yourself blossom,
Then I knew you, then I cried: You live!
And how you cheerfully move around mortals
And heavenly, youthfully send forth
Your radiance from you to each and everyone,
So that all things bear your spirit's color,
So I too greeted life with song,
For your soul was in me and openly

My heart gave itself like you to somber earth,
The suffering one, and oft' in holy might
I promised her fearlessly, faithfully to love
The fateful ones even until death
And to scorn none of her riddles.
Then the rustling was different in the grove
And softly sounded her mountains' springs
And a gentle flame in flower's fragrance
O Earth! your still life touched me.
All your joys, earth! not as you give
Them, smiling, to the weak, but splendid as they ripen,
And come warm and great from love and effort.
All these you gave to me and when I often
294 Sat on distant mountain tops and, wondering,
Contemplated life's divine vagaries,
Deeply stirred by your changing
And sensing my own fate—
Then the ether stirred, as it does with you,
Around my love-wounded breast, healing me
And magically in its depths
My riddles were solved.[117]

Empedocles wants to act on the basis of—indeed, through—this religious consciousness. Thus, the history of his soul unfolds. The motif of its development is the perilous path of the religious genius who turns his lived experience outwards to the external world. For thereby he subjects himself to the finite conditions of religious communication, and becomes dragged down by the forces of the time and of the people to whom he descends.

In his poem to Hölderlin, Hegel describes how every trace of the holy rites of the Eleusinian mysteries disappeared.

To the son of consecration was the high wisdom filled
with unspeakable feelings, much too holy, than that
dry signs should satisfy him of your worth.
Thought did not bind the soul, which sunk in the
infinite presentment of its infinity forgot itself, and
now awoke again in time and space in consciousness.
Who would speak to another of all this, though he spoke
with angels' tongues, would feel the poverty of words.[118]

[117] *GSA*, 4(1):17-18.
[118] Hegel, "Eleusis," pp. 61-62.

This is what Hölderlin felt, too, and he considered it to be the tragic fate of the religious person that at the same time love produces the desire to communicate. There is a kernel of truth in the priest Hermocrates' censure of Empedocles: he "whose one desire was to communicate all . . . seeks to utter the unutterable."[119]

When Empedocles attempts to proclaim himself to the agitated Sicilian crowd of his native city, a second factor that leads to the degeneration of living religious consciousness becomes evident. The Enlightenment summed up this factor in the concept of accommodation. He who communicates adapts himself to his audience, and the ideas that are derived from him and his teachings have an effect upon him in return:

> And with their raving adoration
> Consoles himself, goes blind, becomes like them,
> That superstitious rabble with no soul.[120]

He whom the crowd honors as a god becomes a god in his own mind.

Now a last factor must be taken into account. Those familiar with Empedocles surely know that the greatest of his miraculous effects is the transformation of men's hearts. But other effects of a darker and more dangerous sort also proceed from him, and here lies the chief reason for the corruption of his religious character. Empedocles has a special bond with the powers of nature. He uses his intimate harmony with nature in order to dominate her. He uses what the gods granted him, in order to make himself their equal through miracles. Hölderlin casts Diogenes Laertius' accounts of the miracles in a mysterious light. From this favorite of the gods, there proceed incomprehensible effects. Panthea sees something magical in the way this friend of nature healed her with his potion: 295

> People say the plants take notice of him wherever he walks,
> and the waters of the earth rise up where his staff touches the ground,
> and when he looks into the heavens during a thunder storm,
> the clouds part and the bright day shines out.[121]

Empedocles does not contradict Pausanias' remark:

[119] *GSA*, 4(1):98, 97; *HPF*, pp. 281, 279.
[120] *GSA*, 4(1):94; *HPF*, p. 273.
[121] *GSA*, 4(1):3.

> Are you not intimate with the powers of Nature,
> And like no other mortal easily
> Do you not rule them as you please in silence?[122]

But he who strives in this way to master nature will desanctify and mechanize her. Here the significance of an opposition which is essential for distinguishing between the forms of religious consciousness is revealed to Hölderlin's profound religious sense. Religious respect for divine nature, which he found in Greece and which also permeated him, stands in sharp contrast to the Judaeo-Christian faith which is based on God's dominion over nature and man, which in turn leads to a feeling that man dominates nature. Hölderlin hated the desanctification of nature in Christianity, in the Christian Enlightenment, and in Fichte, whose philosophy in this regard went even beyond the Enlightenment. Undoubtedly the following words allude to Fichte:

> Nature herself,
> Unfit, as well you know, to have her way,
> Is now my servant girl; such honour
> As men accord her still, she owes to me.
> And what indeed would Heaven be and Ocean
> And islands and the stars, and all that meets
> The eyes of men, what would it mean or be,
> This dead stringed instrument, did I not lend it
> A resonance, a language and a soul?
> What are the gods, and what their spirit, if I
> Do not proclaim them? Tell me now, who am I?[123]

Hölderlin's conversations with Hegel undoubtedly influenced these and related ideas. Yet they are, in the last analysis, thoughts that stemmed from Hölderlin's own deepest religious consciousness. During his time in Switzerland, Hegel had already drafted an essay discussing a problem formulated by Lessing: How does Christ's religion become the positive religion which objectifies Christ? It was by working on these problems that the historical conception of the world of this great philosopher gradually took shape. He investigates the following question: Where in the religion of Jesus lies the germ of its transformation? He tries to look into the inner state of mind of the disciples, to determine why they could not preserve the living inner essence of the religion of Jesus. He tries to show how

296

[122] *Ibid.*, p. 109; *HPF*, p. 303.
[123] *Ibid.*

human weakness, which cannot maintain the unifying power of love, externalizes what is divine and projects what is unattainable for it onto another world, and how an external belief in revelation and miracles originates from human mediocrity. Hegel also derives the necessity of positive faith from the relationship of an original religious attitude to the world which it seeks to influence and with which it wants to communicate.

This is how Empedocles became a superhuman being (*Übermensch*). He declared himself a god before the people, who had fallen into an ecstacy of religious adoration. The feeling of his superpower (*Überkraft*) became pathological. There lies his guilt. He knows this guilt better than the priest. The latter sees only relationships of domination and subservience everywhere, and thus he hates and blames Empedocles because he divulged to the people the secret of domination that resides in the power of nature. Empedocles, however, perceives that this guilt lies in amassing such dominating power. This power estranged him from the divine forces:

> Ah, lonely, lonely, lonely!
> And nevermore
> I shall find you,
> My gods, and nevermore,
> Nature, return to your life!
> Your outcast! And, oh, it's true, I paid
> No heed to you then, but thought
> Myself superior to you.[124]

He knows too how that came about:

> For sons of Heaven
> When too much joy, good fortune has been theirs,
> A downfall like no other is reserved.[125]

No divine avenger confronts him, but in his separation from nature and her divine powers and in the suffering therefrom, he experiences the burden of his guilt.

All of these developments precede the tragedy. In one of the first scenes, Empedocles enters as a changed man, in a state of intense mental anguish. This is also the way the raging Ajax first appears, as does Oedipus at the beginning of the tragedy *Oedipus at Colonus*.

[124] *GSA*, 4(1):103; *HPF*, p. 291.
[125] *GSA*, 4(1):107; *HPF*, p. 299.

The artistic form of Hölderlin's tragedy is most intimately related to the form of this, the second Oedipus play by Sophocles; but here 297 a peculiarity of Hölderlin's form, which manifested itself in a different way in his novel, reasserts itself. Sophocles had already provided the dramatic portrayal of the protagonist's guilt in the first Oedipus drama. But in Hölderlin's *Empedocles* the entire development of the protagonist is contained in one tragedy: his pious youthful bliss, his impetuous activity, and his guilt are always present; they are conveyed to the spectator in the speeches of the participants; they are components of the total mood which pervades the tragedy. Such an integration of temporal phases in one state of mind always constitutes Hölderlin's characteristic sense of life, even in his short poems.

The plot proceeds, according to the model of the second *Oedipus*, in a steady, concise line that leads to the voluntary death of the hero. Yet the new content of Hölderlin's tragedy does require a modification in the structure of its plot. I am basing my conclusions here on concepts that Hölderlin himself expounded in the notes to his translations of Sophocles: these notes stem from the period of his insanity, but they contain many ideas that undoubtedly had been held by him for a long time and which extend back to when he was still healthy. They are related to that basic concept of the rhythm of life which came to expression in his writing. Thus the development of a tragedy is for him a rhythm, and what we call a *caesura* in verse appears as the climax or *peripeteia* in the tragic plot where all that had been presented to the spectator is recapitulated in his consciousness; thus this climax becomes a moment of rest which separates the second part of the tragedy from the first part. Of the two forms of rhythm in tragedy that Hölderlin distinguishes, one is characterized by the fact that every subsequent part refers back to a beginning, whereby what is first given is given greater and greater depth. This is the form of his *Empedocles*. It divides into two parts: in the first the suffering caused by guilt pierces the protagonist's soul ever more deeply, and in the second the resolve to die brings about an intensification of his being until his sublime transfiguration.

The structure of the first part acquires a form which diverges from that of ancient tragedy due to Hölderlin's idea of fate, which we have already encountered in *Hyperion* and which now completely distinguishes his tragedy from that of the ancients. The inner and outer events which cooperate in the first part are related to one another by his idea of fate. Because the fate which runs its course in the hero's soul leads him through an inner necessity from guilt to misfortune and from there to atonement, everything that works from without has significance only by intensifying this process and accelerating it. There is a law of life according to which, when a man is internally shattered by his own doing, then everything around him contributes as well, takes power over him, and destroys him. Here tragic fate is not an external relation between guilt and a punishment ordained by the divine order; it is, rather, a causal nexus which results from the reciprocal effects of human forces themselves. In losing his old relationship to the powers of nature and life and thereby losing the certainty with which he dominated people and things, Empedocles himself brings about the moment for which his opponents have been waiting. Hölderlin juxtaposes the regal nature of Empedocles, in which the energy of the ideal is effective, to the priest Hermocrates, a man who surveys the workings of life with a human sense of reality and who is Empedocles' match because he is able to understand him and to capture and lead the masses more skillfully than Empedocles. In the manner of a priest, he makes use of temporal forces to attain his goal.

298

In a great scene when the priest destroys the people's regard for the overwhelming Empedocles, Hölderlin put into words what he then silently carried within himself: his revulsion against the institutional church of his time, his hatred of and contempt for all the human baseness that he had experienced, which had made him solitary, persecuted him with silly gossip, and made even the most modest existence impossible for him. It is the same emotion that he expresses in a few poems from this period, and in the indictments of the German nation in his novel.

The ultimate depth of suffering is reached when the banished Empedocles, who has turned toward Etna, is denied shelter in a peasant cottage. Now comes the *peripeteia*. He resolves to die, and from this moment on weakness and pain are displaced by a sublime peace. The second part of the tragedy begins. It shows Empedocles' transfiguration; before our eyes his figure attains the sublimity of a saint who sacrifices himself for his people in voluntary death.

The personal element in this process is especially moving. Empedocles struggles to suppress the memory of his disgrace: being ashamed, he quietly says to his beloved Pausanias: "We will no longer speak of what has happened."[126] It is, of course, Hölderlin himself who succumbs to the burden of his memories: "It must be

[126] *GSA*, 4(1):52.

quietly suppressed! It is to be buried, deep, deeper than any mortal has yet been buried."[127] The old idea of atonement appears, psychologically enriched by the awareness that lost happiness can recur 299 only at the price of death: "Nothing is granted to mortals free of cost."[128] He can no longer remain on this earth, where everything testifies to what happened to him.

Beyond the personal meaning of his voluntary death there is also a mystical meaning. Reconciled with his compatriots, who returned to him contritely, Empedocles proclaims to them the gospel of nature, the new order of a strong, free people; and with a supreme enthusiasm for action and death, he persists in his wish to voluntarily end his life: for "he through whom the spirit spoke must depart."[129] He calls Etna his place of sacrifice. His death is the miracle needed by the blind populace. But it is really a miracle that takes place in the heart, which feels nature's vitality so intensely that it no longer fears a return to her: "O the death-fearing do not love you, they grow old, in contrast to you—o holy All! Living and fervent."

> Divine nature reveals
> Herself as divine often through men, thus
> Those that venture much recognize her,
> But when the mortal, whose heart
> She fills with her delight, proclaims her
> Let her then the vessel break,
> That it not serve for another use,
> That the divine not become the work of man.
> . . . And if tomorrow you
> Find me nowhere, then say: he was not to grow old
> Nor to count his days, he was not to serve
> Anxiety, unseen he went
> Away and no man's hand buried him.
> And no eye knows of his ashes;
> For it was not fitting otherwise for him, before whom
> The divine cast off its veil
> In the death-rejoicing hour of the holy day—
> He whom light and earth loved, whose own spirit
> Was awakened by the spirit, the spirit of the world.
> In whom they are, to whom I dying return.[130]

[127] *Ibid.*, p. 54.
[128] *Ibid.*, p. 55.
[129] *Ibid.*, p. 73. Text altered by Dilthey.
[130] *Ibid.*, pp. 73-74.

A great politico-religious faith pervades Hölderlin's writings in the various periods of his brief life. This faith appears in its most pure and profound form in the fragments of his tragedy. The intense feeling of an approaching new order of things distinguishes him from Goethe and even from Schiller. He perceived that this would have to be based on a great faith which would intimately unite nature, man, and society. As he came from modest circumstances, full of hardships and worries, and repeatedly fell back into this situation, he knew the meaning of deprivation and could sense the approaching transformation of eighteenth-century society better than these great and fortunate figures. The laws and customs of the past—even the names of the old gods—are to be forgotten: "Forget boldly and like a newborn child raise your eyes to divine nature!"[131] He expected vigor, freedom, and beauty from life: "Shame on you that you still want a king."[132] "This is no longer the age of kings."[133]

300

Compared with the way his drama unfolded in his imagination, Hölderlin found his text inadequate. Drafts of new scenes with stronger action and freer rhythm suggest a plan for reworking it. He himself changed as depression spread its shadows over his mind; he strove to give greater and greater profundity to the voluntary death of Empedocles. His ideas about fate, sacrifice, and death became increasingly like those of his great philosophical friend, Hegel. Thus a new plan of the tragedy originated, of which only three continuous scenes survive. They suggest a religious play. The figures stride and speak in solemn sublimity, as if clothed in the flowing robes of archaic Greek statues. Here one no longer perceives anything of a transgression by Empedocles against the divine powers. He bears that guiltless guilt which, according to Hegel, is borne by the great tragic figures of history: Christ and Socrates. It was his excessive love which evoked the reaction of the world against him and led him to his voluntary death: that is the nature of his fate.

> By Hades! amply I deserved it all.
> And it was good for me; poison heals the sick,
> And we are purged of one sin by another.
> For sinned I have, and greatly, from my youth,
> Never have loved men humanly, but served
> Only as fire or water blindly serves them.
> And therefore too not humanly towards me

[131] *Ibid.*, p. 65.
[132] *Ibid.*, p. 63.
[133] *Ibid.*, p. 62.

They acted, but defiled my face and used me
Like you, all-suffering Nature! And it is you
That hold me now, I'm yours, and between you
And me once more the old love rises up.[134]

As a boy, the presence of divine powers turned to song, a "poetry that was prayer";[135] then the disorder and confusion of his native city touched him. In them he recognized "the departure of [his] people's god."[136] His efforts were in vain, only atonement by death remained to him. The tragic dimension of Greek life that Winckelmann and Goethe had not noticed pervades this Empedocles: Hölderlin understood this dimension. In this world of the Greeks, with its constant rise and fall of city-states, there is no concept of progress of the human race: everything is mere change. In the spirit of his actual historical teachings Empedocles says to his disciple Pausanias: "Go, and fear nothing. Everything recurs. And what's to come already is completed."[137] Hence his yearning for eternal nature. She makes it possible to forget what men have done to him, and to unite that which is now separated. She also produces a harmony which even poetry cannot attain. This too he now leaves behind him:

301

O melodies above me! It was all a jest!
And childlike then I dared to imitate you,
A light unfeeling echo rang in me,
Incomprehensibly reverberated—
More gravely now I hear you, voices of the gods.[138]

Finally, a bold symbolism illuminates Empedocles' atonement through death. On Etna, as Empedocles prepares himself for the end, he is confronted by Manes, a representative of Egyptian culture. Plato had also contrasted the timeless knowledge of these mysterious people with the young, spirited urge of the Greeks to know and to act. A dark, bloodless, inert wisdom comes from the Egyptian. He understands the Christ who is to come, the timeless redeemer of everything human, the Christ who—in order to avoid the world's worship—"breaks His own good fortune, grown too great for him."[139] But he does not understand Empedocles, this

[134] *Ibid.*, p. 122; *HPF*, p. 327.
[135] *GSA*, 4(1):137; *HPF*, p. 357.
[136] *Ibid.*
[137] *GSA*, 4(1):133; *HPF*, p. 349.
[138] *GSA*, 4(1):128; *HPF*, p. 339.
[139] *GSA*, 4(1):136; *HPF*, p. 355.

Greek man who sacrifices himself for the city-state and joyfully devotes himself to an all-living nature. A sketch of a few lines points to further development intended by Hölderlin. The superior Manes, the "Omniscient one,"[140] must learn from Empedocles how this fatal energy with which he feels the decline of his country indicates that he can also have a presentiment or premonition of its new life. With this new insight Manes becomes the executor of Empedocles' testament and proclaims to Agrigentines the last words that the departing Empedocles uttered about the restoration of his city.[141]

Without a doubt there is a connection between this sphere of Hölderlin's ideas and Hegel's religious conceptions. Each had reflected for a long time on the Christian mode of religion and the idea of fate in Greek tragedy. They had moved beyond both ideas. The understanding of life that they were seeking could not be found by linking such concepts as law, justice, punishment, and sacrifice. Nor did they find it in those relations in which the tragic fate-idea of Sophocles is played out. Avoiding all transcendent concepts and all restrictive moral interpretations of life, they found its sense, and the nexus of forces that produces the tragedy of great men, by means of a comparative historical approach which opens itself fully to the great objective realities. At the same time that Hegel was exploring this understanding of life, Hölderlin, now separated from his friend, wrote his *Empedocles* and his new hymns, which are filled with the same spirit of a free comparison of religions. The affinity of their ideas extends even further into their content. "The more vital," Hegel says, "the relations are, out of which, once they are sullied, a noble nature must withdraw himself, since he could not remain in them without himself becoming contaminated, the greater is his misfortune. But this misfortune is neither just nor unjust; it only becomes his fate because his disdain of those relations is his own will, his free choice."[142] "Unhappiness may become so great that his fate, this self-destruction, drives him so far toward the renunciation of life that he must withdraw into the void altogether. But, by himself setting an absolutely total fate over against himself, the man has *eo ipso* lifted himself above fate entirely. Life has become untrue to him, not he to life."[143] "Beauty of soul has as its negative attribute the highest freedom, i.e., the potentiality

302

[140] *Ibid.*

[141] See *GSA*, 4(1):168; *HPF*, p. 366.

[142] Hegel, "Der Geist des Christentums und sein Schicksal," in Herman Nohl, *Hegels theologische Jugendschriften* (Frankfurt a.M.: Minerva, 1966), p. 285; trans. by T. M. Knox in *On Christianity* (New York: Harper Torchbooks, 1961), p. 235.

[143] Hegel, "Der Geist," p. 286; Knox, *Christianity*, pp. 235-236.

of renouncing everything. . . ."[144] These connections between Hegel and Hölderlin could be illuminated in far more detail than I can allow myself to do here by bringing Hölderlin's essay "Grund zum Empedokles" to bear on it.[145]

Thus Hölderlin finally attained the idea of a tragedy in which the artist proclaims the nature of divine things. Art had always been for him an instrument for the highest understanding of the world. While staying within the incontestable rules that derive from the means of representation used by tragedy—rules which were first formulated by Lessing—he explored one of the highest possibilities of future artistic development. What he intended was accomplished by Richard Wagner in *Parsifal* with the richer means of emotional expression offered by music. It was in vain that Hölderlin developed a melody of language, which even exceeds Goethe's achievements in this sphere, for the purpose of writing his tragedy. If at some future time *Wallenstein* and *Faust* can be performed in a national theater, then perhaps our poet's highest longing may also be fulfilled by reviving the religious drama of the Greeks. The adverse conditions of his time prevented him from accomplishing this.

> One summer only grant me, you powerful Fates,
> And one more autumn only for mellow song,
> So that more willingly, replete with
> Music's late sweetness, my heart may die then.
>
> The soul in life denied its god-given right
> Down there in Orcus also will find no peace;
> But when what's holy, dear to me, the
> Poem's accomplished, my art perfected,
>
> Then welcome, silence, welcome cold world of shades!
> I'll be content, though here I must leave my lyre
> And songless travel down; for *once* I
> Lived like the gods, and no more is needed.[146]

303

## THE POEMS

Hölderlin's poetic potential found its most complete expression in his poems. In lyric poetry since Goethe, he holds one of the preem-

[144] Hegel, "Der Geist," p. 286; Knox, *Christianity*, p. 236.

[145] See *GSA*, 4(1):149-162. For more by Dilthey on the relationship of Hegel and Hölderlin, see Dilthey, *GS*, IV, 37ff.

[146] "An die Parzen," *GSA*, 1(1):241; *HPF*, p. 33.

inent places, alongside Novalis, Uhland, and Mörike. It is in this domain of lyric poetry that his full significance first becomes evident, for in music and in lyric poetry, which are related, the creations of the German-speaking nations surpass those of any other people.

Lyric poets have the gift of perceiving, capturing, and raising to consciousness the quiet course of inner states which in others is disturbed by the bustle of external purposes and drowned out by the noise of everyday life. By reviving for us the nexus of our inner life—which once existed in us, too, but not so prominently and self-consciously, nor with such individuality and in such an undisturbed course—their art becomes an instrument for a better understanding of that which lies most deeply in us and for extending our horizon beyond our own emotional experiences. This genius of the heart reveals to each of us his own inner world, and he also gives us access to a world which is foreign and yet nevertheless akin to our own. Through the fullness of these poetic individuals we grasp the richness of human inwardness. Accordingly we understand a lyric poet and recognize his significance when we grasp what is new in his view of human inwardness and in his capacity to express it artistically.

Here again the key to understanding poetry is to be found in lived experience. What we have already encountered in Hölderlin's life and in the two great works in which he represents it can now be integrated by considering his lyric poetry, in which his immortal achievements are found. In our study of his life we found those lived experiences to which his poems relate, and the various periods in the development of his attitude to life which also determined the development of his poetic form. Our study of his novel and tragedy allowed us to grasp his attitude toward life, and the spectrum of moods contained in it, by means of the symbols he established for them. Thus, our account up to this point has also been aimed at making comprehensible the content of Hölderlin's poems; only now can we grasp the relationship between this content and the inner 304 and outer forms of lyric poetry.

I will begin with Goethe, for only thus can what is new in later poets be evaluated correctly. Goethe confronts the world with an incomparable capacity for emotional self-awareness and for succeeding in every situation in life. Since he lives in the moment with all his energy, his poems also derive from lived experience. Everything that could possibly impress a person of an infinitely sensitive nature, one who experiences the full emotional content of things in an intense and lively manner, has been lived through by Goethe and incorporated into his poems in a pure, decisive, and universally valid mode. In so exhausting the emotional content of every situation, the entire relationship of a typical man to the world seems to be mirrored in the immeasurable wealth of his lyric poetry. His poems give us inexhaustible capacity to fully submit to every affective value of the world, as he himself had, without becoming overwhelmed by any. For even in his saddest poems we feel that he will rise above every sorrow, that the sun will rise again, that he will go to meet new situations with the same resolve.

Hölderlin always lived in the context of his whole existence. His present feeling was constantly being influenced by what he had suffered and by what might still happen. He held all of that together in himself. It is as if the moment, in which Goethe lived with such power, had no reality for Hölderlin. Even as a boy he looked on wistfully as other boys would play, because he was unable to submit wholly to the moment. And whether this be his temperament or the effect of his fate, he was never able to live fully in reality with simple, strong feelings. His yearning for the great past of the Greeks destroyed his feeling for the present. His ideals of fatherland, heroism, and freedom only brought him pain and vague hopes that receded more and more into an unattainable distance. Even his love granted him a joyful sense of the present only by virtue of his pure, nonsensual capacity to be content with the mere awareness of being loved. Is there any other poet whose life is woven from such delicate material, as if from moonbeams? And his poetry was like his life! In such a type, who constantly lives in the totality of his inner life, the past has an efficacy just like the present. The existence of the hermit Hyperion is completely saturated by the spirits of what has been. Empedocles feels the pressure of the past so strongly that he can only hope for liberation from it through death. The same cohesive and composite feeling for life is found in Hölderlin's poems. 305 There is nothing playful, light, or winsome in them.

The nexus of his personal existence becomes the nexus of life itself for Hölderlin the philosophical poet. His poems accompany what is happening on the stage of life like the chorus in a tragedy by Sophocles. In his first great hymns, Hölderlin follows the example of Schiller's philosophical poems, where a mood arises from the world of ideas, independently of any particular lived experience. But in his later hymns he goes to a more genuine lyrical form. A mood which evokes an ideal world in him is then developed in accordance with a nexus of feelings: the most beautiful of these poems present us with a sequence of visionary images which is determined by the development of feeling. But the most important creations of his lyric poetry are those in which a universal trait of life discloses itself to him in a lived experience. He works unceasingly to produce an ever more perfect expression for such traits—sometimes by recasting the same poem, sometimes by means of several poems; in this respect he can be compared to Böcklin.[147] Consider the poem "Evening Fantasy," which leads the heart back into itself and lets the strife of the day fade away in peace:

At peace the ploughman sits in the shade outside
His cottage; smoke curls up from his modest hearth.
A traveller hears the bell for vespers
Welcome him to a quiet village.

Now too the boatmen make for the harbour pool,
In distant towns the market's gay noise and throng
Subside; a glittering meal awaits the
Friends in the garden's most hidden arbour.

But where shall I go? Does not a mortal live
By work and wages? Balancing toil with rest
All makes him glad. Must I alone then
Find no relief from the thorn that goads me?

A springtime buds high up in the evening sky,
There countless roses bloom, and the golden world
Seems calm, fulfilled; O there now take me,
Crimson-edged clouds, and up there at last let

My love and sorrow melt into light and air!—
As if that foolish plea had dispersed it, though,
The spell breaks; darkness falls, and lonely
Under the heavens I stand as always.—

Now you come, gentle sleep! For the heart demands
Too much; but youth at last, you the dreamy, wild,
Unquiet, will burn out, and leave me
All my late years for serene contentment.[148]

Sometimes Hölderlin admits a contrast into his state of mind, such as the longing for the bygone Greek world, for the radiant color 306

[147] Arnold Böcklin (1827-1901). Swiss painter known especially for the imaginative power of his works, generally southern landscapes containing figures from myth and fable, manifesting their powers in nature.

[148] *GSA*, 1(1):301; *HPF*, p. 91.

of southern nature, and opposes it to the peaceful happiness of the circumscribed present, the quiet valleys where the Neckar and Rhine flow between meadow and forest, then again a pure, faithful intuition of the omnipresent forces of nature whose violent interactions encompass our own existence. While Goethe's lyric poetry always represents nature in her relation to the poet himself, in Hölderlin nature confronts us as the all-living whole on whose eternal power, as exhibited in stars, forces, and gods, man is dependent. This is one of the most effective aspects of Hölderlin's new poetry as compared with the poems Goethe wrote before he became old.

All these life-relations are joined together in a peculiar mood. An idealistic person extremely receptive to all the values of existence finds himself in that conflict of ideals with the world that Schiller had expressed so movingly; he is led to his own metaphysical intuition which recognizes the transitory as the nature of time itself, the impossibility of establishing beauty, heroism, and power over against the resistance of the inert masses, and the loneliness that a more highly developed individual must suffer. With this attitude toward life, Hölderlin is akin to the young Hegel and Schopenhauer, and his lyrical poetry brings to expression a new feeling about the world. And this is what makes him so extremely attractive to us. To follow the course of his life through his poems, from the time of ideals, from the youthful transfiguration of existence on to this state of mind, is to evoke unbounded pity. How moving is his quiet composure over against the world, his soft and weary tone that works more truthfully than all Schopenhauer's invectives against life, the pure simplicity of his words. In this composed, simple, soft tone, he was like Sophocles and had learned from him. These poems touch our very soul.

Underlying every poem—as well as every instrumental musical composition—there is a psychic process that has been lived through, which relates back to the inner emotional life of the individual. Whether such a sequence of inner states is evoked by a particular lived experience that is determined from without, or by moods that spring up from within, independently of the external world, or even by a body of historical or philosophical ideas, this course of feeling 307 always constitutes the point of departure for the poem and the content which comes to expression within it.

The genius of a lyric poet consists first of all in the peculiarity that he lives through this inner process, purely and fully, according to its inherent lawful development. He submits to it fully and is oblivious to everything that could disturb its necessary course from without. The lyrical genius brings to expression the teleological principle implicit in such a process. Hölderlin was a genuine lyrical genius in this sense. His quiescent inwardness, his distance from the affairs of the world, the contemplative depth of his feeling, all worked to make him receptive to the softly flowing rhythms of the life of our feelings. Thus he saw how an initial state of feeling unfolds in its parts and ultimately returns to itself, and no longer with its initial indeterminateness. By recollecting the process of its unfolding, the feelings can be integrated into a harmony in which the individual parts resonate. He also makes visible how a feeling swells and then slowly wanes as the course of our psychic life shifts; how a conflict of contrasting feelings is resolved, or how the greatest intensification of something all too painful is followed by tranquility.

This succession of feelings and moods, which is the basis of a poem, is not directly mirrored by the creative process; only single tones may resound in the latter. The peculiar talent of the lyric poet consists in preserving the former process, objectifying it for himself, and then forming an expression for it. There are poets, such as Goethe, for whom the progression from lived experience to poetic representation often takes place quickly. Hölderlin, however, worked slowly on his poetic representation. Just as the composer works for an extended period to create a sweeping musical expression for an initial lived experience, during which time new sequences of feelings continually come to his assistance, Hölderlin appears to have worked a long time to articulate the rhythm of the sequence of feelings in its essential features, to link its parts firmly to one another, and to give it expression in the inner flow of language.

The dominant feature of Hölderlin's lyrical creations is that he raises the sequence of our feelings to a nexus in which all the essential parts are made conscious, even those that occurred fleetingly and went unnoticed. It is a special charm of folk songs that the obscure, only half-noticed relations which the stronger feelings have in common—those points in the development of feelings where they continue to flow underground, as it were—do not find expression in words. Goethe made the most felicitous use of these. Hölderlin stylizes the inner process on which the poem is based. He raises it to a conscious nexus. At first, in his strophic, rhymed poems, in which each verse tends to produce its separate effect, he locates this nexus in the syntactical connection of all the parts that unites the verses into one flow. Later this no longer satisfies him; he lib-

308

erates himself from the strophe by means of the hexameter and the elegiac meter, and uses them to reproduce the flow of the feelings. From the strophic lyric poetry of the Greeks and Romans he adopts meters that allow him to express, in the gentle, regular play of stressed and unstressed syllables, the nexus that unites all parts of his poems. And from there he is ultimately driven further to let the flow of feeling complete its development, unhindered, in free rhythms without division into strophes. Only in his last hymns does the unity of this nexus weaken.

Such stylization of the feeling process poses a danger which Hölderlin did not always escape. No matter how the psychic process on which a poem is based may be elaborated and expanded imaginatively through related processes, the poem may ultimately contain only as much as could be given in a real process. The stylization may accentuate something unnoticed, but it may not overstep the indicated bounds. The view of nature contained in a poem seems especially implausible if its content transcends what can be grasped in *one* inner process. Such a poetic view is like a painting that shows more than can be seen at the most opportune moment and from the best perspective. Goethe, who in the beginning always started from a single lived experience and remained faithful to it—and this not only in his songs but also in the dithyrambs of his youth—gives the best example of this lyrical realism. On the other hand, Hölderlin, in dithyrambs such as "The Archipelago," lost sight of the standard for the aspects of moods and perceptions that can be joined together in a psychic process, even if this process originates in the world of ideas. As a consequence, we are no longer able to re-experience the comprehensive whole. In his three beautiful elegies—"Menon's Lament for Diotima," "Fall Festival," "Homecoming"—he sensitively analyzed the comprehensive whole into single moments by means of external signs. He produced the delicate family portrait "Emilie vor ihrem Brauttag" (Emilie before Her Wedding) with greater ease and speed, and precisely because of that it is closer
309 to nature than any other of his longer poems. Mörike's poetic style is most closely related to Hölderlin's in this respect.

Musicality is a further feature of the inner form of Hölderlin's poems. By that I mean not only his treatment of language or of verse, but also the particular form of the inner processes and their structure. I recognize the same form again in the lyric poetry of the Romantics—in Novalis and Tieck, who are Hölderlin's contemporaries, and later in Eichendorff. This whole lyrical movement is contemporaneous with the development of German music. The latter presents a sequence of feelings disengaged from individual lived experience and from the objective references contained in that experience, and there is a similar tendency in these lyric poets. Songs are now written in which the relations to a definite concrete lived experience recede far more than is usual for Goethe. Feelings diffuse into moods which arise from within, without beginning, without end. Or else we find, as in Hölderlin, a complex of feelings and ideas, which hardly needs an occasion to come into being.

The lyric poetry of Hagedorn[149] and Gleim[150] was contemporaneous with the German *Singspiel*[151] and was closely related to the songs of the time which were sung on the various special occasions in the life of the middle class. The lyric poetry of this time is similar to this kind of song and to *Singspiel* in the geometrical precision of its form, its circumscribed verse, its rendering of typical states of feeling. Just as these works are classified into such genres as love songs, drinking songs, religious songs, so, too, the feelings themselves expressed by them are also neatly separated into the domains of the mental economy, so that none is disturbed by the others; the poems are divided into regular verses, each of which comprises a whole in itself. This form of lyric poetry is no longer with us today. Klopstock put an end to it. His genius for the musical aspects of lyric poetry made the structure of a lived experience visible in the form of the poem. That led him at first to ancient meters and to the free forms of his religious hymns. He found the most powerful lyrical expression appropriate for the great themes that he chose. But this was counterbalanced by the barrenness of his thought, his religious pomposity, his dogmatic narrowness, his inability to develop himself and move on. Not until great personalities achieved a maximum freedom of movement in their inner selves did our lyric poetry reach its zenith; it exhibits a beauty and richness that is without equal in modern literature. The greatest of this lyric poetry—the poems of Goethe up to the time when Hölderlin perfected his style and when Tieck and Novalis came on the scene—belongs 310 to the same epoch that saw the rapid rise of our secular music through Mozart's operas. They are simultaneous manifestations of

[149] Friedrich von Hagedorn (1708-54) introduced a new lightness and grace into German poetry. His best-known works are *Versuch in Fabeln und Erzählungen* (1738) and *Oden und Lieder* (3 vols., 1742-52).

[150] Johann Wilhelm Ludwig Gleim (1719-1803). Leading member of the group of Anacreontic poets. Rejecting both Baroque and Enlightenment attitudes, he wrote in a decorative, unpretentious, unidealized manner.

[151] A *Singspiel* is a popular play punctuated with songs.

the same liberation of our secular emotional life, and countless interconnections relate these two modes of expression. The greatest creations of this epoch, Mozart's operas, link musical expression to particular situations and words. Both of the latter provide a determinacy to musical expression which establishes a peculiar affinity among certain determinate, clear form structures in music and in lyric poetry. Then the development of instrumental music in Haydn's last, greatest period, as well as in Beethoven, produces a nonverbal presentation of the nexus of feeling which moves through all parts of the artwork in *one* continuous flow. Hölderlin, Tieck, and Novalis originate a new lyric poetry which expresses the exuberance of feeling, the nonobjective power of mood which arises from the inner recesses of the mind itself, the infinite melody of a psychic movement which seems to emanate from indiscernible distances only to disappear in them again.

All the features we have considered condition the external form of Hölderlin's poems.

Dubos and Lessing already recognized that although words and their combinations provide the means to designate every possible subject matter, the artistic effect of poetry on feeling and imagination requires a peculiar art of choosing words and combining them. Hamann and Herder take these ideas further. Hence, the first task in the analysis of a poet's form is to grasp the means by which he makes words effective. Hölderlin's lyrical art produces its effect first of all by giving each individual expression a stronger intrinsic value through his unique economy with words. Whereas in reading we generally press forward, using the individual word only as a sign for its meaning in the context of the whole verbal structure, here the economy of expression induces us to dwell on the words. Feeling comes forth naked, as it were, from behind its simple designation—in this respect, as well, Mörike's lyric poetry is related to Hölderlin's and is influenced by it. I should like to indicate another artistic means that Hölderlin utilized with the greatest effectiveness. The psyche's attitudes, in whose interactions inwardness consists, are expressed in three syntactical forms: the interrogative, the exclamatory, and the imperative, in which the speaker defines himself or others. The use of these syntactical forms in a poem 311 conveys inner movement more powerfully and directly than the direct use of words such as grief, joy, longing, and desire can. Hölderlin makes greater use of these syntactical forms than almost any other poet, in *Empedocles* as well as in the poems. And he returns them to the function they originally had in the inwardness of the lyrical process by stripping them of everything rhetorical, by displaying clearly and simply the psychic process expressed in these forms—so simply that he approaches the matter-of-factness of prose. And, following the example of the Greeks, he utilizes the freedom of word order permitted by the syntactical structure of the German language to express the inner progression of perceptions and psychic processes in the sequence of words.

The fullness and melodious flow of Hölderlin's verses is unsurpassed by any other writer. However, in terms of strong, natural rhythmic movement and variety of rhythm, he falls far short of Goethe. Indeed, Hölderlin's metrical art results in a certain type of uniformity. But he has the most sensitive feel for our language; in accordance with its spirit, he knows how to bring the values of the words as determined by their meaning context into harmony with the use of stressed and unstressed syllables. In this respect, he compares especially favorably to Klopstock. He is generally able to get his stress to fall on verbal and nominal roots, or in any case on syllables whose emphasis is justified by the meaning in a particular context. Prepositions, prefixes, and suffixes are on the whole unstressed syllables. Thus a natural harmony between normal speech—where stresses are based on meaning—and Hölderlin's verse-form comes about. The principles of connectedness, symmetry, and musical effect are prominently displayed throughout his metrical forms. And they determine the further development of his poetry.

We left the development of Hölderlin's lyric poetry at the point where he transferred the form of his hymns to his personal poems. In the magnificent songs, "Der Gott der Jugend" (The God of Youth) and "An die Natur" (To Nature), the syntactical means of bringing the nexus of feeling to external expression are utilized in a consummate manner. But the effect which results from this is further intensified by a symmetrical ordering which even Schiller had never applied so perfectly.

Hölderlin's poetic principles and his corresponding preoccupation with Greek and Roman poetry subsequently led him to use ancient metrical forms. He knows how to wring unique effects from the hexameter and the elegiac meters. The symmetrical distribution of trochees and dactyls produces a movement in his hexameters by which feeling is carried along as if by waves. By frequently weakening the first stressed syllable of the pentameter, he creates the impression of a crescendo which gives a peculiar charm to his use of the elegiac meter. "Menon's Lament" illustrates this especially

312

beautifully. Assonances serve to enhance the euphony and to strengthen and combine homophonic stressed syllables. Similarly, alliteration has a cohesive effect. Thus Hölderlin's mode of metrical expression is permeated by particularly powerful tendencies which propel it toward a melodious, unhampered flow from verse to verse and toward establishing relations between the parts of the poem. In this way everything serves to give a metrical expression to the course, nexus, and structure of a psychic process. Although the hexameter and the elegiac meter are especially suitable for expressing such a nexus, Hölderlin also knew how to adapt, by the means indicated, some forms of Greek and Roman strophic poetry to produce the same effect. In this respect he went back to Horace; it seems doubtful that he used the remains of Greek lyric poetry as well. No other poet can emulate his application of these verse forms to the German language and to the conditions of modern psychic life. He uses mainly the Alcaic strophe, which Horace also preferred; but with his subtle feeling for rhythms he replaced the late Greek and modified Latin forms with the original Greek form. After the Alcaic strophe, he most frequently employs what has been called the third Asclepiadean strophe, which he also found in Horace, and here he made possible the application of this ancient meter to our language by almost always replacing the spondee at the beginning of each verse by feet which can hardly be considered as anything other than trochees. He once uses the Sapphic strophe as well in the song "Sung beneath the Alps." Here we find a peculiar modification which is based on a transformation provided by Klopstock. He moves the dactyl, which normally would be the third foot in the first three lines of the strophe: in the first line he makes it the first foot; in the second, the second foot; and in the third, the fourth foot.

And once more, the basic tendency of his lyric poetry, which is to express the nexus, flow, and inner rhythm of a particular psychic process, leads Hölderlin to a new form. It appears where he seeks 313 a metrical expression for the strong, advancing movements of the psyche as they are evoked by grand moods and themes. Here his work bears a relationship to Goethe's dithyrambs. Iambs and anapests, trochees and dactyls, that is, rising and falling beats, are constantly alternated and freely mixed together to conform to the movement of the psyche. Here we no longer find a regular strophe formation, but only an articulation into parts that are almost always unequal. Very often the lyric measures of Horace, with which the poet was so familiar, resound. At the very time that he was advancing to this dithyramb and its free forms, his spirit began to succumb to the blows of fate, and hence the development of his lyric art ended prematurely.

## THE END

. . . where are you, light?
Indeed the heart's awake, but, wrathful,
Always astonishing Night constricts me.

Now here I sit alone in silence
Hour after hour, and my mind devises

Shapes for itself—since poison divides us now—
Made up of love's new earth and the clouds of love;
And far I strain my hearing lest a
Kindly deliverer perhaps is coming.[152]

When Hölderlin set out to take up another lowly position far away, his state of health was already extremely precarious. He secretly bore such a burden of memories within himself—pains of every sort, deprivation, humiliation to the point of degradation—that he felt excluded from mankind by his fate. He was engulfed by the total solitude of those who can no longer express themselves. With a sorrowful humility peculiar to him, he begs his family and friends to forgive his silence on several occasions. He was always too bashful to allow his highly devoted mother to see completely what he had to experience and how he felt it. "I must again take up a servile existence,"[153] he writes to her just before his departure for southern France, and then he immediately adds an empty and pitiful solace for himself as well as for her: ". . . and to educate children is a particularly fortunate activity now because it is so innocent."[154] And to his brother he writes, "O my Karl, forgive me so that we can be reconciled."[155]

Once again it was around Christmas that he left home to begin anew the life of a family tutor, this time for the Hamburg Consul in Bordeaux. "Fear nothing and tolerate much"[156]—this is how he 314

[152] "Chiron," *GSA*, 2(1):56; *HPF*, p. 189.
[153] Hölderlin to his family, 1801, *GSA*, 6(1):424.
[154] *Ibid.*
[155] Hölderlin to his brother, 4 December 1801, *GSA*, 6(1):425.
[156] Hölderlin to his mother, 28 January 1802, *GSA*, 6(1):430.

expresses his mood during the journey to France. He walked over the "dreaded snowbound passes of Auvergne."[157] One senses the dreams and horrors of a neurotic man in his account: "In storm and wilderness, in the ice-cold night with loaded pistols beside me in the crude, hard bed—then I prayed what was the best prayer of my life up to now and which I will never forget."[158] At the end of January 1802 he arrived in Bordeaux. A last, curious letter from there shows how he had to keep every excitement from his mind. When his grandmother died he wrote to his mother: "Don't misunderstand me, if I speak concerning the loss more in terms of the necessary composure than of the sorrow that the love in our hearts feels. I must preserve and maintain my spirit which has been tried for so long."[159] In this state of mind he had to face the fact that once again, as before in Switzerland, he did not succeed in meeting the requirements of his modest position. He is reported to have felt demands that he could not fulfill or that he was too proud to fulfill. Without a doubt his self-esteem now suffered a wound that he could no longer overcome. The depressed and exhausted Hölderlin was overpowered by the feeling that he was now a lost man. In June he began the journey back, probably again on foot. It is possible that he suffered a heatstroke in the burning sun of southern France: "The violent element, the fire of heaven, and the silence of men, their life in nature and their narrowness and complacency, have constantly oppressed me—and, as one says of heroes, I can certainly say that Apollo has struck me."[160] Thus he finally turned insane and in this state he returned to his family.

Hölderlin was to live for over forty years in this state of mental illness. After the first acute phases of the illness had abated, one could hope for improvement. He was at that time still in a position to occupy himself intellectually. He translated Sophocles' *Oedipus Rex* and *Antigone*, and the translations appeared in 1804. His rhythmic feeling is undiminished, his language resounds, and he is able to wrest from the language the heart-rending sounds of pain. But he has lost his mastery of Greek, he confuses familiar words with others that sound alike, he loses patience, and translates heedlessly. In the notes, we see his poetics from better times turned into a heap of ruins. One is tempted to probe more deeply into it, but then, having become wearied and disappointed, one just resists find-

[157] *Ibid.*, p. 429.
[158] *Ibid.*, pp. 429-430.
[159] Hölderlin to his mother, Good Friday, 1802, *ibid.*, pp. 430-431.
[160] Hölderlin to Casimir Ulrich Böhlendorff (letter 240), *ibid.*, p. 432.

ing hidden profundities in nonsense. His inability to preserve logical connections is apparent. 315

The same holds for Hölderlin's personal relations. At times, he appeared to his friends as he had in his best days. Then the thread of his thinking would suddenly break again. Such states of mental exhaustion alternated with states of exaltation: he sometimes displayed an overwrought self-esteem and abrupt violent outbreaks, but only to the extent that he could again be calmed. The most loyal of his friends, Sinclair, was still able to obtain a modest position for him as librarian with the Landgrave of Hessen. His salary was, to be sure, paid by the friend himself. What irony that at that time the suspicion was being uttered that the unfortunate Hölderlin only affected insanity from time to time. Hopes for a recovery lasted but a few years. In the summer of 1806 it appeared inadvisable, both to him and to others, for him to be allowed out on the streets of Homburg. Neither then nor later did he suffer from compulsive ideas. His path of suffering was now diverted into a sacred madness, which we should not desecrate by means of reports of curious travelers or indiscrete well-intending persons—especially because no experts on mental illness have written about him. He liked to play and sing at the piano; until the very end he remained receptive to the sounds and rhythms which, it seems, he came into the world to hear. He lived in Tübingen, where he found a quiet retreat in the garden house of the poet Waiblinger.[161] As his thoughts wandered, he looked out upon the city which he had once entered with such proud hopes, and at the Neckar where his poetic dreams had begun—his noble countenance now lifeless, his tall, imposing figure now slightly stooped.

He died in the evening of June 7, 1843. Although in very poor health, he still sat at his open window for many hours to look into the beautiful moonlit night, as he loved to do. Quietly and without drawing any attention, the world's most poor and tired guest slipped away, and it took little notice of his passing.

Our interest, however, remains with the powerful poems that were created just when he approached not only his greatest freedom of lyrical movement, but also the point of madness—he himself gave the poems the mysterious name "Nachtgesänge" (Nightsongs). When the acquired psychic nexus, bound to the functions of the

[161] Wilhelm Waiblinger (1804-30), a Swabian poet. The main character of his novel *Phaeton* (1823) was a sculptor, whose life was modeled in part on Hölderlin's life. In 1827 Waiblinger wrote an account of "Hölderlin's Life, Work, and Madness."

brain, begins to fail, then the formation of individual images obtains a peculiar independence and energy. Ideas of potential effects move beyond the framework of a well-structured, unified artistic form. Unregulated in any way, feeling and imagination follow their own 316 eccentric course. Who can avoid thinking of Robert Schumann or Nietzsche here? Hölderlin writes to a friend, using words that are reminiscent of the proud words of Heinrich von Kleist: "I think that we will no longer need to comment on the poets up to our time, for poetry as such will assume a different character; we cannot go any further with them in their direction, because we are now beginning once again, like the Greeks, to sing as a nation—naturally and even with true originality."[162]

What is so fateful about this last epoch of Hölderlin is that his whole poetic development pressed toward a complete liberation of the inner rhythm of feeling from fixed metric forms, but this last step was only taken by him at the edge of madness. These poems establish a kind of intermediary between Goethe's rhapsodies, such as "Prometheus" and "Wanderers Sturmlied," and the dithyrambs of some of our modern poets. One more time the restlessly advancing Hölderlin sought to improve the great form of the hymn that he had taken over from Schiller. Once more a cycle originates which encompasses the greatest human themes. But it is not concerned with great universal ideals that stand gleaming before us in the bright light of the idealism of freedom. Turned in upon himself, the poet broods upon fate. Once again he represents the fate of the hero in the poem "The Rhine." The gods need heroes:

> . . . For since
> The most Blessed in themselves feel nothing
> Another, if to say such a thing is
> Permitted, must, I suppose,
> Vicariously feel in the name of the gods,
> And him they need.[163]

As darkness descended upon him, the heroes and gods began to take on monstrous dimensions and fantastic forms. It is only through heroes and poets that the divine attains a feeling of itself—but Hölderlin knows what price these heroes pay. He remembers those who lived heroically—Rousseau, Socrates. His vision encompasses the sons of divinity of all lands and religions. Christ appears

[162] *GSA*, 6(1):433.
[163] "Der Rhein," *GSA*, 2(1):145; *HPF*, p. 415.

as the brother of Dionysus and Hercules. Like Michelangelo, Hölderlin sees Christ as a divinely begotten hero. He now grasps the peculiarities of nature more sharply, since his experience of southern France had disclosed the contrasts of her forms. And his language grows in its figurative power to the point of oddness and eccentricity. It contains a unique mixture of pathological qualities and the intimations of a new style of a lyrical genius. A few lines have survived which were certainly fragments of a greater whole, something hastily jotted down with some errors; however, they allow us to see the direction of Hölderlin's new lyrical language.

317

With yellow pears the land
And full of wild roses
Hangs down into the lake,
You lovely swans,
And drunk with kisses
You dip your heads
Into the hallowed, the sober water.

But oh, where shall I find
When winter comes, the flowers, and where
The sunshine
And shade of the earth?
The walls loom
Speechless and cold, in the wind
Weathercocks clatter.[164]

[164] "Hälfte des Lebens," *GSA*, 2(1):117; *HPF*, p. 371.

# GLOSSARY

## German Expressions

*Antrieb*: impulse
*Aufbau*: formation, formative system
*Bedeutsamkeit*: significance
*Bedeutung*: meaning
*Besinnung*: reflection
*Besonnenheit*: pensiveness
*bestimmt-unbestimmt*: determinate-indeterminate
*Bewußtseinsstellung*: attitude
*Bewußtseinstatsachen*: facts of consciousness
*Bildungsvorgang*: formative process
*Einbildungskraft*: imagination
*Einfühlung*: empathy
*Epoche*: epoch
*Erfahrung*: experience
*erklärend*: explanative
*Erlebnis*: lived experience
*Erlebnisausdruck*: expression of lived experience
*Erlebnisphantasie*: experiential imagination
*erworbener seelischer Zusammenhang*: acquired psychic nexus
*Fortgezogenwerden*: being-pulled-along
*für-mich-da-sein*: being-there-for-me
*Geisteswissenschaften*: human sciences (including humanities and the social sciences)
*geistige Tatsachen*: facts of the human world
*geistige Welt*: human world
*Geschichtlichkeit*: historicity
*gliedern*: articulate
*Herausbildung*: articulation
*Innewerden*: reflexive awareness (to be distinguished from reflection)
*Kultursysteme*: cultural systems
*Lebensäußerung*: expression of life
*Lebensbezüge*: life-relations
*Lebenseinheit*: psychophysical life-unit
*Lebenserfahrung*: life-experience
*Lebensführung*: conduct of life
*Lebensgefühl*: feeling of life

*Lebensstimmungen*: moods of life
*Lebenstatsachen*: realities of life
*Lebenswürdigung*: evaluation of life
*Lebenszusammenhang*: nexus of life
*Lebenszustände*: states of life
*Nachbildung*: re-creation, reproduction
*Nacherleben*: re-experiencing
*Nachfühlen*: recapturing feeling, re-experiencing of feeling
*schweigendes Denken*: prediscursive thought
*Seelenleben*: psychic life
*Selbigkeit*: selfsameness
*Selbstbesinnung*: (historical) self-reflection
*Sinn*: sense
*Sprachphantasie*: linguistic imagination
*Strukturzusammenhang*: structural system
*Tatsachen des Lebens*: realities of life
*Tatsachen des Bewußtseins*: facts of consciousness
*Umbildung*: transformation
*unauflösbar*: irreducible
*unergründlich*: unfathomable
*Verhalten*, *Verhaltungsweise*: attitude
*Vorstellung*: representation
*Wechselwirkung*: reciprocal action, interaction
*Weltanschauung*: world-view
*Weltbild*: world-picture
*Weltzusammenhang*: structure of the world, world-nexus
*Wirken*: doing, efficacy
*Zeitgeist*: spirit of an age
*Zusammenhang*: nexus
*Zusammenhang des Seelenlebens*: psychic nexus
*Zweckbeziehung*: purposive relation
*Zweckganzes*: purposive whole
*Zweckmässigkeit*: purposiveness
*Zweckzusammenhang*: purposive system

## English Expressions

acquired psychic nexus: *erworbener seelischer Zusammenhang*
articulate: *gliedern*
articulation: *Herausbildung*
attitude: *Bewußtseinsstellung, Verhalten, Verhaltungsweise*
being-pulled-along: *Fortgezogenwerden*
being-there-for-me: *für-mich-da-sein*
conduct of life: *Lebensführung*
cultural systems: *Kultursysteme*

determinate-indeterminate: *bestimmt-unbestimmt*
doing, efficacy: *Wirken*
empathy: *Einfühlung*
epoch: *Epoche*
evaluation of life: *Lebenswürdigung*
experience: *Erfahrung*
experiential imagination: *Erlebnisphantasie*
explanative: *erklärend*
expression of life: *Lebensäußerung*
expression of lived experience: *Erlebnisausdruck*
facts of consciousness: *Bewußtseinstatsachen, Tatsachen des Bewußtseins*
facts of the human world: *geistige Tatsachen*
feeling of life: *Lebensgefühl*
formation, formative system: *Aufbau*
formative process: *Bildungsvorgang*
historicity: *Geschichtlichkeit*
human sciences: *Geisteswissenschaften*
human world: *geistige Welt*
imagination: *Einbildungskraft*
impulse: *Antrieb*
interaction: *Wechselwirkung*
irreducible: *unauflösbar*
lived experience: *Erlebnis*
life-experience: *Lebenserfahrung*
life-relations: *Lebensbezüge*
linguistic imagination: *Sprachphantasie*
meaning: *Bedeutung*
moods of life: *Lebensstimmungen*
nexus: *Zusammenhang*
nexus of life: *Lebenszusammenhang*
pensiveness: *Besonnenheit*
prediscursive thought: *schweigendes Denken*
psychic life: *Seelenleben*
psychic nexus: *Zusammenhang des Seelenlebens*
psychophysical life-unit: *Lebenseinheit*
purposiveness: *Zweckmässigkeit*
purposive relation: *Zweckbeziehung*
purposive system: *Zweckzusammenhang*
purposive whole: *Zweckganzes*
realities of life: *Lebenstatsachen, Tatsachen des Lebens*
recapturing feeling: *Nachfühlen*
reciprocal action: *Wechselwirkung*
re-creation: *Nachbildung*
re-experiencing: *Nacherleben*

re-experiencing of feeling: *Nachfühlen*
reflection: *Besinnung*
reflexive awareness (to be distinguished from reflection):
*Innewerden*
representation: *Vorstellung*
reproduction: *Nachbildung*
self-reflection: *Selbstbesinnung*
selfsameness: *Selbigkeit*
sense: *Sinn*
significance: *Bedeutsamkeit*
spirit of an age: *Zeitgeist*
states of life: *Lebenszustände*
structure of the world: *Weltzusammenhang*
structural system: *Strukturzusammenhang*
transformation: *Umbildung*
unfathomable: *unergründlich*
world-nexus: *Weltzusammenhang*
world-picture: *Weltbild*
world-view: *Weltanschauung*

# INDEX

Abelard, Peter, 266-267
acquired psychic nexus, 8, 10, 71-72, 103, 106, 115, 122, 199, 213; as a basis for aesthetic norms, 106, 130; of the critic, 131; formation and function of, 97-98; and plausibility of characters, 153; of the poet, 8, 10, 96, 104-106, 381-382; and the spirit of the age, 162-163; as a standard for art, 130
action, 57, 149, 151; dramatic, 141; and feelings, 153; in a poetic work, 147
Addison, Joseph, 189
Aeschylus, 65, 166, 171, 257
aesthetic impression, 47, 120, 121, 197, 198-199, 227; in eighteenth-century aesthetics, 190-191, 192-193; universal validity of, 194
aesthetics: experimental, 12, 188-200, 205; historical, 13-14, 201-205; rationalist, 11-12, 181-187
Alarcón, Juan Ruiz de, 151
Alembert, Jean Le Rond d', 191
Alexander, 181
Alfieri, Count Vittorio, 60, 67, 111
Ariosto, Ludovico, 169, 268
Aristotle, 11, 29, 39, 40, 42, 56, 67, 140; on form and technique, 37-42
Arnim, Achim von, 173
Arnold, Gottfried, 286
Aubignac, François Hédelin, abbé d', 181

Bach, Johann Sebastian, 206, 285
Bacon, Francis, 43
Balzac, Honoré de, 31, 32, 62, 150, 176, 177, 179, 244
Batteux, Abbé Charles, 191
Baudelaire, Charles, 24, 304
Baumgarten, Hermann, 181, 186
beauty, 115, 144, 146, 183-187, 195-196, 198
Beethoven, Ludwig van, 227, 253, 376
*Bildungsroman*, 269, 320, 335-336, 343
Blackwell, Thomas, 48
Boccaccio, Giovanni, 172
Boeckh, August, 16
Böcklin, Arnold, 371
Boileau, Nicholas, 12, 40, 126, 175, 181
Boismont, Alexandre de, 62
Bolingbroke, Henry, 292
Brentano, Franz, 229
Bruno, Giordano, 288
Buffon, Georges Louis Leclerc, Comte de, 190, 285
Burke, Edmund, 145, 191
Byron, George Gordon, Lord, 60, 67, 95, 143, 264, 336, 338, 341

Calderón de la Barca, Pedro, 159
Callistratus, 180
Cardano, Girolama, 246
Carlyle, Thomas, 103, 109, 143
Cassirer, Ernst, 19
Cervantes, Miguel de Saavedra, 65, 169, 219, 221, 257, 268, 293
Chamisso, Adalbert von, 65
character, 57, 77, 149, 151, 155-157, 252; in Goethe, 299-300; in Greek tragedy, 38; in Shakespeare, 138
Chateaubriand, François Réne, Vicomte de, 341
Chrétien de Troyes, 267
Cicero, 180, 182
Claude Lorrain, 189
Clauren, Heinrich (Carl Heun), 123
Coleridge, Samuel Taylor, 264
completion, 8; law of, 104-105, 106, 126
Comte, Auguste, 162, 229, 323
Condorcet, Marie Jean Antoine, Marquis de, 323
Constant, Benjamin, 341

Conz, Philipp, 311
Corneille, Pierre, 33, 40, 65, 219, 294
Cornelius, Peter, 31, 179
Cotta, Johann Friedrich, 326

Dante Alighieri, 66, 94, 145, 221, 242, 275
David, Jacques-Louis, 30
Delaroche, Hippolyte (Paul), 30
Democritus, 67
Descartes, René, 40, 43, 181, 183
Dickens, Charles, 22, 31, 32, 60, 63, 64, 66, 142, 145, 146, 152, 172, 218, 244, 254, 257, 258, 263
Diderot, Denis, 30, 169, 190, 191, 221, 337
Diogenes Laertius, 355, 359
Diomedes, 181
Donatello, 178, 220
Donders, Franciscus Cornelis, 100
drama, 11, 23, 133, 136, 215; historical types of, 165-167; technique of action in, 154
Dubos, Jean Baptiste, l'abbé, 43, 191, 201, 376
Dürer, Albrecht, 179, 219, 226, 297

Eckermann, Johann Peter, 148
Eichendorff, Joseph Freiherr von, 374
elementary aesthetic effects, 79-86, 194-195, 197; universality of, 86
elementary logical operations, 74-75
epic, 41, 133, 135, 139, 150, 155
epochs of aesthetics, 11-14, 180-205
Erasmus, 221
Ermatinger, Emil, 19
Ernesti, Johann August, 30
Euler, Leonhard, 181, 184, 186, 205
Euripides, 66, 257
exclusion, law of, 102, 126, 218, 241
experience. *See* lived experience
explanation, in aesthetics, 5, 7-8, 53, 55, 120, 196

Fechner, Gustav, 7, 62, 82, 84, 86, 87-90, 92, 119, 126, 194, 195, 197
feeling of life, 20, 93, 116; embodied in art, 59
feelings, 86; as the basis of aesthetic effects, 76-93, 105, 137, 243, 373; and interest, 78, 155; spheres of, 6, 7, 15, 77-86; expressed as values, 78, 153, 196
Feuerbach, Anselm, 179
Fichte, Johann Gottlieb, 3, 253, 296, 313, 321, 322, 340, 342, 346, 360
Fielding, Henry, 30, 263, 335
Flaubert, Gustave, 62, 172
Fleming, Paul, 298
Florio, John, 260
form, 22, 32, 40, 49, 81, 82, 83, 212; analysis of, 30, 37, 39, 43, 158; Aristotle on, 37-42; historicity of, 134; in Hölderlin's lyric poetry, 376; inner, 23, 50, 132, 133, 160-161, 216, 292-294; language of, 210-216; poetic, 164-165, 168, 183
Forster, John, 64
Franklin, Benjamin, 192
Frederick the Great, 56, 83, 171
Freytag, Gustav, 127, 134, 154, 219; on types of drama, 165-167
Fröbel, Friedrich, 209

Gallait, Louis, 30
Gautier, Théophile, 62
Gerard, Alexander, 192, 195
Gerhardt, Paul, 298
Gervinus, Georg, 204
*Gesamtkunstwerk*, 15, 177, 211, 214
Gleim, Johann Wilhelm Ludwig, 375
Gluck, Christoph Wilibald, 190
Goethe, Johann Wolfgang von, 3, 4, 10, 11, 19, 20, 22, 24, 31, 33, 40, 41, 43, 45, 48, 50, 57, 58, 61, 62, 64, 66, 80, 83, 92, 95, 109, 125, 137, 143, 148, 153, 163, 169, 172, 175, 200, 204, 208, 211, 215, 221, 230, 235-302, 307, 313, 316, 346, 350, 365, 366, 369, 372, 375; his characters, 299-300; description of his psychic life, 269-274; on epic and dramatic poetry, 41; on history, 276-278; and Hölderlin, 324; his imagination, 107, 244-250; inner form of his poetry, 292-294; limits of his poetry, 300; his lyric poetry, 298-299; on nature, 250, 285-289; his pantheism, 287-288; his poetic development, 294-298; relation of

his works to his lived experience, 278-283; his world-view, 287-292; Works: *Egmont*, 276; *Elective Affinities*, 246, 275, 297, 300; "The Eternal Jew," 275; *Zur Farbenlehre*, 277, 289; *Faust*, 278, 279, 283, 286, 287, 292, 293, 294, 296, 298, 301; "Die Geheimnisse," 295; *Die Geschwister*, 301; *Götz von Berlichingen*, 276; *Hermann and Dorothea*, 249, 278, 293, 294, 297; "Ilmenau," 283; *Iphigenia*, 278, 292, 295, 301, 351; *Die italienische Reise*, 279; *Mahomet*, 286, 294, 301; *Die Mitschuldigen*, 294; "Neueröffnetes moralisch-politisches Puppenspiel," 275; "Die Natur," 287; *Die natürliche Tochter*, 278, 297; *Pandora*, 247, 296; *Prometheus*, 248, 278, 286, 287, 292, 294, 301, 354; *Roman Elegies*, 296; *Stella*, 301; *Tasso*, 278, 292, 301; *Trilogie der Leidenschaft*, 296; *Truth and Fiction*, 275, 277, 282; *Urfaust*, 249; *Werther*, 248, 271, 286, 287, 292, 294, 301; *The West-East Divan*, 296, 298; *Wilhelm Meister*, 248, 275, 278, 282, 290, 292, 294, 296, 298, 336
Goncharov, Ivan Alexandrovich, 110
Goncourt, Edmond and Jules, 179
Gontard, Jacob, 327
Gontard, Susette, 327-331
Gottfried von Strassburg, 267-268
Gottsched, Johann Christoph, 40
Gozzi, Carlo, 148
Greene, Robert, 40, 256
Griesinger, W., 159
Gryphius, Andreas, 299
Günther, Johann Christian, 33

Hagedorn, Friedrich von, 375
Hamann, Johann Georg, 48, 236, 376
Harris, James, 191
Hartmann, Eduard von, 190
Hauff, Wilhelm, 123
Haydn, Josef, 376
Haym, Rudolf, 336
Hebbel, Friedrich, 112, 179
Hegel, Georg Wilhelm Friedrich, 3, 14, 30, 134, 138, 144, 161, 203, 204, 253, 289, 310, 311, 312, 313, 315, 316, 319, 331-332, 333, 344, 347, 348, 357, 358, 360, 365, 367, 368, 372
Heinse, Johann J. W., 327
Helmont, Jan Baptista van, 286
Heloïse, 66, 267
Hemsterhuis, Franz, 187, 346
Henle, Jacob, 208
Heraclitus, 344
Herbart, Johann F., 71, 85
Herder, Johann Gottfried von, 42, 48, 49, 86, 134, 202, 236, 271, 280, 281, 285, 287, 313, 336, 346, 376
hermeneutics, 16-18, 30, 50, 52, 201
Hermogenes, 181
Heyne, Christian Gottlob, 311
historical aesthetics, 13, 201-205
Historical School, 4, 13, 48, 120
historicity: of art and poetry, 49, 166-173, 203; of technique, 6, 11, 160-168, 219
Hobbema, Meindert, 189
Hobbes, Thomas, 43
Hogarth, William, 186
Hölderlin, Friedrich, 3, 4, 10, 23, 24, 26, 253, 303-383; and the French Revolution, 25, 312-313, 334-338; and Hegel, 312, 313, 315, 321, 331-333, 347, 357, 360, 365, 367; his interest in ancient Greece, 25, 306, 311-312, 348, 357, 377, 383; his lyric poetry, 304, 309, 368-383; his madness, 380-381, 382; his pantheism, 315, 321, 344, 345, 346-348, 352; his psychic nexus, 370, 378, 381-382; Schiller's influence on, 309, 314, 315, 316, 318, 320, 322, 323, 324, 325, 372; Works: "Der Abschied," 331; "An die Natur," 377; "The Archipelago," 374; "Eleusis," 331; "Emilie vor ihrem Brauttag," 374; *Empedocles*, 333, 350-368; "Evening Fantasy," 371; "Fall Festival," 374; "Dem Genius der Kühnheit," 318; "Der Gott der Jugend," 377; "Die Götter Griechenlands," 316; "Homecoming," 374; "Hymne an die Göttin der

Hölderlin, Friedrich (*cont.*)
Harmonie," 314, 315; "Hymne an die Liebe," 317; *Hyperion*, 25, 316, 318, 320, 323, 334-350; "Der Künstler," 317; "Menon's Lament for Diotima," 329-330, 374, 377; "Nachtgesänge," 381; "The Rhine," 382; "Sung Beneath the Alps," 378
Homer, 83, 94, 242, 297, 307
Horace, 67, 180, 378
Houdetot, Comtesse d', 66, 267
Hugo, Victor, 145
human sciences, 3, 4, 5, 34, 35, 36, 191, 224
Humboldt, Alexander von, 29
Humboldt, Wilhelm von, 29, 36, 42, 50, 155, 253, 312
Hume, David, 94, 191
Hummel, Johann N., 62
Husserl, Edmund, 229
Hutcheson, Francis, 191

Iffland, August Wilhelm, 34
image-formation, 93-106
images, 8, 61, 63, 64, 66; formation of, 93-106, 239-241, 243
imagination, 8, 60-68, 238-250; and dreams, 67, 100, 102, 108, 185; historicity of, 165; laws of, 5, 101-105, 126, 144; linguistic, 17, 244-245; and memory, 61, 102, 140, 239, 240, 241; and poetic moods, 146-147; psychological basis of, 68-71, 93-106, 239-241
imitation, 38, 39, 43, 46
impression, point of, 217, 218
impressions, analysis of in eighteenth-century aesthetics, 193
inner form, 23, 133, 160-161, 216; defined, 50, 132; of Goethe's poetry, 292-294
insanity and creativity. *See* poetic creativity
intensification, law of, 10, 102, 126, 218, 241

Jacobi, Friedrich, 250, 310, 311, 316
Jean Paul, 87, 109, 146, 253, 335, 340
Jesus Christ, 360, 365, 366, 382
Jonson, Ben, 256, 263
Jung-Stilling (properly Johann Heinrich Jung), 281

Kalb, Charlotte von, 319
Kames, Henry Home, Lord, 12, 13, 191-197
Kant, Immanuel, 13, 14, 46, 47, 48, 86, 188, 193, 194, 198, 202, 230, 251, 253, 281, 285, 296, 310, 311, 312, 316, 319, 346
Keller, Gottfried, 178, 179, 343
Kepler, Johannes, 181
Kestner, Johann Christian, 271
Kingsley, Charles, 103
Kleist, Heinrich von, 111, 382
Klinger, Friedrich M. von, 280
Klopstock, Friedrich Gottlieb, 245, 284, 298, 305, 307, 308, 309, 314, 316, 375, 378
Knapp, Georg Christian, 308
Körner, Christian Gottfried, 29
Kotzebue, August von, 34

Lachmann, Karl, 30
La Motte-Fouqué, Friedrich de, 65
language, 228; of forms, 210-216; Hölderlin's use of, 23-24, 304, 317, 356, 374, 376-378, 383; and poetry, 48, 49, 52, 140-141, 158-159, 244
Lavater, Johann Kaspar, 271, 281, 295
law: of completion, 104-106, 126; of exclusion, 102, 126, 218; of intensification, 102, 126, 218, 241; Lessing's, 141; Schiller's, 45, 47
laws: of aesthetics, 7, 77, 80-92; of art, 33, 41; of imaginative metamorphosis, 5, 20, 101-105, 126, 144; of poetics, 34, 35, 41; of psychic life, 69-70
Lazarus, Moritz, 159
Leibniz, Gottfried Wilhelm, 12, 14, 181, 182, 183, 184, 185, 186, 188, 205, 253, 315, 336
Leicester, Earl of, 257
Lenbach, Franz von, 218
Lenz, Jakob M. R., 280
Leonardo da Vinci, 176, 179, 219, 297
Leopardi, Giovanni, 336, 338
Lessing, Gotthold Ephraim, 3, 11, 33,

40, 41, 131, 172, 175, 179, 181, 187, 190, 191, 202, 213, 236, 280, 284, 285, 294, 295, 310, 313, 336, 350, 360, 368, 376; his law, 141
life-experience, 20, 238; and the meaning of life, 170; relation to lived experience, 57
life-relations, 20, 238, 239, 372
Linnaeus, Carolus, 190
Litzmann, Carl, 307
lived experience, 8, 15-16, 17, 20, 21, 22, 23, 61, 63, 90, 94, 106, 115, 129, 223-230, 237, 242, 348; articulation of, 9, 149; as basis of poetry, 56, 60, 135, 137, 250-254, 278; and lyric poetry, 313, 318, 369-375; and meaning, 16, 59, 225, 231, 348
Locke, John, 43, 94, 182, 191
Lope de Vega Carpio, Félix, 39, 166, 171, 215, 220
Lorrain, Claude. *See* Claude Lorrain
Lotze, Rudolf Hermann, 43, 190
Lubbock, J. (Lord Avebury), 136
Ludwig, Otto, 50, 55, 111, 133, 179, 204
Lukács, Georg, 19
Luther, Martin, 245, 253, 291
lyric poetry, 23, 24, 92, 133, 135, 313, 368-383; of Goethe, 298-299; of Hölderlin, 368-379

Macaulay, Thomas Babington, Baron, 103
Magenau, 309
Manzoni, Alessandro, 92
Marlowe, Christopher, 40, 178, 209, 215, 221, 256
Masaccio, 178, 221
Matthisson, Friedrich von, 309, 318
meaning, 79, 121, 126, 228, 377; of life, 3, 15, 24, 169-170, 173, 230, 348; in literature, 18, 138, 376, 377; of lived experience, 16, 59, 225, 231, 348. *See also* significance
meaning-content, 6, 14, 81, 83, 152, 160-161
means of representation, 14, 41, 54, 87, 147, 157, 203, 252
medium, 14, 17, 203; conditions art, 139-141, 142
Meier, Georg Friedrich, 181, 186
memory, 61, 102, 140, 241; and poetic imagination, 239, 240
Menander, 181
Mendelssohn, Moses, 181, 191
Menzel, Adolph von, 31
metamorphosis, 8, 10, 20, 67, 95, 105, 115. *See also* laws
Meyer, Conrad Ferdinand, 94, 173
Meyer, Johann Heinrich, 31
Meynert, Theodor, 79
Michelangelo Buonarroti, 206, 209, 214, 219, 285, 383
Mill, John Stuart, 143, 229, 254
Milton, John, 94, 255
Misch, Georg, 230
Molière, 32, 33, 125, 151, 259
Montaigne, Michel de, 142, 182, 260
Montesquieu, Charles de Secondat, Baron de, 82, 201
moods. *See* poetic moods
Mörike, Eduard, 305, 319, 369, 374, 376
Moritz, Karl Phillip, 29, 47
Möser, 285
Mosso, Angelo, 100
motif: in a poetic work, 57, 83, 147-149, 252
Mozart, Wolfgang Amadeus, 206, 294, 375
Müller, Johannes, 20, 107, 108, 208, 289
Müller, Kanzler, 148, 247
Müller, Max, 255
music, 3, 15, 17, 48, 77, 111, 184, 186, 189, 212, 214, 217, 369; relation to Hölderlin's lyric poetry, 23, 373-376
Musset, Alfred de, 179

Napoleon Bonaparte, 338
naturalism, 9, 11, 176, 210, 215, 216-222
Neuffer, Christian Ludwig, 309
Newton, Isaac, 292
Nicolai, Friedrich, 34
Nietzsche, Friedrich, 24, 25, 26, 304, 323, 336, 338, 342, 345, 350, 382

Nohl, Hermann, 19
Nösselt, Friedrich August, 308
Novalis (Friedrich von Hardenberg), 253, 335, 340, 369, 374, 375
novel, 23, 42, 172

Oersted, Hans Christian, 200
Ossian, 307, 308
Ovid, 260

pantheism, 345; Goethe's, 287-288; Hölderlin's, 315, 321, 344, 345, 346-348, 352
Paracelsus, 286, 355
Pericles, 199
Pestalozzi, Johann H., 209
Petersen, Julius, 19
Petrarch (Francesco Petrarca), 284
Phidias, 180
Philostratus, 180
Pindar, 316
Plato, 67, 310, 312, 366
plot, 57, 77, 83, 117, 147, 149-151, 252, 362; in Greek tragedy, 38, 39
Plotinus, 92, 180
Plutarch, 180, 260
poetic content. *See* meaning-content; motif; poetic moods
poetic creativity: and dreams, *see* imagination; and insanity, 67, 95, 96, 98-100, 103
poetic form, 164-165, 168, 183
poetic imagination. *See* imagination
poetic moods, 59, 144-148, 252, 373, 376, 378; and laws of imagination, 146-147
poetic technique, 10, 124, 133; defined, 129; historicity of, 35, 39
point of impression, 217-218
Polycletus, 180
Principles of aesthetics. *See* laws of aesthetics
Pseudo-Longinus, 180
psychic nexus, 68, 70, 73, 75, 78, 242, 369; of Hölderlin, 370. *See also* acquired psychic nexus
psychology, 5, 6, 7, 8, 18-19; and lived experience, 228; and universally valid rules, 54
Purkinje, Johannes E., 208

Rabelais, François, 221, 260
Racine, Jean Baptiste, 33, 65, 171, 350
Rählmann, Eduard von, 100
Rameau, Jean Phillippe, 191
Ranke, Leopold von, 255
Raphael, 32, 58, 76, 77, 206, 214, 219, 256, 294
rationalist aesthetics, 12, 181-187, 205
reflexive awareness, 83-84, 90, 118, 223, 224; defined, 16, 69; and spatio-temporal relations, 69
Reinhold, Karl Leonhard, 313
Rembrandt van Rijn, 152, 156, 189, 219
rhythm, 6, 25, 38, 135, 184, 349, 362; and feeling, 77, 80-81, 87
Richardson, Jonathan, 186
Richardson, Samuel, 263
romanticism, 3, 4, 236, 335, 336
Ronsard, Pierre de, 181
Rousseau, Jean-Jacques, 22, 30, 60, 66, 95, 143, 169, 190, 221, 236, 336, 382; description of his psychic life, 264-267
Rubens, Peter Paul, 66
rules of art, 33, 37-38, 39, 126, 187, 212
Rumohr, Carl Friedrich, 204
Ruysdael, Jacob von, 189

Sand, George, 178
Scaliger, Julius Caesar, 158, 167, 181, 203
Schadow, Gottfried, 31
Schelling, F.W.J., 3, 14, 29, 45, 202, 288, 310, 311, 312, 313, 315, 316, 319, 332, 344, 345
Scherer, Wilhelm, 128
Schiller, Friedrich, 3, 11, 13, 14, 31, 33, 40-51, 56, 64, 66, 85, 111, 115, 118, 131, 142-143, 148, 169, 172, 175, 179, 203, 220, 237, 251, 253, 273, 276, 281-284, 296, 307-309, 312, 314, 316, 318, 320, 324-325, 346, 350, 365; his law, 45-47; his theory of living form, 44
Schlegel, August Wilhelm, 29, 45, 49, 50, 175, 333
Schlegel, Friedrich, 14, 29, 42, 49, 50, 165, 167, 172, 203, 313

Schleiermacher, Friedrich, 3, 4, 16, 20, 30, 50, 127, 202, 253, 313, 321, 322, 344, 357
Schnaase, Karl, 204
Schopenhauer, Arthur, 3, 46, 67, 92, 336, 337, 338, 353, 372
Schubart, 307, 309
Schumann, Robert, 179, 382
Scott, Walter, 94, 150, 255, 263
Semper, Gottfried, 15, 178, 179, 190, 200, 204, 208, 212, 214
Seneca, 167
Shaftesbury, Anthony Ashley Cooper, Earl of, 43, 194, 287, 312, 314, 346
Shakespeare, William, 22, 54, 61, 65, 83, 92, 103, 109, 125, 133, 134, 138, 142, 151, 153, 166, 169, 171, 176, 204, 209, 211, 219, 221, 264, 275, 281, 294, 333; contrasted with Goethe, 264; description of his psychic life, 254-264
Shelley, Percy Bysshe, 264
significance, 77, 139, 147, 156, 218, 238, 243, 251, 252
Sinclair, 333
Smith, Adam, 191
Smollett, Tobias, 151, 263
Socrates, 209, 365, 382
Solger, Karl Wilhelm Ferdinand, 144, 202
Sömmering, 327
Sophocles, 65, 257, 259, 275, 285, 350, 352, 361, 370, 372
Spielhagen, Friedrich, 150
Spinoza, Baruch, 92, 182, 281, 286, 288, 310, 316
Staël, Anne Louise Necker, Madame de, 341
Stäudlin, Gotthold Friedrich, 309, 318
Stein, Charlotte von, 159, 273
Stein, Heinrich von, 181
Steinthal, Heymann, 73-74
Sterne, Lawrence, 30, 146, 169
Storr, Gottlob Christian, 308
style, 11, 104, 105, 106, 178, 206, 216, 219-220, 383
sublime, 145, 147, 191, 192, 195-196
Sulzer, Johann Georg, 181
Swift, Jonathan, 146, 169, 337
Swinburne, Algernon, 24, 304

Taine, Hippolyte Adolphe, 176
taste, 46, 47, 183, 187, 194; in rationalist aesthetics, 185
technique, 39, 120, 125; Aristotle on, 37-42; of Boileau and Corneille, 40; claims for universality, 47, 48; of Goethe and Schiller, 42, 48; historicity of, 54, 58, 160-168, 219
Tetens, Johann Nicolaus, 193
Thackeray, William Makepeace, 219, 263
Tieck, Ludwig, 127, 335, 339, 340, 374, 375
Tieftrunk, Johann Heinrich, 308
time, in literature, 152; and lived experience, 225-226
Tobler, Georg Christoph, 287
Tolstoy, Leo, 221
tragedy, 38, 91, 139, 145, 350, 352, 362, 368
Trollope, Anthony, 113
truthfulness, and art, 32, 84, 175, 221
Turgenev, Ivan, 62
Tylor, Edward, 137
types, 116-118, 155-157, 229, 230; versus concepts, 116

Uhland, Johann Ludwig, 305, 369
understanding, 18-19, 20, 137-138, 218, 229-230, 251, 252, 253, 347, 348, 369
Unger, Rudolf, 19
universal validity, 6, 7, 122; in aesthetics, 54, 119, 194, 199-200; in poetic works, 116, 117, 119, 156

Vahlen, Johannes, 140, 149
value, 72, 78, 84, 85, 123, 127, 153, 196, 228, 229, 230, 231, 237-238, 251
Verlaine, Paul, 24, 304
Verrocchio, Andrea del, 178, 221
Virgil, 181
Vischer, Friedrich Theodor von, 160, 203, 204
Voltaire, 83, 171, 221, 280, 292, 337, 356

Wagner, Richard, 15, 67, 110, 170, 177, 179, 214, 368

Waiblinger, Wilhelm, 381
Waitz, Theodor, 135
Webb, Daniel, 191
Weisse, Christian Hermann, 144
Wellek, René, 18
Wieland, Christoph Martin, 284, 295, 307
Winckelmann, Johann Joachim, 13, 165, 167, 202, 203, 281, 285, 311, 366; his hermeneutics, 201
Wittkowski, 100
Wolf, Friedrich, 30, 36, 42
Wolff, Christian, 29
Wolfram von Eschenbach, 242, 267, 268-269
Wood, 191
world-view, 3, 9, 14, 24, 283; aesthetic, 45, 201; Goethe's, 287-292; Hölderlin's, 315
Wundt, Wilhelm, 73-74

Young, David, 43,
Young, Eduard, 191

Zeller, Eduard, 29, 208
Zimmermann, Robert, 43, 190
Zinzendorf, Nikolaus Ludwig, Count, 281, 285
Zola, Émile, 172, 176, 221

LIBRARY OF CONGRESS CATALOGING IN PUBLICATION DATA

Dilthey, Wilhelm, 1833-1911.
Poetry and experience.

(Selected works / Wilhelm Dilthey ; v. 5)
Includes index.
1. Poetics—Addresses, essays, lectures.
2. Literature—Philosophy—Addresses, essays, lectures.
I. Makkreel, Rudolf A., 1939- . II. Rodi, Frithjof,
1930- . III. Title. IV. Series: Dilthey, Wilhelm,
1833-1911. Selections. English. 1985 ; v. 5.
B3216.D82E5 1985 vol. 5 193 s [801'.951] 84-42990
[PN1044]
ISBN 0-691-07297-3 (lib. bdg.: alk. paper)